exploring 3D ANIMATION *with* MAYA 7

exploring 3D ANIMATION *with* MAYA 7

Patricia Beckmann
Phil Young

THOMSON

DELMAR LEARNING

Exploring 3D Animation with Maya 7
Patricia Beckmann and Phil Young

Vice President, Technology and Trades ABU:
David Garza

Director of Learning Solutions:
Sandy Clark

Managing Editor:
Larry Main

Acquisitions Editor:
James Gish

Product Manager:
Jaimie Weiss

Marketing Director:
Deborah Yarnell

Marketing Manager:
Penelope Crosby

Director of Production:
Patty Stephan

Production Manager:
Andrew Crouth

Content Project Manager:
Nicole Stagg

Technology Project Manager:
Kevin Smith

Editorial Assistant:
Niamh Matthews

Printed in Canada
1 2 3 4 5 XX 08 07 06

For more information contact
Thomson Delmar Learning
Executive Woods
5 Maxwell Drive, PO Box 8007,
Clifton Park, NY 12065-8007
Or find us on the World Wide Web at
www.delmarlearning.com

Library of Congress
Cataloging-in-Publication Data:

Beckmann, Patricia.
Exploring 3D animation with
Maya 7 / Patricia Beckmann,
Scott Wells. – 2nd ed.
p. cm.
Includes bibliographical references
and index.
ISBN: 1-4180-5182-9
1. Computer animation. 2. Three-dimensional display systems. 3. Maya (Computer file) I. Wells, Scott. II. Title.
TR897.7.B44352 2007
006.6'96–dc22

2006028706

NOTICE TO THE READER

Publisher does not warrant or guarantee any of the products described herein or perform any independent analysis in connection with any of the product information contained herein. Publisher does not assume, and expressly disclaims, any obligation to obtain and include information other than that provided to it by the manufacturer.

The reader is expressly warned to consider and adopt all safety precautions that might be indicated by the activities herein and to avoid all potential hazards. By following the instructions contained herein, the reader willingly assumes all risks in connection with such instructions.

The publisher makes no representation or warranties of any kind, including, but not limited to, the warranties of fitness for particular purpose or merchantability, nor are any such representations implied with respect to the material set forth herein, and the publisher takes no responsibility with respect to such material. The publisher shall not be liable for any special, consequential, or exemplary damages resulting, in whole or part, from the readers' use of, or reliance upon, this material.

contents

CONTENTS

dedication

For the love of Margot and Helmut Beckmann, Scott, Gerta, two great Young kids, Louise, Thelma, Maxine, and one very special goldfish, Arthur. Ducks, we'll get you next time.

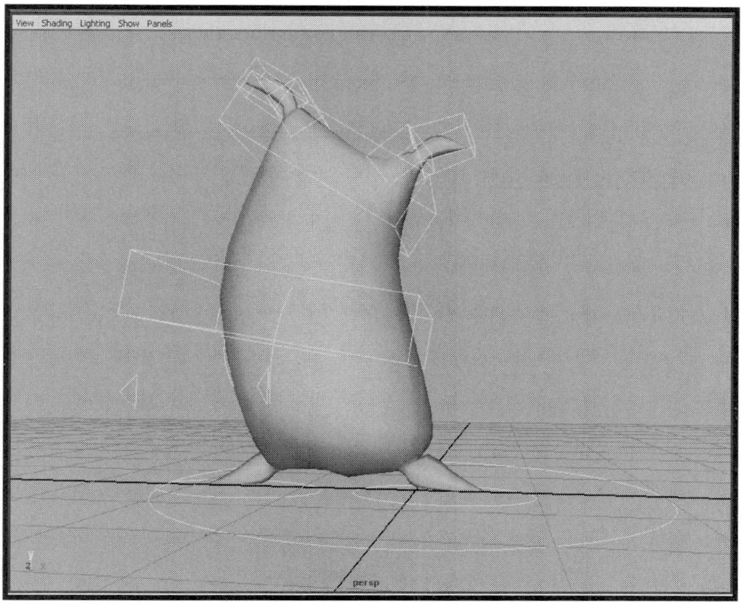

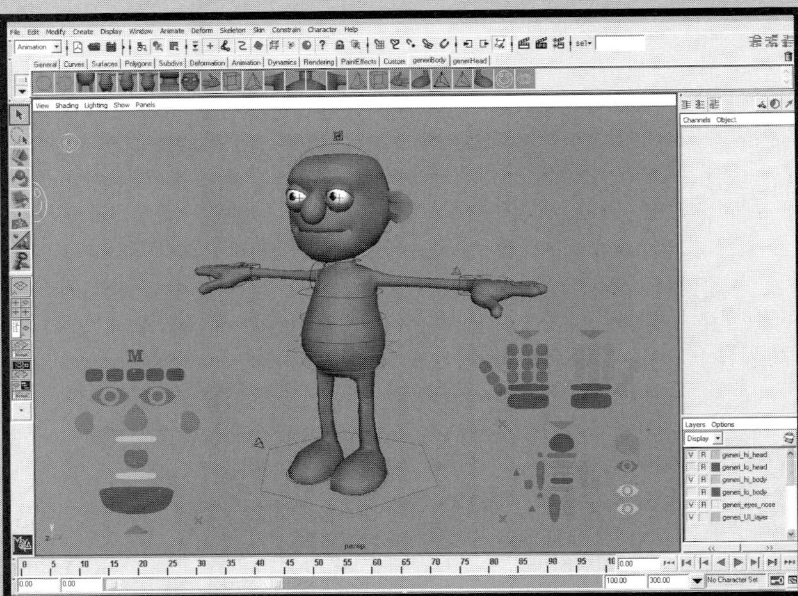
File Edit Modify Create Display Window Animate Deform Skeleton Skin Constrain Character Help
Animation
General Curves Surfaces Polygons Subdivs Deformation Animation Dynamics Rendering PaintEffects Custom generiBody generiHead
View Shading Lighting Show Panels
Channels Object
Layers Options
Display
generi_hi_head
generi_lo_head
generi_hi_body
generi_lo_body
generi_eyes_nose
generi_UI_layer
persp
No Character Set

| preface |

preface

INTENDED AUDIENCE

This book is intended for beginners in animation who want to employ traditional animation technique in their computer graphic films. We take some of the skill sets that have been developed in the last one hundred years of animated film and apply them to the newest animation tool—the computer. The theory remains the same; we just learn how to create with a different tool.

Whether you are new to the field, a traditional animator, or trying to create a more believable movement study in your CG (computer graphic) work, this book will guide you through the basics of character animation in Maya.

EMERGING TRENDS

Computer art is stepping away from the technical and toward the organic. Artists are now finding the medium easier to understand. Digital animation should not be identifiable by its software program; rather, it should serve to achieve the artist's vision using a new pencil. This book strives to bring the technology to the artist in a non-threatening and visual manner.

BACKGROUND OF THIS TEXT

We wrote this book because, as teachers, we found the standard textbooks in use were not addressing the creative interests of our students. We could not find a single book addressing the Graph Editor and how to employ it to create believable movement. We wanted a book that crossed over the divide from traditional to computer-generated movement with respect to the theory that created animation in the first place. We wanted it to be written by industry professionals with credentials.

Phil Young joined Patricia in this cause, bringing valuable traditional experience gleaned from over 25 years as a lead animator at Disney. Together we analyzed our tools and synthesized the subjects a beginner should practice to achieve a solid foundation.

The information presented can be used in all 3D software programs but is specifically targeted at training the beginner animator in Maya 7.0. For effective use of this text, you should have a basic understanding of Maya and have a three-button mouse attached to your computer.

TEXTBOOK ORGANIZATION

Each chapter of *Exploring 3D Animation with Maya 7* asks an essential question and then answers it with clearly thought-out goals and tutorials. The tools included in each chapter are listed on the opening pages. Each chapter is organized in this manner to clearly identify what you are learning and why.

This text will allow you to practice animation by creating thumbnails and key poses and by editing motion curves. We introduce simple CG animation techniques for creating believable movement and study theory shaped by years of development at Disney.

Basic primitive motion will lead you to a flour-sack animation, then to a complex biped rig, and finally a phoneme project on lip synch. You will create a walking, talking character by the end and will have completed studies in follow-through, weight, arc, and the principles of animation applied.

We will also lead you through basic Graph Editor functions and how they relate to believable motion. We will advance through more complex motion theory and rigs to achieve desired motion in a biped character.

The topics covered are as follows:

- Chapter 1 introduces you to the Maya interface and explains how to save files.
- Chapter 2 introduces the main components of Maya for editing movement in the Graph Editor. It covers working with different curves and how movement relates to a tangent.
- Chapter 3 covers the production process of setting up a shot, as well as basic editing techniques in CG. Animation principles are also explained.

- Chapter 4 explains how to use reference images and import them into Maya. The first character animation piece is created involving a flour sack. It demonstrates how to depict a variety of emotions.
- Chapter 5 discusses working with timing charts and setting key poses for the flour-sack character. The goal is to create personality through solid pantomime acting.
- Chapter 6 introduces a complex biped rig that has multiple controls built in for creating personality and movement. This chapter teaches how to identify what is available and what controls to use to move the model.
- Chapter 7 studies wave theory and how to create a practical CG study. Follow-through and overlapping action, and their influence on the believability of a character, are discussed.
- Chapter 8 focuses on theory and practical application in a CG environment. The walk cycle is explored in detail.
- Chapter 9 explains animation theory as it relates to lip synch.

FEATURES

The following list provides some of the salient features of the text:

- Learning goals are clearly stated at the beginning of each chapter.
- The book was written to meet the needs of design students and professionals for a visually oriented introduction to basic design principles and the functions and tools of Maya.
- Client projects involve tools and techniques that a designer might encounter on the job.
- The full-color insert section provides stunning examples of design results that can be achieved using Maya.
- The Exploring on Your Own sections offer suggestions and sample lessons for further study of the content covered in each chapter.
- Review questions are provided at the end of each chapter to quiz understanding and retention of the material covered.
- A CD-ROM at the back of the book contains tutorials and exercises.

HOW TO USE THIS TEXT

The following features can be found throughout the book:

Charting Your Course and Goals

The introduction and chapter objectives start off each chapter. They describe the competencies that you should achieve after completing the chapter.

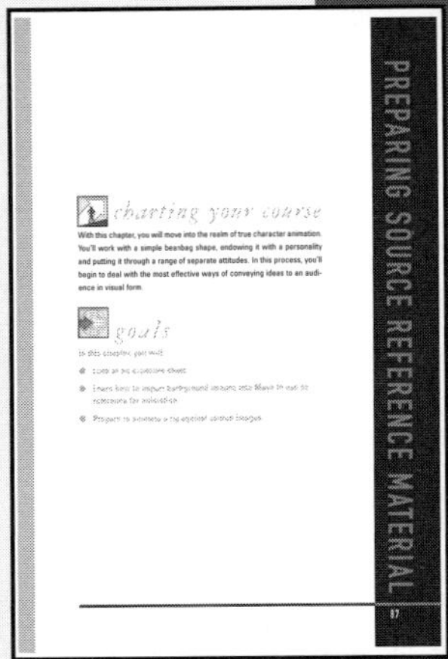
PREPARING SOURCE REFERENCE MATERIAL

charting your course

With this chapter, you will move into the realm of true character animation. You'll work with a simple beanbag shape, endowing it with a personality and putting it through a range of separate attitudes. In this process, you'll begin to deal with the most effective ways of conveying ideas to an audience in visual form.

goals

87

Don't Go There

These boxes appear throughout the text, highlighting common pitfalls and explaining ways to avoid them.

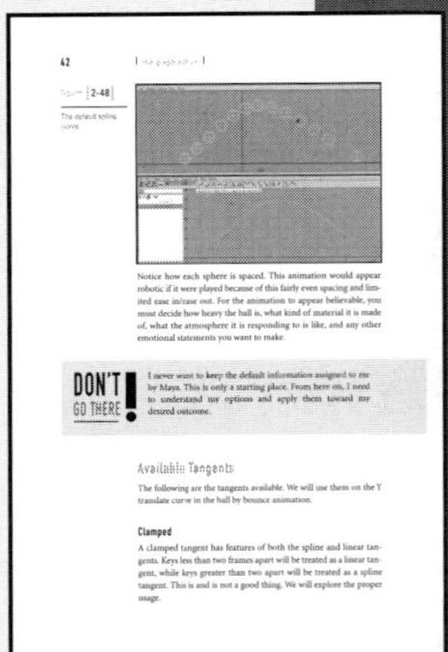
42

figure 2-48

Notice how each sphere is spaced. This animation would appear robotic if it were played because of this fairly even spacing and limited ease in/ease out. For the animation to appear believable, you must decide how heavy the ball is, what kind of material it is made of, what the atmosphere it is responding to is like, and any other emotional statements you want to make.

DON'T GO THERE!

I never want to keep the default information assigned to me by Maya. This is only a starting place. From here on, I need to understand my options and apply them toward my desired outcome.

Available Tangents

The following are the tangents available. We will use them on the Y translate curve in the ball by bounce animation.

Clamped

A clamped tangent has features of both the spline and linear tangents. Keys less than two frames apart will be treated as a linear tangent, while keys greater than two apart will be treated as a spline tangent. This is and is not a good thing. We will explore the proper usage.

Review Questions and Exploring On Your Own

Review Questions are located at the end of each chapter and allow you to assess your understanding of the chapter. The Exploring on Your Own sections contain exercises that reinforce chapter material through practical application.

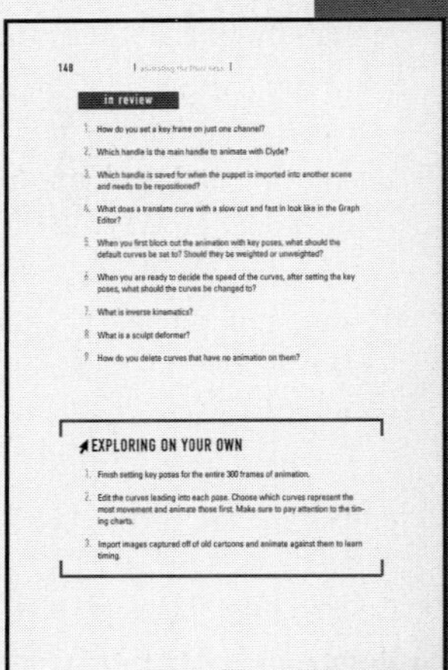
148

in review

1. How do you set a key frame on just one channel?
2. Which handle is the main handle to animate with Clyde?
3. Which handle is saved for when the puppet is imported into another scene and needs to be repositioned?
4. What does a translate curve with a slow out and fast in look like in the Graph Editor?
5. When you first block out the animation with key poses, what should the default curves be set to? Should they be weighted or unweighted?
6. When you are ready to decide the speed of the curves, after setting the key poses, what should the curves be changed to?
7. What is inverse kinematics?
8. What is a sculpt deformer?
9. How do you delete curves that have no animation on them?

EXPLORING ON YOUR OWN

1. Finish setting key poses for the entire 300 frames of animation.
2. Edit the curves leading into each pose. Choose which curves represent the most movement and animate those first. Make sure to pay attention to the timing charts.
3. Import images captured off of old cartoons and animate against them to learn timing.

Adventures in Design

These spreads contain assignments, showing readers how to approach a design project using the tools and design concepts taught in the book.

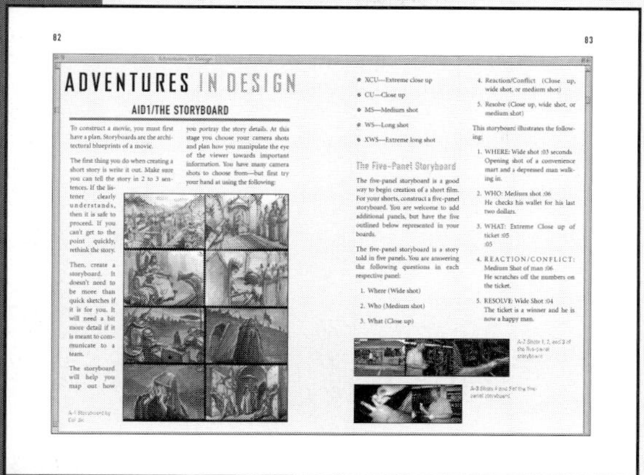

82

ADVENTURES IN DESIGN

AID1/THE STORYBOARD

To construct a movie, you must first have a plan. Storyboards are the architectural blueprints of a movie.

The first thing you do when creating a short story is write it out. Make sure you can tell the story in 2 to 3 sentences. If the listener clearly understands, then it is safe to proceed. If you can't get to the point quickly, rethink the story.

Then, create a storyboard. It doesn't need to be more than quick sketches if it is for you. It will need a bit more detail if it is meant to communicate to a team.

The storyboard will help you map out how you portray the story details. At this stage you choose your camera shots and plan how you manipulate the eye of the viewer towards important information. You have many camera shots to choose from—but first try your hand at using the following:

A-1 Storyboard by

83

- XCU—Extreme close up
- CU—Close up
- MS—Medium shot
- WS—Long shot
- XWS—Extreme long shot

The Five-Panel Storyboard

The five-panel storyboard is a good way to begin creation of a short film. For your shorts, construct a five-panel storyboard. You are welcome to add additional panels, but have the five outlined below represented in your boards.

The five-panel storyboard is a story told in five panels. You are answering the following questions in each respective panel:

1. Where (Wide shot)
2. Who (Medium shot)
3. What (Close up)
4. Reaction/Conflict (Close up, wide shot, or medium shot)
5. Resolve (Close up, wide shot, or medium shot)

This storyboard illustrates the following:

1. WHERE: Wide shot :03 seconds
   Opening shot of a convenience mart and a depressed man walking in.
2. WHO: Medium shot :06
   He checks his wallet for his last two dollars.
3. WHAT: Extreme Close up of ticket :05
   :05
4. REACTION/CONFLICT: Medium Shot of man :06
   He scratches off the numbers on the ticket.
5. RESOLVE: Wide Shot :04
   The ticket is a winner and he is now a happy man.

A-2 Shots 1, 2, and 3 of the five-panel storyboard

A-3 Shots 4 and 5 of the five-panel storyboard

Color Insert

The color insert demonstrates work that can be created when working with Alias/Wavefront Maya.

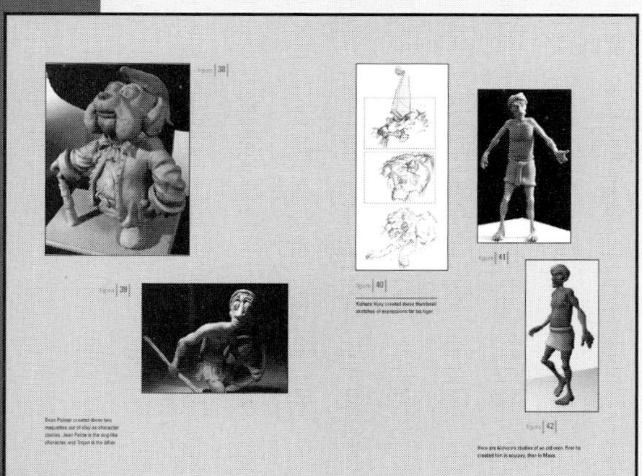

E.RESOURCE

This electronic guide was developed to assist instructors in planning and implementing their instructional programs. It includes sample syllabi for using this book in either an 11- or a 15-week semester. It also provides answers to the end-of-chapter Review Questions, PowerPoint slides highlighting the main topics, and additional instructor resources.

ISBN: 1-4180-5183-7

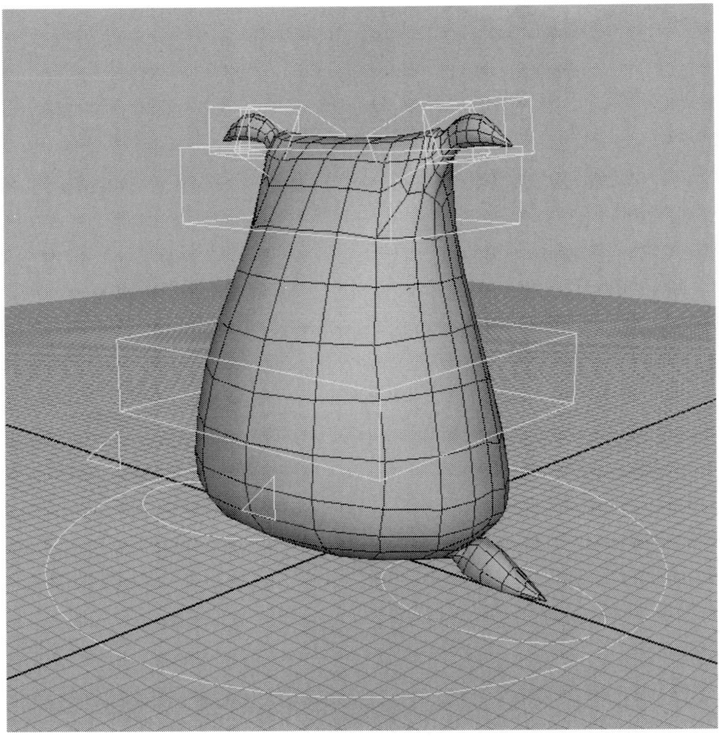

ABOUT THE AUTHORS

▶ Patricia Beckmann-Wells

Patricia presently serves as the Head of Global Training and Technical Development for DreamWorks Animation. There she manages training in the arts and computer graphic programs for all artists on feature animated films. She is also creating short films for festivals. Patricia was previously the Manager of Artistic and Professional Development at Disney Feature Animation.

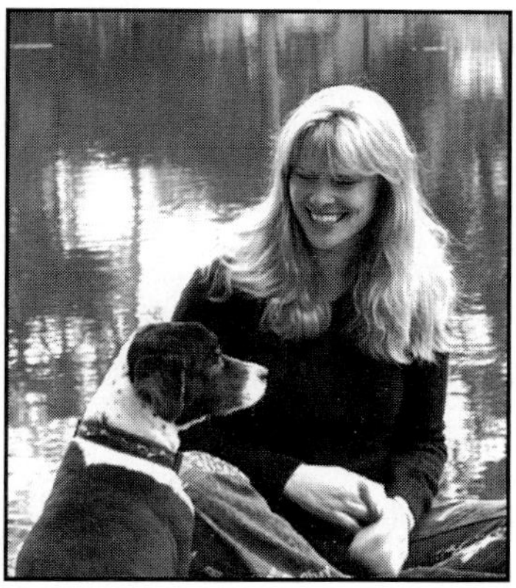

Patricia Beckmann earned her M.F.A. in cinema and animation from the University of Southern California while working as a traditional animator with Phillips Media and holding a fellowship at Silicon Studios in Los Angeles. As a computer graphics artist for Warner Brothers, she created computer graphics effects and animation for the films *Batman* and *Mars Attacks* using high-end software such as Maya. For Film Roman (producers of *The Simpsons* and *King of the Hill*), she managed the computer graphics development department. She was art director on interactive cartoon projects for DreamWorks (*Chicken Run*), ABC (*Norm*), Newline Cinema, E!Online, and Coca-Cola. Her short, *Matilda*, won the Playboy Animation Fest and led to a television pilot for Oxygen Media entitled *Gertrudah and Her Grandmothers.* Patricia spent two years founding the Animation program of a large college in the Southeast as Chair and Professor of a 1,200-student department.

Patricia has received a number of awards, including the Emerging Artist Award at the Rico Gallery Fine Arts Competition in 1999 and was chosen as one of the Top 25 Women of the Web in 2001 by the San Francisco Women of the Web.

She was selected to serve as the Educators Program Chair of the 2005 SIGGRAPH to be held in Los Angeles and continues with SIGGRAPH in the role of Foundation Chair for 2007.

Phil Young

Phil Young is a professor of animation at Savannah College of Art and Design. Phil previously worked at Walt Disney Feature Animation and DreamWorks Animation on popular films such as *The Little Mermaid, Beauty and the Beast, The Lion King, Dinosaur, Tarzan*, and *Sinbad*—among many others. He has worked as a lead traditional animator with these companies for over 25 years and is a well-known artist in the animation community.

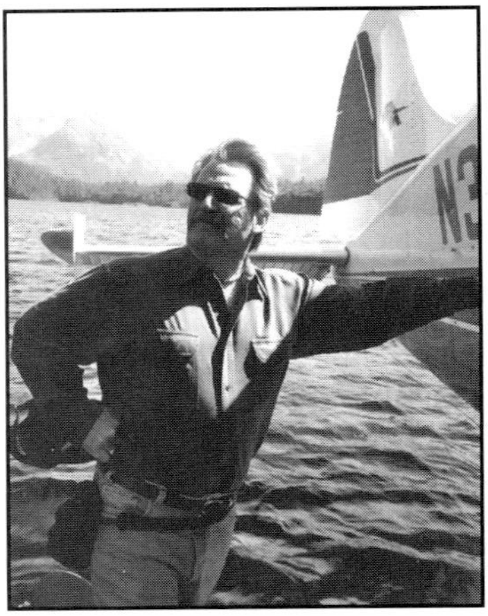

Phil has traveled the world on behalf of Disney and his artistic efforts. He is presently completing his masters in sculpting and has created a series of bronze sculptures currently on exhibition.

Phil is currently working on his own short films and sculpture in Savannah, where he lives with his wife Gerta and goldfish Arthur.

ACKNOWLEDGMENTS

The authors would like to thank Andrew Silke (www.cane-toad.com) for providing the Generi rig used in this book and Scott Wells (www.animaxdesign.com) for providing the flour-sack rig.

Sincere thanks also goes to all of the students who contributed work to the interior color pages. Each is credited where their work is displayed.

Thomson Delmar Learning and the authors would also like to thank the following reviewers for their valuable suggestions and expertise:

Cecilio Acosta
Digital Media Design Department
Texas State Technical College
Waco, TX

Royal Winchester
Art Department
Digipen Institute of Technology
Redmond, WA

Marc Hess
Chair, Multimedia Department
College of Westchester
White Plains, NY

A very special thank you goes to Kendrick Wallace for his technical edit of this material.

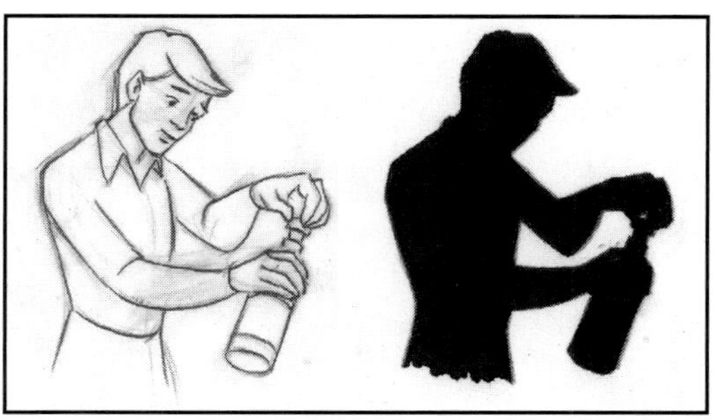

Patricia
Beckmann &
Phil Young
2006

QUESTIONS AND FEEDBACK

Thomson Delmar Learning and the authors welcome your questions and feedback. If you have suggestions that you think others would benefit from, please let us know and we will try to include them in the next edition.

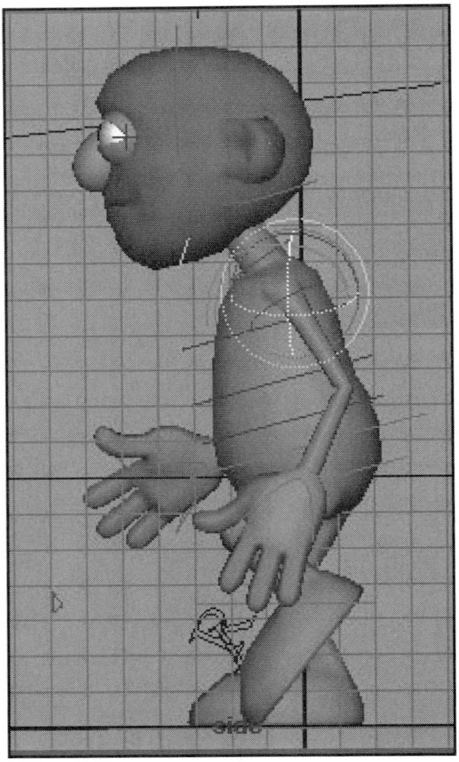

To send us your questions and/or feedback, you can contact the publisher at:

Thomson Delmar Learning
Executive Woods
5 Maxwell Drive
Clifton Park, NY 12065
Attn: Media Arts & Design Team
800-998-7498

Or the authors at:

Patricia Beckmann
Savannah College of Art & Design
P.O. Box 3146
Savannah, GA 31402
bunsellapb@yahoo.com

Phil Young
Savannah College of Art & Design
P.O. Box 3146
Savannah, GA 31402
payoung@scad.edu

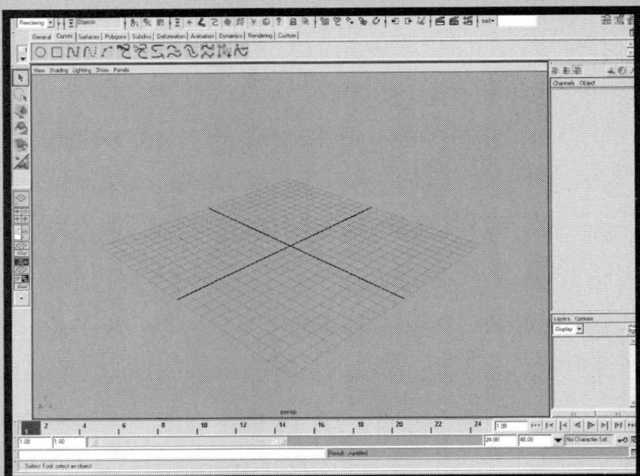

1

a discovery tour

charting your course

The computer is just another pencil; don't let the initial complexity overwhelm you.

Three-dimensional (3-D) software can help you build anything you can imagine. Everyone learns the same buttons, but your own individual imagination will create the art.

This chapter will introduce you to the different places wherein you will find your tools. First, you must understand the interface. Once you become comfortable with it, learning will get easier.

goals

- To discover the four main modules in Maya Complete and where they lead you.
- To learn the basics of the interface and mouse interaction.
- To set up a file directory to save your work.
- To get comfortable with navigating in Maya Complete.

NAVIGATION

Consider the interface to be a giant file cabinet with four main drawers. Inside these drawers are files. These files contain envelopes. The envelopes contain tools. The secret to getting the tool you need is to know which drawer, file, and envelope to look in. This becomes second nature after a bit of practice. Then you will be prepared to look deeper into the cabinet for the smaller folders containing the more complex tools. In this book, we will concentrate on practicing the tools found in the Maya Complete program.

Before we move ahead, make sure your interface looks like that shown in Figure 1–1.

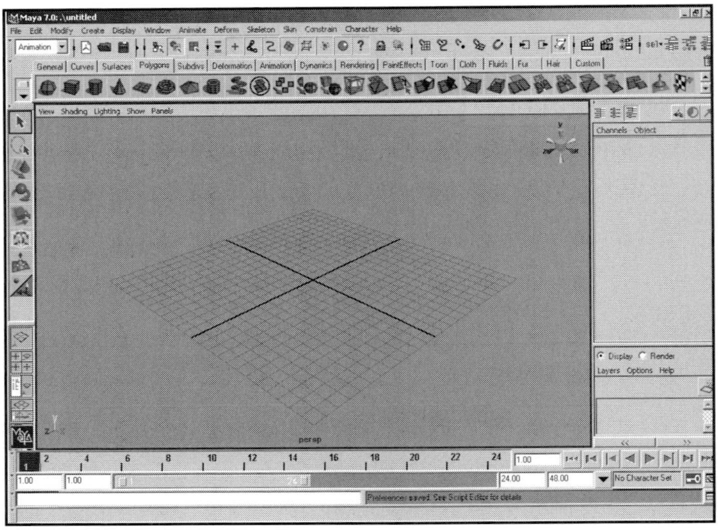

figure 1-1

The Maya interface.

Select the following:

Display > UI Elements

Make sure there is a check mark next to each interface item (Figure 1–2).

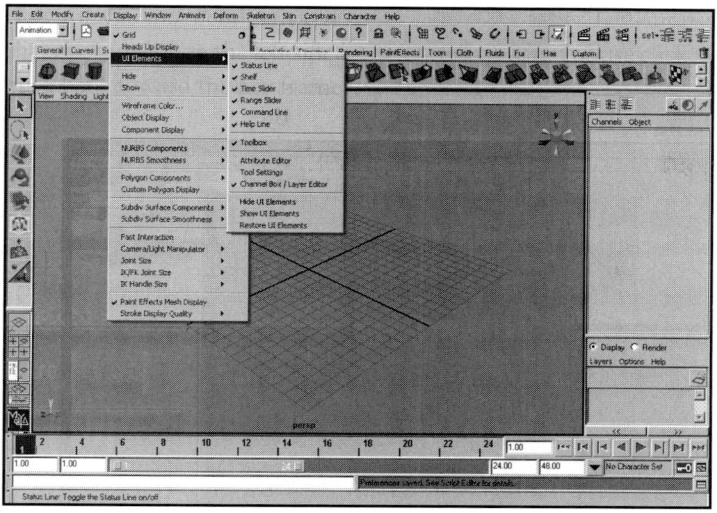

figure 1-2

Display interface items using the Display > UI Elements command.

In a school, many people will have access to the same software and computer you are working on. Each user will change the interface and customize it to his or her own individual work habits. Someone may turn off all interface menus. The next person who logs on will just see the perspective view and nothing else. You can get all of your navigation windows back by using:

Display > UI Elements

Just check or uncheck your desired options.

DON'T GO THERE!

THE DRAWERS

Maya Complete consists of four base modules. Consider these your drawers to the cabinet. These four modules organize the thousands of tools available in Maya as they pertain to animation, modeling, dynamics, and rendering. When you are in the Animation module, you will find the tools you need for setting up a skeleton and key-framing movement. In the Modeling module, you will find the tools you need to model a ship. The Dynamics module allows you to program physics into your models. The Rendering module gives you access to tools to process the scene for viewing.

You will find these modules in the upper-left corner of the interface. Click on the pull-down menu to reveal all of the four modules for Maya Complete (Figure 1–3).

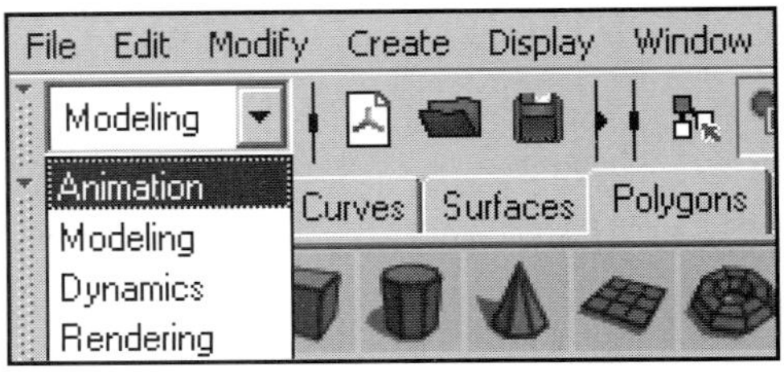

figure 1-3

The four basic modules in Maya Complete are Animation, Modeling, Dynamics, and Rendering.

Select each module in turn. Nothing really changes on the interface except for the pull-down menus at the top.

THE MAIN FILE FOLDERS

The area at the top of the application window is called the menu bar (Figure 1–4). The menu bar changes depending on which module you are in. Consider these titles to be the names of folders in the drawers of your file cabinet. Make sure you are in the Animation module, and then examine the menu bar titles.

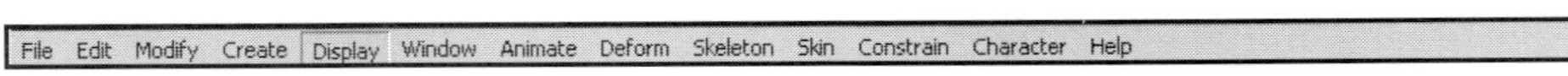

figure 1-4

The menu bar. Can you determine which mode this is?

Each module has the same six folders beginning the menu. These are File, Edit, Modify, Create, Display, and Window. These menus drive preference features you can access in any module of the interface.

To follow our file cabinet analogy, consider the choices available in these submenus to be the "envelopes" inside your "folders" (Figure 1–5).

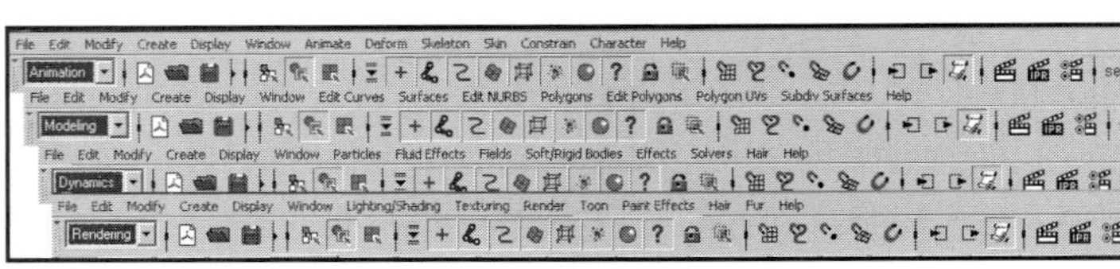

figure 1-5

Each module has the same six folders beginning the menu.

! MAYA'S HOTBOX

You can also access the modules and subfolders by holding down the space bar. When you hold down the space bar, Maya's Hotbox will appear. The Hotbox contains the main folders and subfolders plus the modules, as well as recent commands and the Hotbox display options. The Hotbox is a quick and easy way to access tools in Maya that can be customized to help speed up the workflow (Figure 1–6).

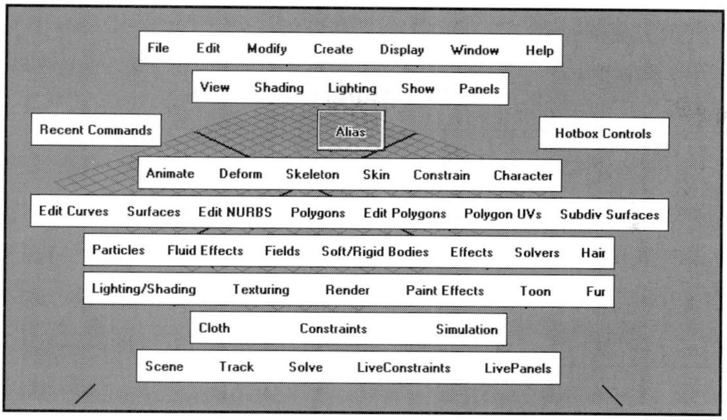

figure 1-6

Hold down the space bar to access the Hotbox.

THE TOOLS

Pull down a menu bar and tear off a dialog box.

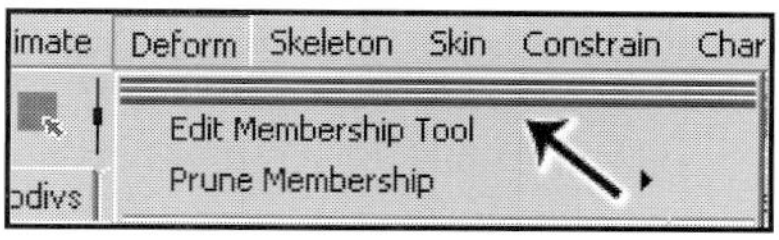

figure 1-7

The double blue line is at the top of the drop-down box.

To do this, highlight a menu item and look for the double blue line. Left mouse click on the lines, and the menu will float in the interface (Figure 1–7).

Left mouse click on one of the directories. These are your tools.

Do you notice the little boxes to the right of the tools? Left mouse click on one of them. A new box opens as shown in Figure 1–8. These are called options boxes. They allow you to modify the creation settings for that command. You do not always need to modify these settings. Most of the time, it is fine to use the default. If you are

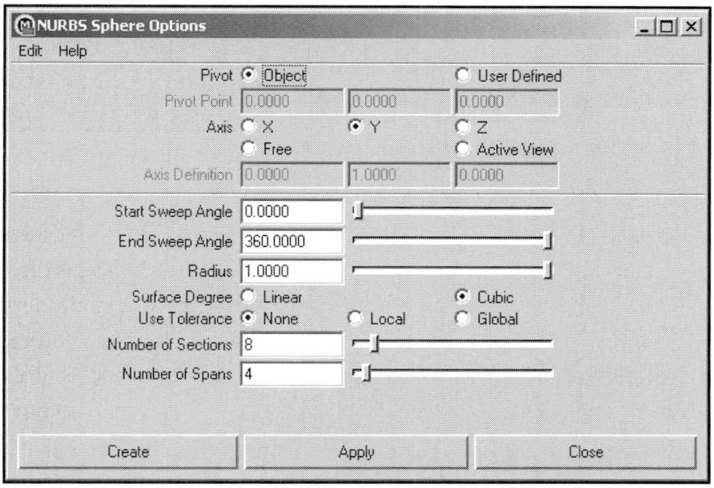

figure 1-8

The options box allows you to modify the settings of your tools.

a student sharing a machine with many others, make sure you reset these settings by using > **reset settings.** Then close the options dialog box. When you have done so, you are ready to use your tool.

THE STATUS LINE

The Status line (Figure 1–9) contains tools to edit your scene as a whole, by object, or by detail. The mode selector is at the far left. Look to the right of it, and you will see the Collapser icon. Left mouse click on it. The menu collapses or expands, depending on its initial setting.

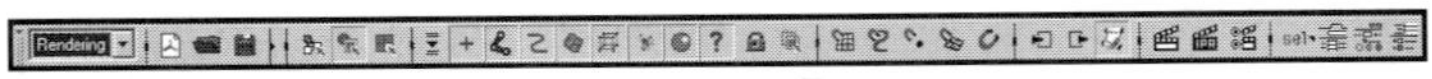

figure 1-9

The Status line.

This is used to hide a section of the Status line and eliminate clutter. When the Collapser shows an arrow, something is hidden. When it shows a box, you have the ability to hide the items on the right. These icons are shown in Figure 1–10.

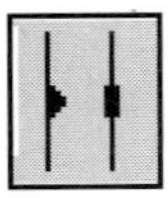

figure 1-10

The Collapser with an arrow and a box.

The next important area to discover is the Hierarchy/Object/Component mode (Figure 1–11). This very important group determines how you select objects in the scene for editing. Hierarchy selects an entire grouped object, such as a model of a car, and all the elements. Object will pick a piece of the car, such as a tire, for example. Component will allow you to select a piece of the car, such as a tire, and then select the points in space that make up the tire.

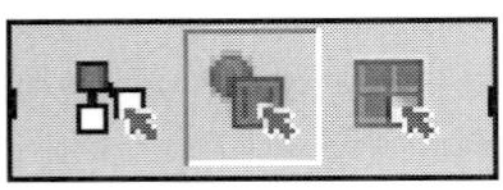

figure 1-11

Hierarchy mode, Object mode (selected), and Component mode icons.

As you click on each of these, you will notice that the section to the right on the Status line changes. These icons represent what can be edited while in that mode. Hierarchy icons manipulate the grouped objects as a whole. Object mode icons affect base objects, such as primitives. Component mode icons affect smaller components of the model, such as lines, hulls, and vertices.

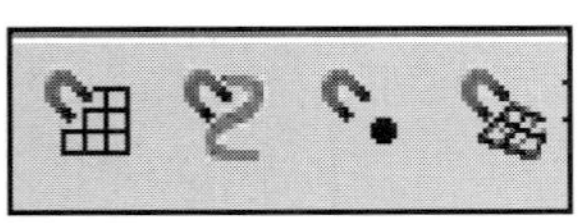

figure 1-12

Snap to Grids, Snap to Points, and Snap to Planes icons.

The next section is Snap modes (Figure 1–12). When you snap to something, it is as if the object has a magnet luring your object to the selected Snap mode. We will explore these later.

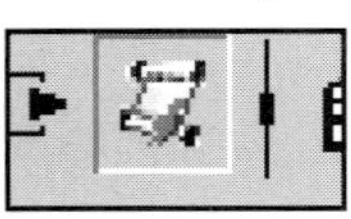

figure 1-13

Construction history icon.

Construction history (Figure 1–13) is the next important button. It looks like a scroll and feather.

Construction history records all of the commands used to create an object. The construction history is used as a reference so that when you edit an object, all related information gets updated with it. Do not continually leave this feature on. You should only use it when you need to because it uses considerable random access memory (RAM).

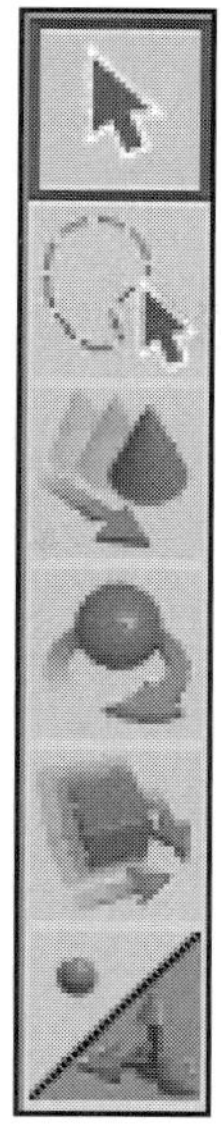

figure 1-14

Scene icons.

The Scene icons (Figure 1–14) represent the different rendering modes in Maya. A render is the final graphic output of the scene showing model, lighting, texture, and possibly animation. It is as if you are shooting a reel of film with your camera as you model, light, texture, and animate, and then you take the reel of film to the one-hour-photo shop for developing.

On the left side of the interface is the Toolbox (Figure 1–15). These tools are the most often used, and they relate to positioning objects in the scene.

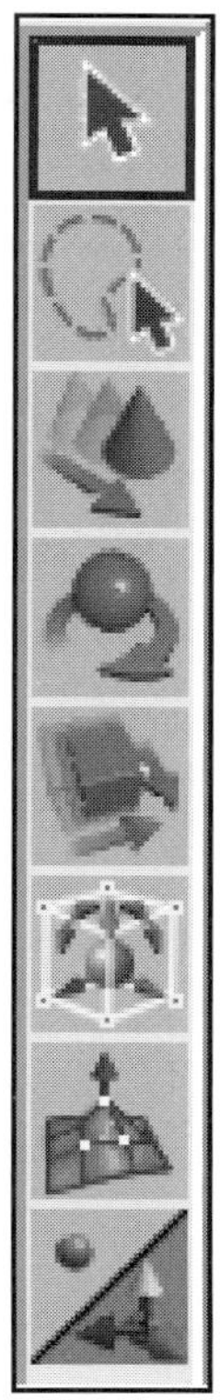

figure 1-15

Toolbox.

The first tool in the Toolbox is the Select tool. This allows you to select an object by left mouse clicking on it. Next, the Lasso tool allows you to draw a shape around an object to select it. The third tool is the Move tool, which allows you to translate an object through *x*, *y*, and *z* space. The Rotate tool allows you to rotate an object in *x*, *y*, and *z* space. The Scale tool is fifth, and it allows you to scale in *x*, *y*, and *z* space. The sixth tool in the Toolbox is the Universal Manipulator. This is new to Maya 7. This tool combines the functions of the Move, Rotate, and Scale tools into a single manipulator. The seventh tool in the Toolbox is the Soft Modification tool. This tool allows you to push and pull on geometry as if you were a sculptor working with clay. The eighth tool in the Toolbox is the Show Manipulator tool. This tool displays a manipulator that is modified to fit the specific node that is selected and the particular task at hand. It is used frequently when modeling with the polygons as well as creating and adjusting lights and cameras.

The Quick Layout buttons (Figure 1–16) are below the Toolbox. These allow you to pick different views of your model. Click through them to get comfortable with finding your Four-Panel view, Perspective view, and others. You can enlarge any of the individual layout windows to Full-Screen view by first selecting the viewport and then tapping the space bar. Tap the space bar a second time to return to Layout mode.

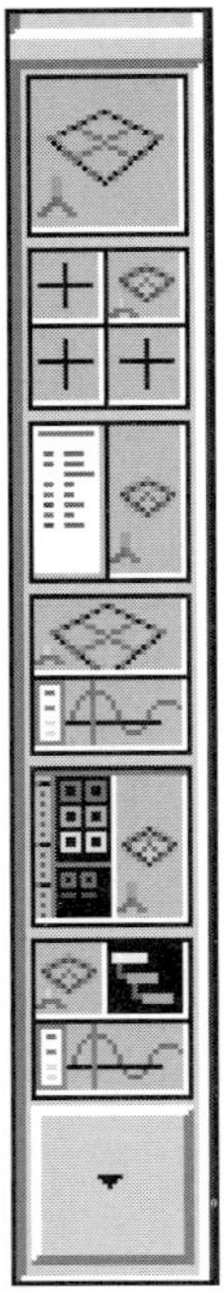

figure 1-16

Quick Layout buttons.

The largest portion of real estate on our interface is the View Panel (Figure 1–17). This is the stage that is used to construct your artwork.

Go to the Quick Layout buttons and select the Four-Panel view, it is the second button from the top of the list. This configuration of views offers the artist one of the most advantageous ways to view the scene file. The Four-Panel view is so advantageous because it incorporates the use of both orthographic and perspective view ports.

The Perspective view is a true 3-D view. The other kind of view offered in Maya is Orthographic, which includes views such as Front, Left, Back, Top, Bottom, and Side views. Lines do not converge at a distance in Orthographic view, but they do in Perspective view, which is how the two views differ.

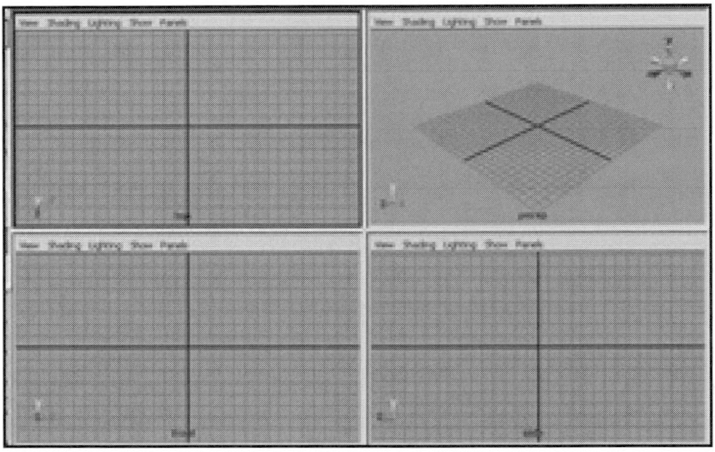

figure 1-17

The View Panel, in the Four-Panel view.

VIEW COMPASS

New to Maya 7 is the View Compass button (Figure 1–18) located in the Perspective viewport. The View Compass button is a quick and easy way to move from the Perspective view to any one of the six Orthographic views. The Orthographic views include Front, Left, Back, Right, Top, and Bottom (Figure 1–19). To move from the

Perspective view to an Orthographic view, simply click any of the arrows on the View Compass. To return to the Perspective viewport, simply click the blue box in the center of the View Compass.

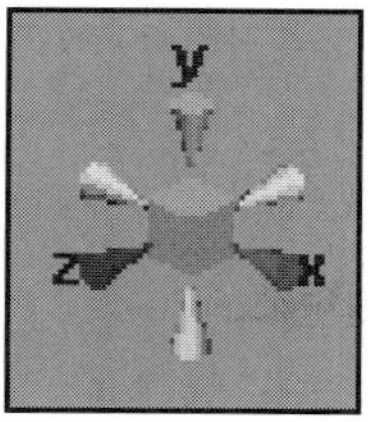

figure 1-18

View Compass button.

You should be using a three-button mouse with this software. Avoid two-button mice with

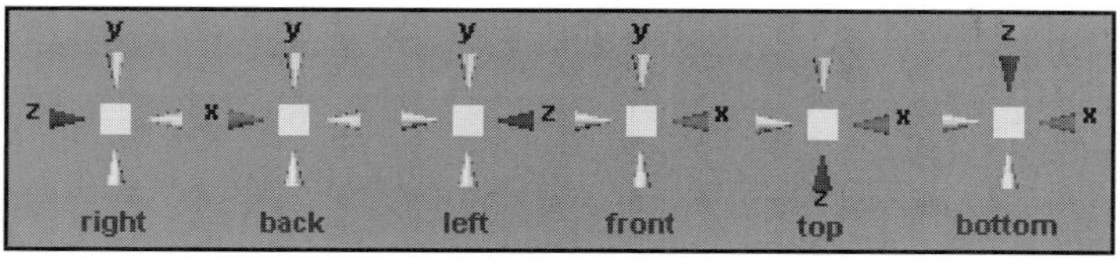

figure 1-19

Orthographic views in View Compass.

scrollwheels, though they can be used. Each of the three buttons has a unique purpose in Maya. Try the following combinations of buttons and keyboard controls for navigating the View window (Figure 1–20):

- Put your mouse icon in the Perspective view. Press the left mouse button (LMB) and the Alt key at the same time and hold them down. By moving your mouse, you rotate around the window. This method only works in the Perspective view.
- Press and hold down the middle mouse button (MMB) and the Alt key at the same time. By moving the mouse, you pan around the window. This method works in all window views.
- Hold down the left and middle mouse buttons (LMMB) and the Alt key. By moving your mouse, you dolly in and out of the window. This method works in all window views.

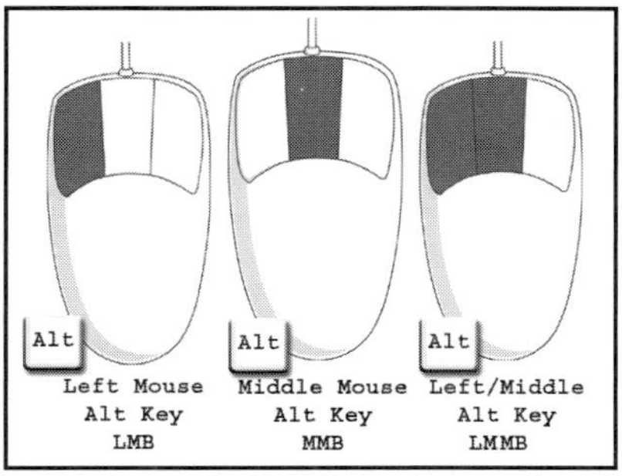

figure 1-20

LMB (rotate), MMB (pan), and LMMB (dolly).

On the right of the interface, you should have your Channel Box (Figure 1–21). This window allows you to put in mathematical values for Translate, Rotate, and Scale. You may also make adjustments to newly created objects. You can also change this window to the Attribute Editor or Tool Settings window by selecting one of the icons in the upper-right corner of the interface (Figure 1–22). We will use this area quite often.

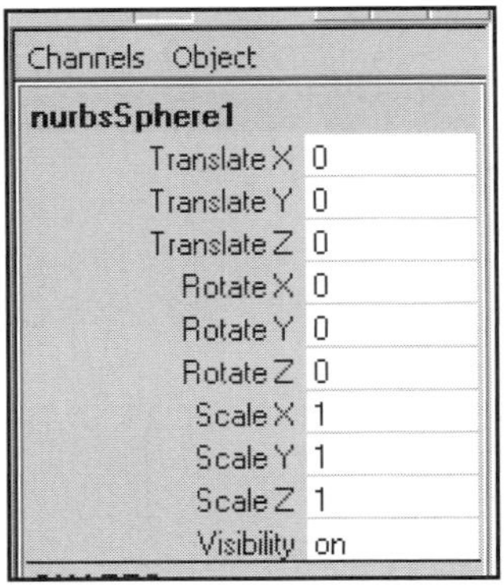

figure 1-21

Channel Box with a sphere selected.

At the bottom of your interface, you will find the Time slider, Playback controls, and Range slider (Figure 1–23). When you animate, these controls will identify at what point in time you are adding information.

Below the Range slider is a blank rectangular field known as the Command line.

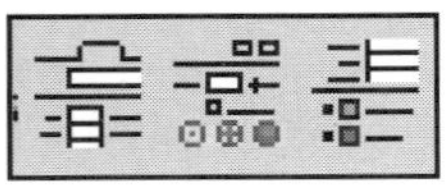

figure 1-22

Attribute Editor, Channel Box, and Tool Settings icons.

The Command line (Figure 1–24) allows you to type MEL commands directly into Maya. (MEL is the programming language used in Maya.) Maya operates through script commands. Every icon on the interface merely represents a script command. If you wish,

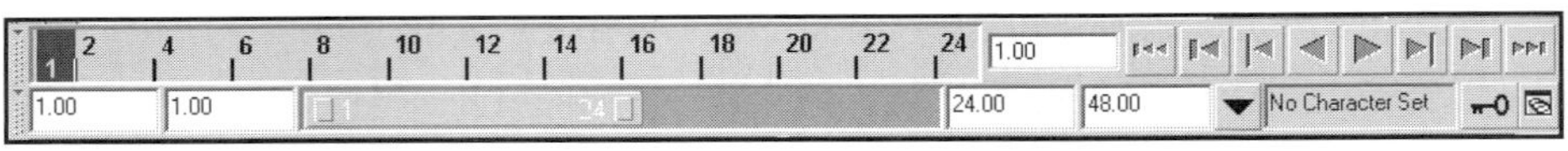

figure 1-23

Time slider, Playback controls, and Range slider.

you can bypass the icons and directly type in the commands to create artwork in Maya.

If you are uncertain of what an icon represents, move your mouse over it and look at the Help line (Figure 1–25). This will give you a written definition.

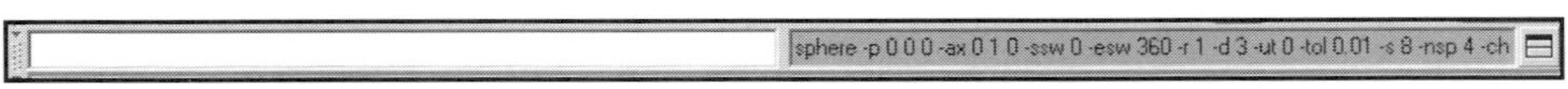

figure 1-24

Command line.

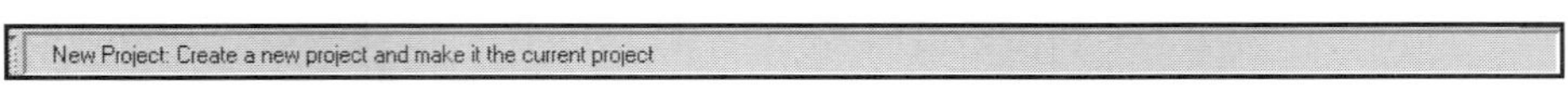

figure 1-25

Help line.

SETTING UP YOUR ACCOUNT

Correctly saving files will keep you from losing or misplacing scene files containing many hours of work. Always remember to do a double backup of your files. Countless artists have lost beautiful work because of misplaced disks, corrupted media, and computer crashes. No teacher, production manager, or client will accept the excuse that you lost your file when the project is due. It is recommended that you back up your files on a daily basis.

TUTORIAL: SETTING UP YOUR FIRST PROJECT

To set up your project directory, follow the steps outlined here.

As shown in Figure 1–26, select the following:

File > Project > New

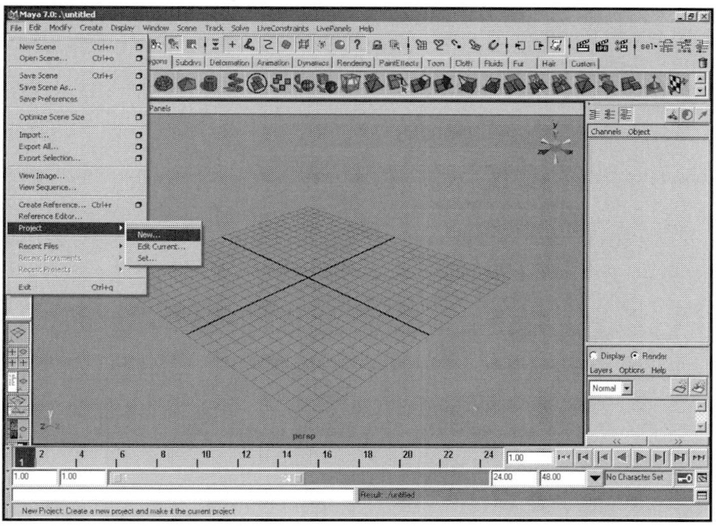

figure 1-26 Creating a new project.

The New Project window opens (Figure 1–27). This window shows a directory holding all the folders for this project. In this directory, you will store your textures, scene file, rendered pictures, and all other data. This is where you will look for information pertaining to your project. Make sure this directory is backed up onto your personal backup media when you are done.

In the Name box, put your name or the word "Tutorials." For the Location box, click on Browse. This opens your computer, and you can locate an area on your computer disk where you can store this directory. You may also store directly to your personal media. Choose the location you want, and click OK. The location you have chosen will show up in the Location path. The location may be a drive other than C, a recordable CD, DVD, or flash card.

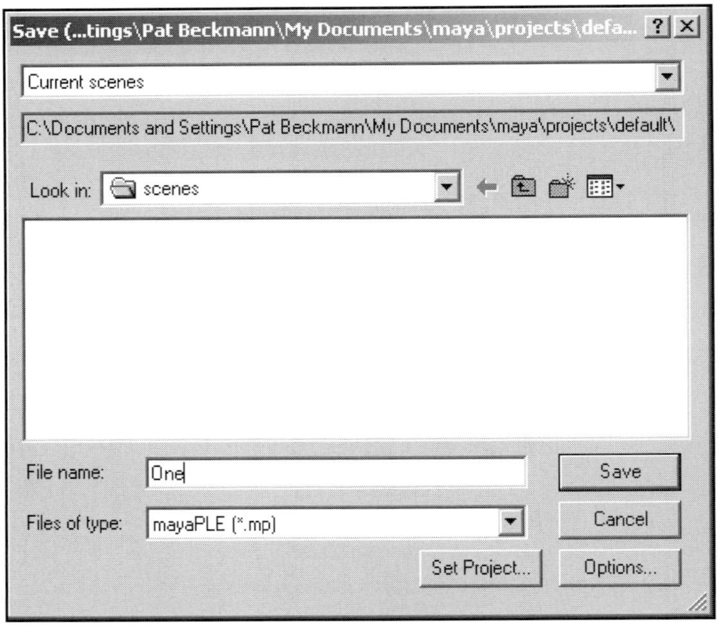

figure 1-27 New Project window.

At the bottom of the box, click Use Defaults. Folders will be named with default directory names. Click Accept. You now have a directory in the location specified. Search for the directory you have created to make sure you know where it is.

Now save your first file. Go to the main pull-down menu, and select the following:

File > Save Scene As...

A new window pops up. These are your save settings. Look in the window under Current scenes. This is the directory path leading to where your file will be saved. You can navigate away from this directory in special circumstances, but for now leave it here. Name the file "One," and select Save (Figure 1–28).

Look at the top of the Maya interface. The directory path to your file is presented here. If you need to access files from your directory, you can find them using this path. All data created in your scene will be found in the folders in this directory.

When you back up this directory, don't forget to include such things as your textures and scripts. They will be linked from different folders contained in the directory. If you are missing any information, you will have to reconstruct it the next time you consult your project.

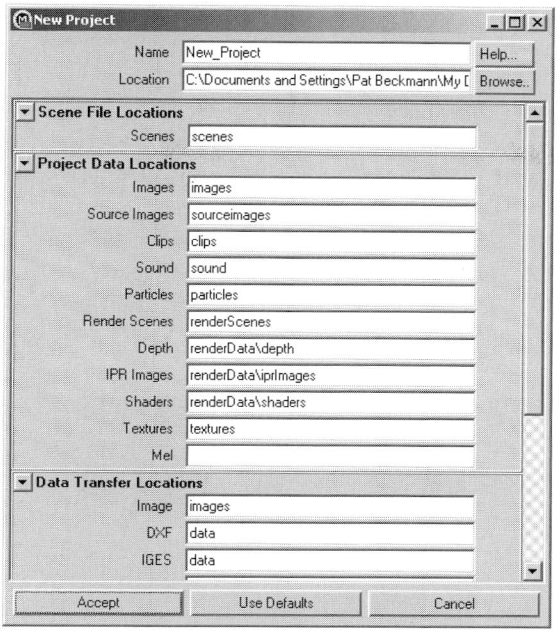

figure 1-28

Saving the new project.

DON'T GO THERE!

Don't make the biggest mistake that digital artists make. Don't forget to double back up your work!

Make two backups of your work at the very least. Keep a backup in a box in a safe, dry place. Keep one with you. You *will* lose your files. Your disk *will* eventually corrupt. Disks are easy to abuse—and they exact revenge. Once that happens, your competition three states away will be that much closer to getting your dream job. Protect yourself with double backups.

SUMMARY

Congratulations on making it through the introduction. You have absorbed some very important basic material. The interface is your map. If you don't know where you are going, you will get lost. You should also now understand how to pack your treasures away and take them with you.

Now close the book, and think about what you have learned. Play with the software, and do the tutorial again without referring to the book. Then answer the review questions and perform the homework exercises in this chapter.

in review

1. What are the four main modules in Maya Complete?
2. What keyboard entry is required with the left mouse button that allows you to rotate around in the Perspective view?
3. How do you turn on the display of different user interface elements?
4. What are the differences among Hierarchy, Object, and Component modes?
5. How do Orthographic and Perspective views differ?
6. How do you set up a project directory?
7. How often should you back up your work?

EXPLORING ON YOUR OWN

1. Access the Help menu option to view introductory learning materials that are provided with Maya. Here you will find tutorials, a method of looking up unfamiliar terms, and learning movies.
2. View the Essential Skills Movies under Help/Learning Movies. They will help you learn the interface.
3. Work on the tutorials in addition to what you will do in this book. These tutorials can be found under the Help button.
4. Examine the Help file information pertaining to system and document preferences.

notes

2

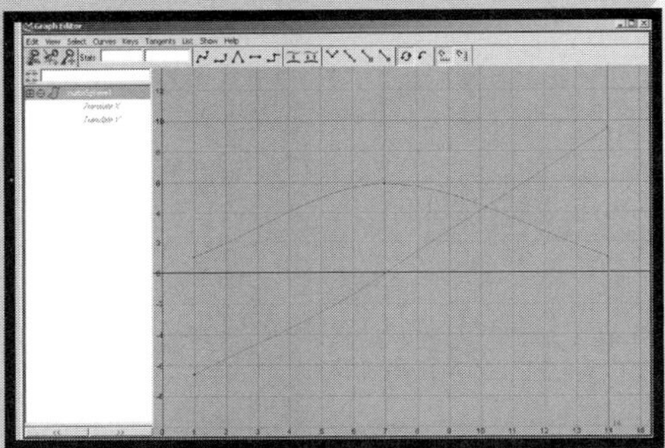

principles of animation

charting your course

The secret to believable animation resides in the Animation Graph Editor. Understanding this graph is the secret to finding out where your animation is going right and where it is going wrong. Knowing how to apply weight, follow-through, and anticipation to curves can mean the difference between bad and phenomenal animation.

Animation moves in arcs. Weight is determined by how fast or slow mass moves through these arcs, how it reacts, and so on. The Animation Graph Editor is a visual representation of all arcs in your 3D animation.

goals

In this chapter, you will:

- **Understand the principles of animation.**
- **Discover the Animation Graph Editor.**
- **Learn the curve shapes of different kinds of movement.**
- **Get familiar with editing curves.**

THE CLASSIC PRINCIPLES OF ANIMATION

What makes it work? It is necessary at this time to discuss some of the basic principles that have been developed over the past 100 years or so by the pioneers in the animation industry. Keep in mind that these are not separate concepts. They are interlocking pieces of the whole in creating a piece of animation that communicates ideas to the audience.

Mechanics

The following are some basic concepts on mechanics:

Timing: In the bouncing ball test, timing will be one of the first principles you deal with. Timing is the main determinant in the meaning of your drawings when they are assembled in a series for the purpose of animation. In the case of the ball, the timing is determined by the frequency of each bounce. As you will learn, each arc in the bounce is designed to be a bit shorter than the one before. In this manner, the timing is regulated by the time it takes to complete each bounce. The second factor in determining the visual elements in the bounce is spacing, which is discussed next.

Spacing: This refers to the way the ball drawings are closely grouped at the top of each arc and to the way they incrementally become spaced apart throughout the arc until hitting the widest spacing on either side of each impact point. This principle will be examined with more variation in the beanbag exercise in the following chapters. The principles of timing and spacing that you will learn in the first two exercises will remain constant factors in each piece of animation you will execute from here on.

Hard and soft accents: Throughout our scenes, there will be points of emphasis deriving from the dynamics of weight and speed applied to movements. Each of these accents can be varied through the use of timing and spacing to achieve a varied feeling in the action and to prevent a sameness that can detract from visual interest.

Next, referring once more to the way the drawings will be spaced in the beginning exercises, we are able to discuss another term used quite often in animation.

Slow in and slow out: In discussing spacing and timing, you will become aware that the slowing down of an animated object is accomplished by the "bunching up" of drawings in a series. By utilizing an extreme slowing down of drawings, you can very nearly stop a movement entirely. This will be a very handy thing to remember when you want to slow down an action in order to show an important point in a scene or to showcase a facial expression inferring a thought process or a change of emotions in a character. The terms "slow in" and "slow out" refer to this process as it applies to movement, as in "slowing in" to a movement from a static pose or "slowing out" of a movement and into a more static pose.

Moving holds: This term is used for the drawings leading into and out of those more static poses in our animation. They supply a very necessary function in that they keep the movement of an animated object going, regardless of how slight that movement may be. This is very essential because movement is the only element that keeps the feeling of reality and life maintained for the audience. As soon as a series of animation drawings is reduced to one held drawing, the illusion vanishes, the drawing goes flat, and the viewer is reminded that he or she is looking at something that is really only a drawing. There are some actions you can use to keep things lively in your animation during moving holds, and we will discuss those later in this section.

Squash and stretch: This term is among the most well-known principles when discussing animation. It applies to the most essential function of movement—the changing of shapes. This shape is the characteristic that differentiates living things from hard or inanimate objects.

The use of squash and stretch in the bouncing ball exercise in the next chapter is a minimal use of the principle. In the beanbag exercise, it will be used in more broad applications. There are many ways to use it in the context of animation.

Think of the crouch of an athlete about to execute a standing broad jump. Then picture the explosive extension of the body as the jump is executed, and then imagine the bend and flex of knees and waist as the landing is completed: squash, stretch, and back to squash.

Facial expressions are another place where squash and stretch is not only helpful but necessary. Our facial muscles enable us to convey a complete range of expressions from a squint-eyed, compressed-mouth picture of anger to a wide-eyed, open-mouthed example of surprise and then to a relaxed, smiling countenance.

Full-body attitudes are another example of where squash and stretch come into play, and several of these will be evidenced in our beanbag exercise (see Figures 2-1 through 2-5):

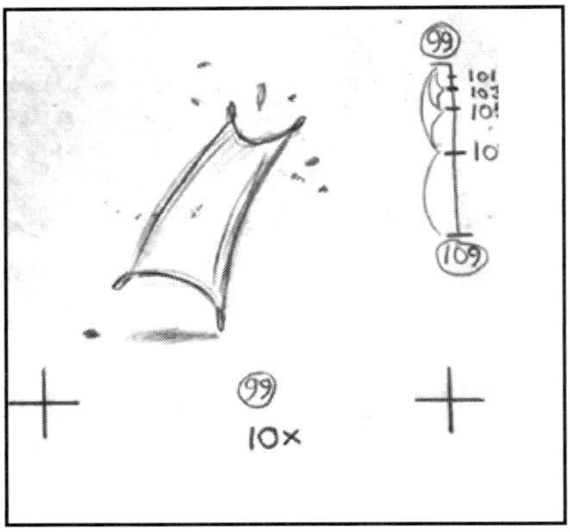

figure 2-1

The "fright" reaction = stretch.

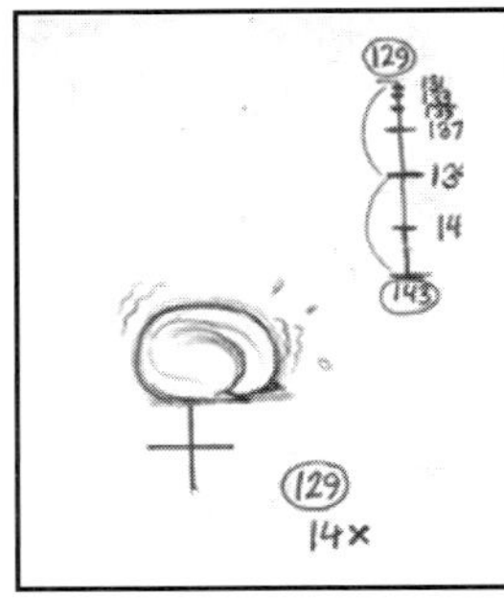

figure 2-2

Cowering crouch = squash.

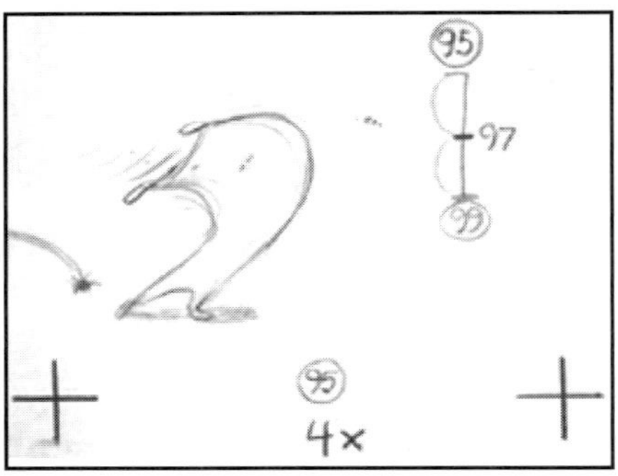

figure 2-3

"Attack" pose = stretch.

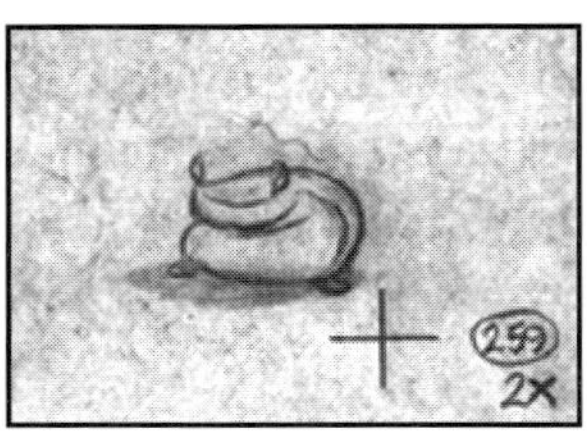

figure 2-4

Anticipation to the leap = squash.

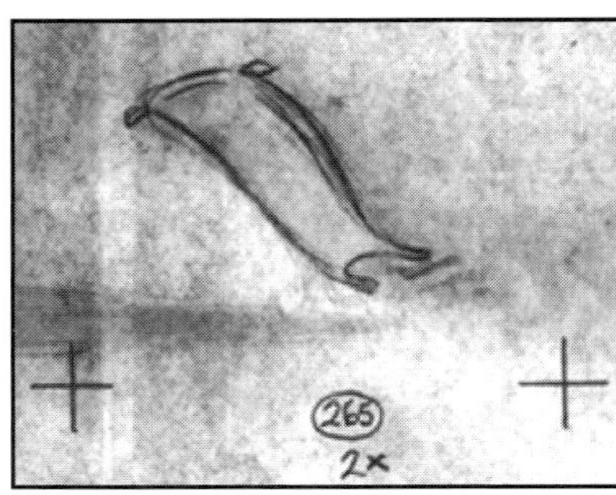

figure 2-5

The leap = stretch.

Other issues you will encounter during the beanbag exercise are as follows:

Straight ahead and pose-to-pose action: These are two basic approaches to animating. Most professionals today do not consider either of them "the only way to work" at the exclusion of the other.

Straight ahead is simply starting with a drawing and then working through the animation one drawing at a time to the end of the scene. The animator is aware of what needs to happen in the course of the scene to advance the story but has no hard, set plan, which allows his imagination to take him on a kind of stream-of-consciousness path filled with spontaneity and surprises. In the best scenario, the surprises inject a quirky element into the story that can be an asset.

On the other hand, the down side to this approach may contain several pitfalls. The control factor is thrown more or less to the wind; the size and volume of the drawings tend to fluctuate, which creates drawing problems that cause an inordinate amount of time and labor to correct. The timing and movement may become repetitive and assume a uniformity of intensity that can easily become predictable to the viewer.

Now we will consider the pose-to-pose approach. In this method, the scene is carefully planned out in advance. Thumbnail sketches of the action are defined so that the needed action of the scene is addressed. The size relationships in the drawings are more easily controlled, which results in less time spent on drawing corrections, which is a fact appreciated by the assistants who will handle the work as it moves down the production line.

There are a few drawbacks to the exclusive use of the pose-to-pose method as well. With everything planned out in advance, spontaneity may suffer or be altogether lacking. Stiffness may result, and the entertainment could be lacking, which produces boredom in the audience.

Since there are advantages and disadvantages to either approach, the judicious use of both methods within our animation seems to be the best method for most animators. By taking this course of action, a variety of visual expressions can be attained, which produces the element known to animators as "Texture" within our scenes.

The beanbag exercise will be animated using this combined method of pose-to-pose and straight ahead. The use of the initial thumbnails translated into animation poses is an example of pose-to-pose planning. A good example of straight ahead will be found in the "Fright-take" and midair scramble into the crouch position that our character will use in reaction to the spider.

Ones or twos?: The standard screen time allotted to an animation drawing is two frames of film. We will back up a little at this time and explain a bit about frames and how they are fitted into continuity in motion picture technology.

To start at the beginning, a 35mm camera shoots 24 frames for each second of screen time. This produces one and one-half feet for each second of picture that the audience sees on screen. As a rule, each animation drawing shot at the 2-frames-per-drawing rate will approximate natural movement. That means 12 drawings are required for each second of screen time.

If the motion that is represented in the animation is very fast or complex, the animator may need to resort to making one drawing per frame in order to smooth out the animation and eliminate strobing or jerkiness in the images. This results in the number of drawings for each second increasing by double to 24 drawings for one second of screen time.

In Computer Graphics, you automatically animate on ones. You can create an interesting look by rendering out the animation done on ones, deleting every second frame, and then duplicating every first. For some, this appears more natural.

Composition

Staging: As in any element of presentation, the staging is primarily dictated by the need to advance the story being told. Each idea needs to be showcased so that its clarity is unmistakable. The shots in sequence should take the audience on a review of the story points, which directs attention to each part of the whole with a minimum of distraction.

The camera needs to be at the correct distance for the action or story point being shown in each scene:

- A long shot is used when everything in a large space needs to be seen.
- A close-up can feature personality.
- A master shot can start out taking in a large area and then move in for a closer aspect.
- Short-cut shots can skip from place to place to feature several important objects or locations.

Clarity is of the essence in staging a scene and includes the elimination of any conflicting movement or element within the composition that might "upstage" or attract the attention of the viewer during the shot.

In the case of animation, clear expression of ideas may be attained through the use of silhouette in the poses. Action is best shown through having the center of attention outside the lines of the character drawings rather than trying to have the action played straight in front of the actor (see Figures 2-6 and 2-7).

In this illustration, the actor is removing a cork from a bottle that is directly in front of him and in our line of vision.

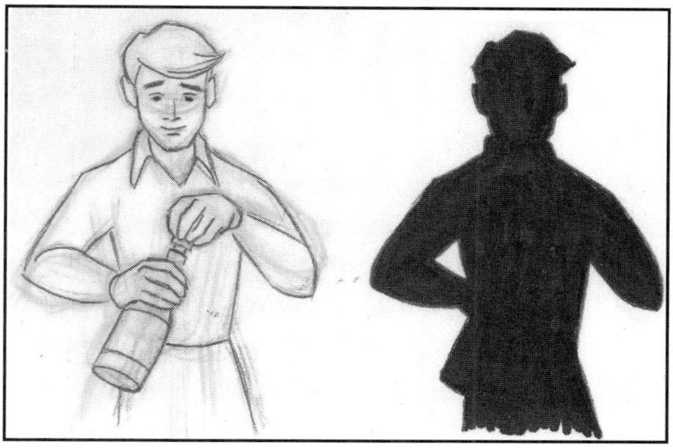

figure 2-6

A bad silhouette.

Now we see the same bit of business staged in clear silhouette, which results in much more easily seen staging of the action.

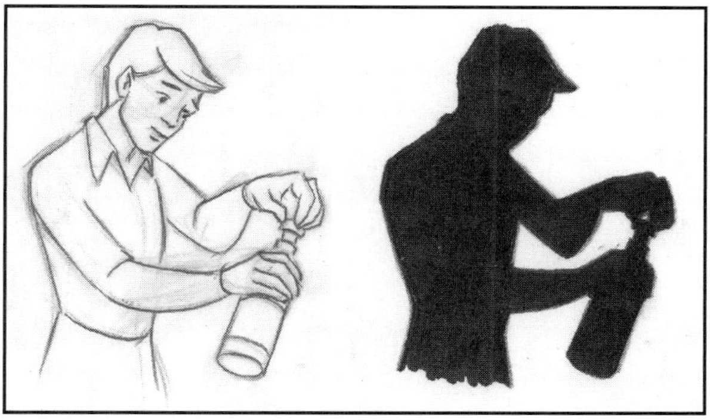

figure 2-7

A good silhouette.

Using the same idea of clear expression of ideas, the use of carefully planned arcs in the action being animated is of utmost importance. As you will learn in the bouncing ball exercise, an arc is the natural line through which most things move, and it is one of the most vital elements in character animation. An arc is the best way to help the viewer follow an action without confusion, which unifies the motions within the animation and eliminates the bumps and rough spots in the movements.

After posing out a piece of animation, the next item of importance is to check all the arcs within the movement for smoothness and the placement from one to the next in the progression.

An example of the arcs within the animation of a tennis serve and how they should be employed is shown in Figure 2-8.

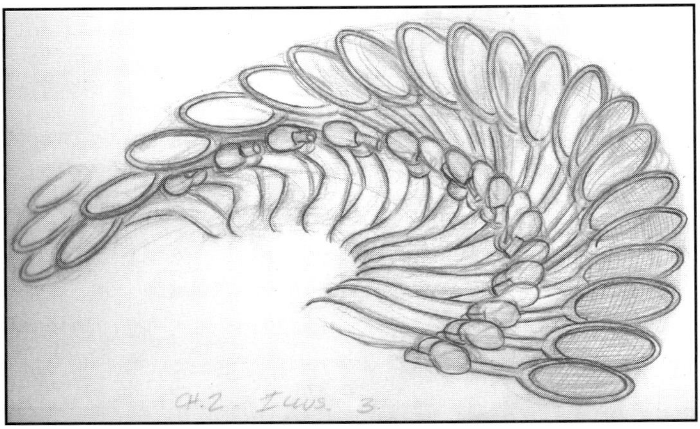

figure 2-8

Arcs within the animation of a tennis serve.

Acting

The following are some basic concepts on Acting:

Exaggeration: The drawings in an animated scene can most often be classified as caricature. By the same standard, the actions being depicted should be caricatured versions of the "real thing"; that is to say, the animator must push reality a bit into the realm of caricature.

This exaggeration of reality can actually enhance the "real" feeling of a mood or action for the audience. In effect, the contact is established more solidly even though we are not necessarily depicting realism.

In summary, the attitude should be to push the broad action as far as possible while keeping it believable.

Anticipation and follow-through: It is difficult for an audience to understand events being depicted on the screen without a planned sequence of actions leading one activity to the next. The proper exposition will set up the audience to expect the next movement before it happens.

The principle here is to precede each action with a specific move that anticipates what is about to happen for the audience. The move may be as small as an expression change or as large as a broad physical action. An example might be the drawing back of an arrow on a bowstring prior to the release of the arrow. It can be the gaze of a character at an object, then raising the hand just before reaching for, and picking up the object. Even a surprise gag needs to be set up with anticipation, or the punch may fail to pay off.

The natural result of anticipation is the follow-through that comes after it, which is the release of the arrow in our previous analogy. The artful employment of anticipation should make this the easy part, as long as the staging is effective and unhampered by upstaging or other distractions.

The previously mentioned surprise gag can be made effective by setting up the audience to expect a certain follow-through and then introducing a completely different result. If this happens unintentionally, you had better brush up on your storytelling skills!

Overlap and secondary actions: These terms were developed to apply to some of the means that were discovered to keep animated characters from coming to a complete stop between active modes or when going into a held pose. As was mentioned previously in the section on moving holds, a held, single drawing becomes very flat and unnatural.

Overlapping and secondary actions refer to the movements of other elements in a drawing that continue a moving momentum when a character starts or stops a primary action. Examples of these kinds of elements can be appendages, such as long ears, tails, hair, and clothing, or any articulated objects attached to or being carried by the character.

Any accessory objects or materials used in overlaps or secondaries must have a believable feeling of weight and a movement pattern that is natural looking and does not feel self-generated. For example, it is not a good idea to have clothing that appears to have a life of its own.

Body parts on a heavy, fleshy character can stretch, catch up, twist, and contract as internal forms work with and against each other. Any or all of these actions can be used to add a punch line of their own to primary action.

Drawing

A pencil is still a useful tool in 3D.

Design unity: Whether working in a traditional or computer-generated format, design is the prime consideration in constructing a character. One need not get "trapped" in a particular formula in character design, but it is a good idea to be practiced and well versed in many of the styles that have developed over the years, as the reasons for their existence are usually well founded on functionality. That is to say, they are proven to work!

The goals are elusive at times, but it is useful to keep certain principles in mind when attempting to come up with a character design that is successful. Design unity is exemplified in a character that blends visual characteristics to add up to a harmonious whole. The starting point leading to this successful application is to learn to draw as well as possible.

Solid drawing: Through the effort of constant practice, we can bring our abilities up to the levels of expertise required to create drawings with weight, depth, and balance. Experience is usually the best teacher, and only through trial and error can we attain that experience. Studies in perspective and anatomy are of equal importance in this combined effort.

The goal, once again, is not simply to replicate reality, but to learn the tangible aspects of realism and use them as a starting point on which to express your individual presentation, exaggerating and de-emphasizing as needed to attain a caricature (there is that word again!) of reality.

Appeal: This term is not reserved for cute kittens and baby ducks; it includes anything in a character that draws our interest in a positive (or sometimes negative) way. Whether dealing with a noble, heroic character or a base villain, both types must have enough appeal, or the audience will lose interest in what they are doing. In a live actor, we use the term "charisma." Here is a list of a few items that give a character appeal:

- Charm
- Pleasing design
- Simplicity
- Communication
- Magnetism

Simple, direct attitudes make the best animation drawings. Delicate expressions are easy to misinterpret; we do not want to confuse our audience! Attempting too much refinement can make the presentation so restrained or involved that it may interfere with communication.

Un-appeal: This is the term we have chosen to represent the flip side of appeal. Unfortunately, we are witness to un-appeal in the movie and TV animated products we see on an almost daily basis. It does not mean we need to lower our standard and settle for less, and it certainly does not mean we need to emulate it. An ugly drawing may have an initial shock value, but usually it lacks the strength it would need to carry a story, such as character building and audience identification.

Here are some of the things that contribute to un-appeal:

- Weak drawing
- Complicated; hard to read
- Poor design
- Clumsy shapes
- Awkward moves

Line of action: This aspect is one of the very basic necessities in an animation pose. It represents the main thrust or function of a specific action and is the very first consideration when an animator begins a pose. In a very broad movement, the line of action can point straight into the movement being depicted. Even in a resting pose, the line of action can be evident in the depiction of the center of gravity that balances the figure or the leaning of a figure against a solid object.

The ability of an artist to immediately address the line of action in a pose is a function that is continually sharpened through the process of life drawing sessions as well as informal sketching of observed subjects in various locations. These activities should be considered an ongoing process, as there is never the need to feel we have learned all there is to learn from observation. It must become a lifelong habit.

YOUR MAIN TOOL—THE GRAPH EDITOR

The Animation Graph Editor can be found by going to: **Window** > **Animation Editors** > **Graph Editor** (see Figure 2-9).

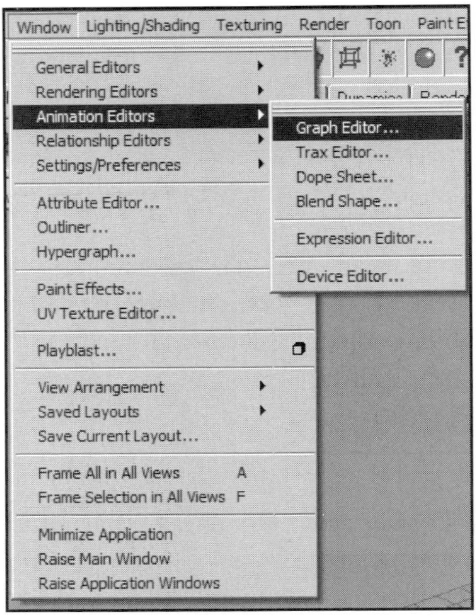

figure 2-9

How to find the Graph Editor.

A new window opens. This is the Animation Graph Editor interface (see Figure 2-10).

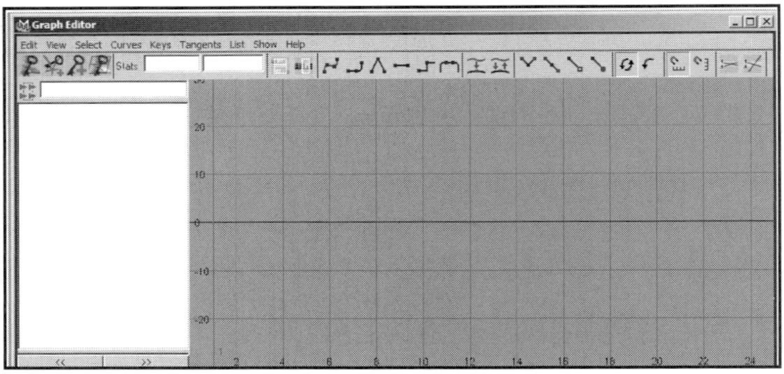

figure 2-10

Graph Editor interface.

Within this interface, the arcs of movement you create in your animations are represented. You can easily see where problems have developed and can interactively make changes. We will not go through every tool at this beginner stage, but we will give an overview and show you the techniques for correctly using the most active buttons.

The top of the Graph Editor has eight pull-down menus. Left-mouse click on these pull-down menus to see the extra tools available (see Figure 2-11).

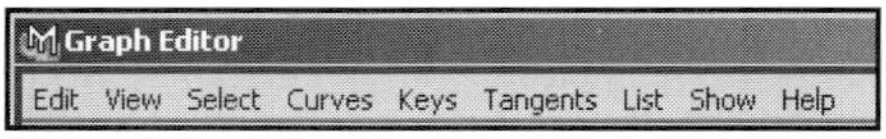

figure 2-11

The pull-down tools available.

These tools are the heavy hitters. Each pull-down menu lists a new set of tools available to you. The titles of each set are self-explanatory, and we will review each set. The individual tools you will use most often in this book are explained later in this chapter. You can read about the rest by going to the Help menu in Maya and typing in their names.

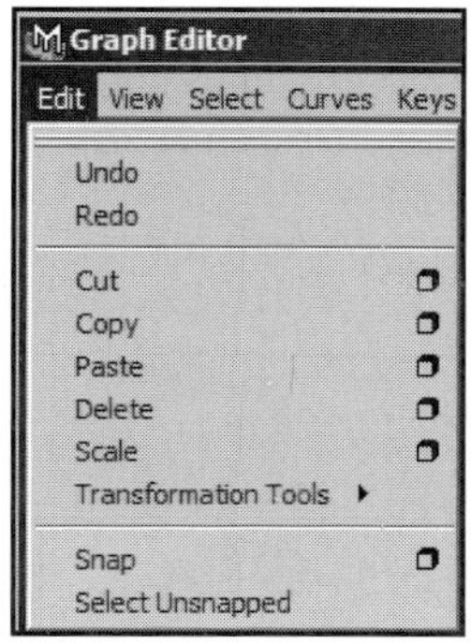

figure 2-12

The Edit tools.

Edit Tools

The Edit tools are basic commands much like those found in a word-processing program (see Figure 2-12).

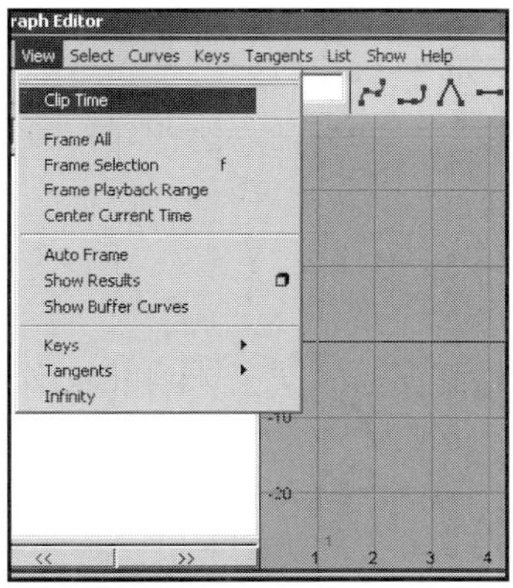

figure 2-13

The View tools.

View Tools

The View tools assist with setting up the window for optimal navigation (see Figure 2-13).

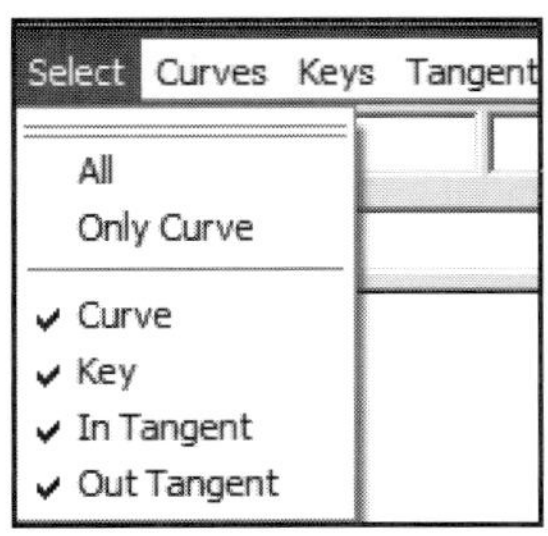

figure 2-14

The Select tools.

Select Tools

The Select tools allow you to simplify the selection process (see Figure 2-14).

Curves Tools

The Curves tools provide you with an excellent resource for advanced entire-curve editing and manipulation (see Figure 2-15). Here you are able to bake channels, cycle animation, and alter the weight of tangents, among other things.

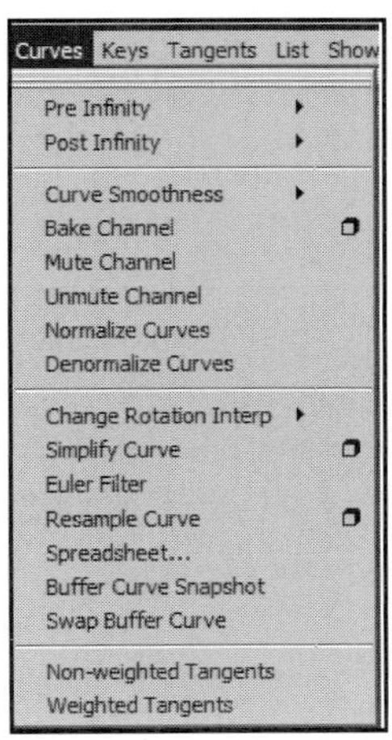

figure 2-15

The Curves tools.

Keys Tools

The Keys tools allow you to hone in on the keys themselves and modify specific tangent, spacing, and weight issues (see Figure 2-16).

figure 2-16

The Keys tools.

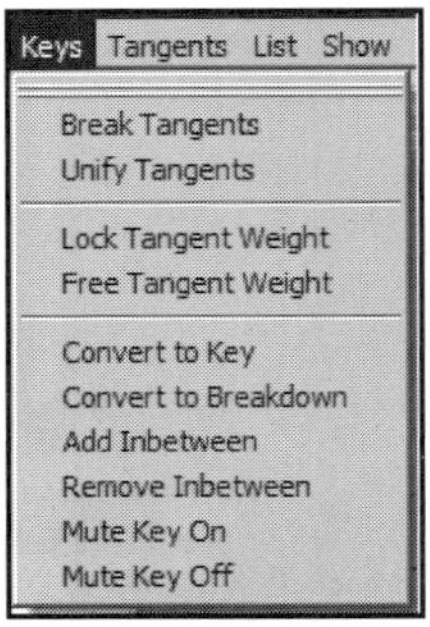

Tangents Tools

The Tangents tools allow you to change how the points on the curve are connected (see Figure 2-17). This greatly alters the movement of your object.

figure 2-17

The Tangents tools.

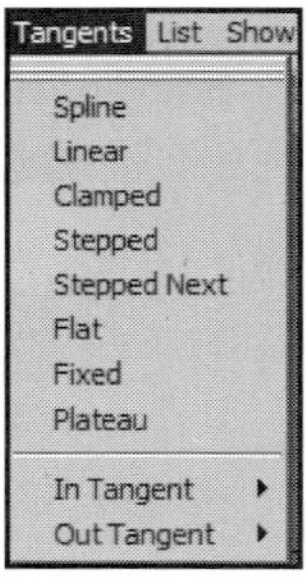

List and Show Tools

The List and Show tools assist you in organizing objects for viewing within the Graph Editor (see Figures 2-18 and 2-19).

figure 2-18

The List tools.

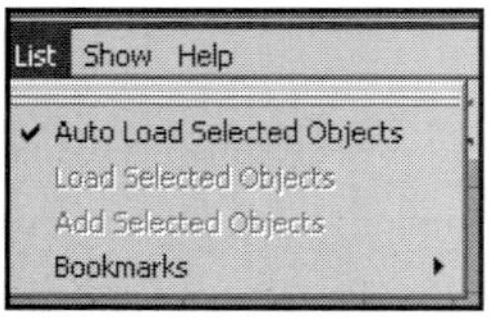

figure 2-19

The Show tools.

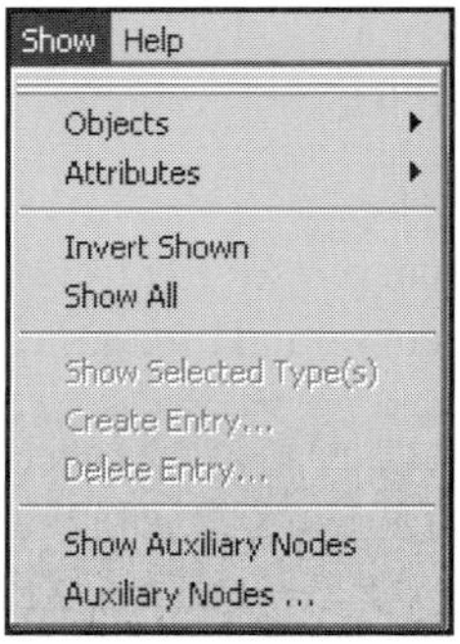

Help Menu

The Help menu leads you to software documentation and online manuals (see Figure 2-20).

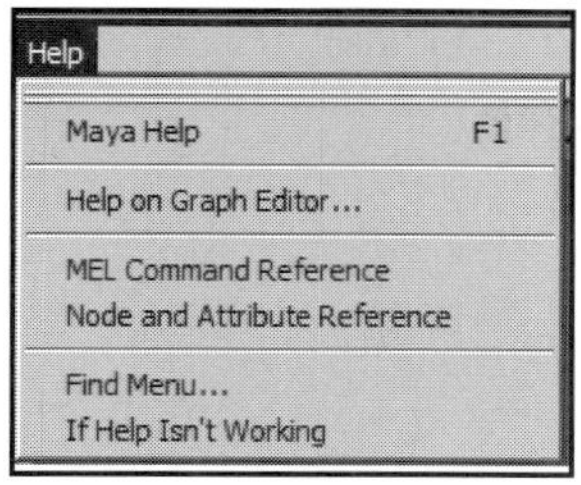

figure 2-20

The Help menu.

Graphic Interface

The second line of the graphic interface contains shortcut symbols to more commands (see Figure 2-21). They are here because they are used quite often.

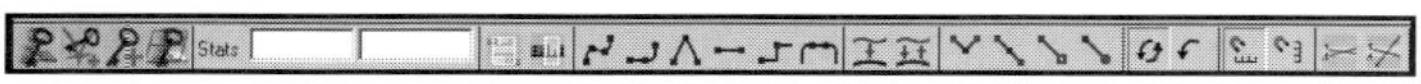

figure 2-21

The graphic shortcuts.

Move Nearest Key Picked Tool

This tool moves the nearest key picked (see Figure 2-22). You could have several key frames selected in the graph, but when you middle-mouse click and move the mouse, only the nearest key frame is edited. The mouse needs to be over the selected key frame.

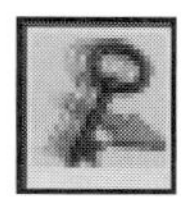

figure 2-22

The Move Nearest Key Picked tool.

Insert Keys Tool

The Insert Keys tool will place new keys on an existing animation curve (see Figure 2-23). Left-click to select the curve to which you will add a new key.

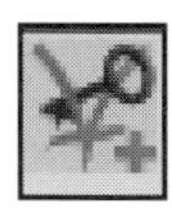

figure 2-23

The Insert Keys tool.

Middle-mouse drag to set the location of the new key. A black line with a square will appear, locating the insertion point of your new key. Releasing the mouse button places the key. The new key will have tangents that preserve the original animation curve segment's shape.

Add Keys Tool

The Add Keys tool inserts a new key frame directly on the curve (see Figure 2-24). Left-mouse click to select the curve, and middle-mouse click to create a key frame. This

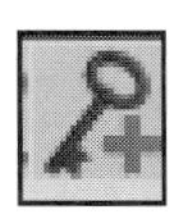

figure 2-24

The Add Keys tool.

works differently than the Insert Keys tool in that you get fresh tangents that need editing, which are consistent with the tangents of the curves but are in the default placement.

figure 2-25

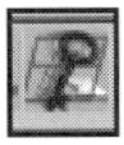

Lattice Deform

The Lattice Deform tool allows you to move multiple keys on the Graph Editor by creating a lattice around the desired keys. When the lattice is created, you can move all the keys within the lattice by simply moving the lattice points. The Lattice Deform tool helps save time when you want to move multiple keys at once (see Figure 2-25).

Stats

The Stats window allows you to mathematically enter exact placement of your point (see Figure 2-26).

figure 2-26

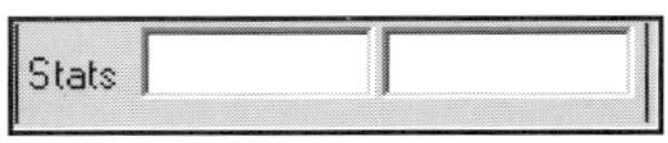

Stats.

figure 2-27

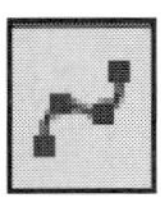

The Spline Tangents tool.

Spline Tangents

This is the default tangent. This creates a very smooth interpolation (see Figure 2-27).

figure 2-28

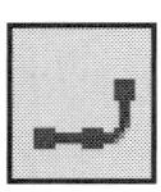

The Clamped Tangents tool.

Clamped Tangents

These are a combination of linear and spline tangents. Your in and out tangents will usually be spline when using this curve, unless the points are very close, in which case they are linear (see Figure 2-28).

figure 2-29

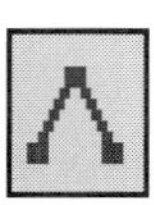

The Linear Tangents tool.

Linear Tangents

A linear tangent creates a curve as a straight line joining two keys. This results in an evenly paced (almost robotic) movement. It is often used in conjunction with the stepped curve for setting the key poses (see Figure 2-29).

figure 2-30

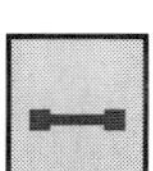

The Flat Tangents tool.

Flat Tangents

The in and out tangents of a flat curve have a slope of 0 degrees (see Figure 2-30).

Step Tangents

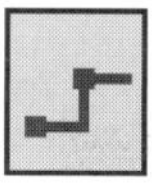

figure 2-31

The Step Tangents tool.

This curve is used when creating the key poses. It strobes from pose to pose when played back (see Figure 2-31).

Plateau Tangents

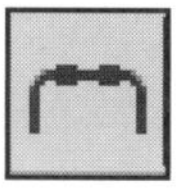

figure 2-32

The plateau tangents feature is new to Maya 7. Plateau Tangents help prevent key frames from "overshooting" their minimum and maximum values. Plateau Tangents are similar to Clamped Tangents and are recommended for setting keys for things like feet when you do not want the foot to "overshoot" the floor causing the foot to go under the floor (see Figure 2-32).

Graph Window

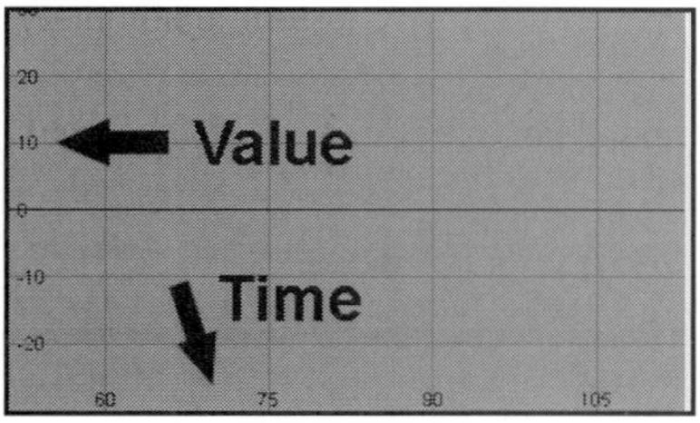

figure 2-33

Coordinates.

The Graph window contains an X,Y coordinate of points in space (see Figure 2-33).

The main section of the Graph Editor is the Graph window. At the bottom of the window, the Time is represented. Along the left side of the window is Value.

You can read the window by looking at the bottom to see what frame you are on. You can also see the change in the Translate, Scale, or Rotate value by looking at the Value Line. Over time, these changes are represented by the curves. The movement of the key-framed object is influenced by the tangency of these curves.

If you right-mouse click in this window, a floating pull-down menu of the top interface menu appears.

Your Turn to Play

Make sure your interface looks like Figure 2-34. If it is different, go to **Display** > **UI Elements** and make sure the options shown in Figure 2-35 are checked off.

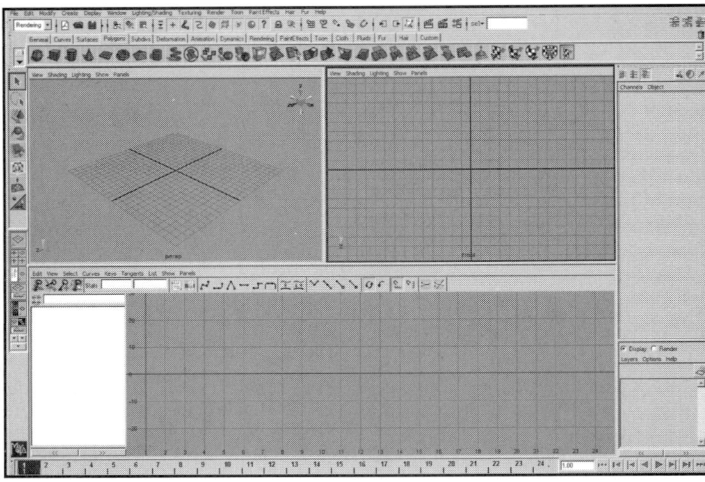

figure 2-34

The correct interface for this chapter.

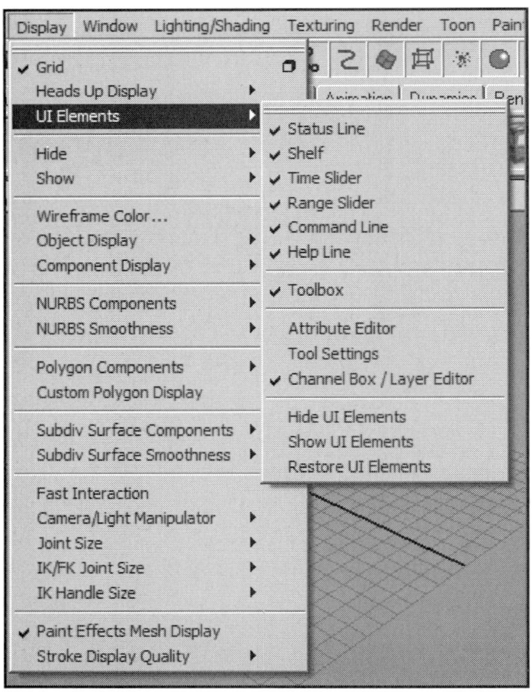

figure 2-35

The UI options.

Set your panels by going to **Panels** > **Layouts** > **Three Panes Split Top** (see Figure 2-36).

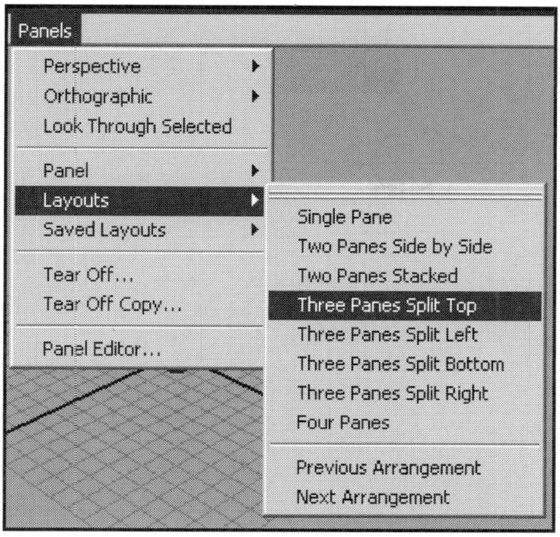

figure 2-36

Layout Settings.

Make the bottom panel your Graph Editor. Close any open Graph Editor windows and then go to **Panels > Panel > Graph Editor** (see Figure 2-37).

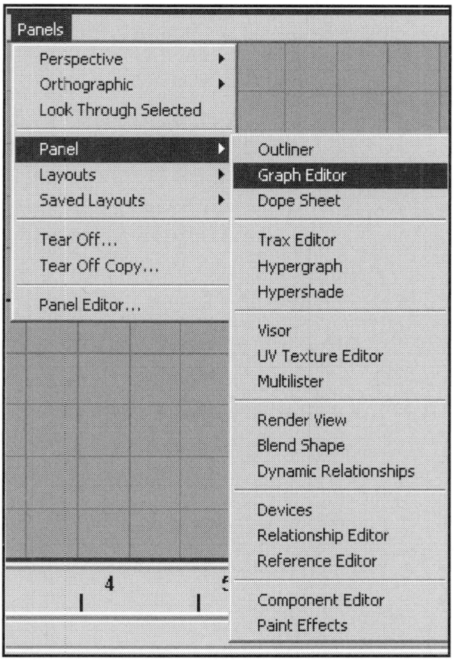

figure 2-37

The Graph Editor.

Open the file "ball_keyed," and experiment with it while learning the following basics about the Graph Editor. Examine the following curves in the Graph Editor.

What Motion the Curves Represent

Figure 2-38 shows the default motion that Maya gives you when you animate a ball bouncing straight up and down.

figure 2-38

The default spline curve.

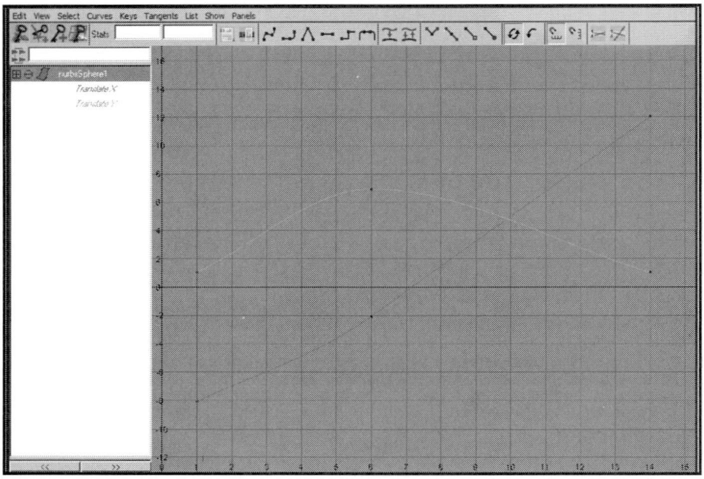

When an animation looks floaty, this is the usual culprit. Maya assigns a default spline curve to all movement. It evenly spaces all interpolation between key frames. Figure 2-39 shows what the animation will look like.

figure 2-39

The default animation.

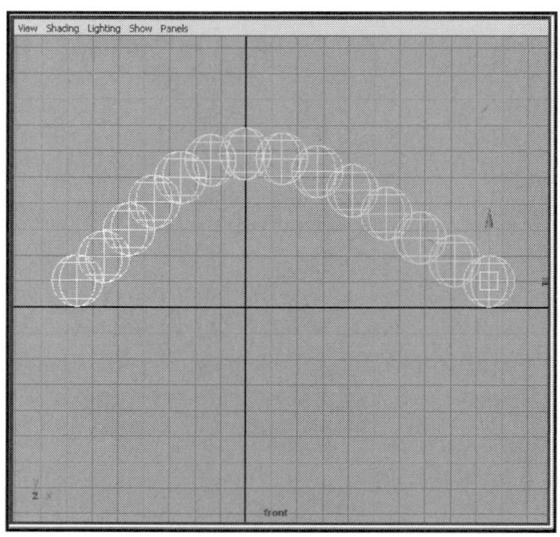

No real weight or timing exists. Learn what information the different curves, channels, and tools provide, and you will create more believable animation.

Figure 2-40 shows the animation you want. It shows weight and timing. It involves some understanding of Curves and Editing tools to get this correct.

The curves for a ball bounce like this resemble those in Figure 2-41.

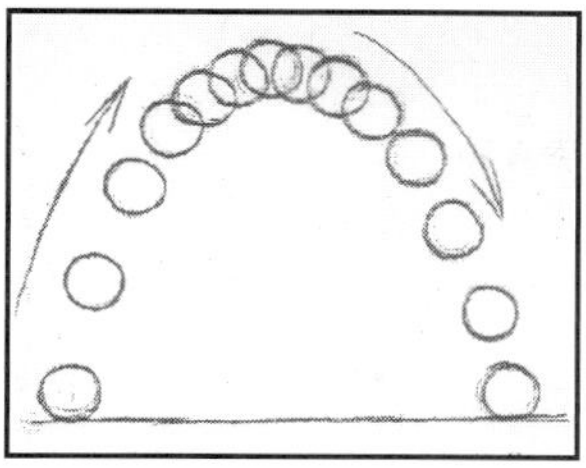

figure | 2-40 |

The *correct* ball bounce.

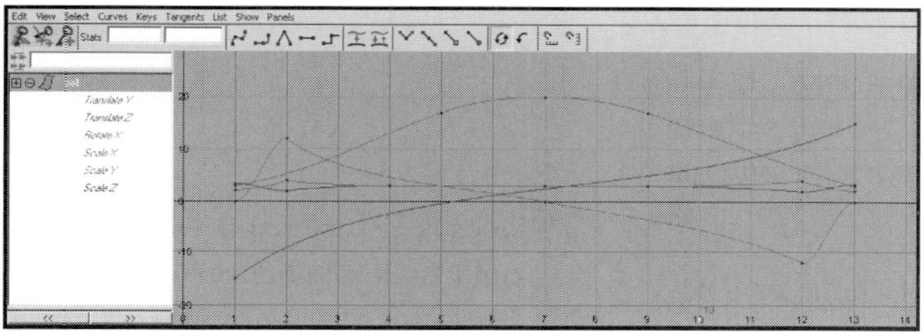

figure | 2-41 |

The curves for an unedited ball bounce.

Let us find out what all the curves represent.

Each curve is the color of the coordinate it represents. X is red. Z is blue. Y is green. Look for the Coordinate icon in your Camera view (see Figure 2-42), and you will be able to understand where each curve is moving your view.

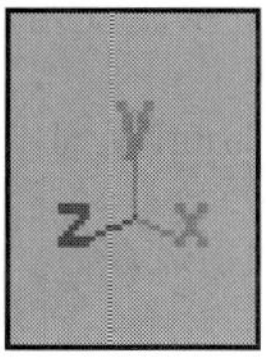

figure | 2-42 |

The coordinate icon.

We are working in Y up space, which means Y is the up and down axis. These curves are being explained as they react in a Front view window.

X, Y, Z Translate

Translate stands for the amount of movement in space. A movement from the left to the right of the screen would be represented here, as would a movement up and down or toward you. It represents the spacing generated by the Move tool (see Figure 2-43 and 2-44).

NOTE

Interpolation is the term used for the motion "in between" the key frames you set. The software creates this motion. This interpolation is represented by the curves in the Graph Editor.

figure 2-43

The default X translate and its effect on the sphere.

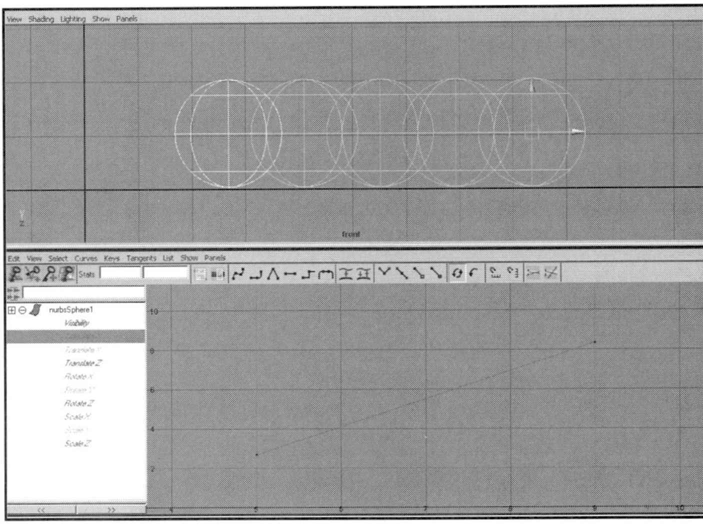

X moves left to right across the screen. Y moves up and down. Z moves forward and back.

figure 2-44

The default Y translate and its effect on the sphere.

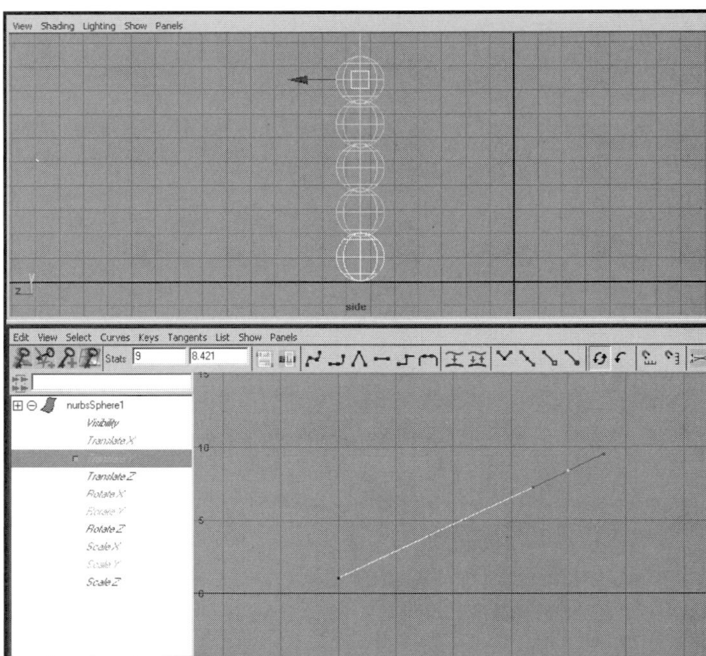

X, Y, Z Rotate

Rotate stands for rotation around an object's pivot, which is the local coordinate system for the object.

X rotates the object towards you. Y rotates the object like a spinning top on the floor. Z rotates the object like a pinwheel.

NOTE

Don't understand pivot? Take a piece of paper and lay it on your desk. Place your finger in the middle of the sheet and press against the table. Spin the sheet. The paper rotates around your finger. Move your finger to the bottom of the paper. Rotate again. In Maya, the pivot will have the same effect against the object as your finger does against the paper.

X, Y, Z Scale

Scale stretches the object on one or two channels or increases and decreases the size of the object as a whole (see Figures 2-45 through 2-47).

X scale

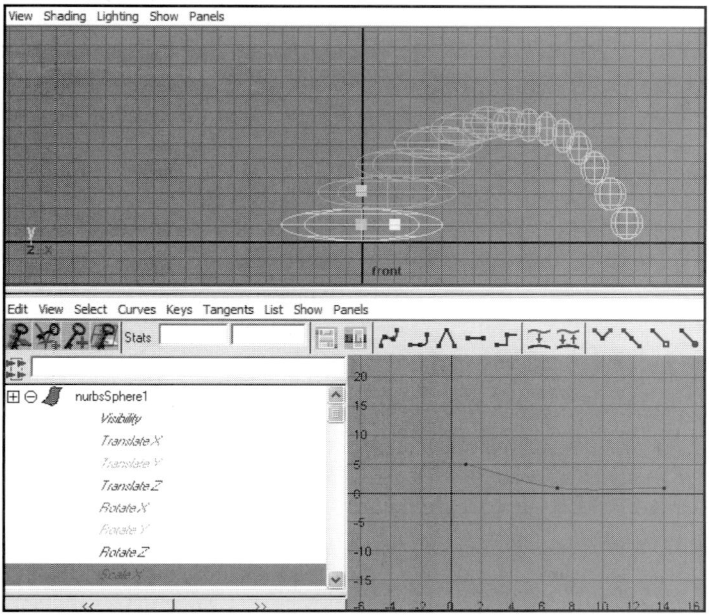

figure 2-45

X scale.

Y scale

figure 2-46

Y scale.

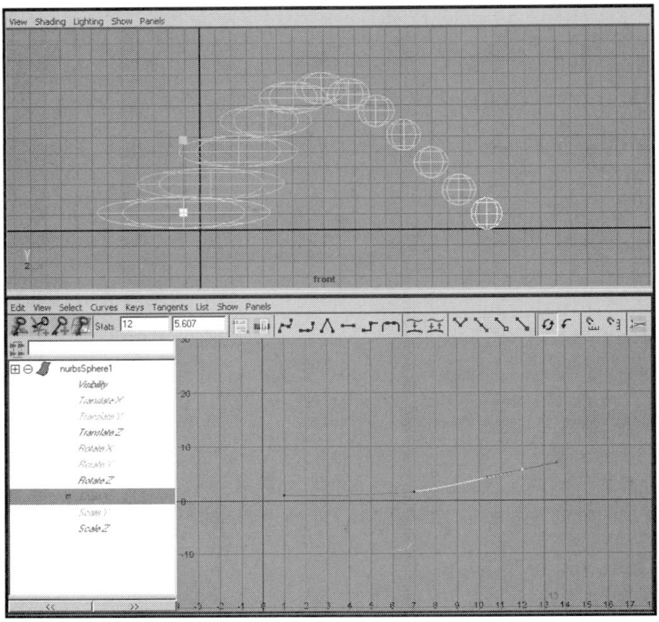

Z scale

figure 2-47

Z scale.

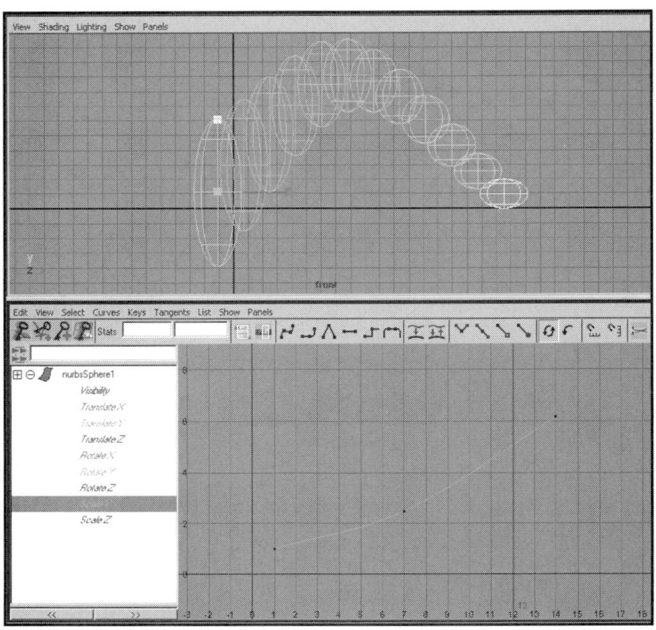

These are the three scale values available.

Can I See the Motion of My Object by Looking at the Curve?

You can see the motion of an object by looking at the curve. Once you understand your curves and the production process well enough, you will be able to see motion without playing the animation. Know your tangent shapes and how they affect Translate, Rotation, and Scale values.

To demonstrate the impact of tangency, let us use a basic primitive sphere and a simple animation. Open 14framebounce_worker.mb to work along.

Select the Y translate curve. Then select **View > Frame All** in the Graph Editor interface (see Figure 2-48). You want the Y translate curve to fill the window.

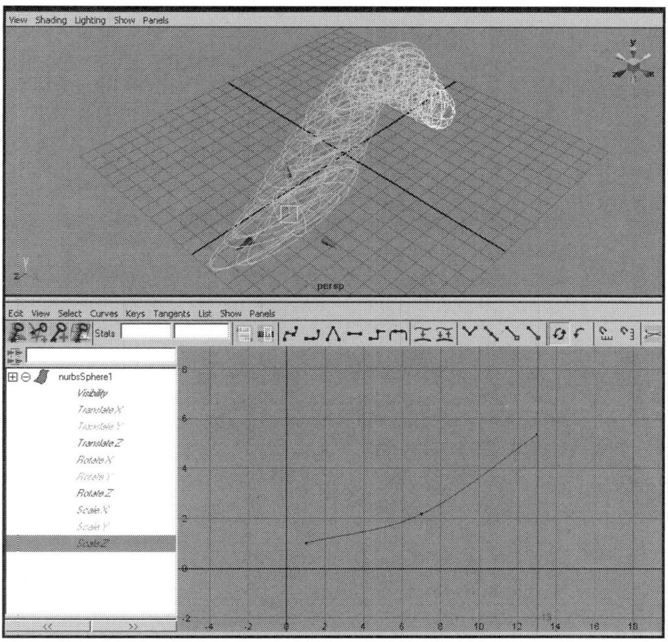

figure 2-48

Maya will assign default curves and animation (see Figure 2-49).

Notice how each sphere is spaced. This animation would appear robotic if it were played because of this fairly even spacing and limited ease in/ease out. For the animation to appear believable, you must decide how heavy the ball is, what kind of material it is made of, what the atmosphere it is responding to is like, and any other emotional statements you want to make.

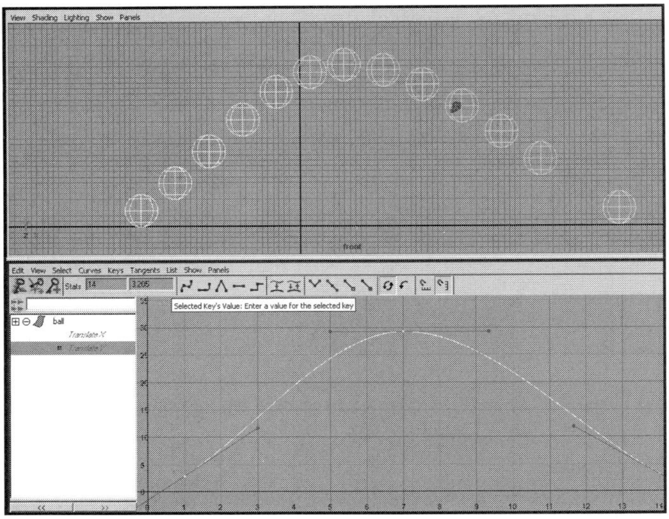

figure 2-49

The default spline curve.

DON'T GO THERE

I never want to keep the default information assigned to me by Maya. This is only a starting place. From here on, I need to understand my options and apply them toward my desired outcome.

Available Tangents

The following are the tangents available. We will use them on the Y translate curve in the ball by bounce animation.

Clamped Tangent

A clamped tangent has features of both the spline and linear tangents. Keys less than two frames apart will be treated as a linear tangent, while keys greater than two apart will be treated as a spline tangent. This is and is not a good thing. We will explore the proper usage.

Spline Tangent

A spline tangent is a curve that is smooth between the key before and the key after the selected key (see Figure 2-50). The co-linear tangents of the curve (both at the same angle) ensure that the animation curve smoothly enters and exits the key.

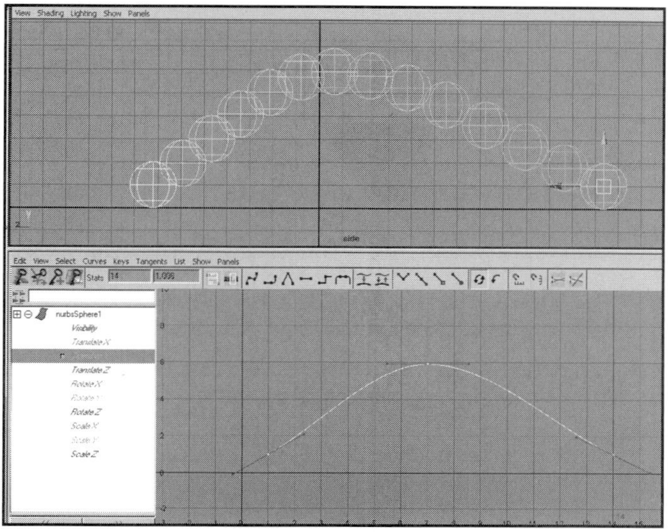

figure 2-50

Spline tangent.

Linear Tangent

A linear tangent creates a straight line joining two keys (see Figure 2-51). The curve segment before the key is a straight line. The curve segment after the key is a straight line. A sharp angle connects them.

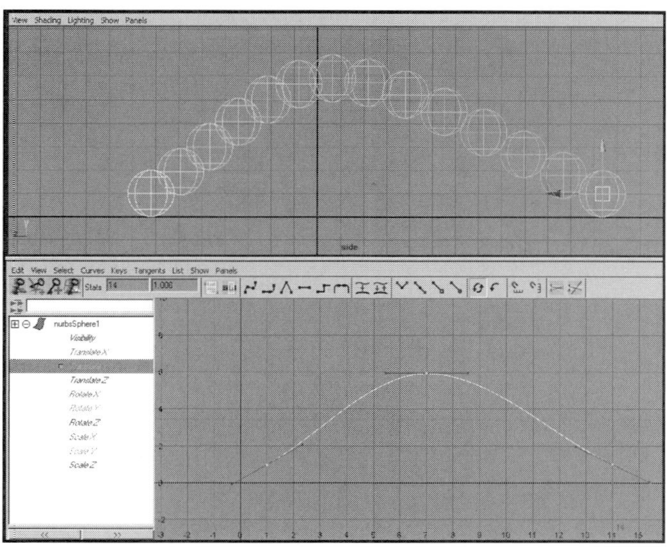

figure 2-51

Flat Tangent

Flat sets the in and out tangents of the key to be horizontal, with a 0 slope (see Figure 2-52).

figure 2-52

Linear tangent.

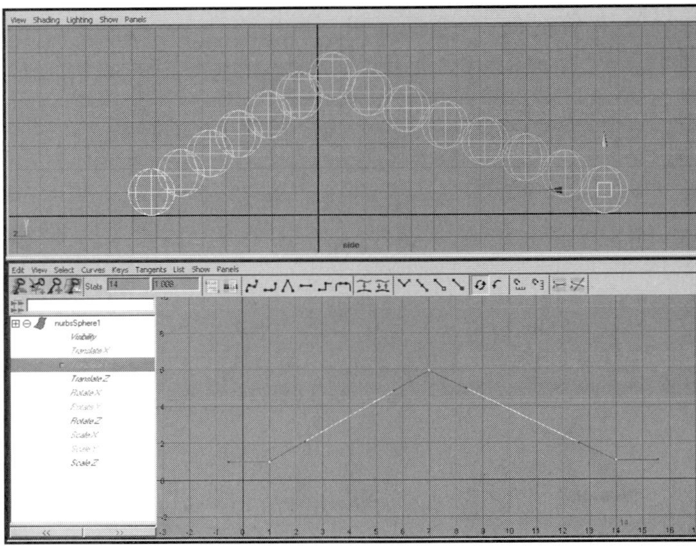

A stepped tangent creates a flat curve on the out tangent of the key frame (see Figure 2-53). The curve segment is flat.

figure 2-53

Flat tangent.

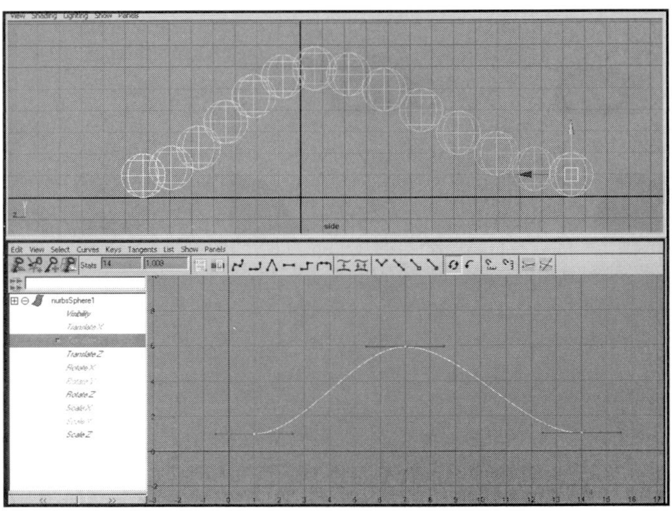

Stepped Next Tangent

Similar to stepped tangent, the stepped next tangent creates a flat tangent at the beginning of two set keys instead of the end. This is useful when setting up key frames.

Fixed Tangent

Fixed retains the slope assigned when edited. This is a good option when you want to edit the value but retain the slope you had adjusted before the edit.

Plateau Tangent

Plateau tangents are similar to clamped tangents and are new to Maya 7. Plateau tangents flatten the uppermost and lowermost keys to keep the animation from "overshooting" the key frame (see Figure 2-54).

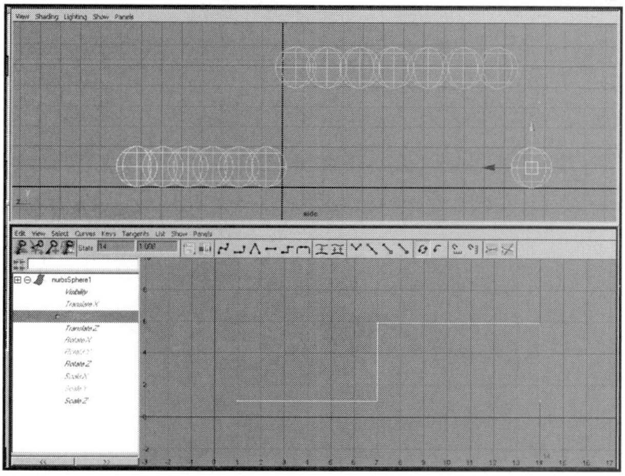

figure 2-54

How the ball is spaced.

MINI TUTORIAL: EDITING

You will first try to make a proper bounce in the Y translate by changing the ease in and ease out of the Y translate curve.

You can use the file 14framebounce_worker.mb on the enclosed CD. Open the Graph Editor by going to **Windows** > **Animation Editors** > **Graph Editor.**

Select the Translate Y curve in the left-hand column so that only the Y translate curve is viewable in the window (see Figure 2-55). Left-mouse select the first key frame on the curve.

Select **View** > **Frame All** to get the best view of this curve.

Left-mouse select the first key frame on the green Y translate curve. Now look at the round-tipped arrows on the key frame. They point in opposite directions. These are your tangents (see Figure 2-56), and the arrows are called "control handles."

Tangents describe the entry and exit of curve segments from a key. Manipulating these tangents enables you to change the shape of the curve. Thus, the spacing of the ball will change as it enters and leaves a key, which allows you to infer Weight, Timing, and other movement choices.

figure | 2-55 |

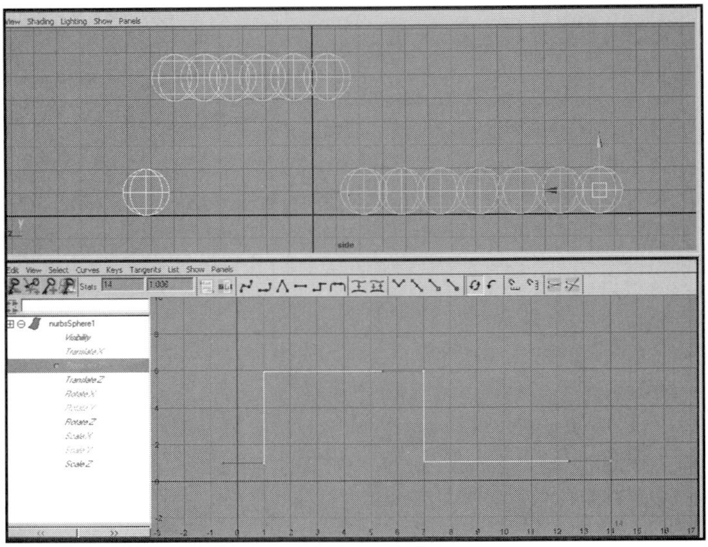

figure | 2-56 |

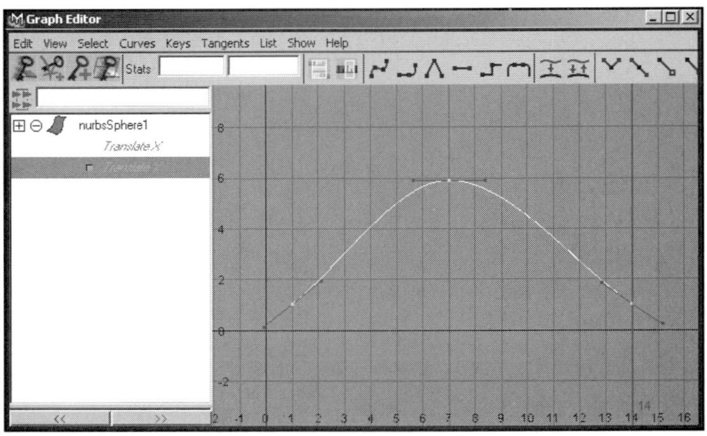

figure | 2-57 |

How the ball is spaced.

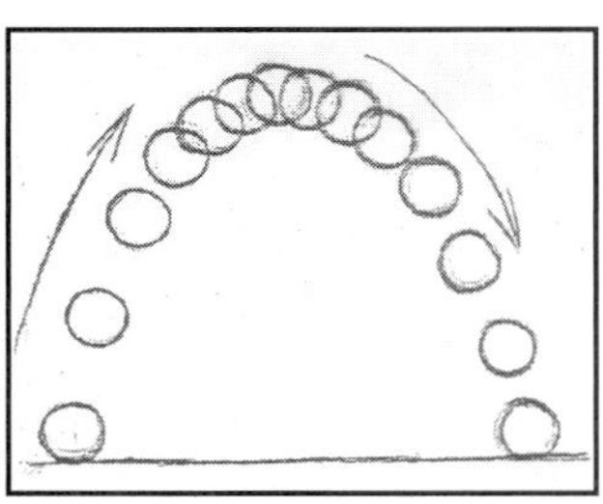

A typical bouncing ball in a traditional animation looks like Figure 2-57.

Notice that there are fewer spheres close together immediately after leaving the ground, but many balls are close together when the ball "floats" in midair. The spacing between the balls infers speed. If there is a wide gap between two images, the ball moves quickly. If there is a small gap between images, the ball moves slowly.

To emulate this effect in Maya, you will change the ease in and ease out of the Y translate curve. In the Graph Editor, choose **Select > Out Tangent** (see Figure 2-58).

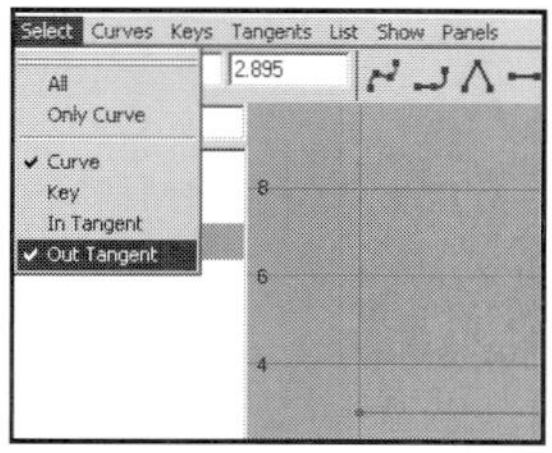

figure 2-58

Select > Out Tangent.

Select the arrow to the right of the key frame in the Graph Editor (see Figure 2-59).

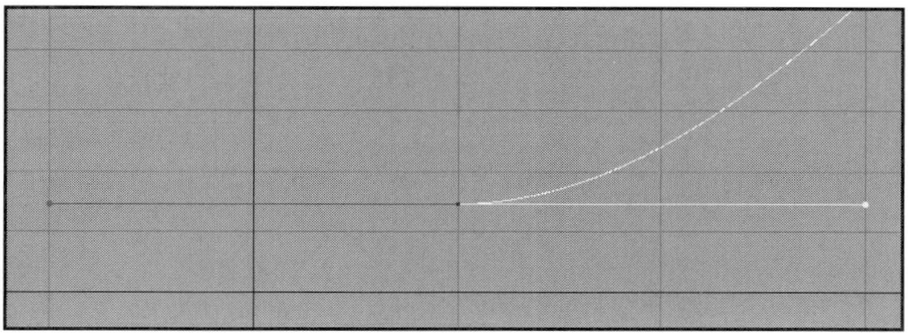

figure 2-59

Tangents on key frame one.

Click on the Move Nearest Picked Key tool at the very left of the Graph Editor (see Figure 2-60).

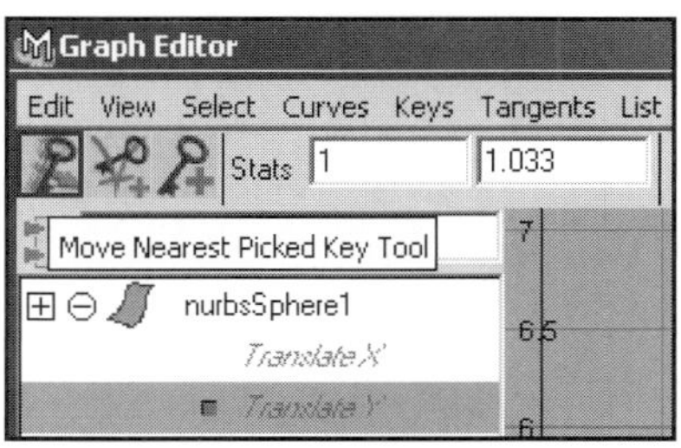

figure 2-60

Move Nearest Key Picked tool.

Hold down your middle mouse button, and select the tangent. Move your mouse, and the tangent changes. Make your curve look like Figure 2-61.

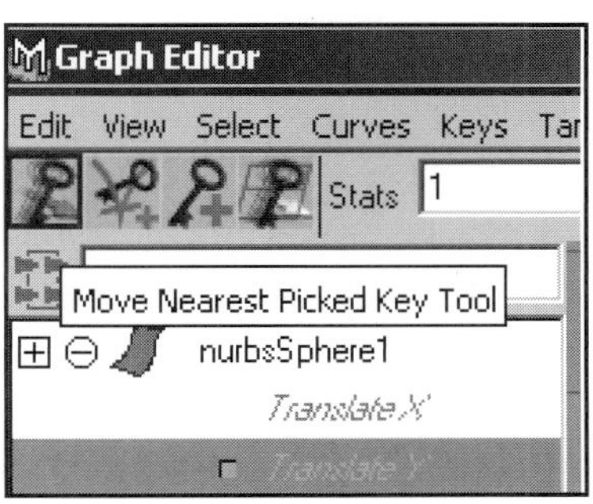

figure 2-61

Do the same with the key frame at 14 (see Figure 2-62).

figure 2-62

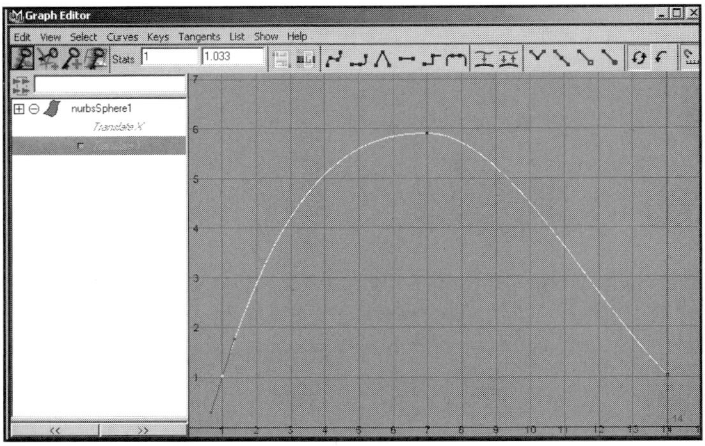

Notice that the spacing of the ball has changed. When you play the animation, it will appear to quickly leave the ground, float in midair, and then quickly approach the ground (see Figure 2-63).

figure 2-63

Here is a curve with the in tangent edited.

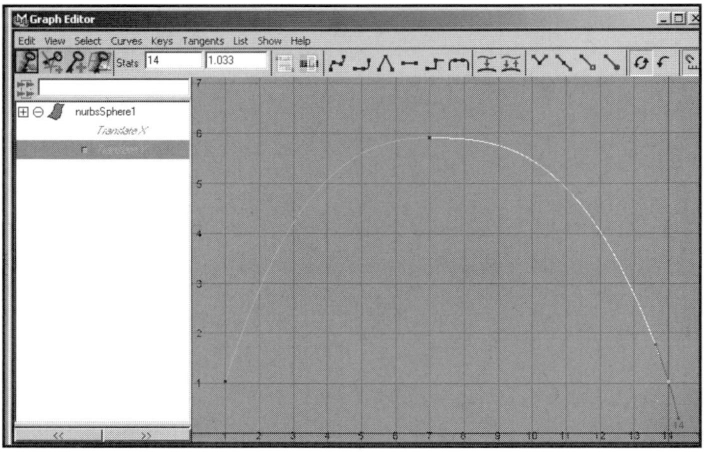

Now let us make the curve a little more believable. The float position is undesirable at this point and should happen at 7.5 instead of at key frame 7. Next edit the position.

Left-mouse select the key frame at 7. Turn off Time Snap On Off in the Graph Editor. In the Stats window in the upper-left of the Graph Editor, type in 7.5. The key frame is now at 7.5.

Play your animation.

Suppose you want the float to last longer and the ball to more quickly leave the ground. The tangent will not let you do it. You need to use another tool to weight the tangent.

Left-mouse select the key frame at 7.5. Select **Curves** > **Weighted Tangents** (see Figure 2-64).

The tangents change a bit.

NOTE

Tangent weights dictate the amount of influence a tangent has over a curve segment. Curves are non-weighted by default.

Nonweighted tangents have short tangent handles that only control the angle of the tangent.

Weighted tangents have long tangent handles that control the angle and weight of the tangent. Weighted tangents provide finer control over your animation curves.

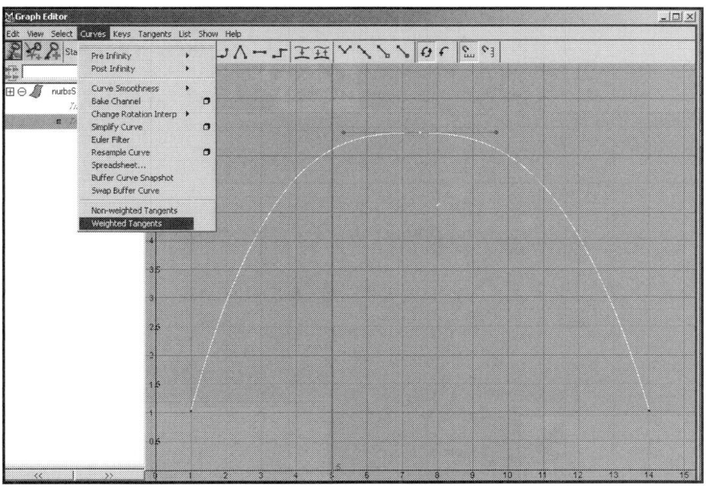

figure 2-64

Now select the Free Tangent Weight button (see Figure 2-65). The tangents now have boxes at their ends.

Left-mouse select one of the tangents. Middle-mouse select the tangent, and pull it away from the key (see Figure 2-66).

Look at how much float you can have now (see Figure 2-67)! Unfortunately, this does not look good when you play it, but it illustrates how you can edit in the Graph Editor.

figure 2-65

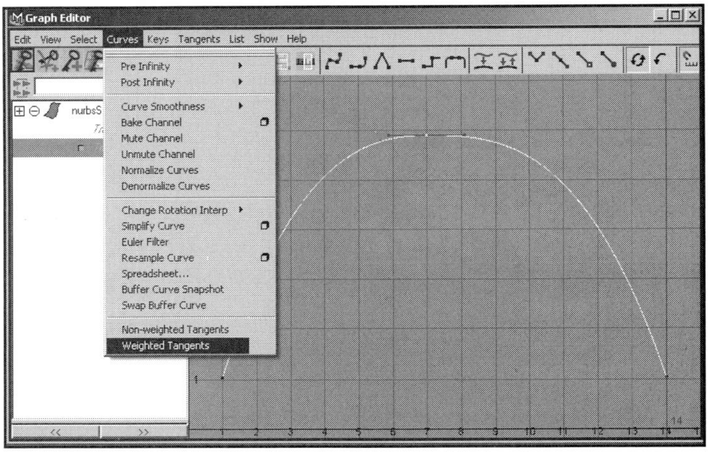

figure 2-66

Free Tangent Weight.

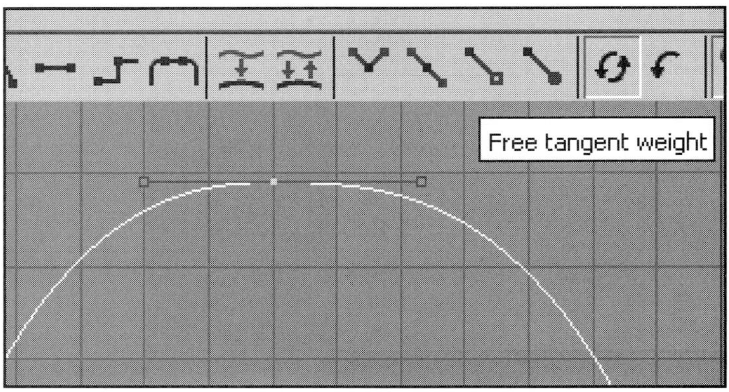

figure 2-67

The edited curve.

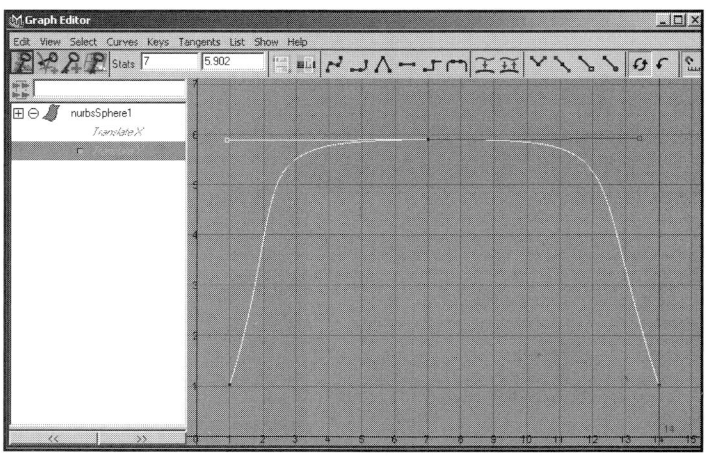

figure 2-68

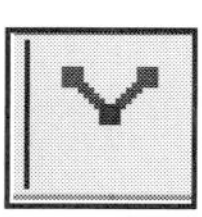

Break the tangent so that you can independently manipulate either side. Left-mouse select the key frame at 7.5, and use the Break Tangents button (see Figure 2-68).

Now you can independently edit either side of the other. Left-mouse click the tangent on the left side to select, and middle-mouse click to push back toward the key frame (see Figure 2-69).

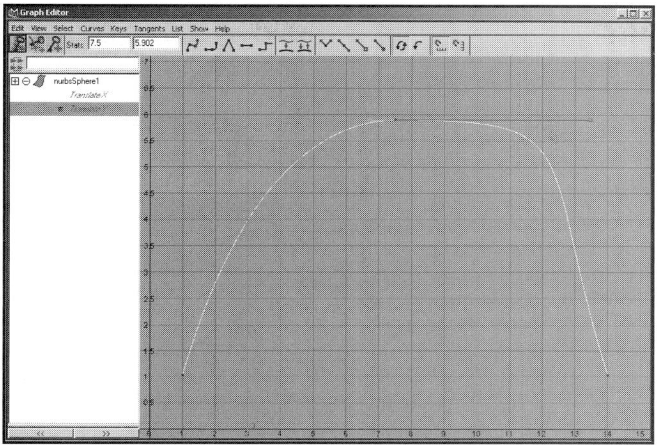

figure 2-69

Edit independently

The tangent on the right side is unaffected. Weighting the tangents and breaking them gives you dexterity. You can do anything you want with the curves now. Try to match what is shown in Figure 2-70.

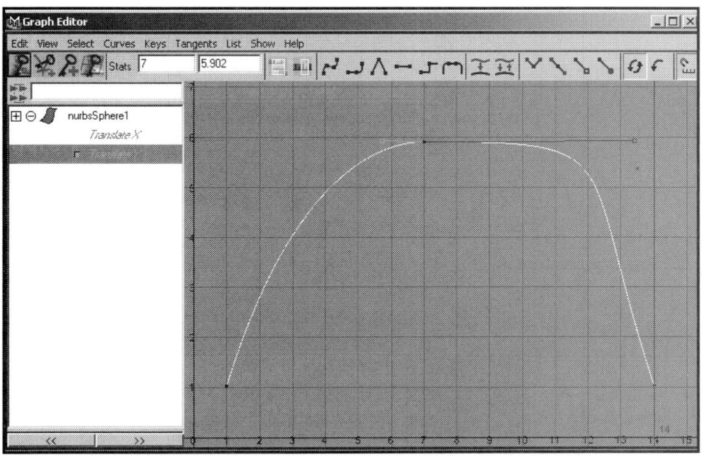

figure 2-70

You are left with the strange animation in Figure 2-71.

Be encouraged to play with the curves and get used to what shapes give you what kind of animation result. Your Graph Editor is the root of all great motion. Get to know it well.

Now edit the points in space, and look at your sphere while doing so. Let us try this with the Y translate.

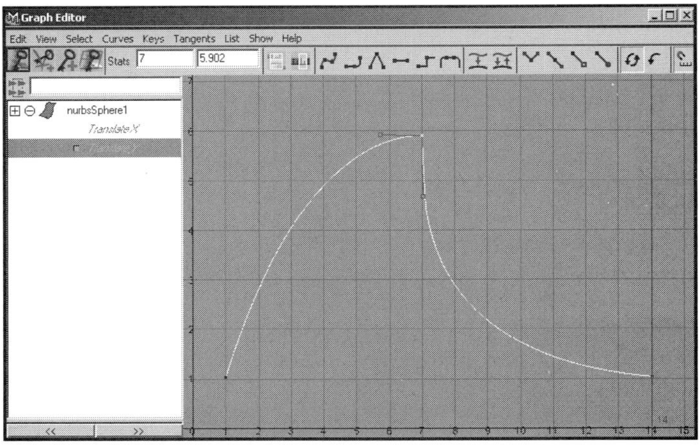

figure 2-71

A new curve.

Select the key frame at 7.5, and move it up in the Graph Editor. You can manually do this with the middle mouse button and the Select Nearest Key Picked button. Slide the key frame to a new position, or you can type a new value into the Key Value box (see Figure 2-72).

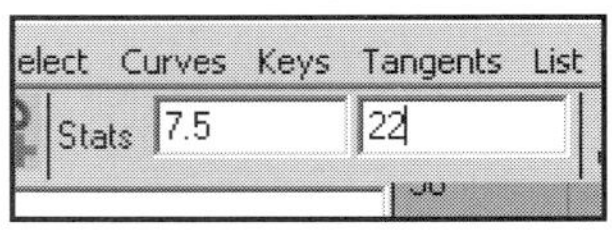

figure 2-72

The Key Value box.

Play your animation. The ball bounces higher. Lower the value, and make your ball bounce lower. Edit the other curves, tangents, and keys to see what happens.

Why Does This Object Not Move the Way I Key-Framed It?

Two points in space create a curve based on the appointed tangency. A third point can greatly affect the previous two.

Here are two points for the Y translate of a sphere (see Figure 2-73). At frames 1 and 7, a value of is key-framed.

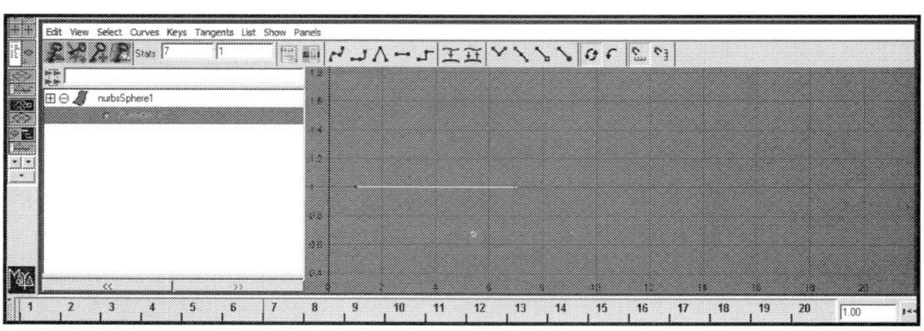

figure 2-73

Two key curve.

At frame 10, a value of 2 is key-framed. Notice how the new key frame affects how the curve reacts to frames 1 and 7 (see Figure 2-74).

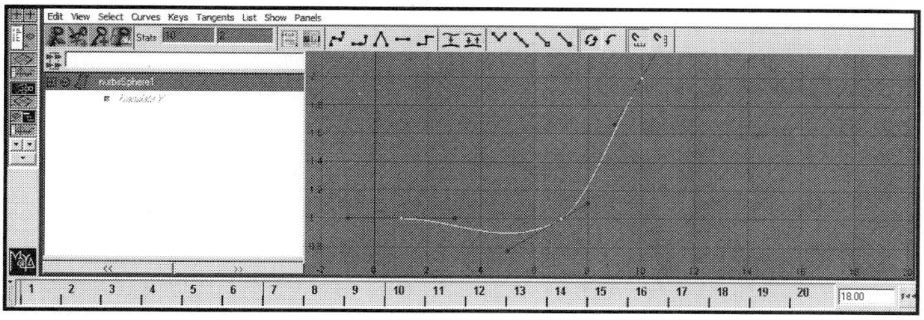

figure 2-74

Overshoot.

It creates an overshoot. This is why the Graph Editor should be open as you animate. Watch how new key frames are affecting your curves. An overshoot will affect any animation because the object is now moving past the chosen key pose.

Don't over key-frame your animations. You should be in control of the curves and use as few key frames as possible to complete the action. Too many can distort the curves and cause jarring jumps and flaws in motion.

DON'T GO THERE!

Common Software-Inspired Mistakes

1. Most beginning animators accept the default curve and do not modify it.

2. Figure 2-75 shows a curve muddied by too many key frames.

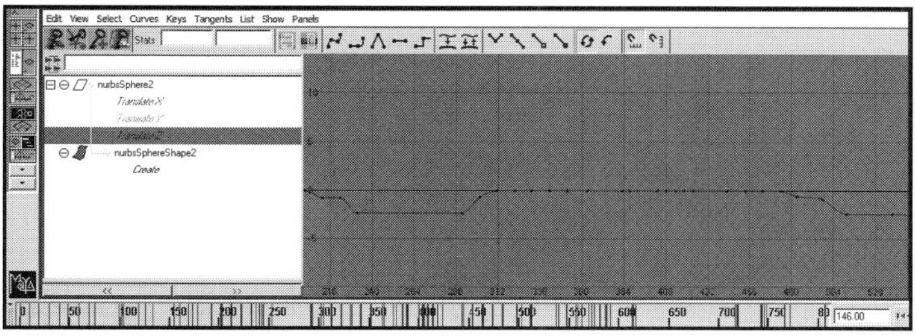

figure 2-75

Too many unnecessary frames.

3. Figure 2-76 shows a curve that hyperextends before the next key frame.

figure 2-76

Overshoot.

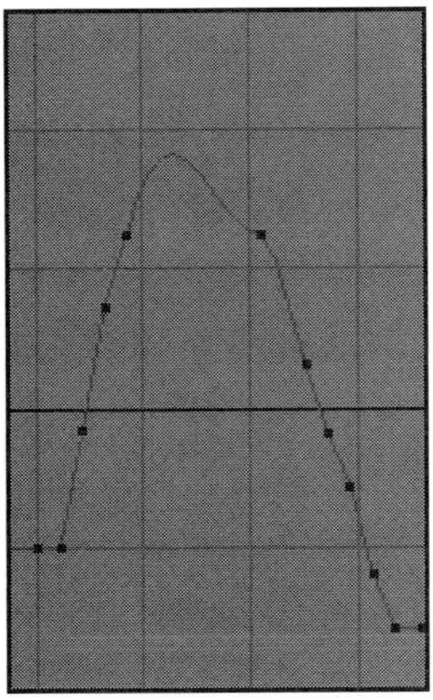

4. Hitting the S key as a shortcut for key frames sets a key frame for every channel. This only serves to clutter your file and make it bigger, which potentially lengthens your renders.

SUMMARY

Animation is a complex art in computer graphics. Not only do you need to understand the principles of animation, you must also understand how to apply them to a software program.

The Graph Editor is the most important tool you have available. It details every movement and provides you with the tools to improve it if necessary.

in review

1. What are the "Mechanics" of animation?
2. What is "Composition" in animation?
3. What is "Acting" in animation?
4. What is "Drawing" in animation?
5. Should you make a key frame on every key? Why or why not?
6. Should you have values recorded in every animatable channel?
7. What are the names of the tangents available in Maya, and what motion do they represent?
8. What are some common mistakes made by the beginning animator?
9. What is overshoot?
10. What is tangent weight?
11. What is the Graph Editor used for?
12. Can I see the motion of an object just by looking at the curve?

EXPLORING ON YOUR OWN

1. Make a simple 30-frame, 3-key frame animation with a sphere. Experiment with all of the curves and tangents in this chapter until you feel confident with the differences in each tool.

notes

notes

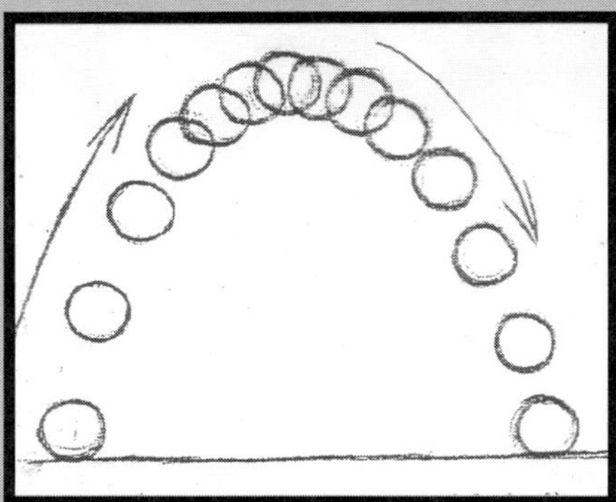

3

the bouncing ball

charting your course

The first assignment that a traditional animator receives is to complete the "bouncing ball" exercise. Here, if you can add convincing appeal to a mundane object, you are ready to apply those skills to a more complex object. We will try bouncing a ball as our first computer animation.

goals

In this chapter, you will:

- **Animate the motion, scale, and rotation of a primitive object.**
- **Apply changes in the Graph Editor.**
- **Learn how to create a pose test.**
- **Practice timing, squash and stretch, and volume.**

TOOLS USED

- **Key Selected.** The Key Selected command captures the placement information of your object in *x, y, z* space (see Figure 3-1). This information is kept in a node.

figure 3-1

Key Selected.

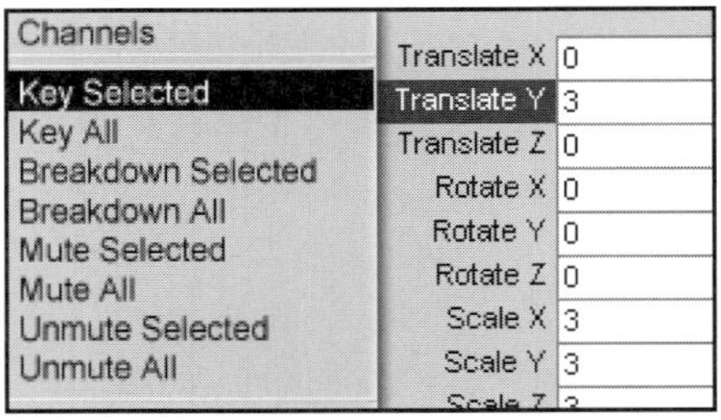

- **Node.** A node is like a file folder for keeping documents tidy (see Figure 3-2). A node rests on top of an object in the Hierarchy window. It stores mathematical information relating to the object as attributes. Nodes are attached to an object in a hierarchy, and an object can move in different ways depending on where the math is placed.

figure 3-2

A node in the outliner window.

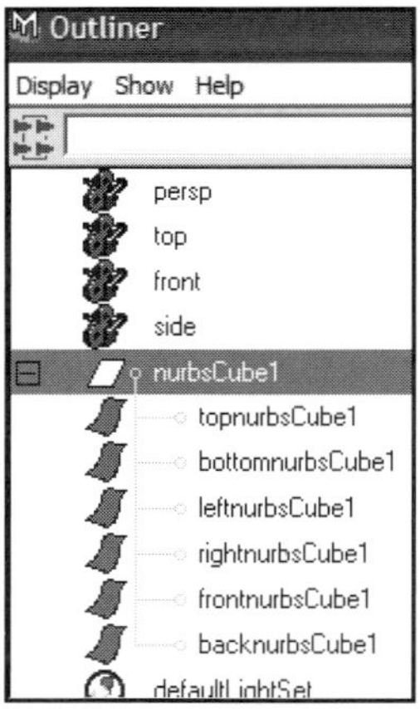

A TRADITIONAL APPROACH

This assignment has been given to beginning animators since the art form first came into its own, and it accomplishes several important things with a minimum of time and difficulty. Using this deceptively simple test, a potential animator is introduced to the mechanics of animating a scene while also learning hands-on about the principles of spacing, timing, and squash and stretch.

There are a couple of things to consider when beginning this exercise. First, there is the shape of the arc that a bouncing object makes. One might suppose that the arc would be a simple half-circle, somewhat like a Roman arch. Actually, the shape is more like the end of an ellipse due to inertia and momentum. Figures 3-3 and 3-4 show the shape comparisons.

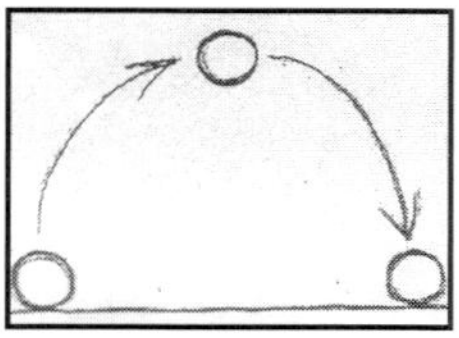

figure 3-3

The half-circle approach (wrong).

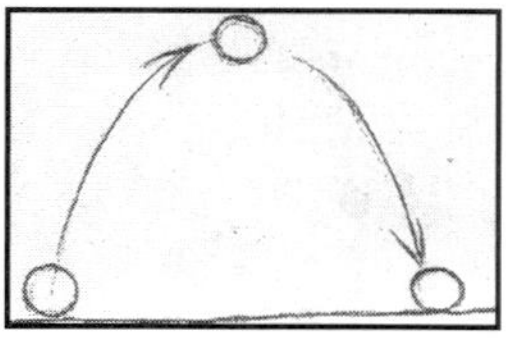

figure 3-4

Using an ellipse (right!).

The spacing of the drawings as the ball goes through the arc is the second consideration as you begin. An even spacing would get the object moving in the arc pattern, but it would do so with no feeling of weight and believability. On the other hand, if you group the drawings closer together at the top of the arc (the slowest point) and space them out as the ball travels up and down (the fast part of the bounce), a natural feeling of a real object with weight is created. The difference in shaping is shown in Figures 3-5 and 3-6.

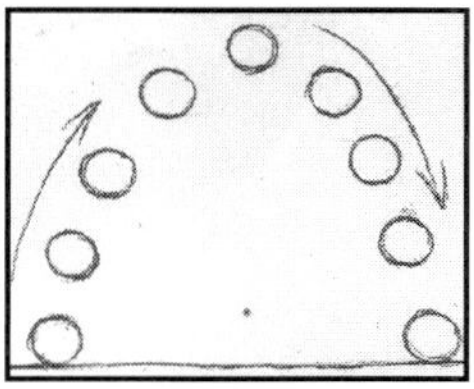

figure 3-5

Evenly spaced (wrong).

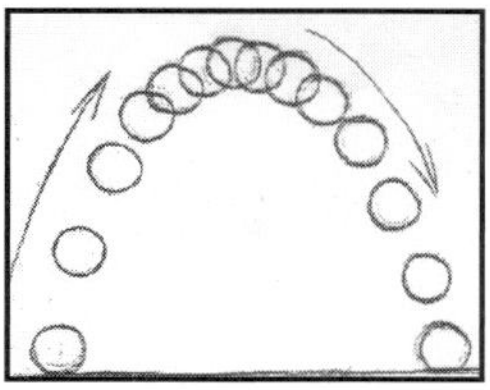

figure 3-6

Grouping at the top (right!).

Now that you have worked with the path of travel (the arc) and the spacing and timing of the bounce, we move on to another basic element of animation mentioned earlier: squash and stretch.

Early animators who experimented with the bouncing ball found that in the fast parts of the bounce, the speed of the ball could be enhanced by a slight elongation of its shape into an oval, with the axis along the path of travel. In further tests of this sort, the ball was also flattened at the point of each impact in the bounce. This caused a shape change that enhanced the effect of the ball hitting the ground and rebounding (see Figure 3-7).

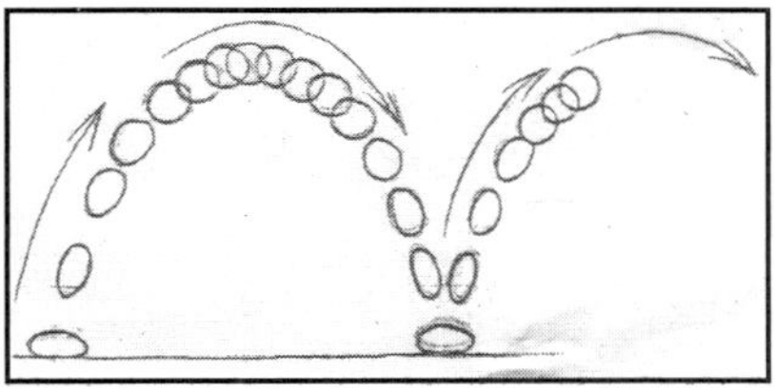

figure 3-7

Impact.

This is a good point at which to introduce one more variable into this experiment: the material used in the ball itself. While the squashy-stretchy example shown up to this point is a good representation of a soft rubber ball, what about something made of a heavy, unyielding type of material, such as a bowling ball or a cannon ball? It is clear you need a slightly different approach for an example of that sort.

Considering the weight of this new object, you know it is not going to bounce nearly as high as the bouncy little subject of the preceding example. Think of the comparison in terms of something audible. If the rubber ball goes "boing! . . . boing! . . . boing!" along the course of its bounce, the heavy ball by comparison would make a sound such as, "BAM! . . . ba-dum bum." The mass would permit maybe one fairly large rebound, and then the arcs of bounce would rapidly diminish to a couple of "rattles" against the surface (see Figure 3-8). In addition, you would need to minimize the amount of squash and stretch when animating a ball of heavy, unyielding character to avoid destroying the believability of its weight and hardness.

figure 3-8

The arc diminishes.

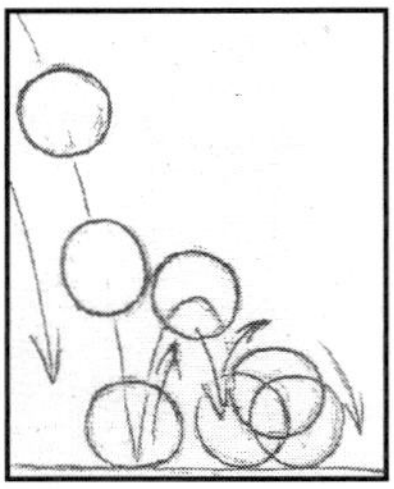

A 3D BOUNCING BALL

Figure 3-9 shows a bouncing ball drawn in traditional animation.

figure 3-9

Animated bouncing ball.

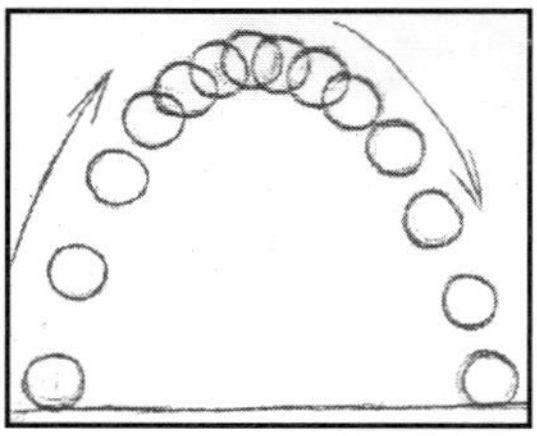

You will create the preceding animation in Maya, emphasizing timing, squash and stretch, and volume. You will animate over 13 frames. Like traditional animators, you will set up key frames and then add your in-betweens. You will learn the basics of the bounce and then apply those basics to different bounce situations.

figure 3-10

The Animation module.

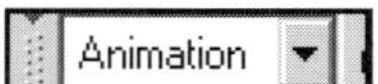

First, make sure you are in the Animation module (see Figure 3-10).

Enter "13" as your playback end time and final end time (see Figure 3-11). Playback end time is the amount of time you will view while working. Final end time is the duration of the entire animation.

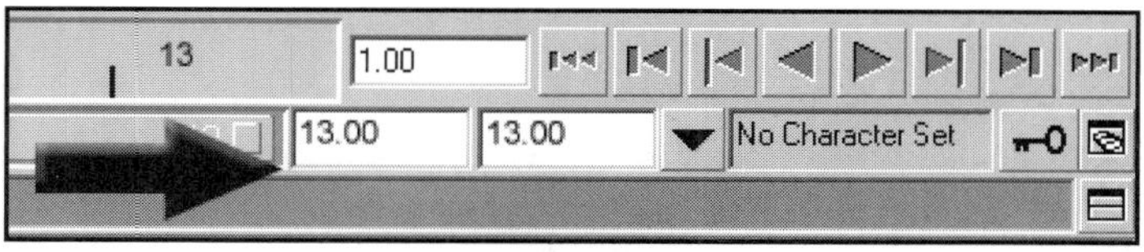

figure 3-11

Playback end time and final end time.

Go to:

Create > NURBS Primitives > Sphere.

Do not deselect the sphere. It appears in your Channel Box as nurbsSphere1.

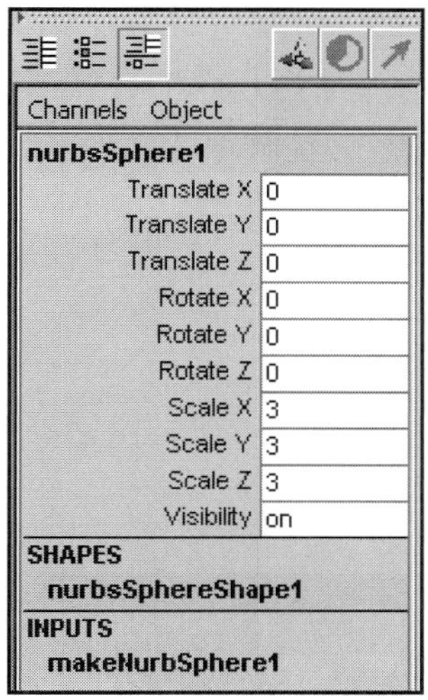

figure 3-12

The Channel Box with the sphere selected.

Scale the sphere using your Channel Box (see Figure 3-12).

Scale X: 3

Scale Y: 3

Scale Z: 3

Notice how the sphere reacts when you change each Scale option. It squashes and stretches as the values are changed. You will be using the scale options in the squash and stretch portion of your animation.

You now have a sphere of scale (3, 3, 3) at origin. You will animate the Scale option later. With the sphere selected, go to the Channel Box and rename "nurbsSphere1" to "ball." Remember to press Enter when you are finished (see Figure 3-13).

Now you will move the pivot to the bottom of the ball. This will allow all scale actions to refer to the pivot as the contact point. The contact point is where the ball hits the floor.

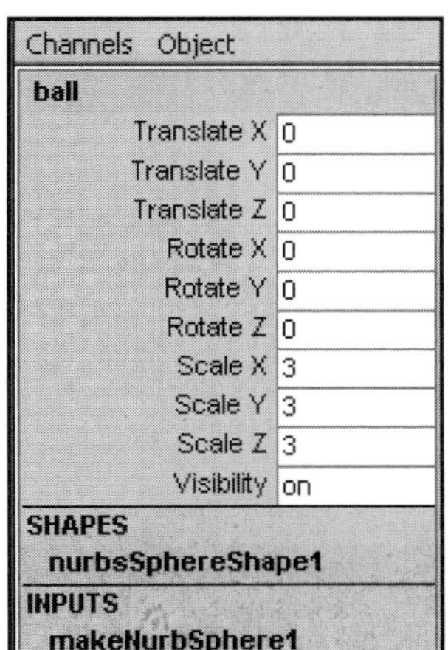

figure 3-13

Rename the default title.

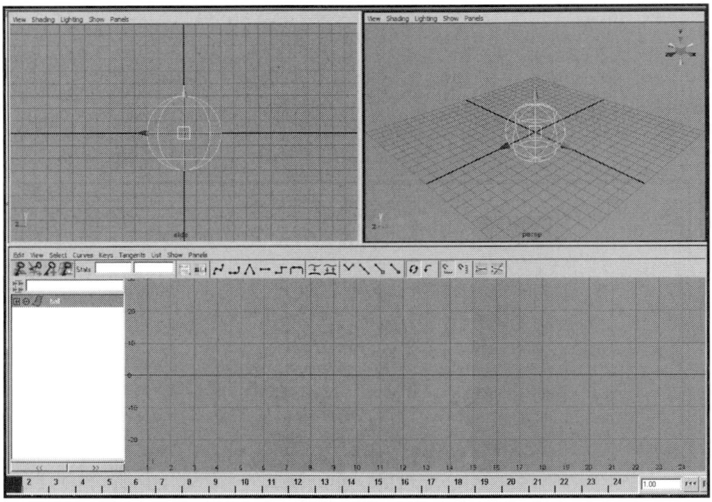

figure 3-14

Three-panel view.

Make sure you are in three-panel view, as shown in Figure 3-14.

You can get to the view by using the pull-down menu shown in Figure 3-15. Select the following:

Panels > Layouts > Three Panes Split Top

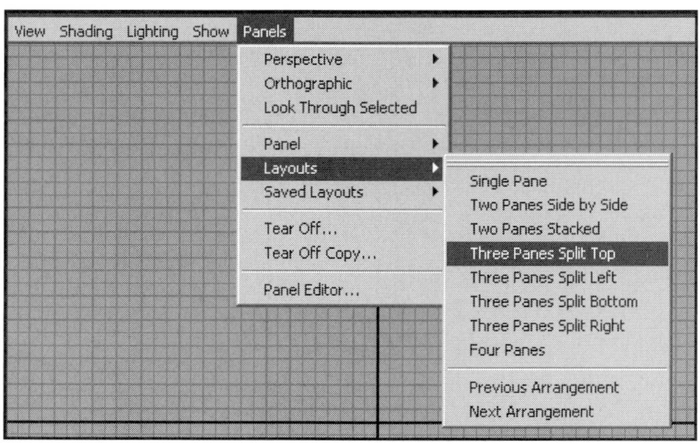

figure 3-15

How to get to three-panel layout.

We suggest that you use the Perspective and Front Camera in the top left and right window view to keep an eye on your movements. Also keep an eye on your Graph Editor when you animate. In the lower panel, go to the pull-down menu, and select the following (see Figure 3-16):

Panels > Panel > Graph Editor

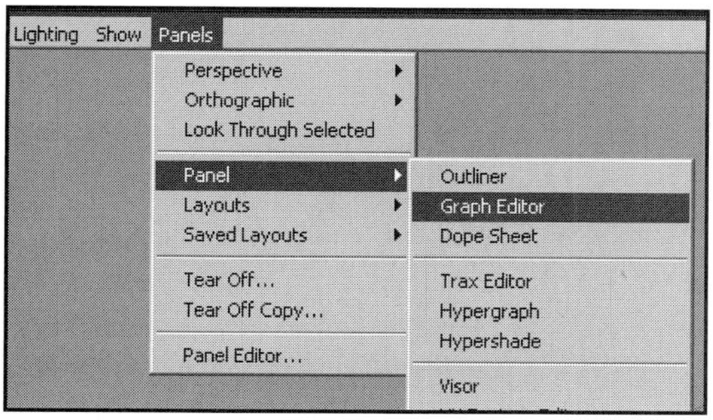

figure 3-16

Three-panel view with the Graph Editor.

We will later create a shot camera that will frame your work for final approvals.

Select the Move tool. (The Manipulator icon will not show up if you have not selected the Move, Rotate, or Scale tool.)

With the ball selected, press the Insert button on your keyboard. (On most keyboards, the Insert button is above the arrow keys on the right-hand side.)

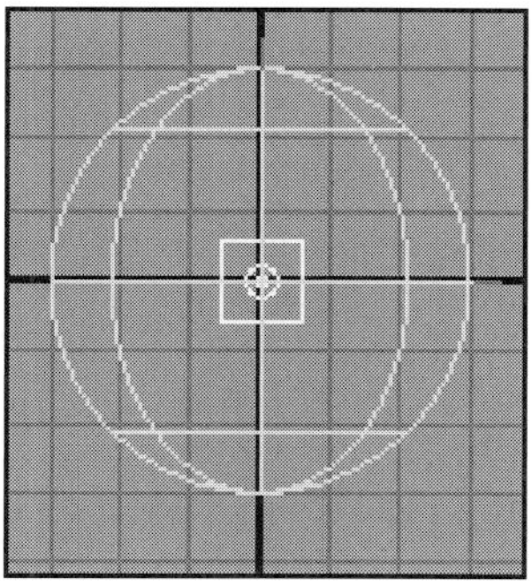

figure 3-17

The manipulator changes to a yellow box icon.

The manipulator is now a pivot and looks like a yellow square with a circle inside (see Figure 3-17).

Move this square with your left mouse button (LMB), and center it on the bottommost contact point of the sphere (see Figure 3-18).

Press Insert again to turn off the Translate Pivot option. The translate manipulator returns.

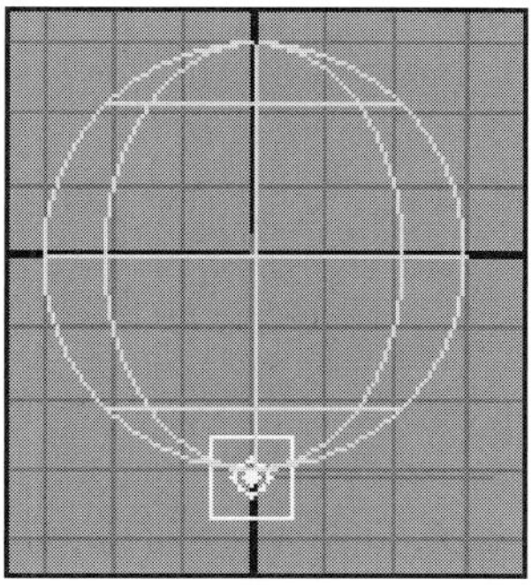

figure 3-18

Select yellow axis only.

Play with different Scale entries to see how the sphere reacts to the new pivot. Changing the Y value in the Scale function will give you the most interesting reaction (see Figure 3-19).

Select the green arrow of the translate manipulator. Move the ball along the Y axis so that the new pivot rests on top of the origin (0, 0, 0). If you want to continue using the Channel Box, type “3” into Translate Y and keep Translate X and Z at 0.

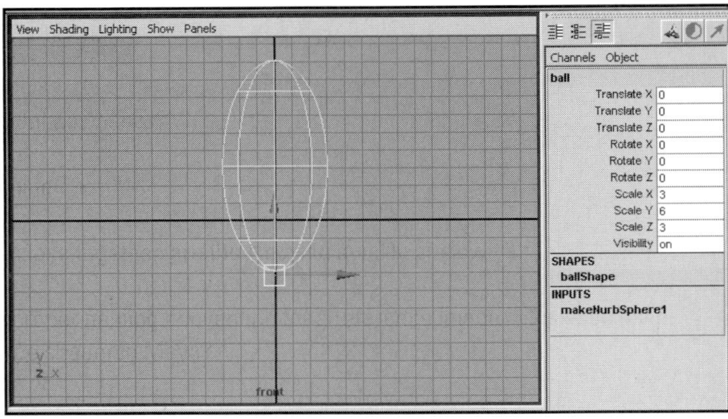

figure 3-19

Changing the Y value in the Channel Box.

Before you begin to key frame, reset the default settings in Maya for your tangents. Go to your preferences (see Figure 3-20):

Window > Settings/Preferences > Preferences

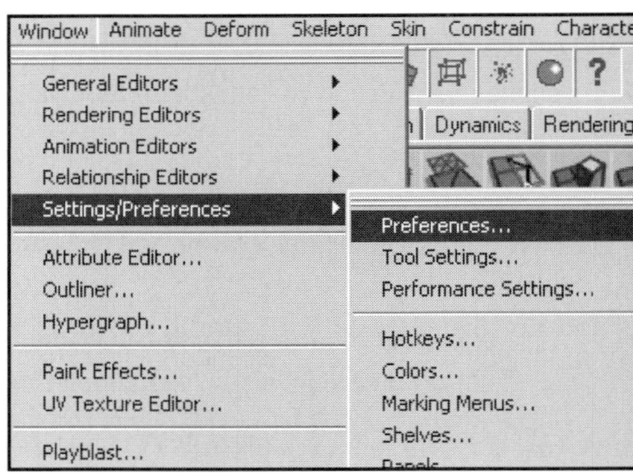

figure 3-20

Here is one way to get to your preferences.

Go to Animation in the Preferences, and change the "in" tangents to "linear," the "out" tangents to "stepped," and turn on "weighted tangents" (see Figure 3-21). This will allow you to have static poses. Later, you will tweak the curves to create believable movement.

Save and close.

At this stage, define your key poses. The key poses are the silhouettes which determine the acting in the scene. We use linear and stepped because you want static poses at certain points in time.

Set a key frame for ball at "frame 1," using the following:

Animate > Set Key

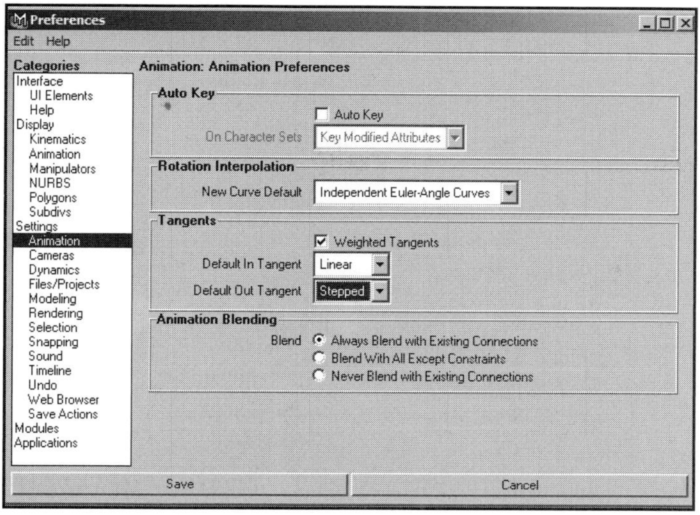

figure 3-21

Change the tangents under Keys in the Preferences.

The shortcut for default key-framing is "s."

Notice how all the Channel Boxes went from white to beige. This means key-frame animation has been attached to every channel (see Figure 3-22).

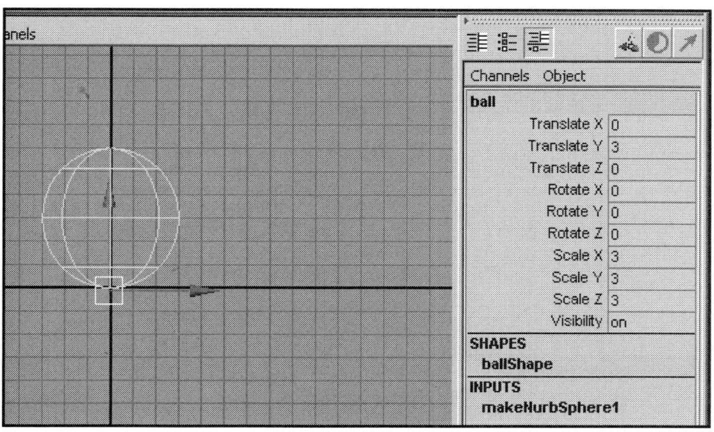

figure 3-22

The area next to key-framed channels should turn beige.

A red tick should now be on your timeline. This indicates that a key frame has been set.

By pressing "s" you set the default setting in creating a key frame in Maya. The default setting is undesirable because the beige color signifies a key frame in every channel in your Channel Box. You do not want a key frame in every channel because this makes your animation heavy, difficult to edit, and messy overall.

For this part of the tutorial, you will only concentrate on the Y Translate. For a clean slate, go to (see Figure 3-23):

Edit > Delete All By Type > Channels

figure 3-23

All animation is removed with this command.

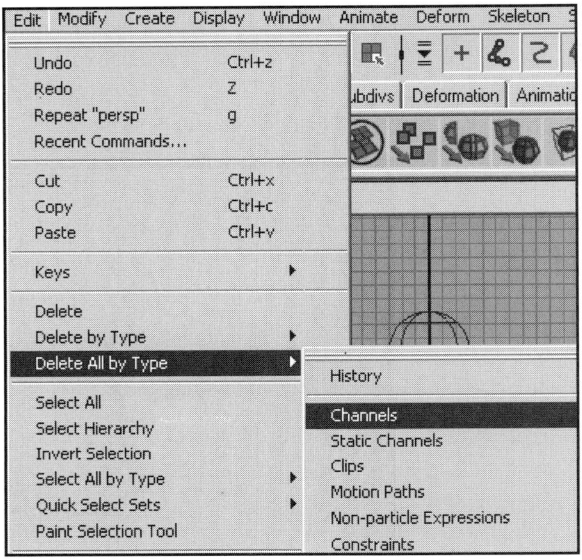

All the beige should be removed from your Channel Box.

Again, set a key frame for ball at frame 1. Do not use the shortcut "s" key. Instead, go to the Channel Box.

Left-mouse select the Y Translate channel. It will turn black. Right-click over the Y Translate channel to reveal the menu (see Figure 3-24). Hold down the right mouse button (RMB).

figure 3-24

A hidden menu.

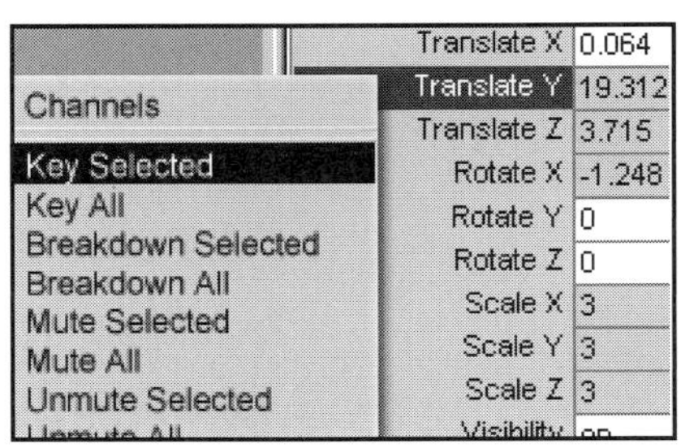

Select Key Selected. Now you will see that only the Y Translate channel is beige (see Figure 3-25).

Go to frame 13. Right-click over the Y Translate, and select Key Selected again. You will see red ticks on the line at frames 1 and 13.

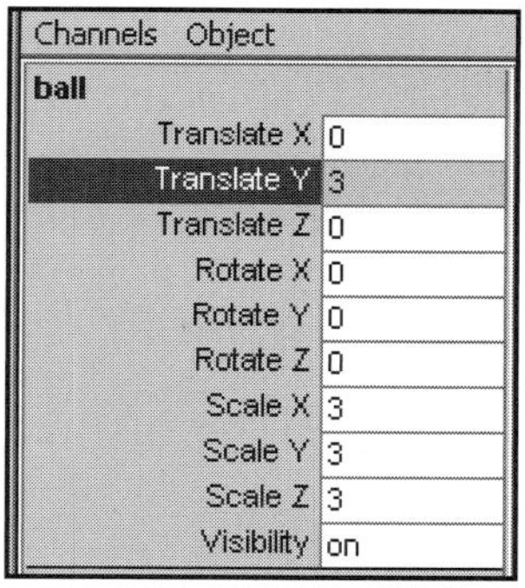

figure | 3-25

Y Translate is beige.

The first and last frames of a loop must be the same or else there will be a pop in the animation. The animation will appear halted where the extra frame adds additional 'hang' time to the movement. When you get more sophisticated in movement, you will want to make the last frame precede the first so that the movement does not slow on contact.

Now, in your timeline, change playback end time to 12 (see Figure 3-26).

| NOTE |

Remember to always go to the next frame before setting a key frame. Otherwise, you will likely overwrite your previous key frames.

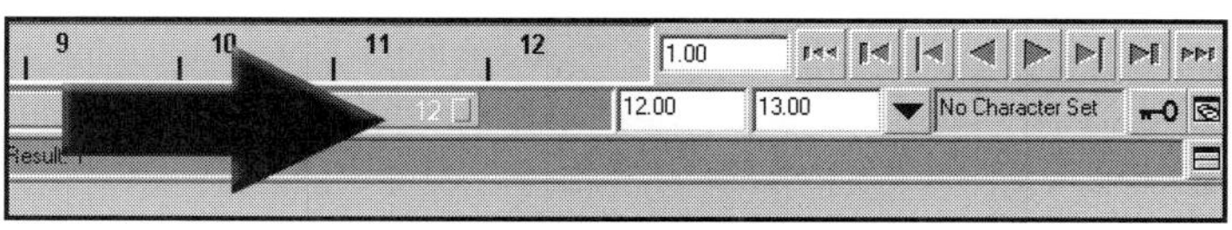

figure | 3-26

Change playback end time to 12.

When you loop this animation, you do not want to play the same key frame twice or it will hold. Frames 1 and 13 are the same key frames right now.

Go to frame 7. Type "20" into the Translate Y field. Set a key frame. This is the "float" position (see Figure 3-27).

Select a window as your playback view. Perspective or Front view is your best choice.

Play your animation using the controls (see Figure 3-28). (They look like a VCR or DVD control window).

This is a pose test. It is your first opportunity to view the timing. It is supposed to be choppy. Now, to capture the timing found when the ball loses upward momentum and gains downward momentum, you will set two more key frames.

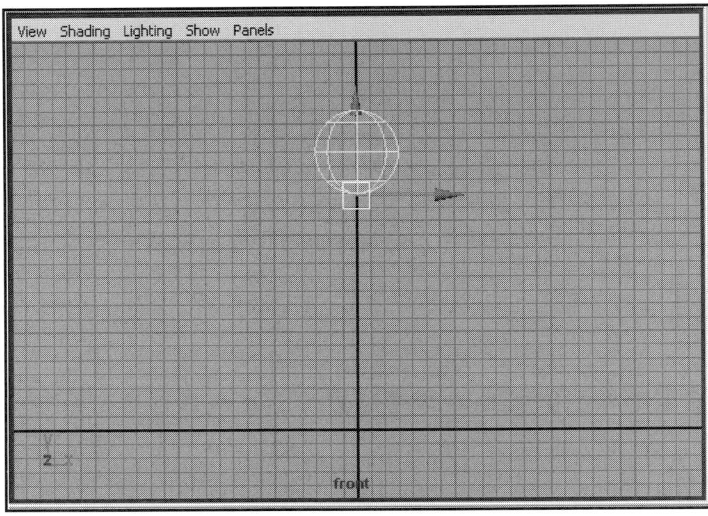

figure 3-27

Float position.

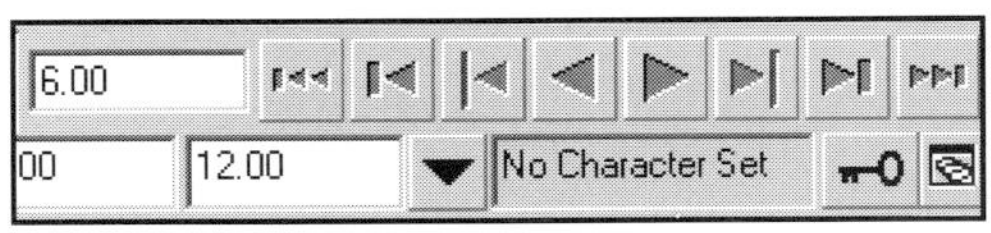

figure 3-28

The Controls.

Go to key frames 5 and 9, and set a value of 17 in the Y Translate. Your curve should look like Figure 3-29.

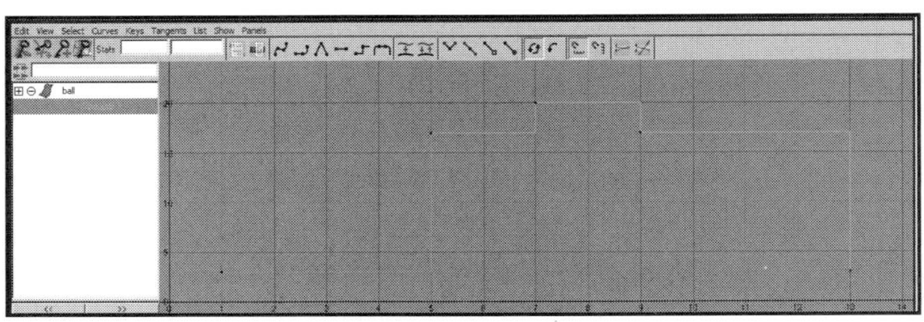

figure 3-29

Your curve should look like this.

Play the animation. At this stage in production, if you were working in a studio, you would need to get approval for the timing before you work on movement.

If the animation is too fast to see, check your animation preferences and make sure you are playing at 24 or 30 fps (frames per second).

You have created the basic timing of the bouncing ball. Traditional animators call this "setting the key poses."

To see a representation similar to the traditional bouncing ball sketch, turn on ghosting. Make sure the sphere is selected. Then turn on the following and see Figure 3-30:

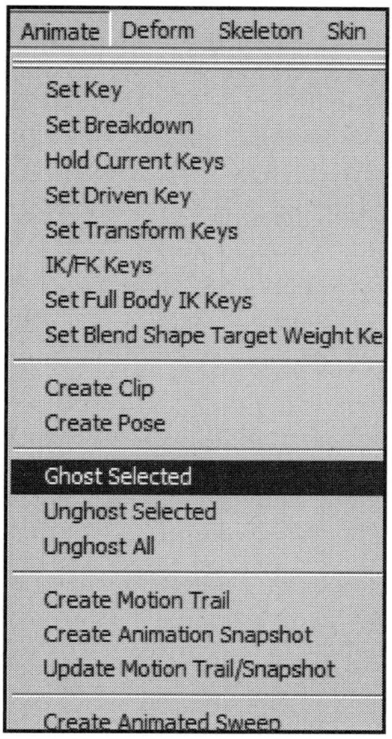

figure 3-30

The Ghost selected.

Animate > Ghost Selected

Play the animation. You will see spheres for every frame of animation selected in the Ghosting Options box. To turn off ghosting, use the command Animate > Unghost Selected. Open the Options box, and check out all of the different ways you can ghost.

Create a shot camera by going to (see Figure 3-31):

Panels > Perspective > New

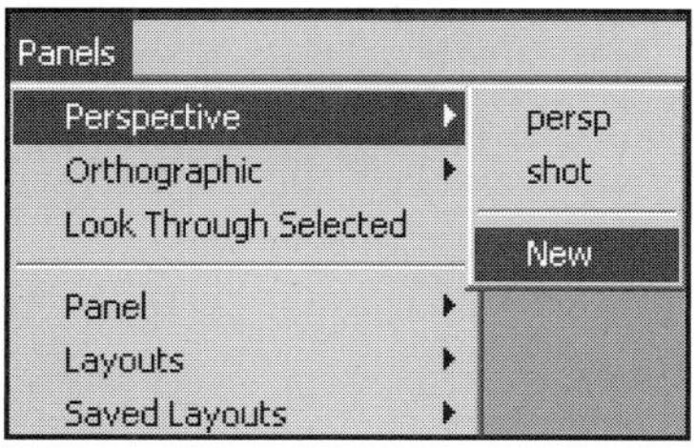

figure 3-31

Create a shot camera.

Look for the new camera you just made by going to the outliner: **Window > Outliner**

The new camera is called persp1 (see Figure 3-32). Rename it "shot."

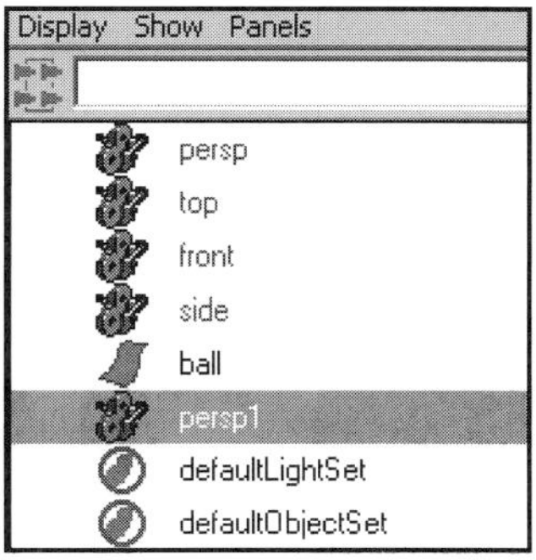

figure 3-32

Find the new camera in your outliner.

You can also change the name in the Channel Box.

Select the shot camera, and set the view you want to see through the camera. You can dolly, pan, and zoom to frame the shot.

Set your shot, and lock the camera. To lock a camera, select it in the outliner. Then, in the Channel Box, select all the channels. Right-click over the selected channels, and choose Lock Selected. Locked channels will appear as gray in the Channel Editor.

At this point, the animator goes to the art director for approvals on timing and staging. Once approved, you move on to adding motion.

Adding Motion

Now you can add motion between key frames. In the Graph Editor, select each key frame and change it to a clamped tangent. To do this, select the key frame and then right-mouse click to get a hidden menu. Select (see Figure 3-33):

Tangents > Clamped

figure 3-33

Select clamped tangents.

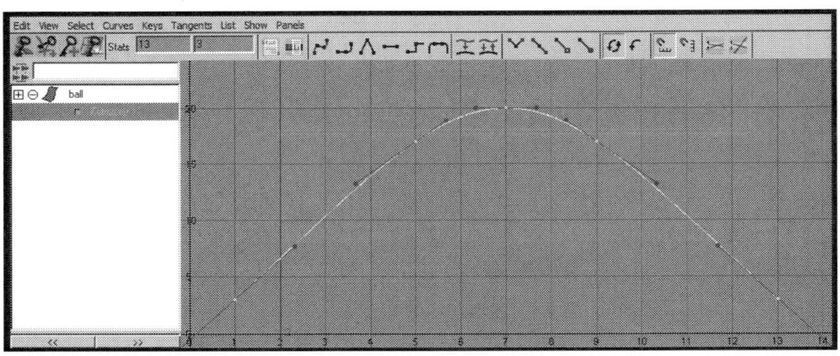

Notice how curvy the tangents are. At this time, you choose the value of the slope to reflect your needs for the ease in and out of the motion. Play the animation for an example of this. The motion is not very believable.

Select the key frames at 5, 7, and 9, and shape them like the 5, 7, and 9 shown in Figure 3-34.

figure 3-34

Select a key frame, LMB the tangent, and MMB the tangent up or down.

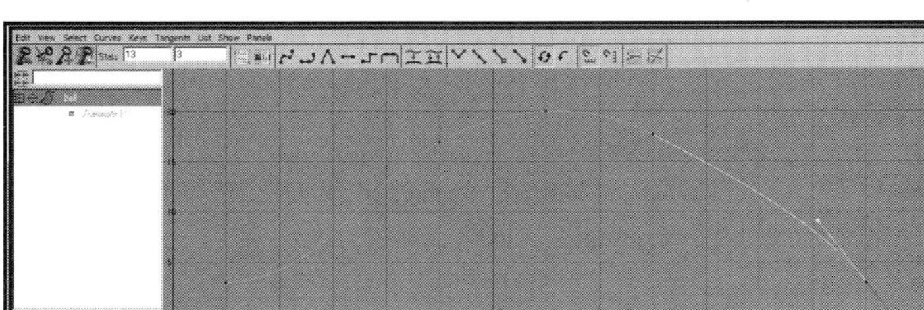

Remember, to shape them, you left-mouse select the key frame (only one at a time for this purpose). Then left-mouse select the tangent and middle-mouse move the tangent up or down.

Play the animation and notice that the timing is decent. Next we need squash and stretch.

Squash and Stretch

Go to your preferences. You already know how to get there through the pull-down menus, so now use the graphic shortcut. Click on the icon next to your automatic key-frame button on the lower right of the interface (see Figure 3-35).

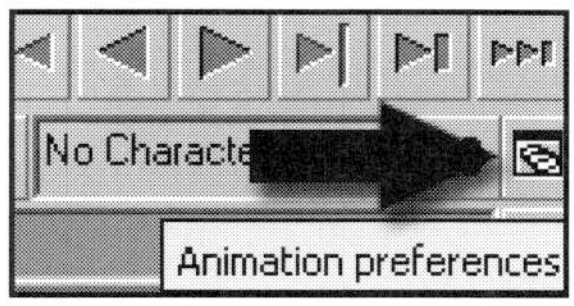

figure 3-35

The Preferences icon.

The Preferences window opens (see Figure 3-36). Select Animation. In the Keys area, change the default in and out tangents to flat. Keep them weighted. Click save.

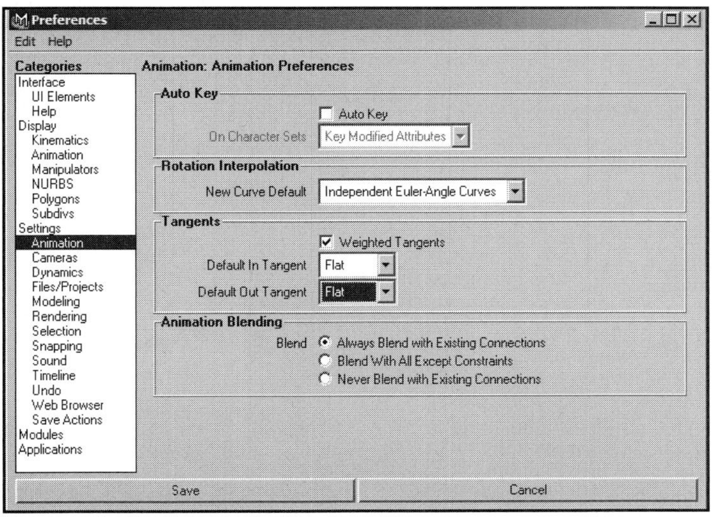

figure 3-36

Key preferences.

You have finished the pose test. Your tweaking from this point on will contain movement.

Go to frame 7. Make sure the values for the X, Y, and Z Scale are 3.

Set a key frame for the three Scale channels. Remember to use Key Selected so that only these channels are key-framed (see Figure 3-37).

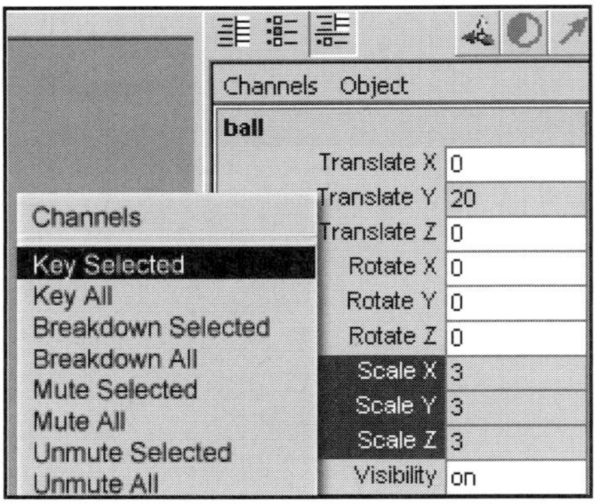

figure 3-37

Set keyframes for the X, Y, and Z Scale.

Make sure to set the same values for key frames 5 and 9.

Go to frame 12. Change the Scale values to the following:

Scale X: 2

Scale Y: 4

Scale Z: 2

Set a key frame for the scale values. Do the same at key frame 2. You now have stretch.

Now go to frame 13. Key the following values:

Scale X: 3.4

Scale Y: 2.2

Scale Z: 3.4

Play all 13 frames. You now have squash.

Notice that you shaved .8 off the Scale Y value and added .4 to the Scale X and Scale Z values. Maintain a consistent volume by maintaining a total x + y + z value of *q*.

The movement is a little like a bag of ooze. Tweak the in and out tangents of the Scale values to give a crisper transition.

Edit your tangents in the Graph Editor. Move the in and out tangents to create believable movement. In the Graph Editor, select only the X, Y, and Z scale curves. Then use the Graph Editor pull-down menu and select (see Figure 3-38):

View > **Frame All**

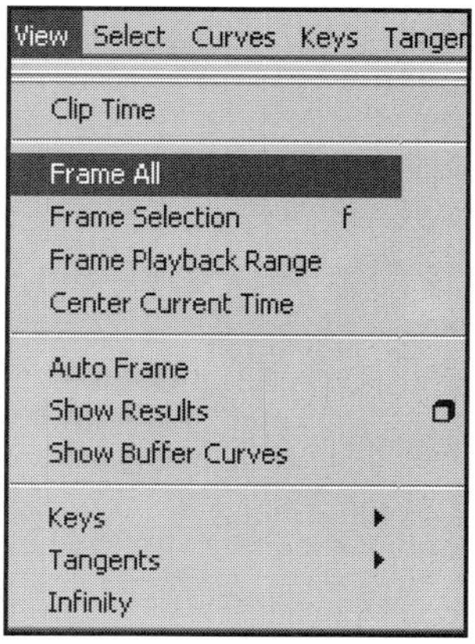

figure 3-38

View > Frame All.

You will now see just the Scale curves close up (see Figure 3-39). It is easier to work this way.

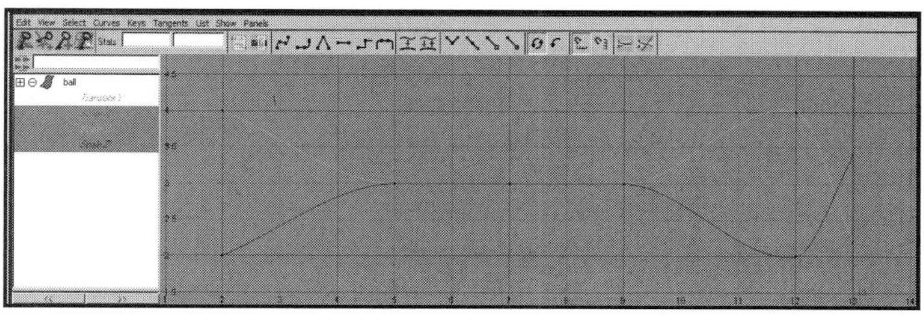

figure 3-39

Scale curves viewed close up.

Sometimes a shift of movement is hidden, so you need to look closely at your curves. The author prefers scale curves be edited this way for this bounce (see Figure 3-40).

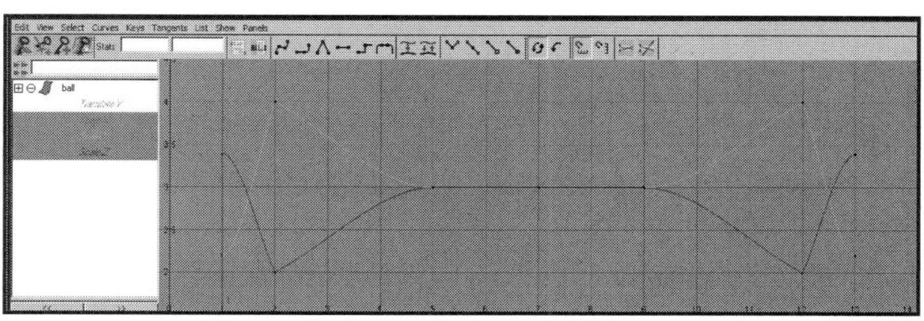

figure 3-40

My Scale curves.

Be very careful with curves. Look out for overshoots. If the curve extends beyond your key frame, it is hitting a key pose you did not create. Break the tangent in these cases, and edit the curve by doing the following: Choose a key frame, and use the Break Tangents tool (see Figure 3-41).

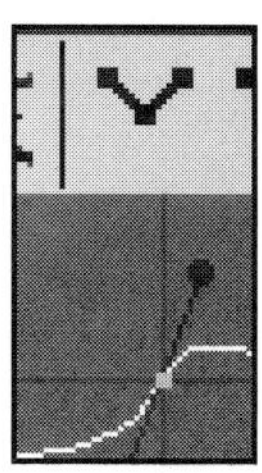

figure 3-41

The Break Tangents tool.

Left-mouse click the tool after the key frame is selected. The tangent is now broken.

You will notice that the in and out tangents are now two different colors: red and blue. When you select one and move it, the other side does not respond (see Figure 3-42).

NOTE

I am applying cartoon physics. When an object bounces, the volume of the object adjusts to the force of contact. Note that volume does not disappear; it displaces. You can observe this firsthand when you take a water balloon and place it on a table top. A ball that was skinny and tall while you carried (see Figure 3-43) it is now short and fat as it lies on a table. The weight and appeal of the object will determine the physics you apply.

figure 3-42

Fix the overshoot.

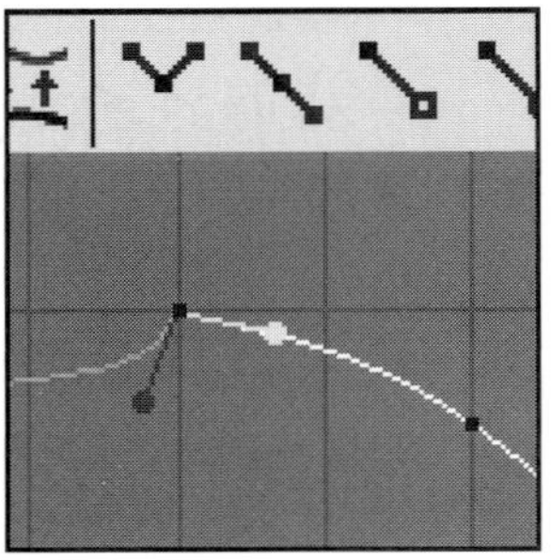

If you play the key frames now, you will notice you have a little bit of believable bounce, but only a little bit. You will be using additional tools to create more believability.

You will add a few more keys. Save this version of your file before continuing. Name the file ball_base_v1_0101. Replace 0101 with today's date. If you save multiple versions of your file with dates attached, you will be able to access older versions of your files.

figure 3-43

A water balloon is elastic.

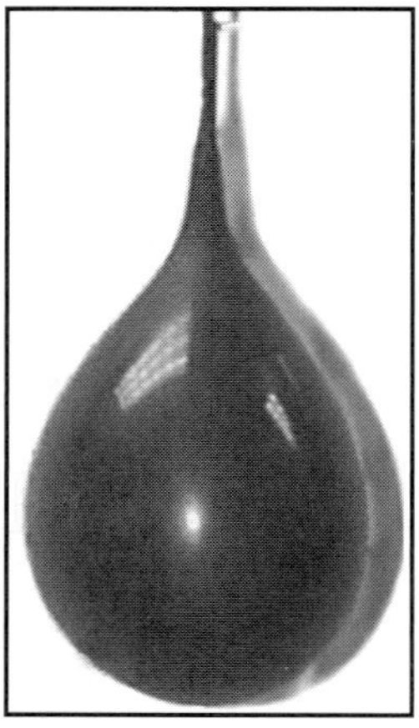

Interactive Editing

Highlight "ball" in the Graph Editor by left-mouse clicking on it. This will allow us to see all four curves.

Make sure you are on frame 7 in the timeline. Select Ball in the Front View window. In the Graph Editor, click on the Move Nearest Key Picked tool (see Figure 3-44). Your arrow icon in the Graph Editor window should turn into an arrow pointing to a box.

figure 3-44

The Move Nearest Key Picked tool.

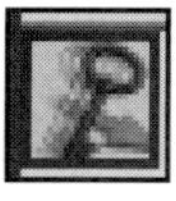

Select the uppermost key frame on the Y Translate curve. If you have correctly done this, the key frame changes from black to yellow, and the affected curves turn white.

Click and hold down the middle mouse button (MMB); then move the mouse toward you. The key frame should follow. Watch the ball in the Front view; it should be moving in response to where you move the key frame. Move the key frame up and down. See that the ball moves up and down as well because you are changing the information in Y Translate. Watch Y Translate in the Channel Box; look at how the numbers are changing as you move the key frame.

When a typical ball bounces, it speeds up as it rises from the floor. It then slows down as it loses momentum and gets pulled by gravity, floats for a bit, and then gravity pulls it back to the ground. Notice how the curve arches (see Figure 3-45). It is experiencing a change in forces from push to retract. As these forces balance, the ball appears to float momentarily before succumbing to gravity.

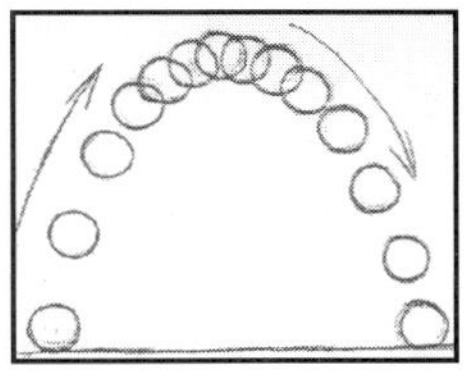

figure 3-45

Note the slow and fast portions.

Tweak your frames until you are happy with the movement. Save your file, this time as version 2 with today's date.

Using the Lattice Deform Keys

For this tutorial, change how high the ball bounces by using a lattice with the Lattice Deform Keys tool.

With the ball highlighted, select the Translate Y channel in the Graph Editor.

Select the Lattice Deform Keys button in the Graph Editor (see Figure 3-46).

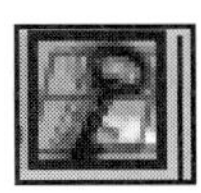

figure 3-46

To create the lattice, left-mouse click and drag a box around the entire Y channel in the Graph Editor (see Figure 3-47).

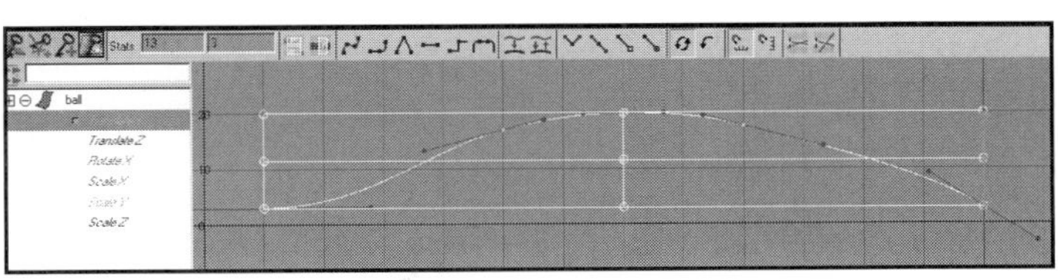

figure 3-47

To edit the lattice, move the lattice points to modify the Keys on the Curve Editor (see Figure 3-48).

figure 3-48

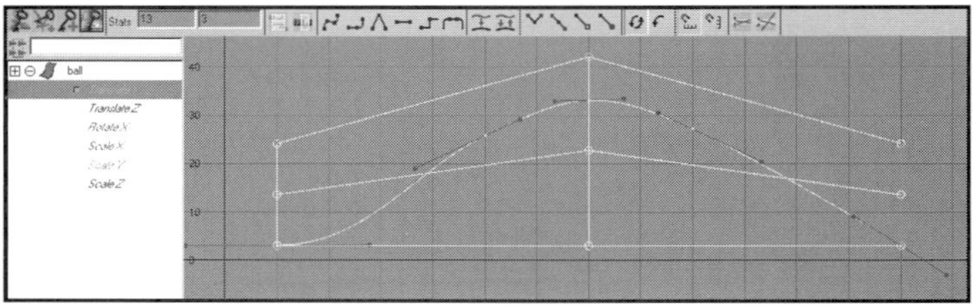

Move the Ball Across the Screen

Now you will bounce the ball across the screen. You can do this using which two channels.

The two channels you can use are X Translate and Z Translate because they represent movement forward and backwards or left to right. You will move forward and backwards using the Z Translate.

Look at the ball in the Side view window. Move to frame 1 on the timeline. Set the value for Z Translate in the Channel Box to –15. Set a key frame for only the Z Translate channel. Go to frame 13. Move the sphere to the right side of the screen, Z Translate 15. Set a key selected for the Z Translate channel.

This is what your Z Translate curve looks like (see Figure 3-49). We reverse the ease in and ease out because we want the ball to move faster when it lands and takes off and to slow at the float position.

figure 3-49

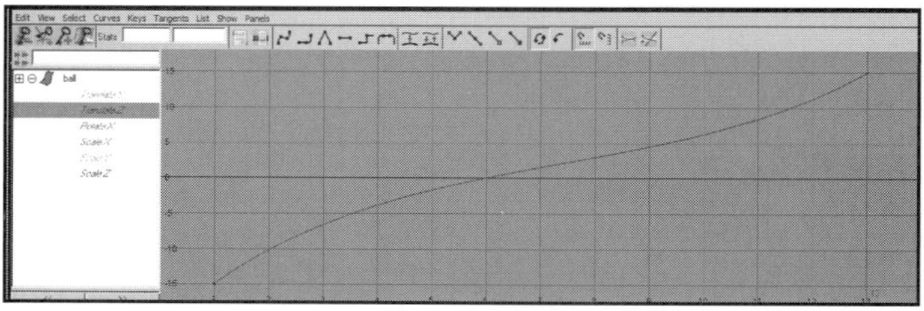

Z Translate curve.

Play the animation. The ball now bounces toward you in the Perspective view.

To add the final beauty to your ball bounce, you will add one small rotation to the X axis. When your ball moves forward, it must lean forward. When your ball lands, it must land from the trajectory.

Go to frame 1. Set a key frame in X Rotate to 0. Go to frame 2. Rotate the sphere to the right to 12. Set a key frame. Go to frame 7, and set X Rotate to 0. Go to frame 12. Rotate the sphere to the left to –12. Set a key frame at frame 12. Go to frame 13, and set X Rotate to 0. Set a key frame at frame 13.

Figure 3-50 shows the X rotate curve. It is edited so that it will transition more quickly.

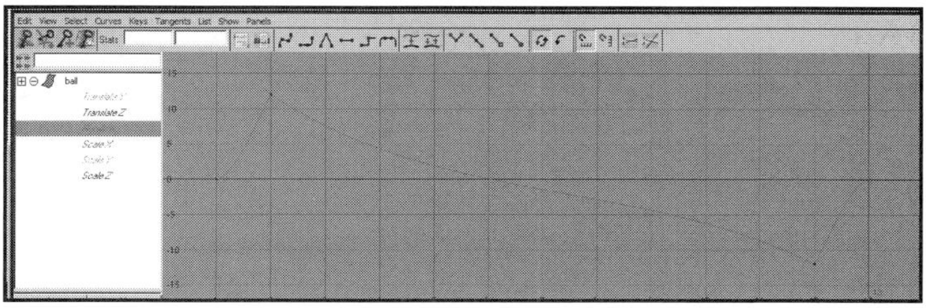

figure 3-50

X rotate curve.

Play the animation.

Figure 3-51 shows the final curves for this animation. Yours does not have to look like that which is shown in Figure 3-51. You only need to have mastered the buttons to achieve the motion you desire. Do this chapter over again until you can do this animation without the book.

You can certainly cycle this animation; however, it is unneccessary to do so after all the effort you put into achieving a believable

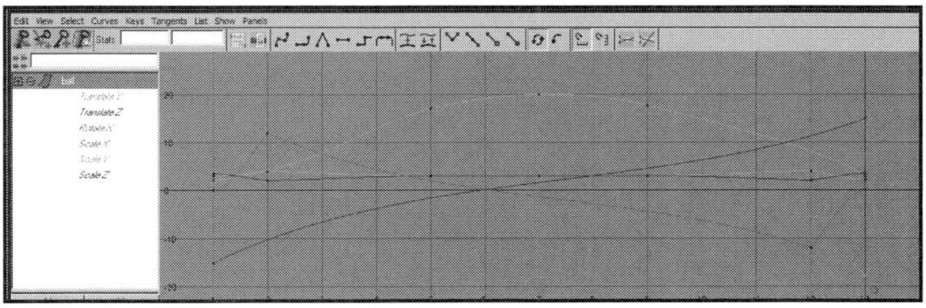

figure 3-51

Final curves.

bounce. Bouncing balls loose height and momentum as they move forward, and cycling keeps all momentum constant. It would take only a few key frames and a few tweaks to create a believable bouncing ball that eventually slows with a roll forward and then ends with a slight tip backwards.

Edit your ball to bounce forward a few more times. We advise that you move ahead one bounce at a time. Each time, shorten the movement in the Y and Z Translates. Also, reduce the squash and stretch.

Now you know all the tools you will need to edit this bouncing ball to look like any kind of ball you want to create. Try your hand at editing the function curves to emulate the motions of two distinctly different balls, like a bowling ball and a ping-pong ball. Make reference footage of the balls you will be working with. You will find believable detail by observing the object firsthand.

The Ping-Pong Ball

A ping-pong ball has a hard, inelastic shell. It is light and very responsive to force. When it achieves momentum, it travels much farther than a heavier object, like a bowling ball. Which curves would you edit if it bounced on smooth concrete?

A ping-pong ball bounces higher and faster than the average ball and floats for a little longer. The Translate Y will need to be brought up to a much higher value to allow for a higher bounce. You should lengthen the float in the Z Translate channel. The ping-pong ball also requires less bounce and stretch because it is made of an inelastic substance. Thus, the Scale values would need to be tweaked. Edit the Scale X, Scale Y, and Scale Z to be much closer to the initial Scale value of 3. You may only want a variance of .05 for squash and stretch.

The Water Balloon

A water balloon has a soft, elastic shell. It is heavy and jiggles in response to force. It does not travel up in Y when it responds to momentum; rather, it tends to spread out more and respond internally. Which curves would you edit to create the water balloon bouncing on a shag rug?

There is little or no float time on the bounce. The bounce is low and shallow after the drop. You will need to bring down the Y Translate value to achieve the lower bounce. The ballon will travel a shorter distance, so the Z Translate curve will need to be adjusted. It squashes and stretches more than the average ball and has much more elasticity. You will need to edit the Translate Y, Scale X, Scale Y, and Scale Z again, but in a vastly different direction. The Scale values should be pushed to further extremes. The balloon squashes in more deeply, jiggles, and almost does a double bounce.

Two or three bounces happen in the same space of time as an average ball bounce. You will need to shorten the timeline and edit the frame playback to accommodate the timing change.

SUMMARY

A bouncing ball is the basis for most movement in animation. A frog jumping and landing will require similar arc, bounce, and stretch. The fleshy parts of a larger person jogging will require bounce and stretch, timing, and arcs. Knowing how to use your tools to create the principles will make your animation much more convincing.

in review

1. What is the shortcut for setting a key frame?
2. What is a clean and efficient way to set a key frame?
3. Which translate curve represents the up-and-down motion of the ball in this chapter?
4. What command do you use to delete all of the animated channels?
5. How does volume change when a ball squashes and stretches?
6. When you first set the preferences for your tangents, what is your default "in tangent" when key-framing for the pose test? What is your default "out tangent"? Are tangents weighted or free?
7. What are these values changed to when you are ready to edit the curves?

EXPLORING ON YOUR OWN

1. Collect different balls: ping-pong ball, basketball, bowling ball, tennis ball, playground ball (half deflated), beach ball, volleyball, racquetball, and super ball.

   Take the balls to different surfaces and bounce them. Take note of the different reactions that each ball gives to each different surface: nubbled concrete, wood, running track, ice, steel, smooth concrete, and stone.

   Now try to re-create the different movements in your animation so that you can visually read what kind of ball you are animating and what kind of surface the ball is reacting to.

2. If you are confident in your skills, animate two balls as if they were feet walking forward. This is an excellent way to practice timing. Watch people walking. The feet are similar to bouncing balls, except they are also responding to a load of weight. Thus, the volumes may be a bit more crucial to giving information. Make one ball the left foot and one ball the right foot. They will spend more time on the ground than a ball, and they will move with a directed purpose when achieving each step.

notes

notes

Adventures in Design

ADVENTURES IN DESIGN

THE STORYBOARD

To construct a movie, you must first have a plan. Storyboards are the architectural blueprints of a movie.

The first thing you do when creating a short story is write it out. Make sure you can tell the story in 2 to 3 sentences. If the listener clearly understands, then it is safe to proceed. If you can't get to the point quickly, rethink the story.

Then, create a storyboard. It doesn't need to be more than quick sketches if it is for you. It will need a bit more detail if it is meant to communicate to a team.

The storyboard will help you map out how you portray the story details. At this stage you choose your camera shots and plan how you manipulate the eye of the viewer towards important information. You have many camera shots to choose from—but first try your hand at using the following:

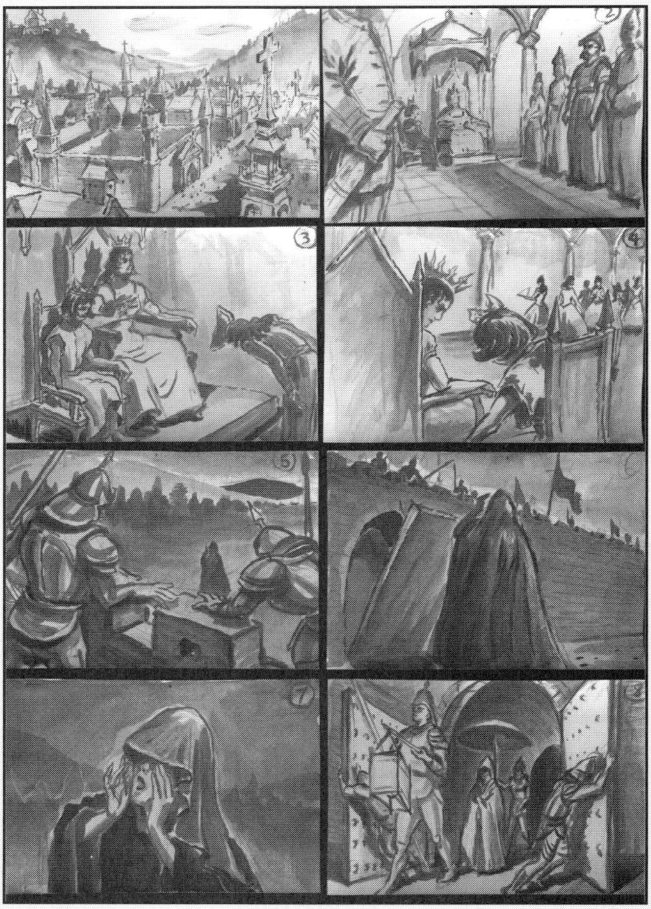

A-1 Storyboard by Cui Jin.

- XCU—Extreme close up
- CU—Close up
- MS—Medium shot
- WS—Long shot
- XWS—Extreme long shot

The Five-Panel Storyboard

The five-panel storyboard is a good way to begin creation of a short film. For your shorts, construct a five-panel storyboard. You are welcome to add additional panels, but have the five outlined below represented in your boards.

The five-panel storyboard is a story told in five panels. You are answering the following questions in each respective panel:

1. Where (Wide shot)
2. Who (Medium shot)
3. What (Close up)
4. Reaction/Conflict (Close up, wide shot, or medium shot)
5. Resolve (Close up, wide shot, or medium shot)

This storyboard illustrates the following:

1. WHERE: Wide shot :03 seconds
   Opening shot of a convenience mart and a depressed man walking in.
2. WHO: Medium shot :06
   He checks his wallet for his last two dollars.
3. WHAT: Extreme Close up of ticket :05
4. REACTION/CONFLICT: Medium Shot of man :06
   He scratches off the numbers on the ticket.
5. RESOLVE: Wide Shot :04
   The ticket is a winner and he is now a happy man.

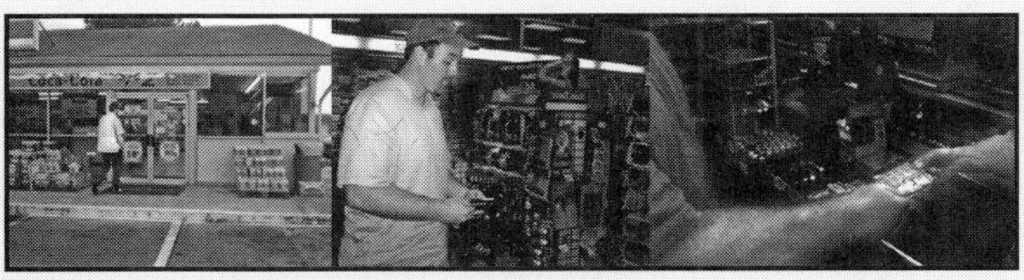

A-2 Shots 1, 2, and 3 of the five-panel storyboard.

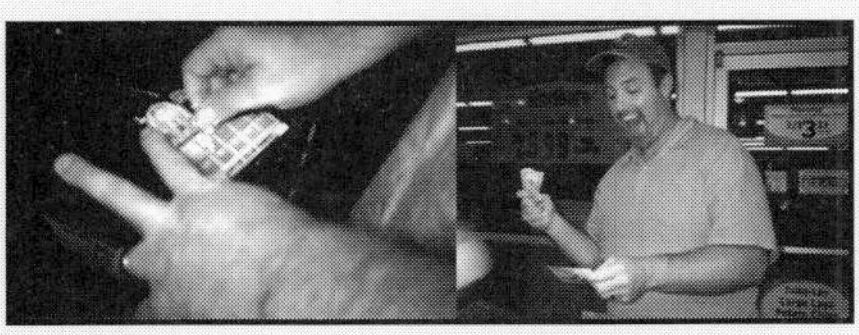

A-3 Shots 4 and 5 of the five-panel storyboard.

Adventures in Design

When you have chosen the shots, then assign an amount of time to each shot. A few rules of thumb are:

1. Wide shots are generally longer—7 seconds or more, because there is a lot of information for the viewer to absorb. I break this rule here.

2. Generally, shots are no longer than 9 seconds (although editing has pushed this shorter and shorter in recent days).

3. Close ups tend to be shorter in duration, though typically no less than 1.5 seconds.

4. Do not make all of your shots the same length of time.

5. Editing is like writing music—be aware of rhythm.

These are not absolute rules. You will find many music videos have incredibly short edits. On the other extreme, Director Robert Altman (*The Player, Ready to Wear*) starts many of his movies with a several minute opening shot.

Follow these rules for the creation of the five-panel storyboard. Try to keep your five-panel storyboard to exactly 25 seconds. This will force you to budget your time, like they do in commercial production.

If you want to make a Hollywood story, add a sixth/seventh panel. This is the "twist." To the five-panel storyboard above, I will add two panels.

6. Wide shot (:05)
   Man runs away joyfully with his winnings.

7. Medium shot (:07)
   Man is hit by bus.

To make your own five-panel storyboard, do the following:

1. Write down a one- to three-sentence description of the story encapsulating the main essence of the action.

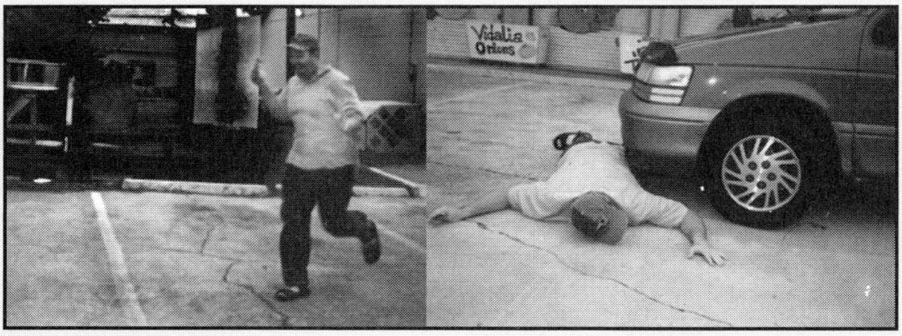

A-4 Shots 6 and 7 added for the Hollywood story.

2. Draw your five boxes and label them *where, who, what, conflict/ reaction,* and *resolve* in the upper left hand corner of each box.

3. Transfer your ideas to these boxes, translating your story to answer the five labels. Write the action below the boxes.

4. Time out your scenes, and label each scene with how many seconds will be awarded the shot underneath the box.

5. Draw sketches in each box illustrating the primary activity in that shot. Frame it as you want the camera to frame it.

6. Label your camera shot in the upper right hand of the frame.

This is a great way to churn out ideas for a short film. Start with a simple story, then plot out the major elements this way. On your second pass, you can add more details and shots, but you will start out with a basic story that answers the questions your audience will want answers to.

Now that you have a five-panel storyboard, you will need to create an animatic. The next Adventures in Design (see pages 00–00) will give you advice on how to create one.

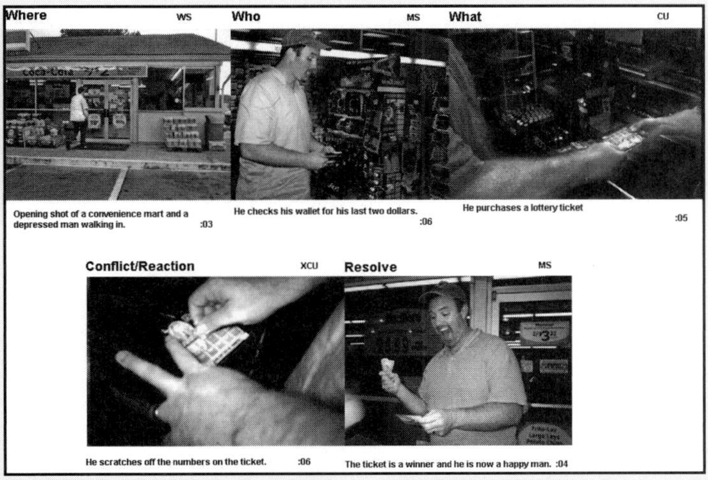

A-5 Final storyboard.

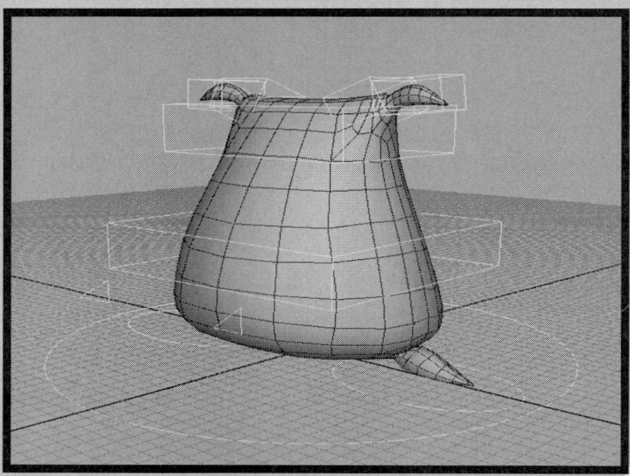

4 preparing source reference material

charting your course

With this chapter, you will move into the realm of true character animation. You will work with a simple beanbag shape, endowing it with a personality and putting it through a range of separate attitudes. In this process, you will learn the most effective ways of conveying ideas to an audience in visual form.

goals

In this chapter, you will:

- **Look at Animation timing charts.**
- **Learn how to import background images into Maya to use as reference for animation.**
- **Prepare to animate a rig against source images.**

TOOLS USED

- **Multilister.** Reference images for an animation can be linked to a plane using the Multilister (see Figure 4-1).

figure 4-1

Materials Editor.

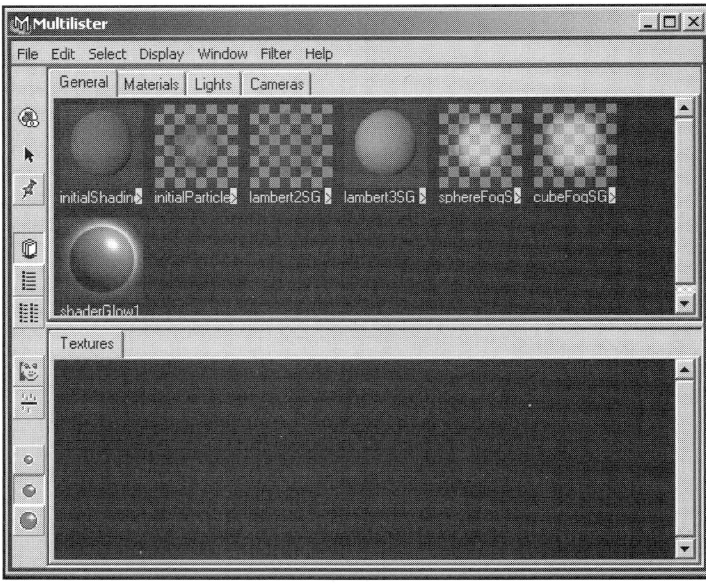

Figure 4-1

- **Targa image files.** Maya likes Targa files and easily imports them (see Figure 4-2). We will learn the proper naming convention.

figure 4-2

Targa files

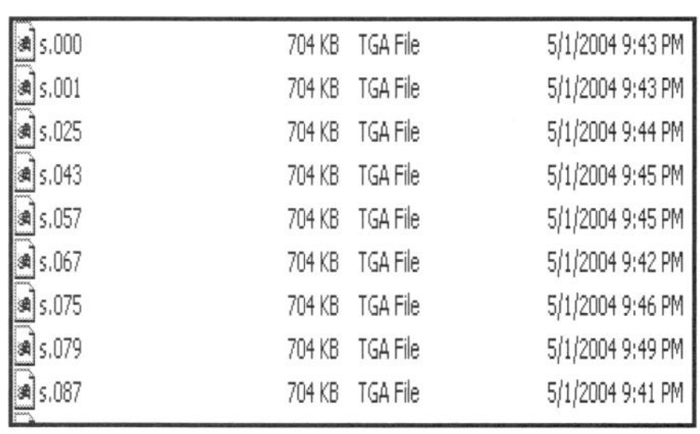

s.000	704 KB	TGA File	5/1/2004 9:43 PM
s.001	704 KB	TGA File	5/1/2004 9:43 PM
s.025	704 KB	TGA File	5/1/2004 9:44 PM
s.043	704 KB	TGA File	5/1/2004 9:45 PM
s.057	704 KB	TGA File	5/1/2004 9:45 PM
s.067	704 KB	TGA File	5/1/2004 9:42 PM
s.075	704 KB	TGA File	5/1/2004 9:46 PM
s.079	704 KB	TGA File	5/1/2004 9:49 PM
s.087	704 KB	TGA File	5/1/2004 9:41 PM

- **Shaded view/hardware texturing.** You can see image files in your 3D work area when the right parameters are turned on in our window (see Figure 4-3).

- **The Attribute Editor.** The Attribute Editor contains details pertaining to an object (see Figure 4-4). It is a filing cabinet of links and mathematical information.

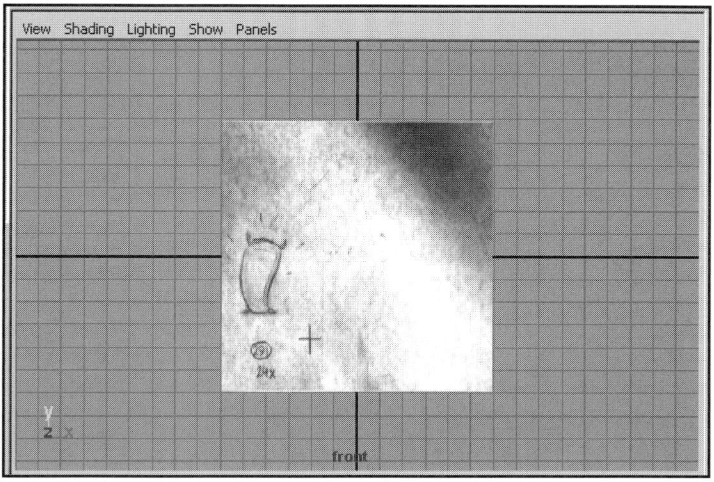

figure 4-3

Shaded view/hardware texturing.

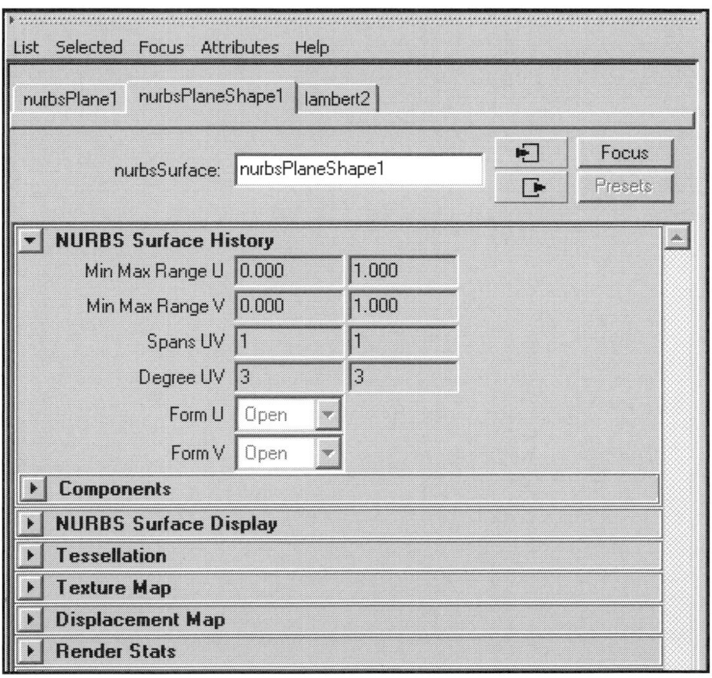

figure 4-4

The Attribute Editor.

Using a Beanbag to Express Some Physical Attitudes

You will now be introduced to your "performer": a half-full beanbag that is able to assume a full range of forms that imply attitudes and emotions. Using a simple and direct line of action running through the form, you can express enough varying shapes to act out a simple story line in pantomime.

Let us start with a series of thumbnail sketches to outline the story points of the presentation (see Figures 4-5 and 4-6).

1. Here is your star, a respectable young beanbag named Clyde. You see him here in a "neutral" pose, waiting for the beginning of a situation in which he can perform.
2. A spider enters stage left.
3. The spider attracts Clyde's attention; he turns to take a look.
4. Clyde is curious and takes a cautious step to look at the spider.

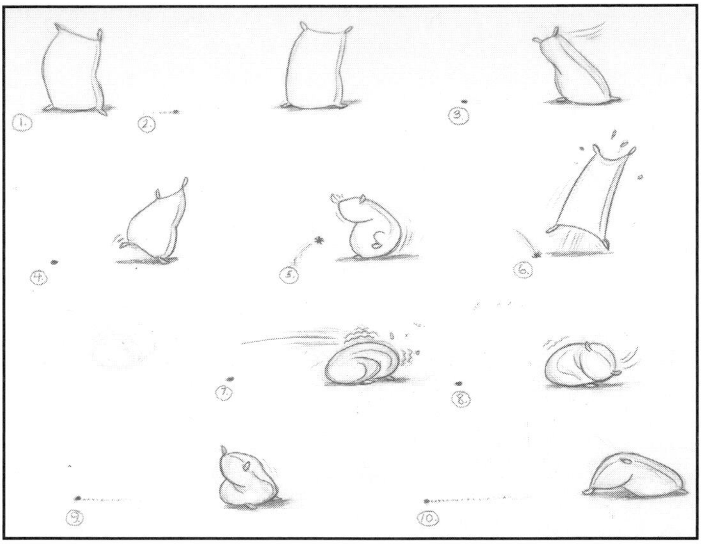

figure 4-5

Thumbnails 1–10.

5. The spider jumps toward him, perhaps realizing that the best defense is an offense.
6. Clyde reacts with a big "fright take" . . .
7. . . . and then zips into a crouch and cowers in terror.
8. After recovering a little of his nerve, he takes a tentative peek back at the spider.
9. The spider begins to walk away.
10. Picking himself up off the ground, Clyde watches the spider walking in the other direction.
11. Gaining courage, Clyde goes into "attack" mode . . .

12. . . . and then into anticipation . . .

13. . . . and then a lightning-fast leap into the air toward the doomed spider.

14. He lands with a hefty "stomp."

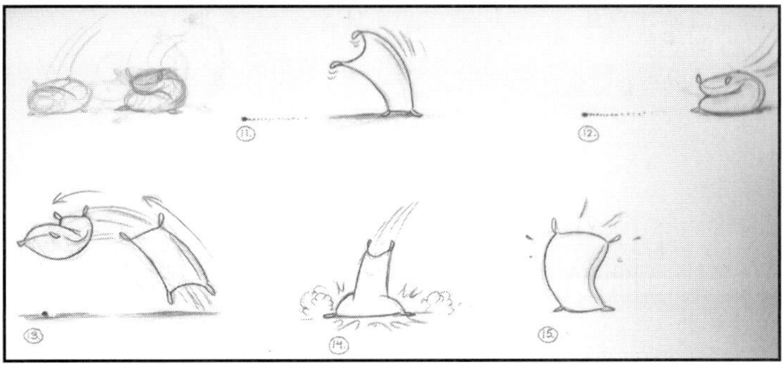

figure 4-6

Thumbnails 11–15.

15. Having overcome his fears and defeated his foe, Clyde strikes the "hero" pose.

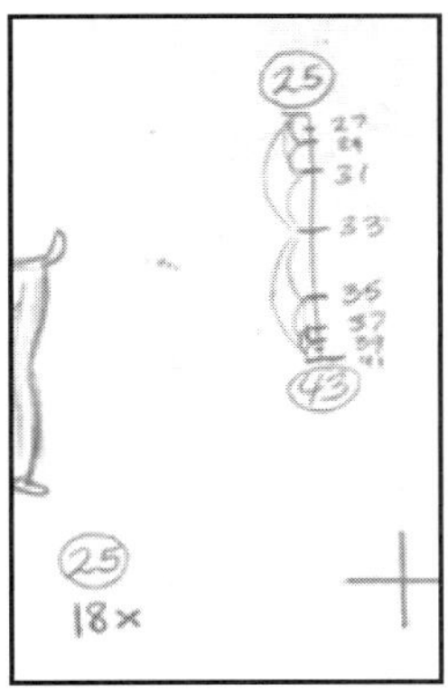

figure 4-7

Timing chart example.

Now that you have a set of thumbnail poses to outline your story, it is time to begin the actual animation. The thumbnails were used in the actual process of animating the ideas. Each drawing will have a number indicating the number of frames that were assigned to it in the sequence (see Figure 4-7). The notation "x" means frames (example: 12x = 12 frames).

There are also charts on the right side of each drawing to indicate the way in-between drawings would be used to break the animation down to either one or two frames each, which is the standard for presenting full animation. As you learned in the first exercise with the bouncing ball, grouping drawings closer together slows them down, and spreading them further apart speeds them up. Therefore, when you want to slow down a pose enough to allow the viewer to clearly see it, you very closely group the drawings. The timing charts reflect that sort of spacing and allow you to replicate the motion on your own, even adding the in-between if you wish. Animation charts are a visual way to see the timing of the animation and are primarily used by traditional 2D animators.

Pay special attention to the in-between pose on the timing chart. This is the exact mid pose. It will not always be the exact in-between "number."

Say you have a key pose and drawing for frame 50, and a key pose and drawing for frame 62. The mid pose will not necessarily be 56 (62−50 = 12, then divide by 2, add that sum to 50 which is the number of the first pose). It may be 58, or even 61. This number is chosen by the lead animator and depends on the movement the animator wants the object to have. This will soon be very important, as we explain how to edit movement.

figure 4-8

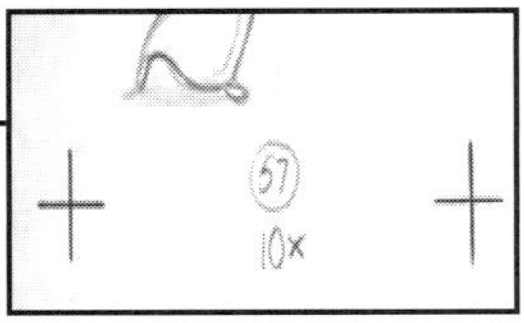

Drawing 57 timing chart.

The cross marks along the bottom of each drawing (see Figure 4-8) allow for the proper registration of each succeeding drawing to the one before.

So, here we go!

Drawing 1 is held for 24 frames. How can you tell? Look at the chart on the side of the drawing (see Figure 4-9).

Drawing 25 begins the movement of Clyde (see Figure 4-10). He has 18 frames until he hits drawing 43.

You will notice that the poses from the thumbnail sketches were utilized and then "fleshed out" to describe the full movement for the execution of the ideas as an animated presentation (see Figures 4-11 through 4-46). Many times, with more complex characters, there will be a few sets of timing charts on your sheet. You may have them for hair, arms, legs, and body, as well as any other objects in the scene.

figure 4-9

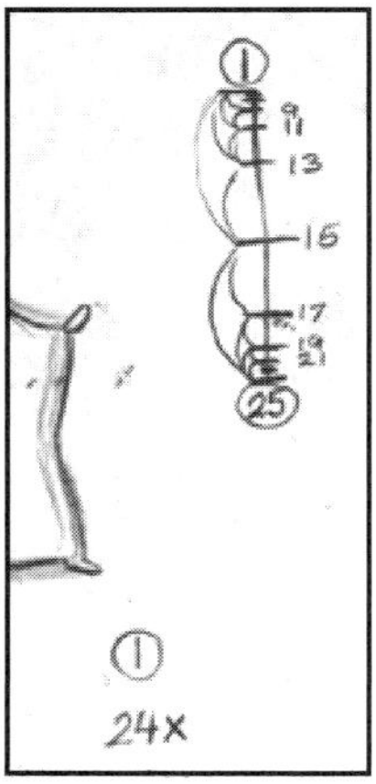

Drawing 1 timing chart.

figure 4-10

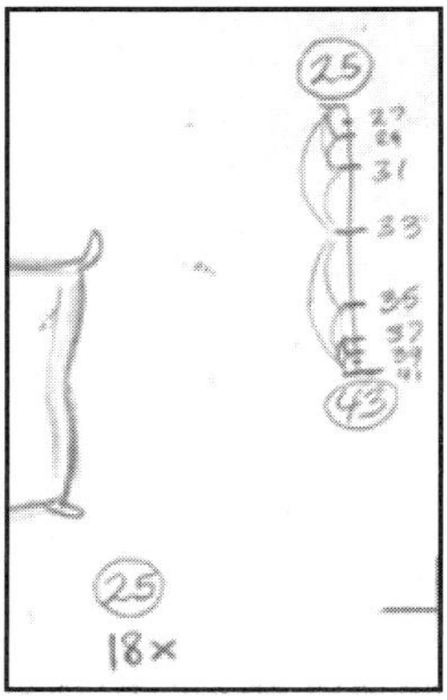

Drawing 25 timing chart.

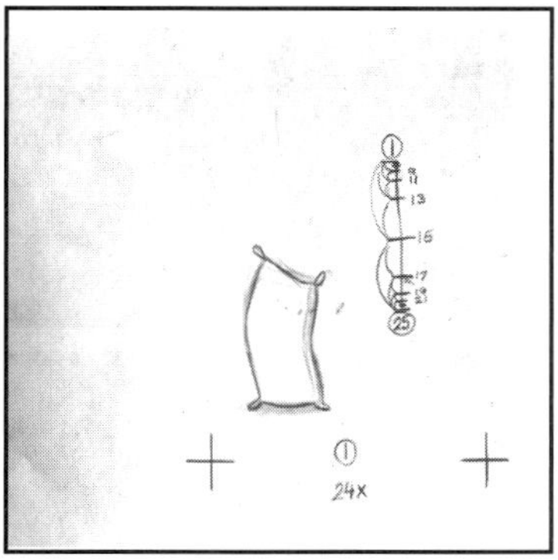

figure 4-11

Drawing 1.

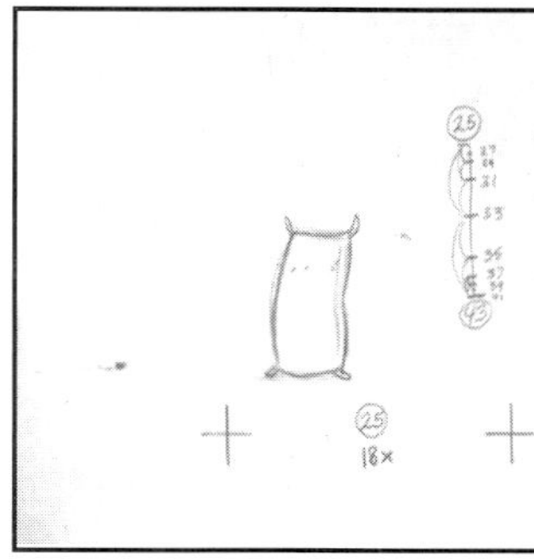

figure 4-12

Drawing 25.

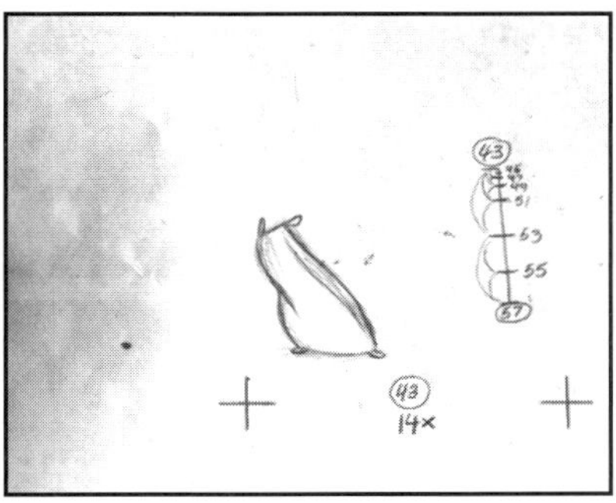

figure 4-13

Drawing 43.

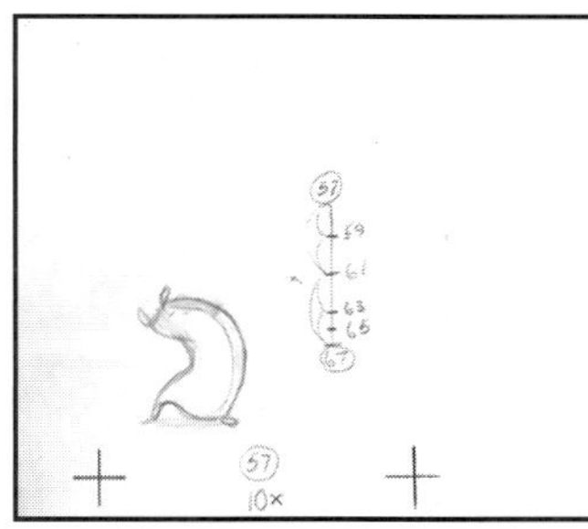

figure 4-14

Drawing 57.

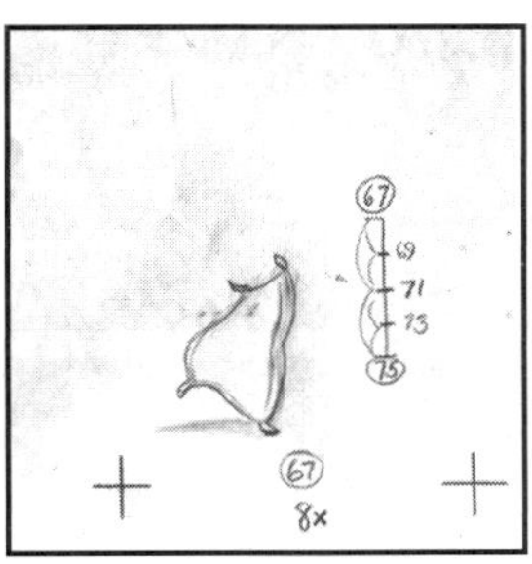

figure 4-15

Drawing 67.

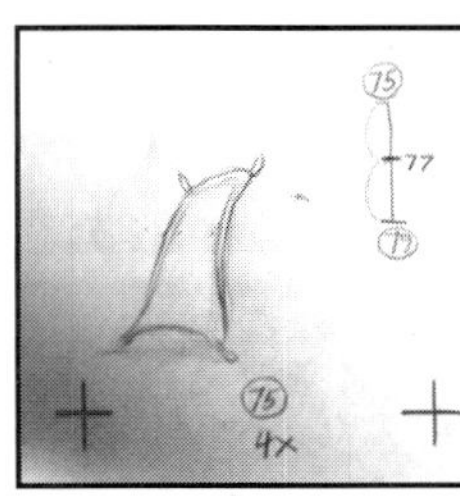

figure 4-16

Drawing 75.

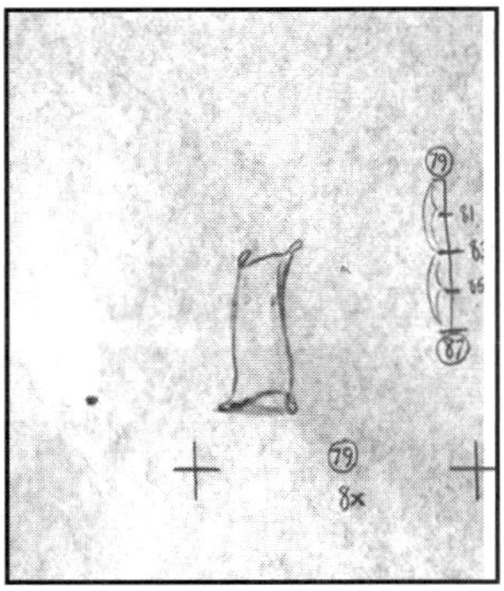

figure | 4-17

Drawing 79.

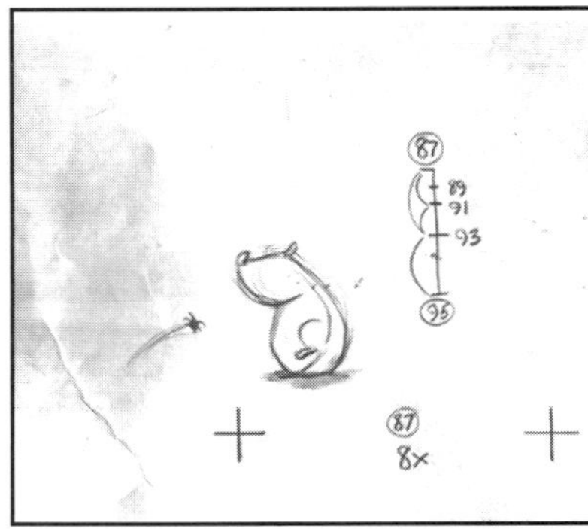

figure | 4-18

Drawing 87.

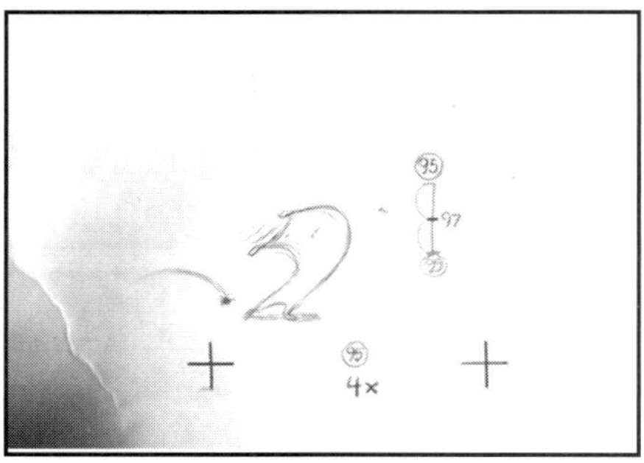

figure | 4-19

Drawing 95.

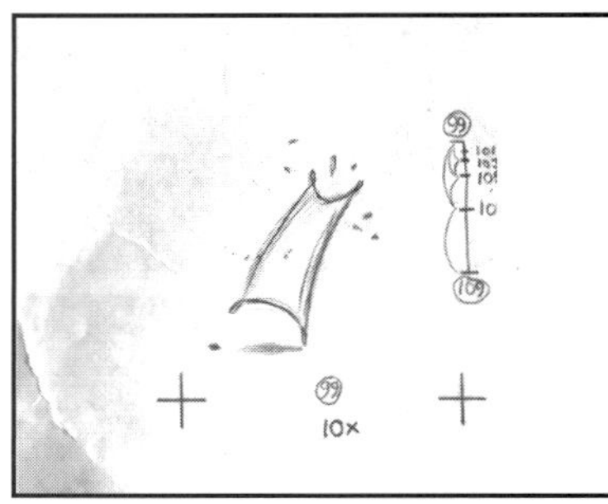

figure | 4-20

Drawing 99.

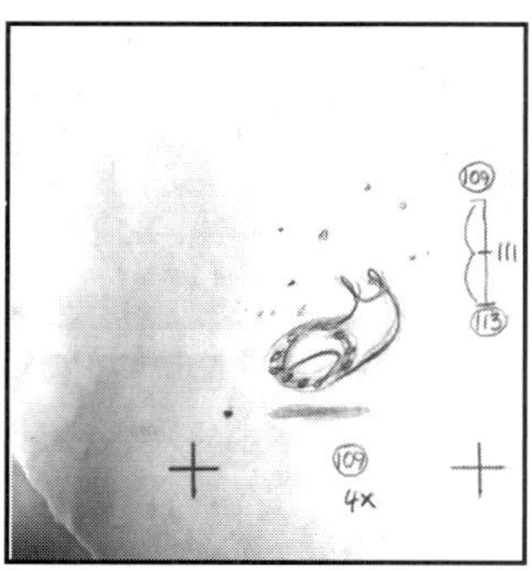

figure | 4-21

Drawing 109.

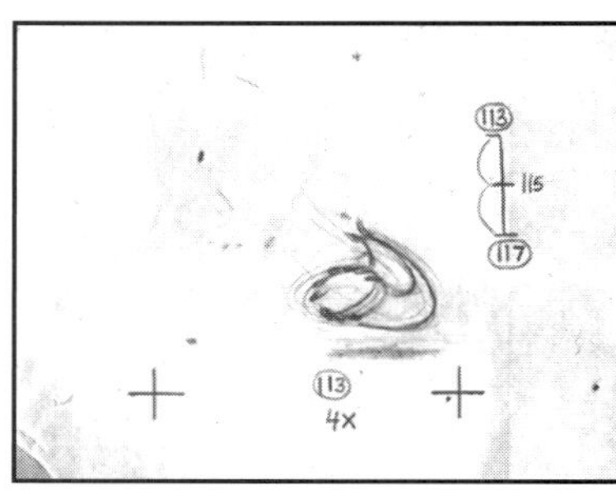

figure | 4-22

Drawing 113.

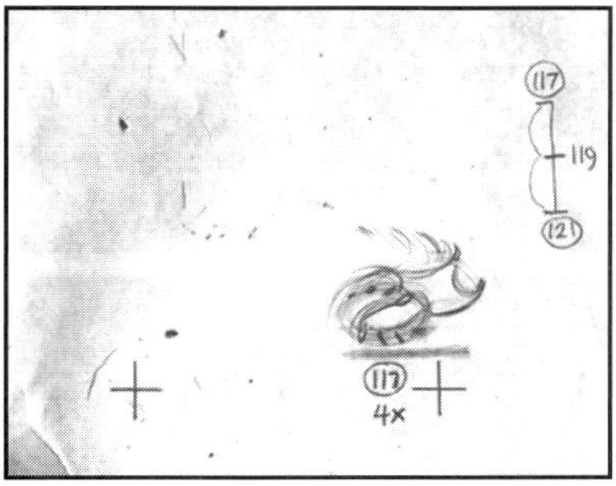

figure | 4-23 |

Drawing 117.

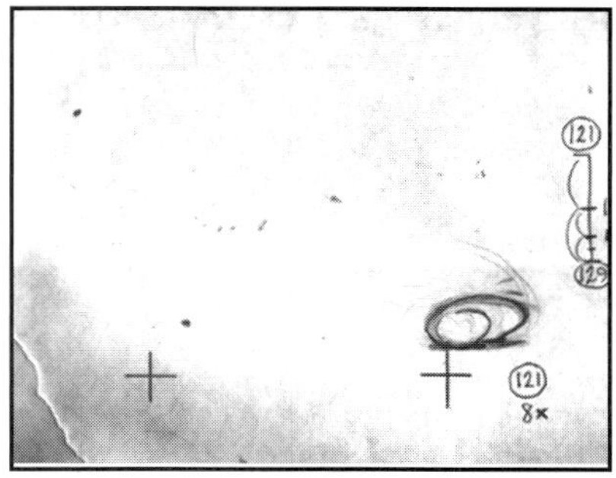

figure | 4-24 |

Drawing 121.

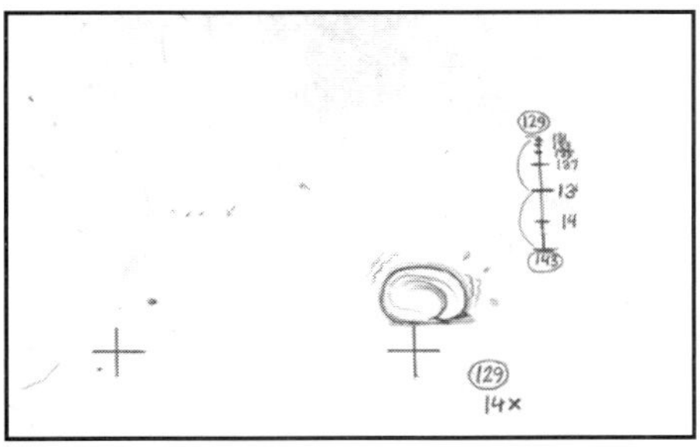

figure | 4-25 |

Drawing 129.

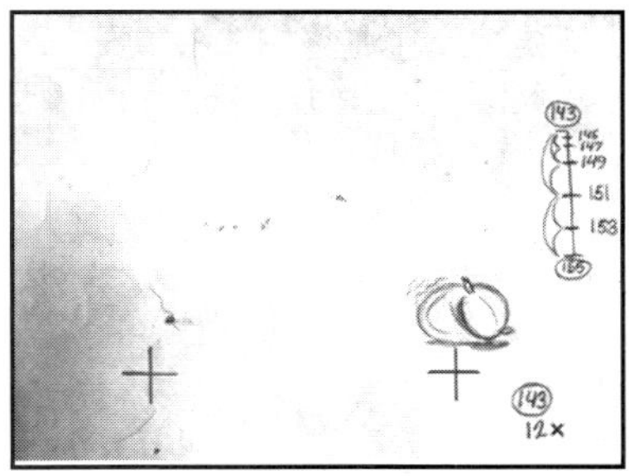

figure | 4-26 |

Drawing 143.

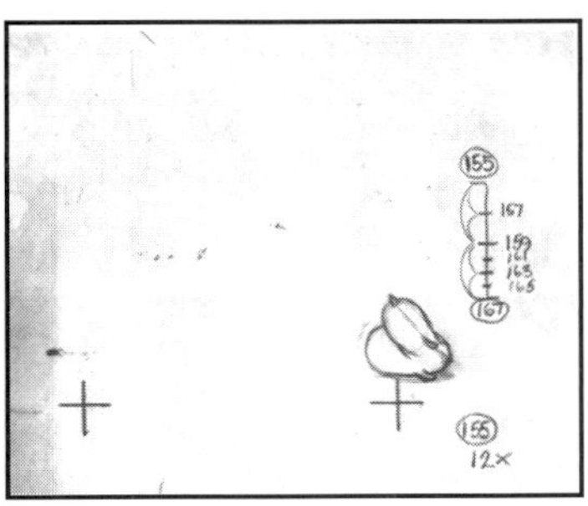

figure | 4-27 |

Drawing 155.

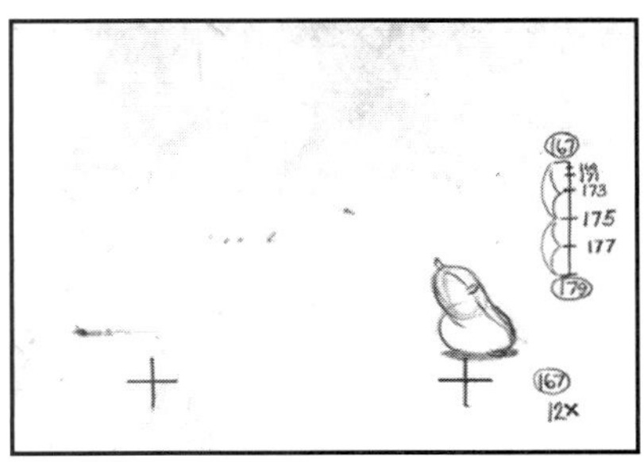

figure | 4-28 |

Drawing 167.

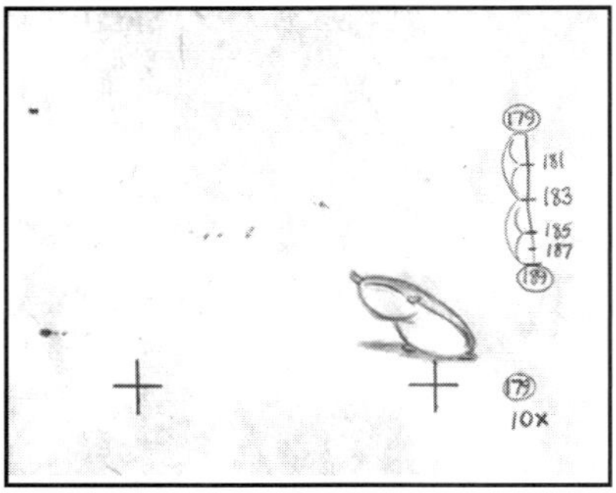

figure | 4-29 |

Drawing 179.

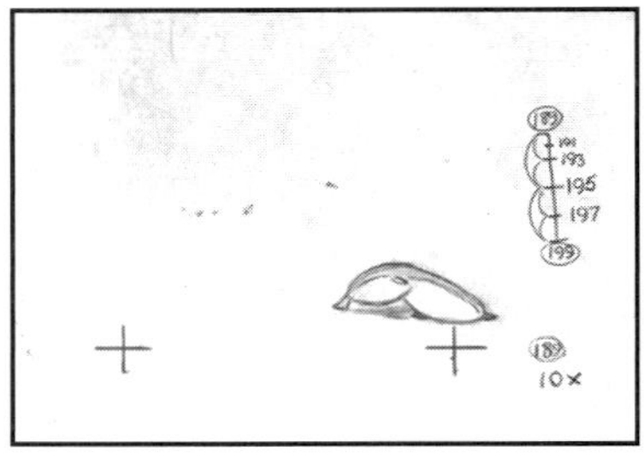

figure | 4-30 |

Drawing 189.

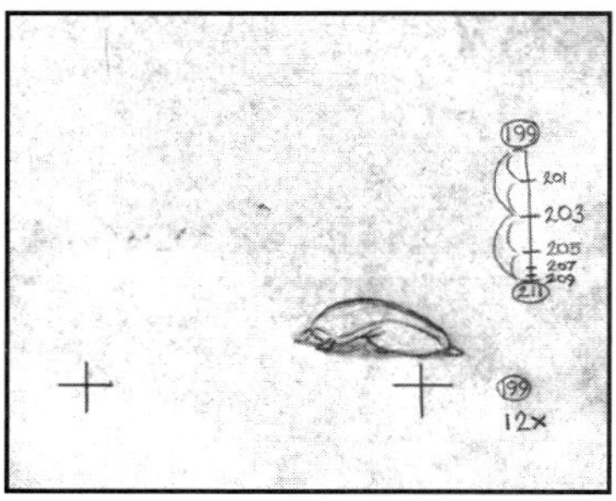

figure | 4-31 |

Drawing 199.

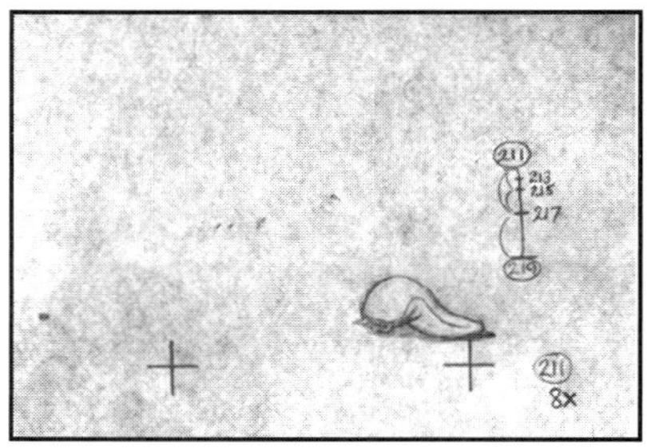

figure | 4-32 |

Drawing 211.

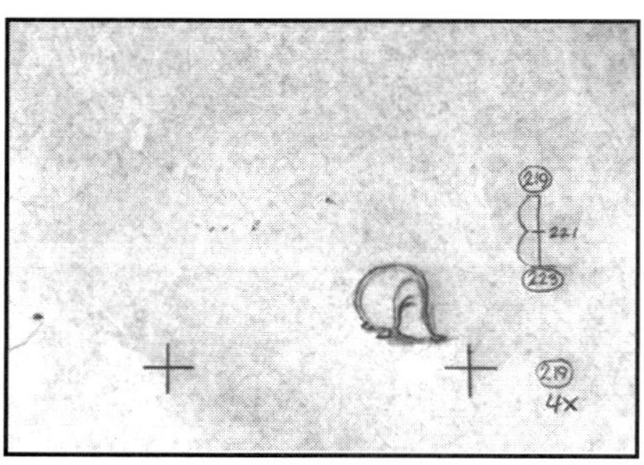

figure | 4-33 |

Drawing 219.

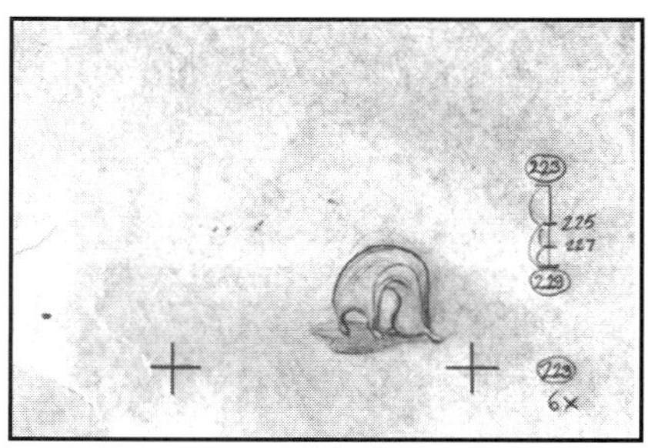

figure | 4-34 |

Drawing 223.

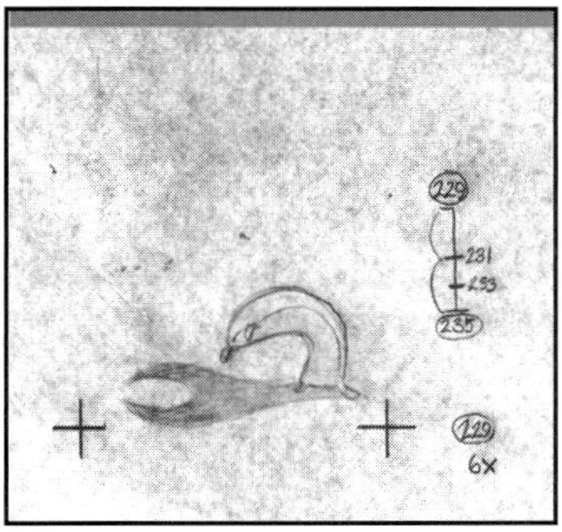

figure 4-35

Drawing 229.

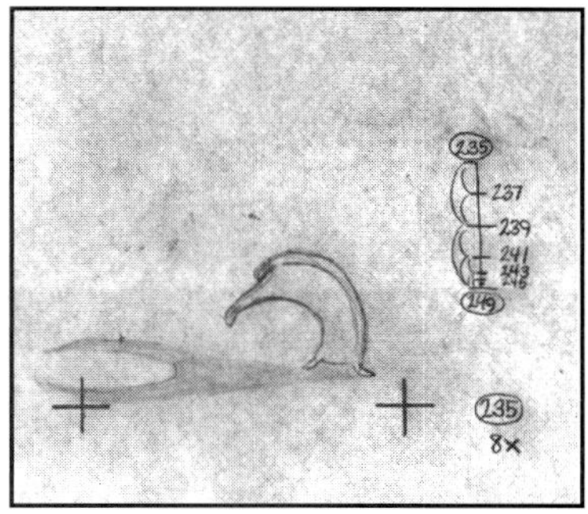

figure 4-36

Drawing 235.

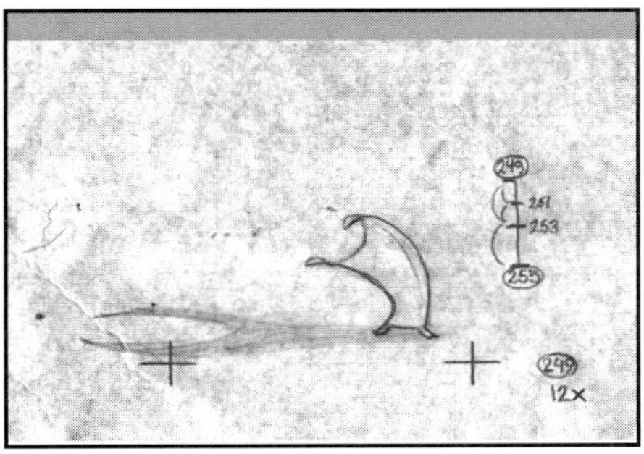

figure 4-37

Drawing 249.

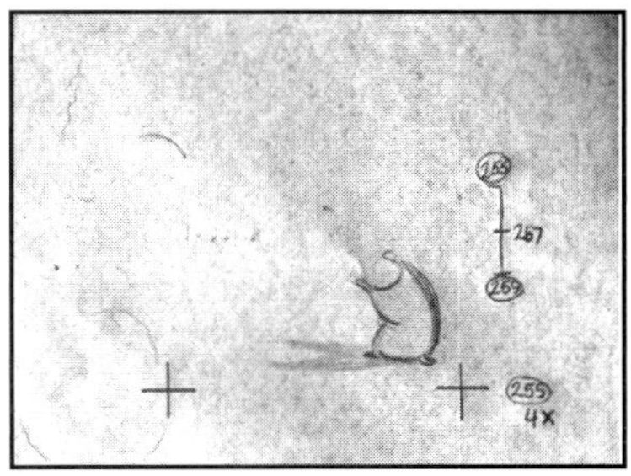

figure 4-38

Drawing 255.

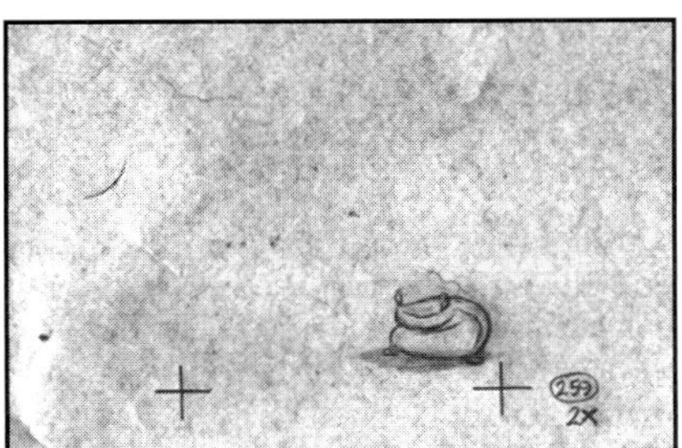

figure 4-39

Drawing 259.

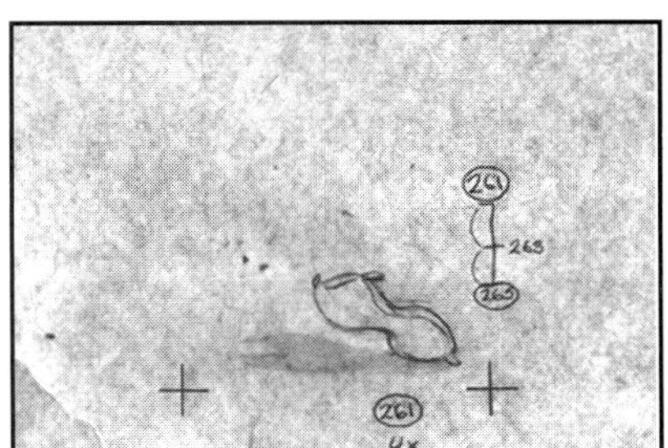

figure 4-40

Drawing 261.

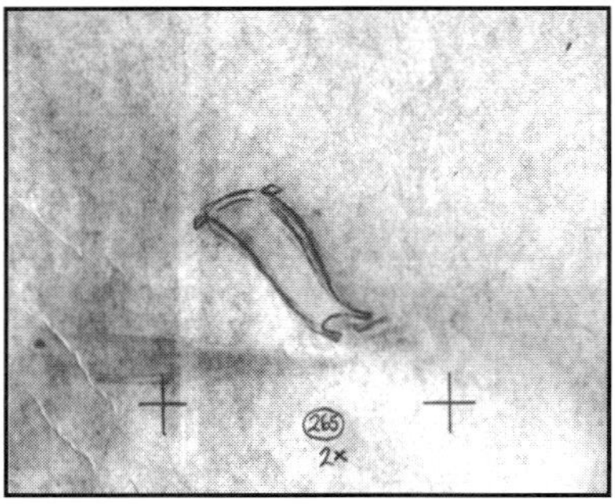

figure 4-41

Drawing 265.

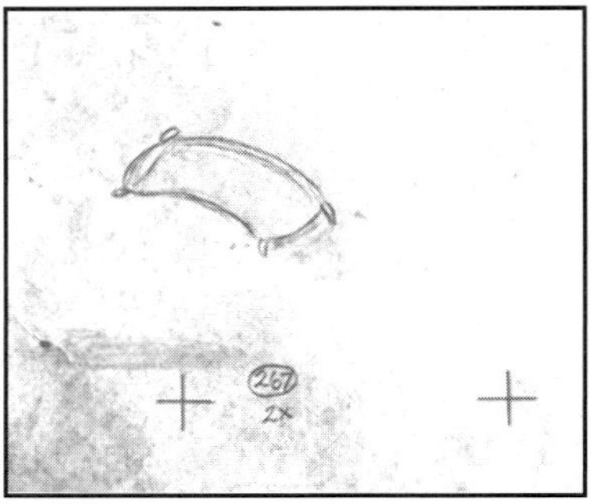

figure 4-42

Drawing 267.

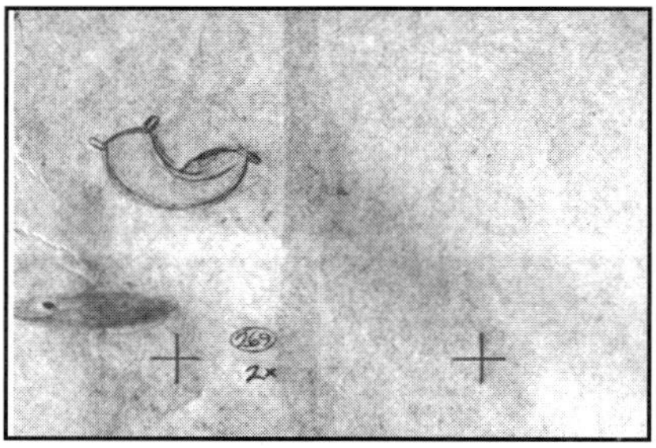

figure 4-43

Drawing 269.

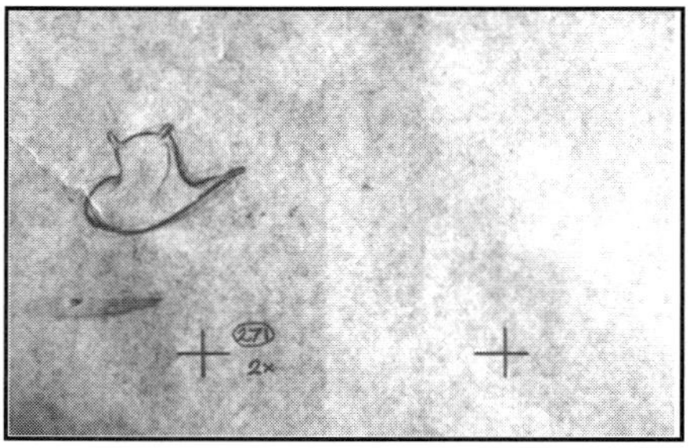

figure 4-44

Drawing 271.

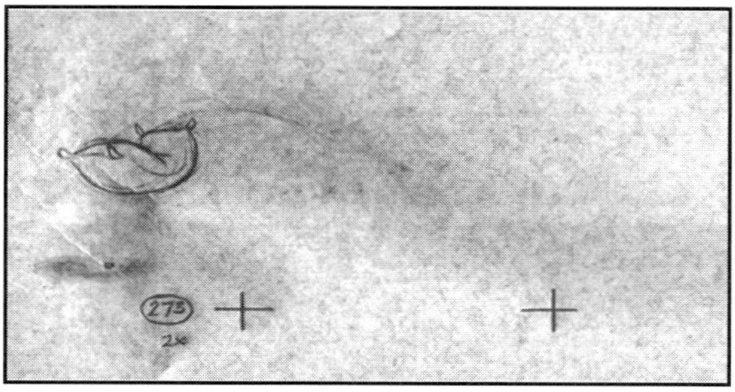

figure 4-45

Drawing 273.

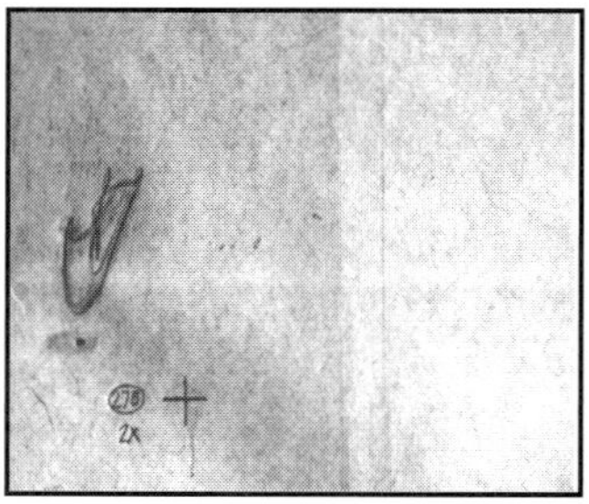

figure 4-46

Drawing 275.

This exercise has demonstrated some basics of animation theory and has done it with a minimum of embellishment. Although the beanbag was a deceptively simple character presentation, it contains most of the elements that are fundamental principles in animation (see Figures 4-47 through 4-51).

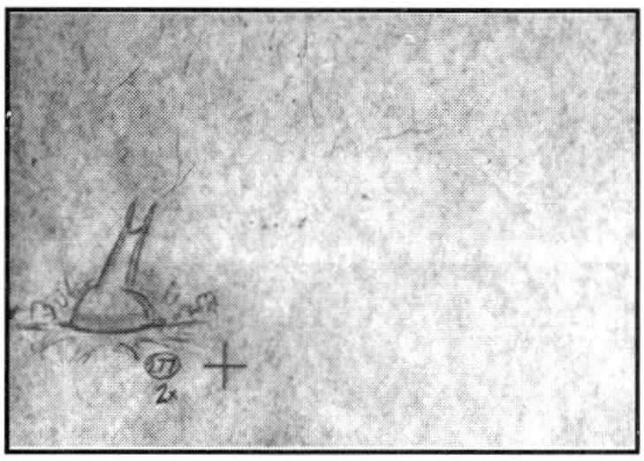

figure 4-47

Drawing 277.

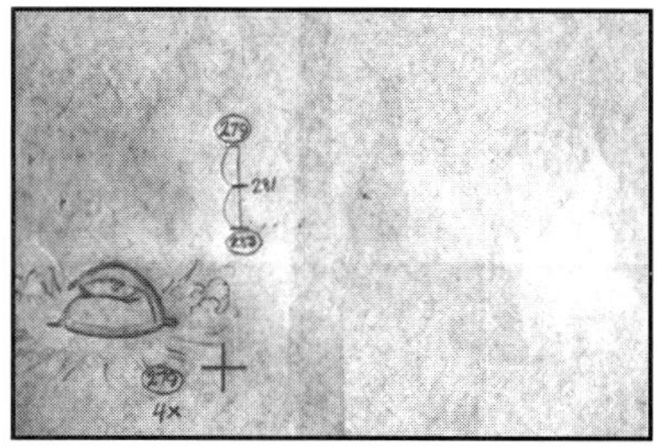

figure 4-48

Drawing 279.

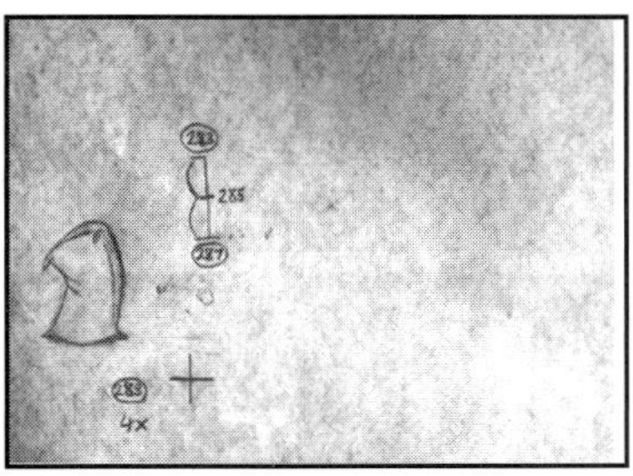

figure 4-49

Drawing 283.

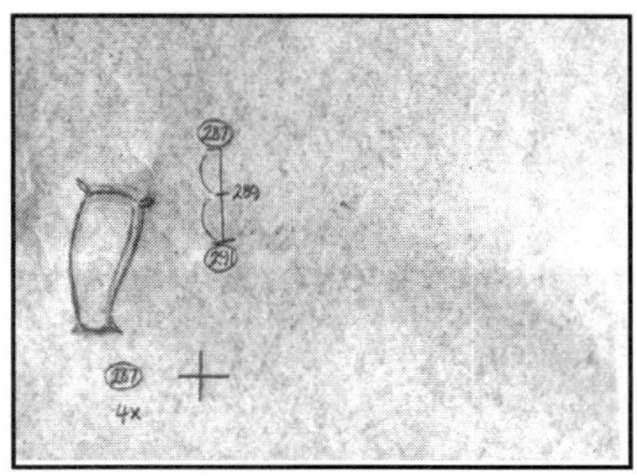

figure 4-50

Drawing 287.

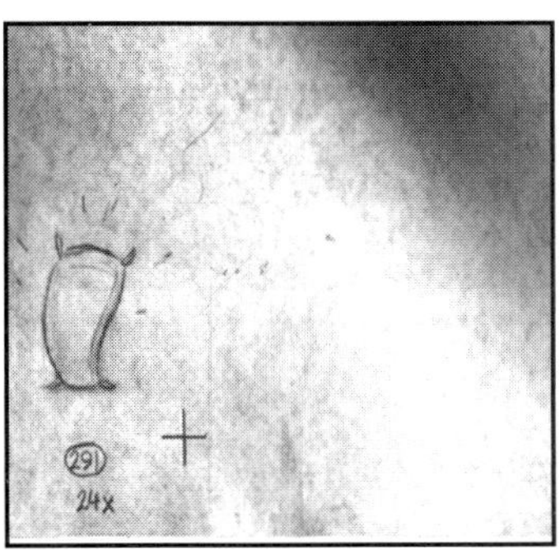

figure 4-51

Drawing 291.

IMPORTING IMAGES INTO MAYA TO USE AS RESOURCES

First, make sure you are in the Animation module (see Figure 4-52).

figure 4-52

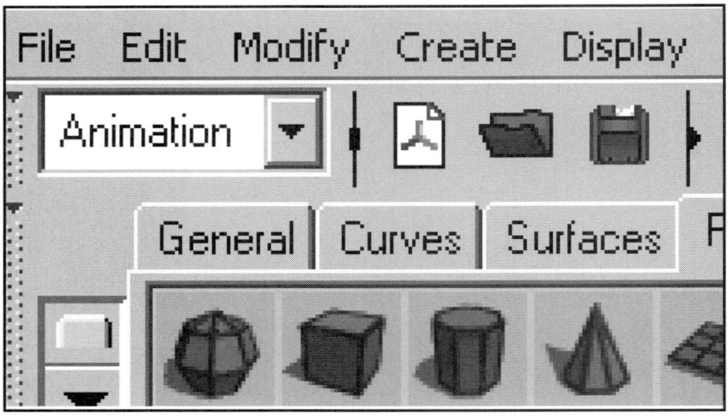

You will find the images listed in Figure 4-53 on the enclosed CD. You now need to transfer these images from the CD to your animation file in Maya.

figure 4-53

Thumbnail images you will import as a reference.

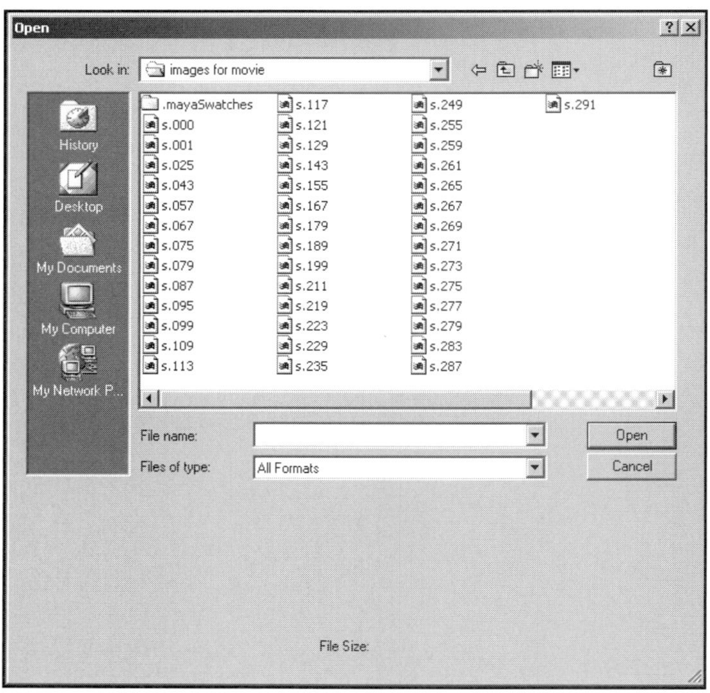

Notice how the images are named (see Figure 4-54).

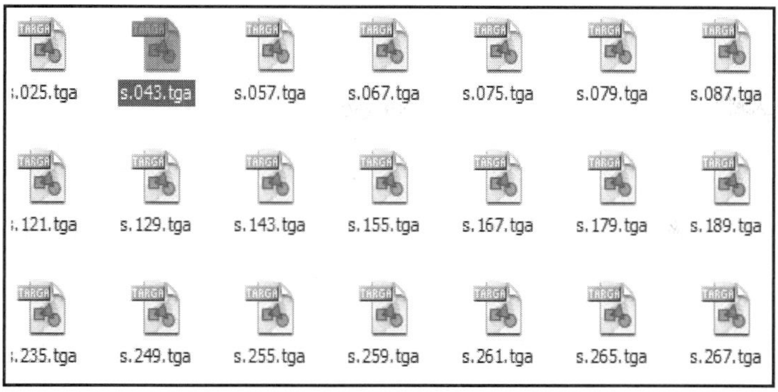

figure 4-54

Targa naming convention.

Each image is a Targa, beginning with a name (s), a period to separate, an image number (057), another period to separate, and file convention identification (tga) (see Figure 4-55).

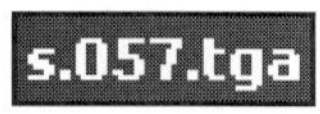

figure 4-55

The naming convention.

Maya needs sequenced image files to be named this way so that it can import the images in order. The name, (s), identifies the target group of images. The period separates the group from the sequential placement. The number identifies the image place in the sequence. The text period separates the number from the file identity. The file identity identifies the format as acceptable to Maya.

Create a plane by going to **Create** > **NURBS Primitive** > **Plane** (see Figure 4-56a).

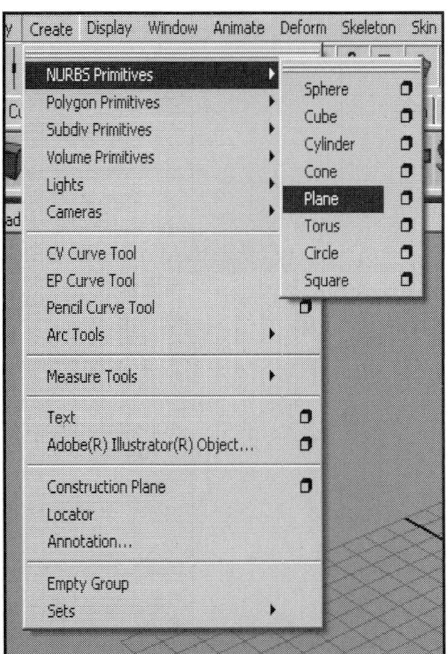

figure 4-56a

How to create a plane.

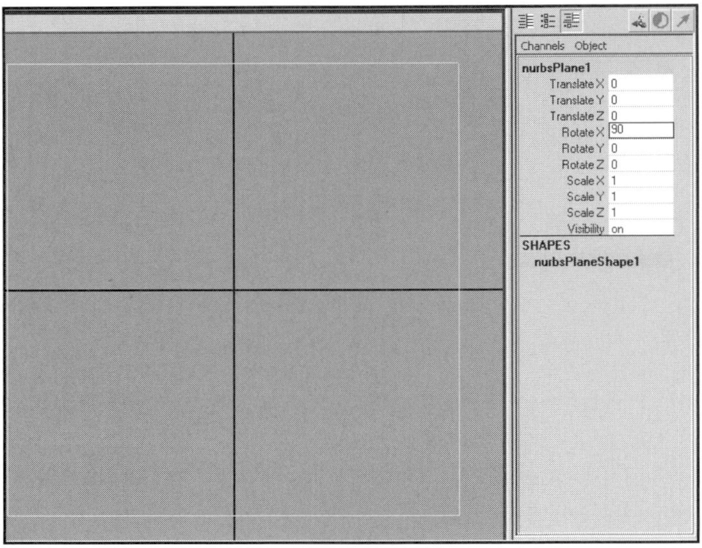

figure 4-56b

The plane in the Front window, rotated 90 degrees in X.

Rotate the plane 90 degrees in X so that it is visible in the Front window (see Figure 4-56b).

Open the Multilister to create a shader by going to **Window** > **Rendering Editors** > **Multilister** (see Figure 4-57).

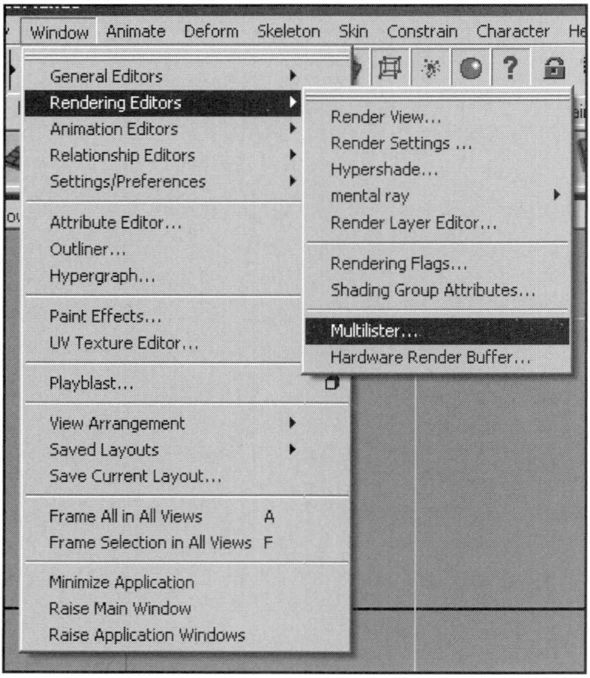

figure 4-57

How to open the Multilister.

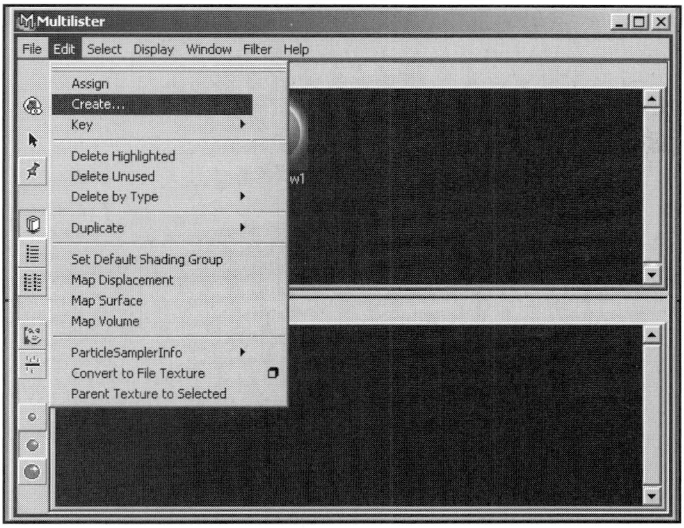

figure 4-58

Edit > Create.

Create the shader in the Multilister using **Edit** > **Create** (see Figure 4-59).

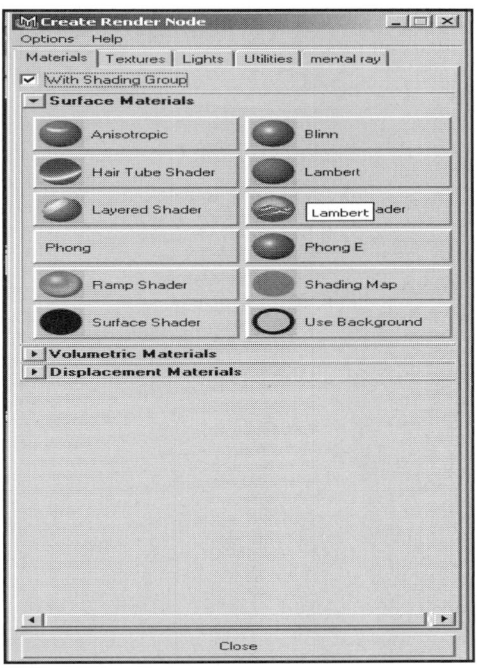

figure 4-59

The Create Render Node window.

A new interface window called the Create Render Node opens (see Figure 4-60). Here it lists all the shaders you can pick. These are outlined in our book entitled ***Exploring 3D Modeling in Maya***. For your uses here, pick Lambert because it has no highlight and thus is a flat shader.

After you have selected Lambert, close the Create Render Node window and look at your Multilister. A new icon is present. Rename this icon by double-clicking on the title lambert2SG and renaming it **Source** (see Figure 4-60).

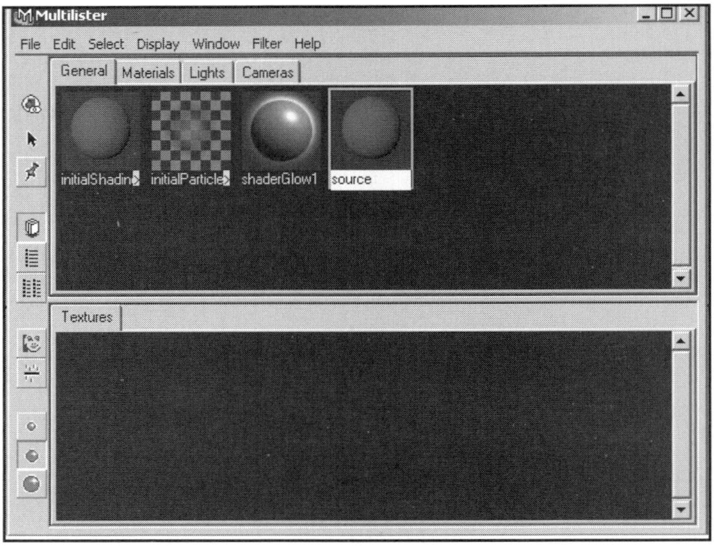

figure 4-60

Rename the icon Source.

Double-click on the Source icon to bring up the Attribute window (see Figure 4-61).

Left-mouse click on the black-and-white Checker icon to the right of Color to attach our series of animated reference images to the color channel of the shader (see Figure 4-62).

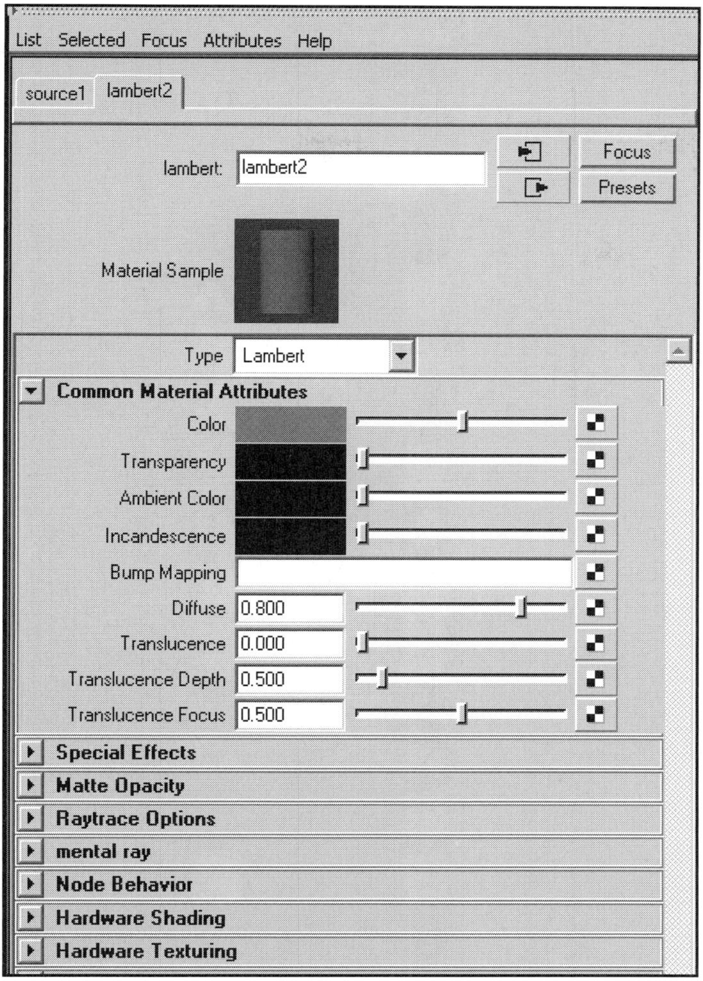

figure 4-61

The Attribute window.

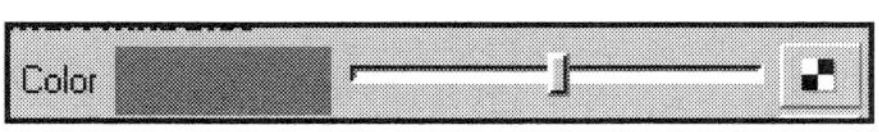

figure 4-62

The black and white Checker icon.

figure 4-63

The Create Render Node window.

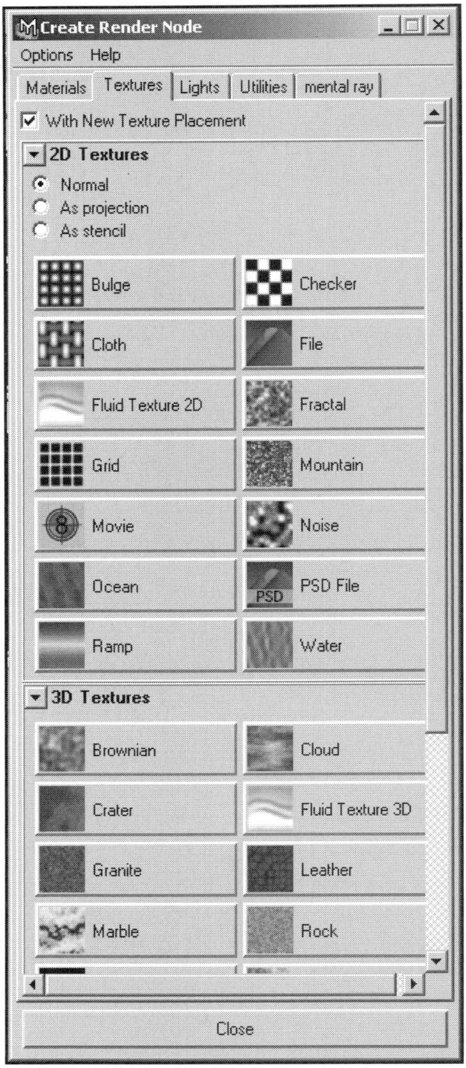

The Create Render Node window opens and is shown in Figure 4-63, where you can select a texture for your node.

figure 4-64

The File button.

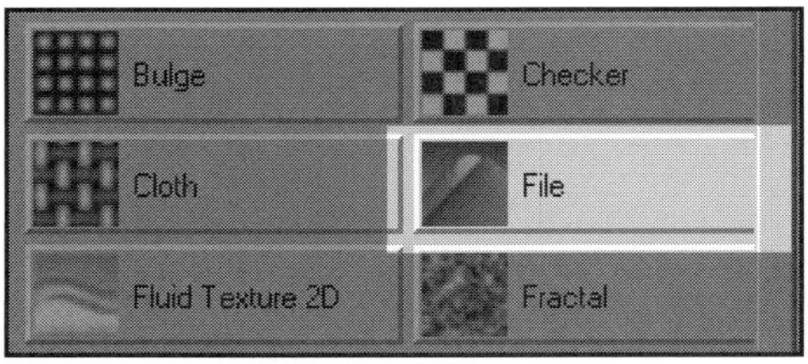

Left-mouse click the File button in the right column, below the word Checker (see Figure 4-64).

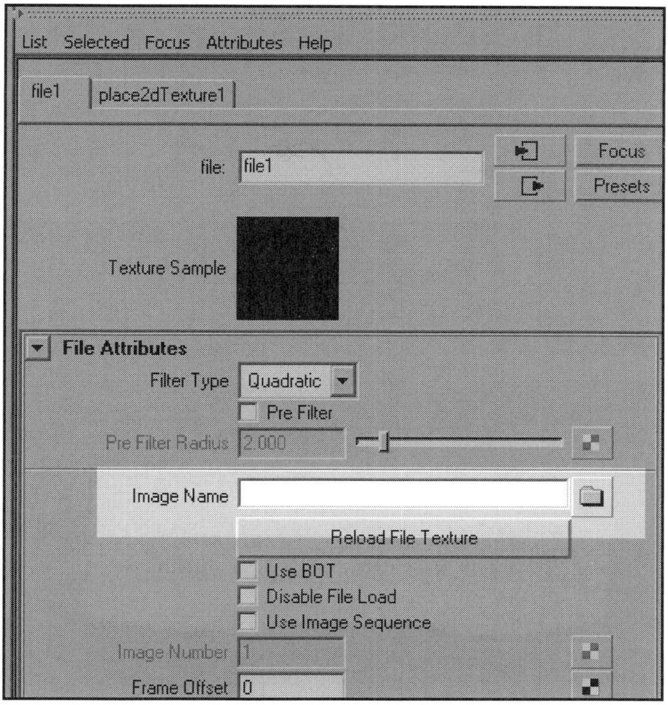

figure 4-65

The Attribute Editor.

Your Attribute Editor will reflect your selection (see Figure 4-65). Under File Attributes, left-mouse select the file icon to the right of Image Name.

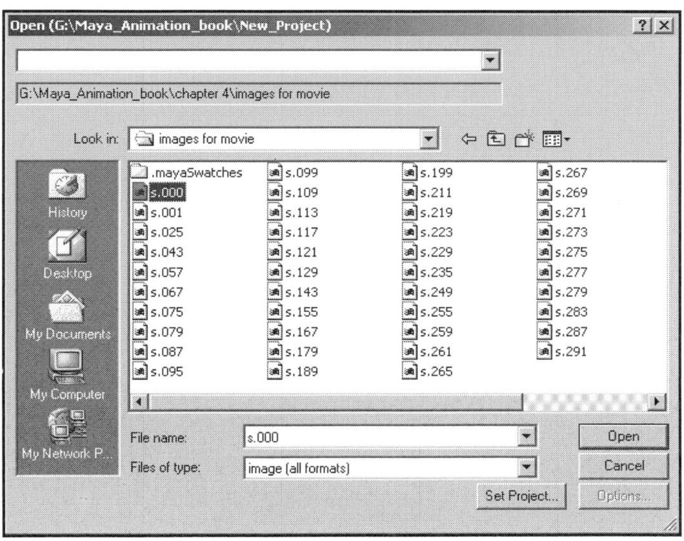

figure 4-66

The reference images.

A new window opens. This window is your navigator to the file holding your reference images (see Figure 4-66). Open the image

folder found on the attached CD under the heading for this chapter. We suggest that you use the images on the CD and place them in the source image folder under your project directory before completing this step.
Find your first image in the sequence called s.000, and left-mouse click to select it.
Select Open. You should see that image on your source node in the Multilister (see Figure 4-67).

figure 4-67

The node with image attached.

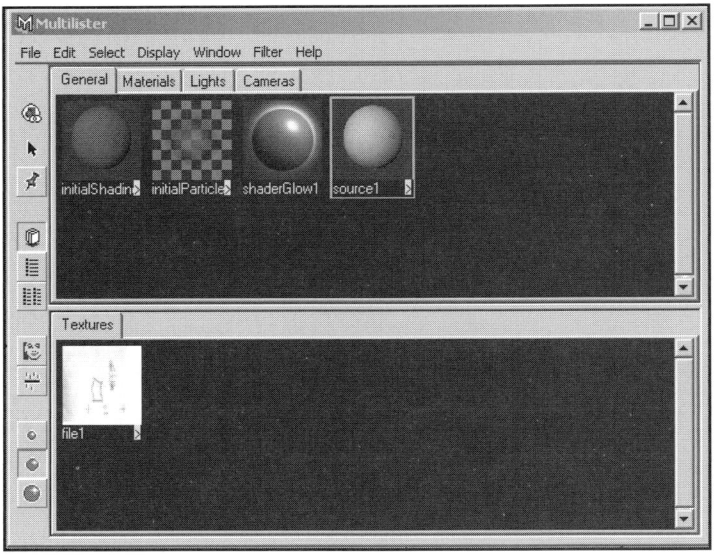

Select file1 in the Multilister.
Now you will need to make some changes in the Attribute Editor.

Make your Attribute Editor look like Figure 4-68 by selecting Use Image Sequence and Interactive Sequence Caching Options. Sequence Start is 1, and Sequence End is 291.

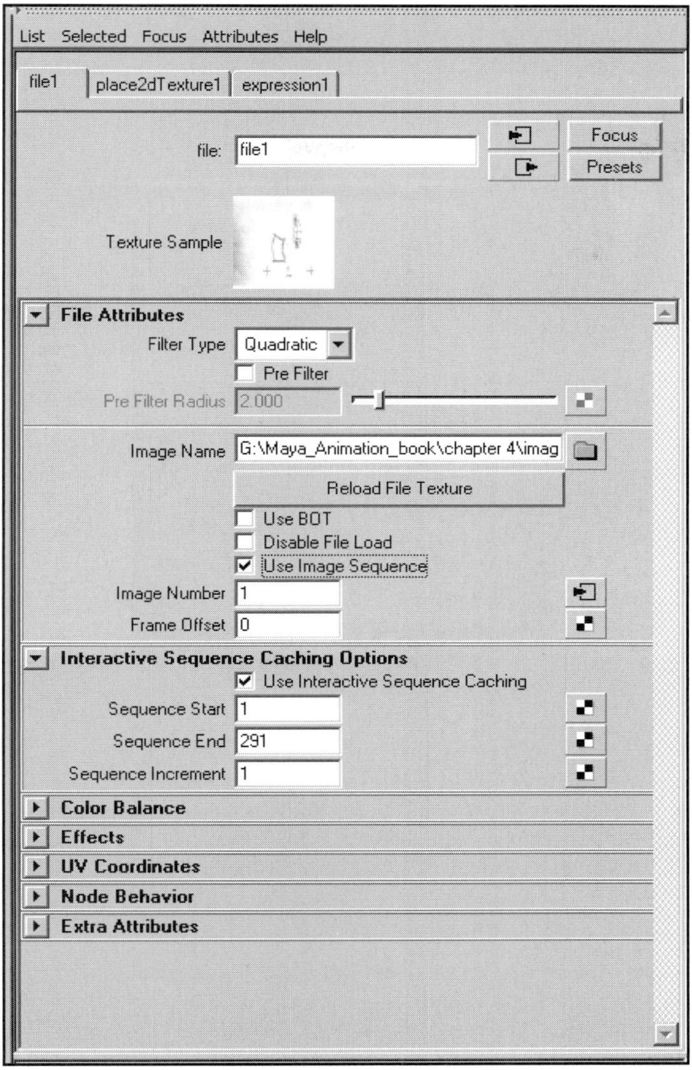

figure 4-68

Change your attributes to look like these.

Activate the Front Window camera view in your main Maya interface by clicking the left mouse button (LMB) anywhere in the window. In the window, select from the drop-down windows at the top:

Shading > **Smooth Shade All**

Shading > **Hardware Texturing**

Now attach the new shader to your plane. Middle-mouse select the Source icon that you just made from the Multilister window. Drag this icon over to your plane, making sure to drop the icon onto the actual geometry.

Close the Multilister window.

You should now see your plane with the image sequence attached (see Figure 4-69).

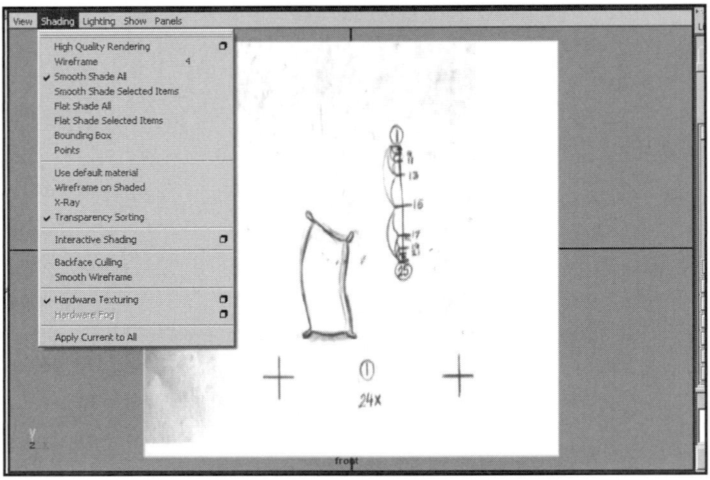

figure 4-69

Plane with image attached.

Set your control playback window like Figure 4-70. Enter 1 as the first frame and 292 as the last.

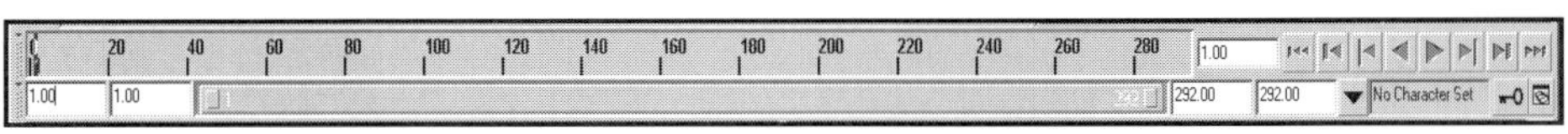

figure 4-70

Control playback window.

Press Play. You will notice that many of the images are blank. That is correct as you only want the key poses and a visual of the timing chart as your reference (see Figure 4-71).

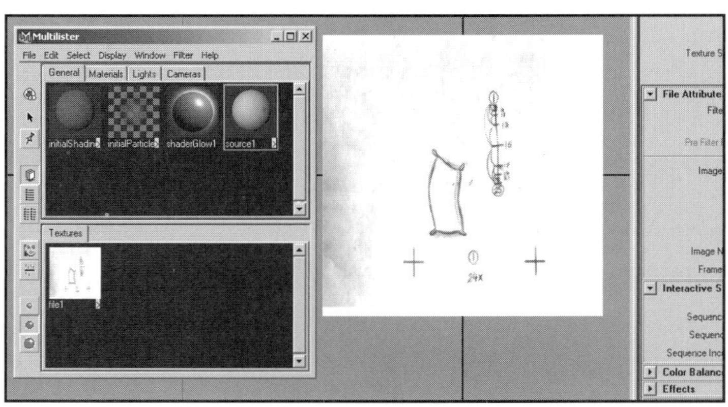

figure 4-71

Plane with image attached.

Make a playblast of your Front Window view of the image plane and save it for reference. To make a Playblast, select **Window > Playblast.**

SUMMARY

Reference imagery may not seem important to you now and certainly not worth all the trouble. However, as you get more experienced, you will find it invaluable. There is a character and looseness available in the drawn image that is tougher to conjure in 3D. Drawing is faster and easier to push. 3D can easily become stale without good thumbnails.

in review

1. What are thumbnail poses?
2. What is a timing chart?
3. If poses are close together, are they moving quickly or slowly?
4. What is the proper naming convention for a reference image if it is to be used as a sequence shader in Maya?
5. How do you key-frame a sequence shader?
6. How do you find the in-between pose?

EXPLORING ON YOUR OWN

1. Thumbnail out an animation scene, and determine the key poses. Make timing charts.
2. Draw a series of images, and try to import them into Maya using the methods described in this chapter.
3. Watch animation on a frame-by-frame playback and re-create the timing charts for the scene. Make charts for hands, feet, facial movements, and clothing.

notes

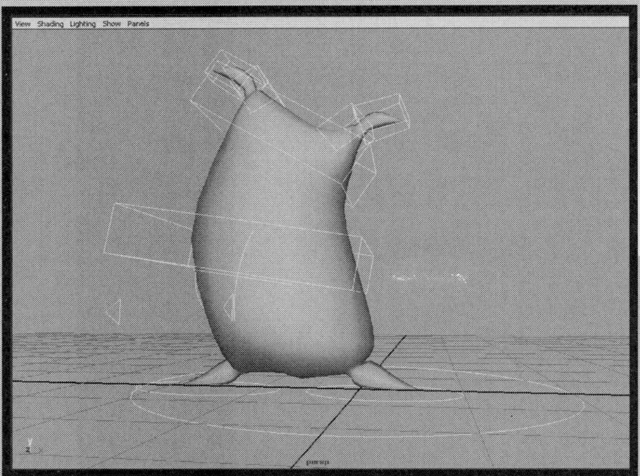

5

animating the flour sack

charting your course

Theory and practice will converge in this chapter as you explore a basic Maya rig applied to a simple flour sack. You will learn to work with a variety of Maya controls. You will also practice editing your Graph Editor curves and reading timing charts.

goals

In this chapter, you will:

- Define inverse kinematics.
- Gain exposure to a simple rigged puppet.
- Read timing charts.
- Master the advanced controls used on this puppet.
- Edit curves to achieve the principles of animation.
- Animate Clyde.

TOOLS USED

- **Inverse kinematics.** Inverse kinematics (IK) uses something called an end effector to move the bones. This is attached to a skeleton inside the character. It works like a marionette by attaching a string-like end effector to a skeleton. Imagine that an animator attaches a string to the hand of a puppet. The animator moves this string, and the puppet arm follows. The arm rises and bends according to where the hand is placed (see Figure 5-1).

figure 5-1

Skeleton arm animated with IK.

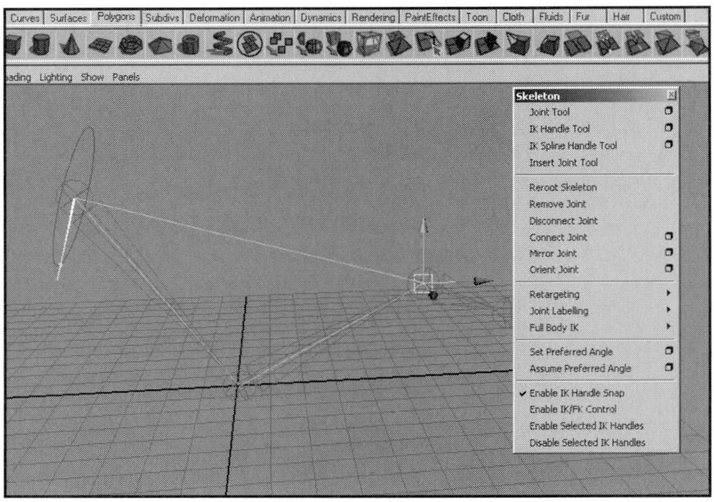

- **Graph Editor Transformation tools.** Maya 7 has tools for scaling and translating the Graph Editor curves. Transformation tools in the Graph Editor now let you work with a lattice to scale entire portions of curves (see Figure 5-2).

figure 5-2

Transformation tools.

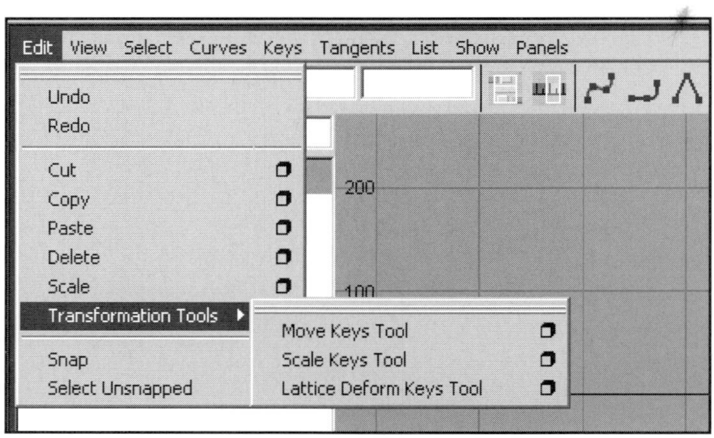

- **Sculpt deformer.** The sculpt deformer will be used to provide additional character detail and squash/stretch (see Figure 5-3). The sculpt deformer is useful in displacing geometry that is difficult to deform within the rig.

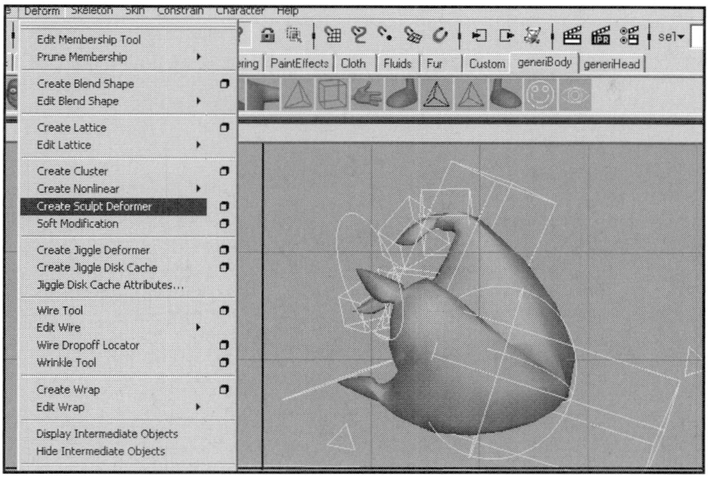

figure 5-3

Sculpt deformer tools.

INVERSE KINEMATICS

Open the file ArmIK.mb on the enclosed CD. This is a basic IK skeleton for an arm (see Figure 5-4). You are expected to animate it using IK in this exercise. Late in Chapter 7 we will practice forward kinematics (FK). There is a line present on the model itself and an IK handle in the Outliner.

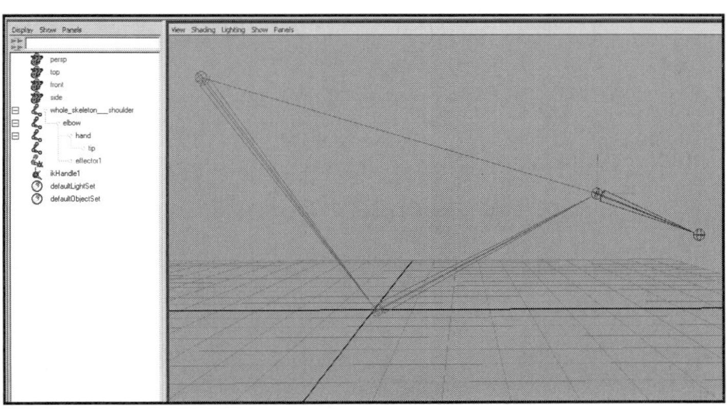

figure 5-4

The arm with an IK handle.

First, select the ikHandle in the Outliner (see Figure 5-5). Go to the Camera view of the arm, and you will see a Manipulator icon. Select the Move tool from your tool box. Move the manipulator (the IK handle) around with your left mouse button (LMB). Notice how the entire arm follows along.

figure 5-5

The IK Handle.

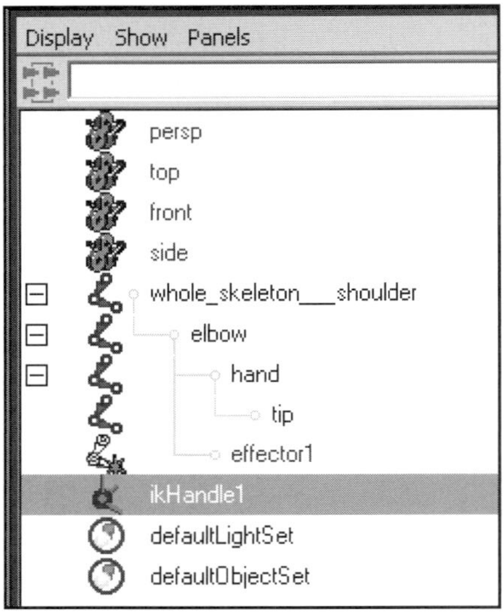

Enter values of **0** for Translates X, Y, and Z in the Channel Box (see Figure 5-6). Set a key frame at frame 1.

figure 5-6

Enter Translate Values.

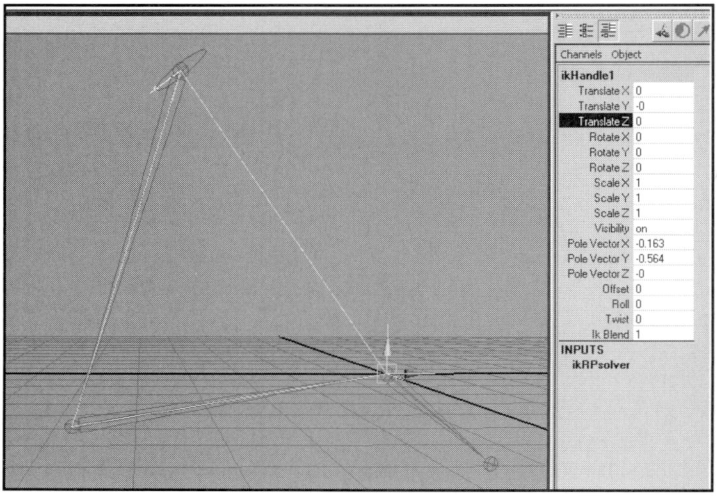

Go to frame 30 and enter a value of **4** for Translate X and 14 for Translate Y (see Figure 5-7). Set a key frame for the Translate Values.

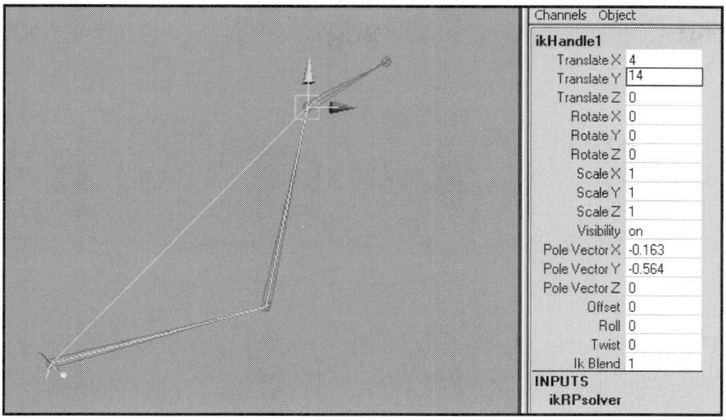

figure 5-7

Enter Translate Values.

Play the animation, and you will see a simple move of the arm. Notice how the elbow and upper arm follow the hand.

Close this file. You do not need to save it.

SCULPT DEFORMER

Open the file BallSS.mb on the enclosed CD.

There is an added control present in this skeleton that you have not seen before. It is called the sculpt deformer. It looks like a sphere

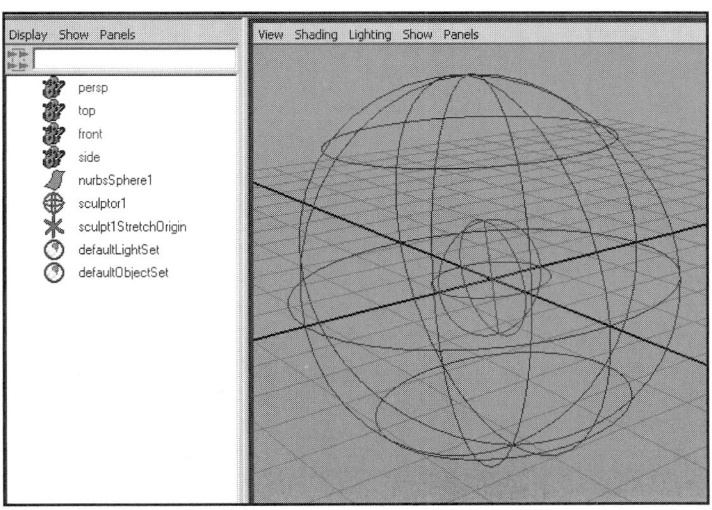

figure 5-8

Sculpt Deformer.

NOTE

There are a hundred ways to do anything in Maya. I am taking you through one way of animating and will introduce you to more controls as we go along. As you grow more comfortable animating, you will find more interesting ways to make things move.

(see Figure 5-8). Look in the Outliner. You will see an item called sculptor1 and another called sculpt1StretchOrigin.

Select sculptor1. Use the Scale tool and enlarge the icon so that it is no bigger than the original sphere in your Camera view. Notice how the sphere reacts. Now move the icon left and right using the Translate tool. The sphere distorts when the icon crosses the exterior of the sphere.

Experiment with this control by setting key frames for it.

Close the file.

Clyde the Flour Sack

Open the file flourSack.mb on the enclosed CD.

This is a fully rigged puppet to accompany the following material (see Figure 5-9). This rig employs the advanced animation tools explained at the beginning of this chapter.

figure | 5-9

FlourSack.mb.

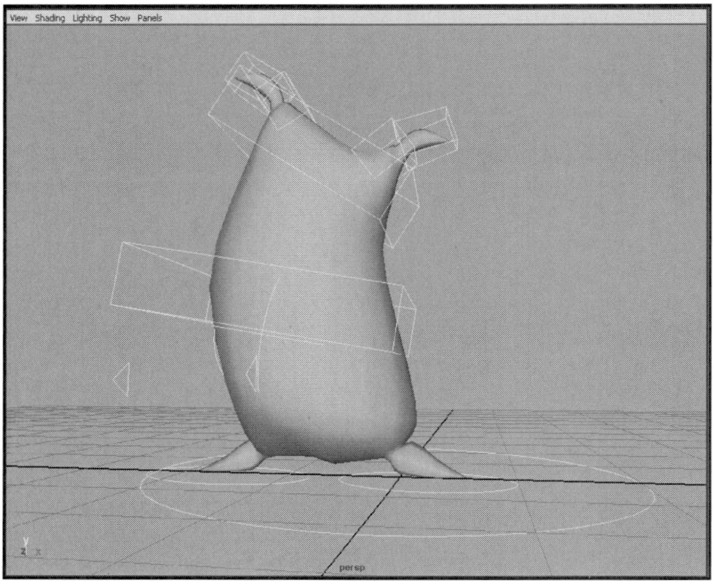

Close the file FlourSak.mb. Open the reference file you made in the last chapter. If you do not have this file, open and use Animation reference.mb on the enclosed CD. If you are working from the CD, you may have to reload the source TGA files in the Multilister (see Chapter 4). Make sure each of your Camera views is set to Smooth Shade All and Hardware Texturing (see Figure 5-10).

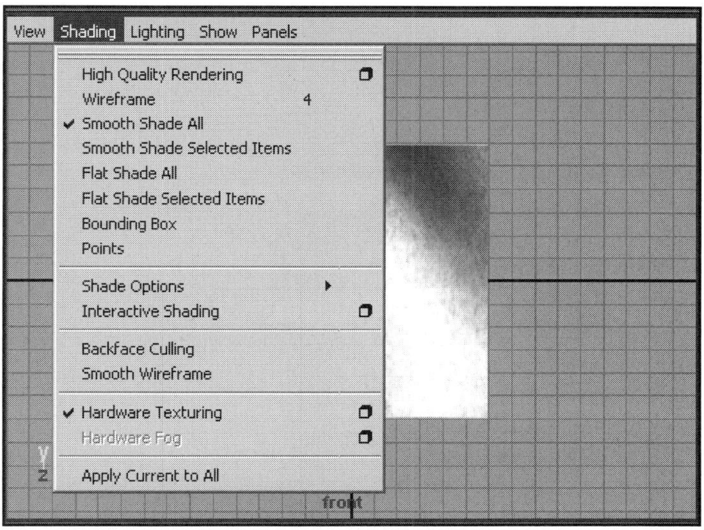

figure 5-10

Camera view port set so that you can see the images.

Clyde and the Spider

Enter 300 as your playback end time and final end time (see Figure 5-11).

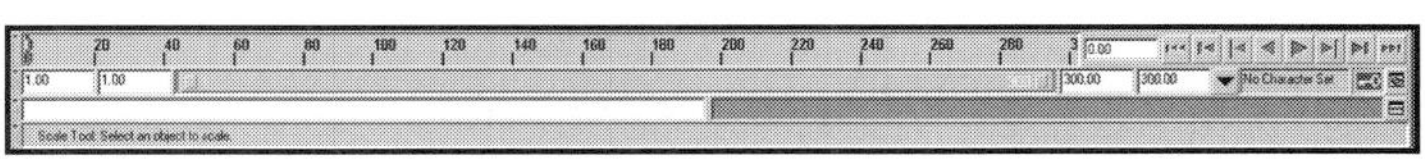

figure 5-11

Playback end time and final end time set to 300.

Set the automatic key-frame toggle to "on" (see Figure 5-12). It is on if it is red. You will set a key frame for every animatable channel in this exercise. In this chapter, you should be more concerned with understanding poses and how to create a successful in-between.

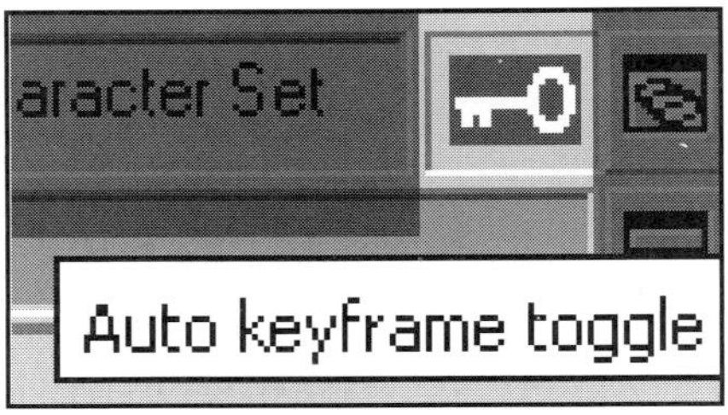

figure 5-12

The automatic key-frame toggle turns red when it is on.

Make sure your curve tangents are set to Linear and Stepped with Weighted Tangents, as in the bouncing ball animation (see Figure 5-13). Make sure Auto Key is set to Key All Attributes in the Animation preferences dialog box.

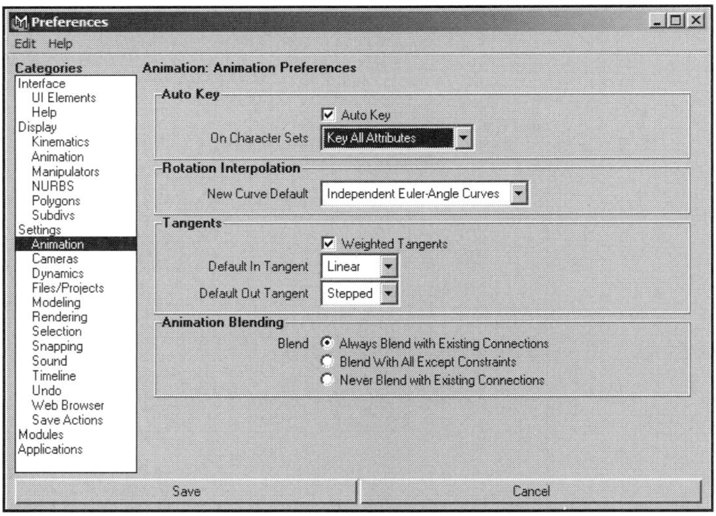

figure 5-13

The Preferences window.

! DON'T GO THERE

You do not need to use the same rig for every scene in an animation.

Very often, several rigs will be available for one puppet. Animators will work closely with riggers to create characters that can perform the movement requested by the director. Rigs may vary from shot to shot, depending on the movement required.

There are many ways to rig a puppet, and you will experience ones that work—and ones that break.

You will be creating a flour sack animation to express some physical attitudes.

Your setup should look like Figure 5-14.

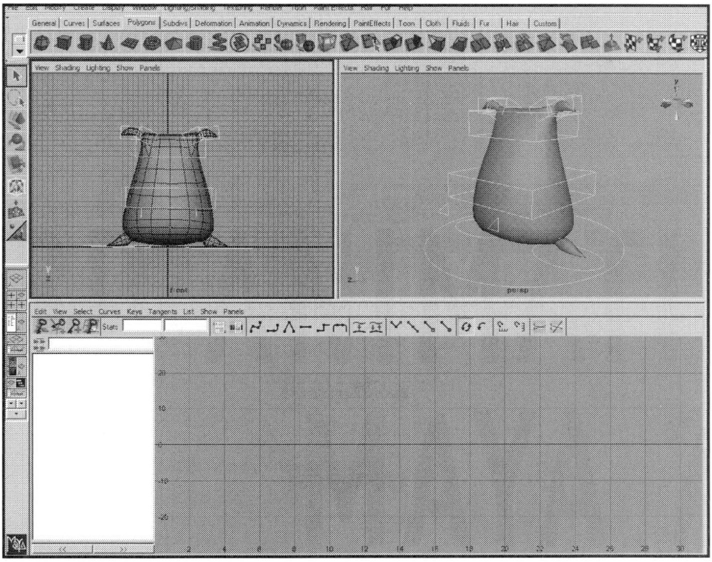

figure 5-14

Window Setup.

Locate the file FlourSack.mb you had open earlier. You will import the flour sack into your present scene using the **File** > **Import** command (see Figure 5-15).

Import the file (see Figure 5-15), and locate it in your directory.

Press open. Your window should now look like Figure 5-16. You have just imported Clyde the sack and are now able to work with him against the reference images you imported in the last chapter.

Zoom in on Clyde, and check out his controls (see Figure 5-17).

Open the Outliner, and you will see the names of these controls (see Figure 5-18). When you see a + or – sign in front of an item in the outliner, this means it is part of a hierarchy.

Left-mouse click on a + sign to see all elements.

Left-mouse click on a – sign to close the hierarchy.

Press the shift key and LMB together to open the entire hierarchy.

figure 5-15

Import Clyde.

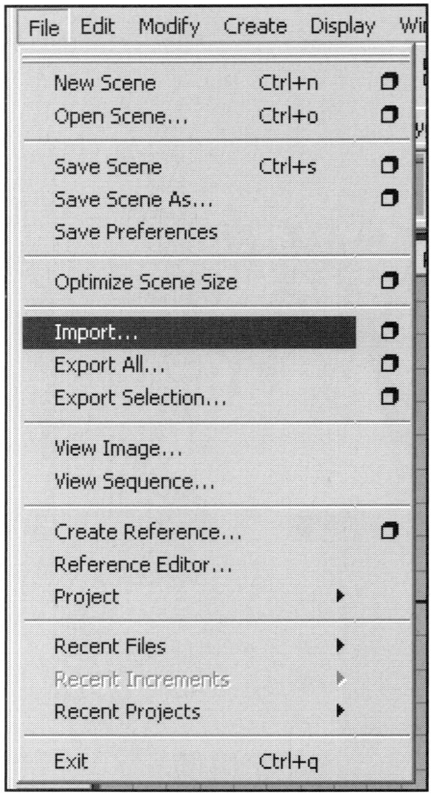

figure 5-16

Ready to begin.

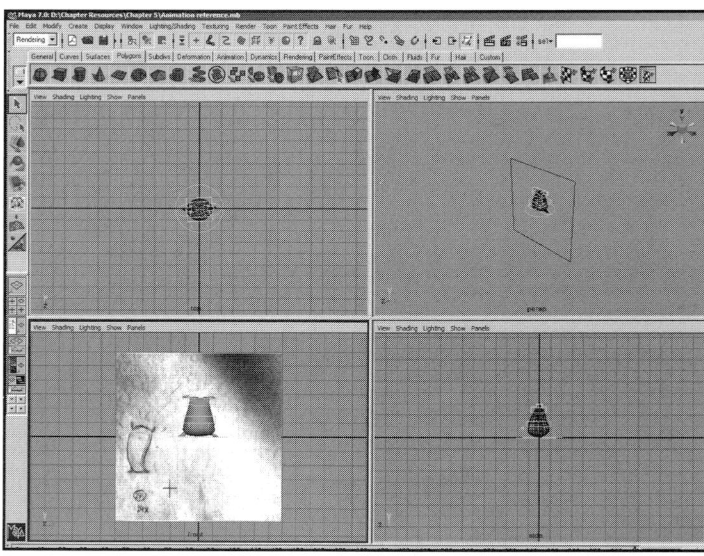

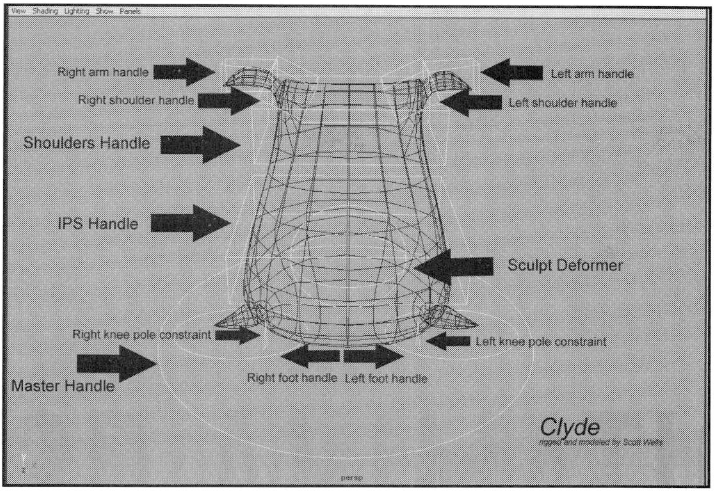

figure 5-17

Clyde and his controls, modeled and rigged by Scott Wells.

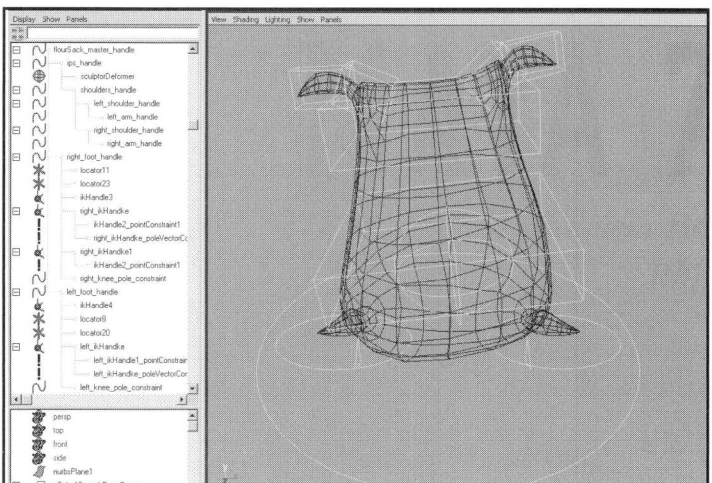

figure 5-18

Controls represented in the Outliner are identified by Curve graphic.

The sideways S-curves preceding the names represent the handles you should animate with. Do not animate any of the other objects. The main control you will see is **flourSack_Master_Handle** (see Figure 5-19).

To see the entire hierarchy of the puppet, press Shift + LMB over the little plus sign preceding the name **"flourSack_Master_Handle."** You will now see the whole tree (see Figure 5-20). Many elements go into the creation of a puppet.

You will not need to select your controls from the Outliner. You can select the controls off the puppet itself. You can directly select the

figure 5-19

The main control flourSack_Master_Handle.

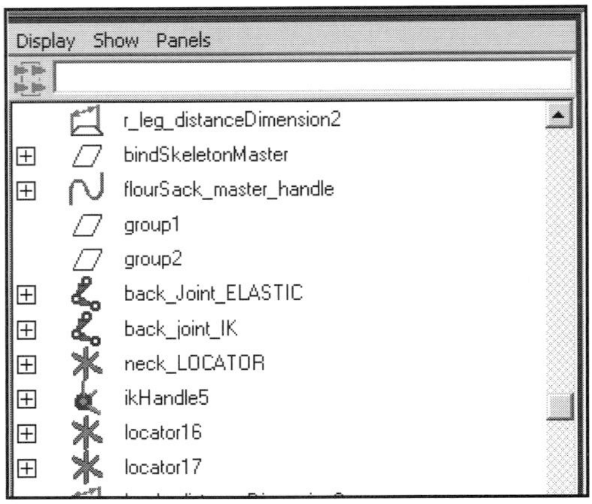

figure 5-20

The whole tree.

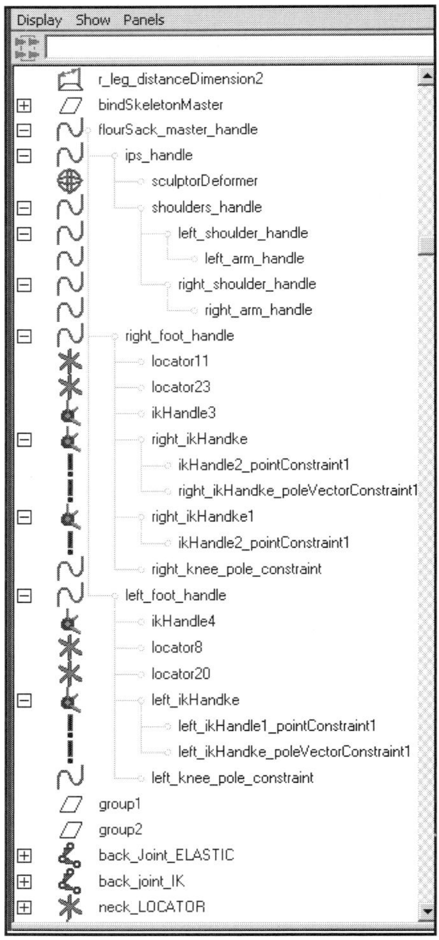

animatable elements in the puppet interface. Notice the boxes over each of the limbs. You can select these and rotate or translate them.

Select the boxes to animate this puppet. Make sure you are in object mode and that your Channel Box is open. The Channel Box will reveal the attributes available for the handle. You can either plug mathematical values into the channels, or you can interactively move the handle. If you want to scale a handle and Scale is not in the Channel Box, you cannot scale. You can only do what is offered in the Channel Box.

Master handle: The master handle moves the entire puppet. This handle should not be animated. This handle exists so that you can accurately place the fully animated puppet into your scene. When you are done animating, you will be able to import the entire animated puppet into whatever scene file you want.

IPS handle: This is the handle you should use to move the puppet in space. Because it is the main control, it is the first handle you adjust when animating a puppet. Whether up and down or in *x, y, z* space, this is the correct handle to animate for full puppet motion because it is the parent in control of the shoulders and ears.

Shoulders handle: The shoulders' handle moves the upper torso of Clyde. This control is a child of the hips, meaning that it is below the hips in the hierarchy and thus affected whenever the hips are moved.

Sculpt deformer: The sculpt deformer is used to flesh out an area that may be stretched out by a pose. The sculpt deformer acts like air in a balloon. It can inflate an area if placed properly. It needs to be placed within the puppet to work. It can be left outside of the puppet when you do not need it. It requires key frames like any other handle.

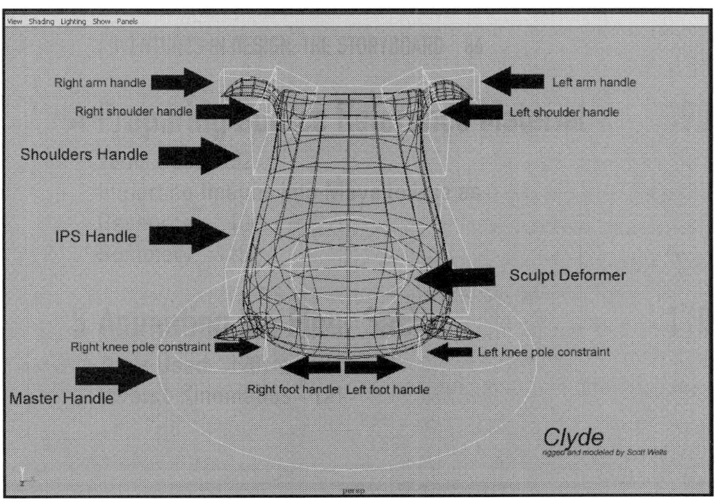

figure 5-21

Clyde and his controls, modeled and rigged by Scott Wells.

Shoulders handle: This will give you control over the shoulders, or the "head" of the puppet. It will not affect the lower extremities. The arm handles are parented to this shoulder handle, so they move whenever the shoulder is moved.

Right/left shoulders handles: These controls let you move the arms of Clyde. They are parented to the shoulders and move when the shoulders are moved.

Right/left arm handles: These controls let you move the outermost arms of Clyde. They are parented to the shoulder handles and move when the shoulders are moved.

Right/left foot handles: These handles move Clyde's feet. They can translate and rotate. When they are key-framed, they are constrained to an area in space and do not move when the rest of the body is moved. Successful positioning of the feet relies heavily on the correct placement of the right and left knee pole constraints.

Right/left knee pole constraints: These constraints tell the knees where to point. They are necessary for keeping the geometry in the right place when animating.

figure 5-22

Lining up the reference plane.

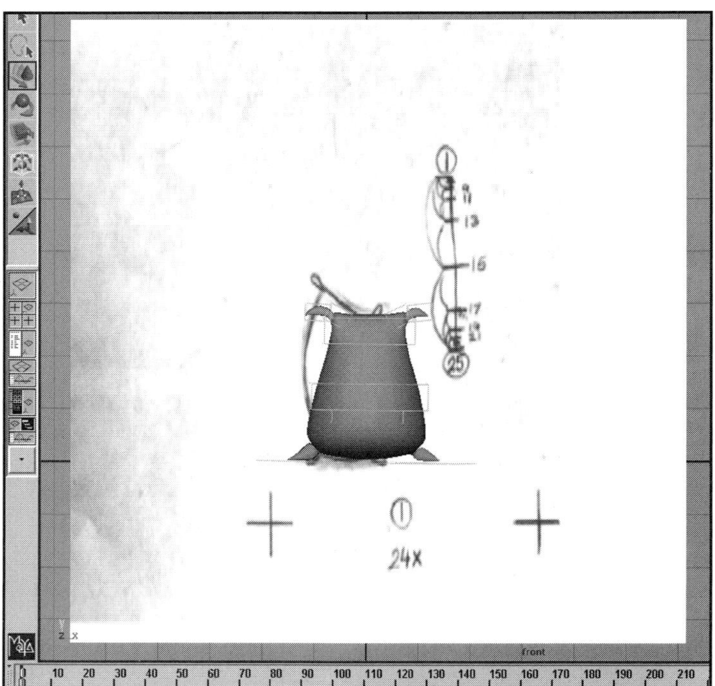

Go to frame 1 in the timeline. In the Front viewport, select the reference plane and move it upward so that the first drawing of Clyde sits on the graph line and Clyde is lined up (see Figure 5-22).

Notice at the bottom of the reference image that a timing notation has been specified. The key framer wants this animation to run at 24 frames per second (24x = 24 frames per second).

You need to make sure your animation is timed correctly, so go to the Preferences to verify. Select the Preferences icon in the lower right of the interface (see Figure 5-23).

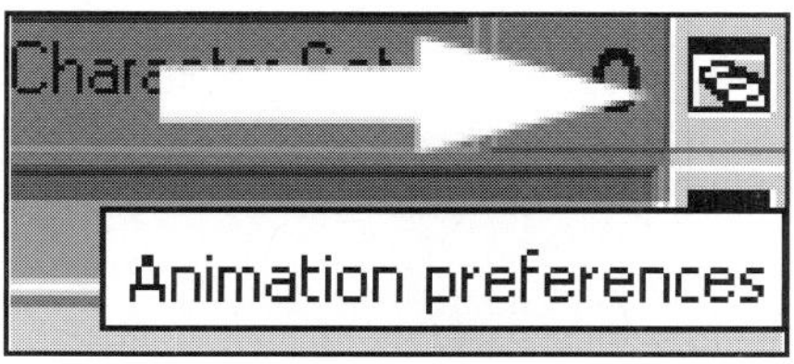

figure 5-23

The Preferences icon.

A new interface window opens (see Figure 5-24).

Make sure your interface looks like Figure 5-24. Be sure to select 24 fps as the playback.

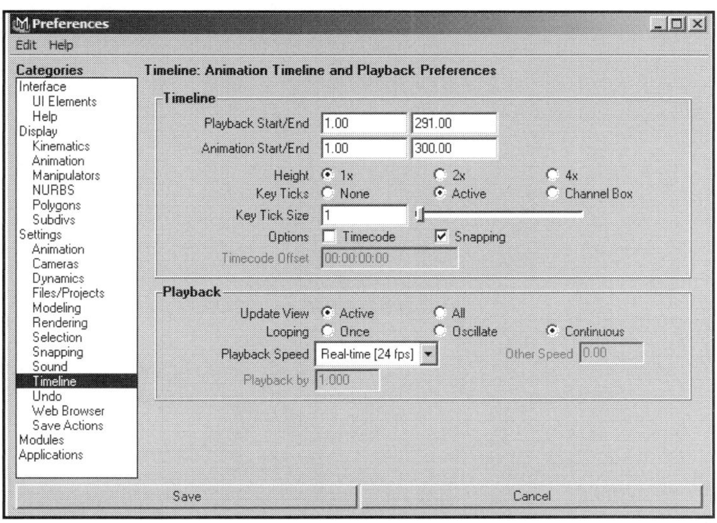

figure 5-24

The Preferences window.

Set up your Maya interface like Figure 5-25 to make the maximum use of your "real estate" (the viewing space on your screen). You want to be able to see all the controls influencing your movements while you work. Refer to Chapter 3, "The Bouncing Ball," if you have forgotten how to do so.

Now you are ready to make Clyde shake, rattle, and roll!

figure 5-25

The proper setup for this tutorial.

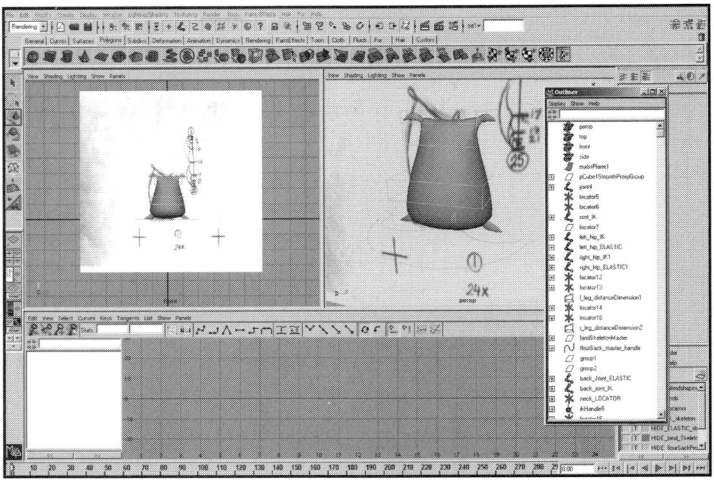

First, Check Out the Controls

The sculpt deformer is used to add "meat" to the puppet when poses stretch it too far out. Open the file Clyde_deformed.mb on the enclosed CD. This contains Clyde in a pose that could benefit from the use of the sculpt deformer (see Figure 5-26).

figure 5-26

The sculpt deformer used on Clyde.

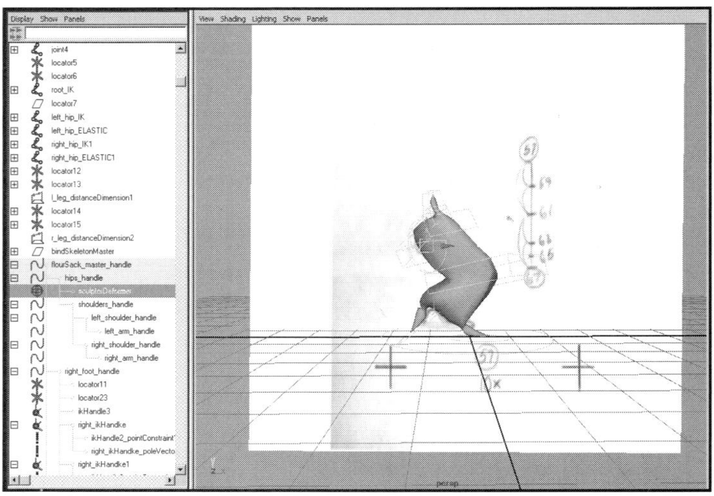

The reference image shows Clyde in a very rubbery pose. This is often hard to achieve with puppets when just using the basic rig.

Fortunately, this rig was built with squash and stretch, and you have access to a sculpt deformer.

Go to reference image 57, on key **57**. Look at this scene, and see how Clyde is posed. Turn off Clyde's visibility by going to the Layers box and turning off the V next to the Flour Sack smooth layer (see Figure 5-27).

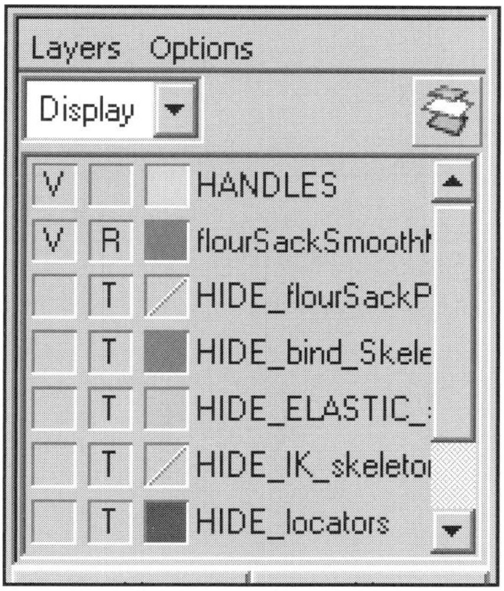

figure 5-27

LMB click over the V.

The image gives Clyde a little meat in the facial area. Otherwise, the 'squash' would have deleted much of his volume. Turn on Clyde's visibility again.

Go to the Perspective view, and select the sculpt deformer, which is a large sphere inside Clyde.

Make sure you are using the Move tool.

Move the sphere left and right away from Clyde (see Figure 5-28). Notice how Clyde shrinks and grows in response to the sphere?

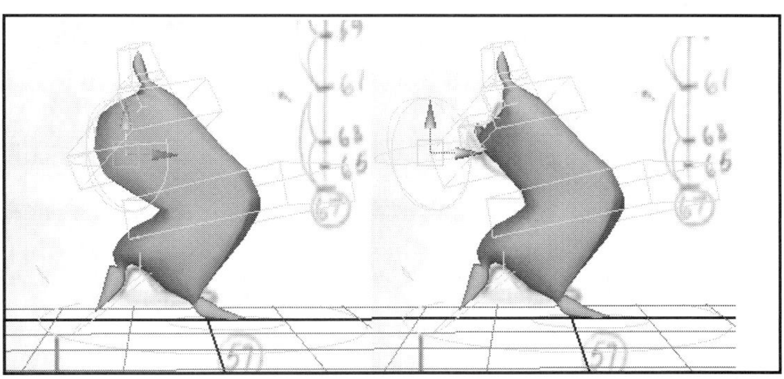

figure 5-28

Clyde with and without the sphere deformer.

Move the sphere around Clyde, and notice the influence. Scale the sphere up and down.

This will assist you in shaping the puppet when the skeleton deforms Clyde too much.

The left and right knee pole constraints are very important. They are used to point the knees of Clyde in the correct direction. If they are out of place, the puppet will crease or fold over itself (see Figure 5-29).

figure 5-29

Poorly placed knee pole constraints.

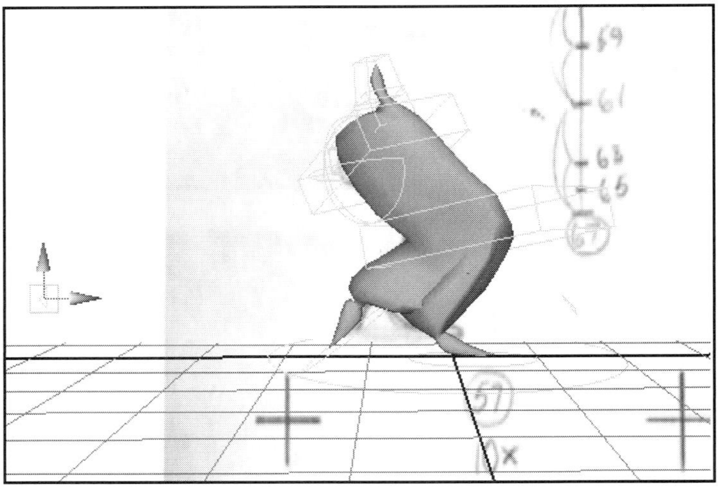

Posing Clyde

The main control you will use with this puppet is the ips_handle. You will pose this first. You will then follow with the feet, then the shoulders, and then you do the ears. You never use the flour-Sack_master_ handle, which is only used for placing the character into a scene.

You will begin by posing Clyde against the reference picture (see Figure 5-30).

Clyde has a nice lean to him in the first image. Begin by selecting the IPS handle and sliding it left (see Figure 5-31).

Then slide the feet to the left a bit to line up with the feet in the image by individually selecting each foot handle. Also select and rotate the shoulders handle until the figure looks like Figure 5-32.

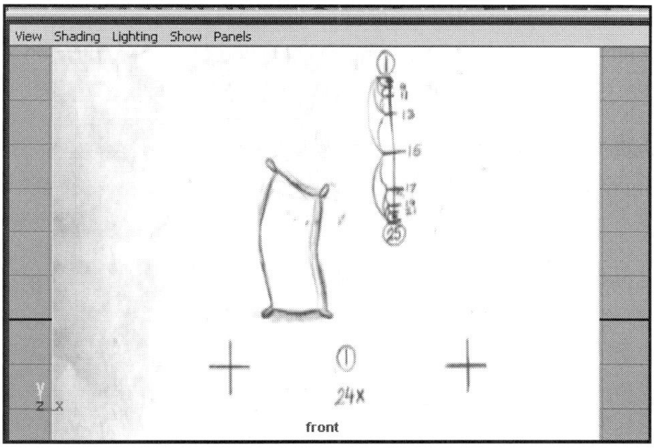

figure 5-30

Reference picture 1.

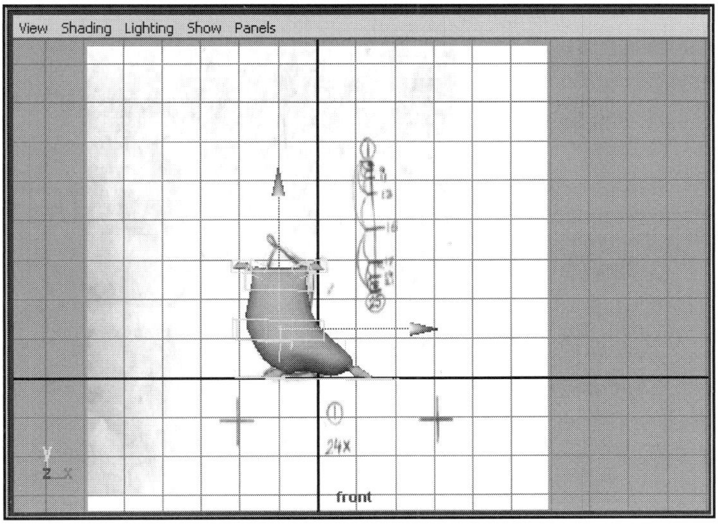

figure 5-31

Slide the IPS handle left.

TIP

If you find that your manipulator icons are too large or too small, go into your Preferences and change them. Go to **Window > Settings/Preferences > Preferences.**

In the new window, select Manipulators from the sidebar and then scale down the global scale to about .5 (see Figure 5-34).

figure 5-32

Clyde in stance.

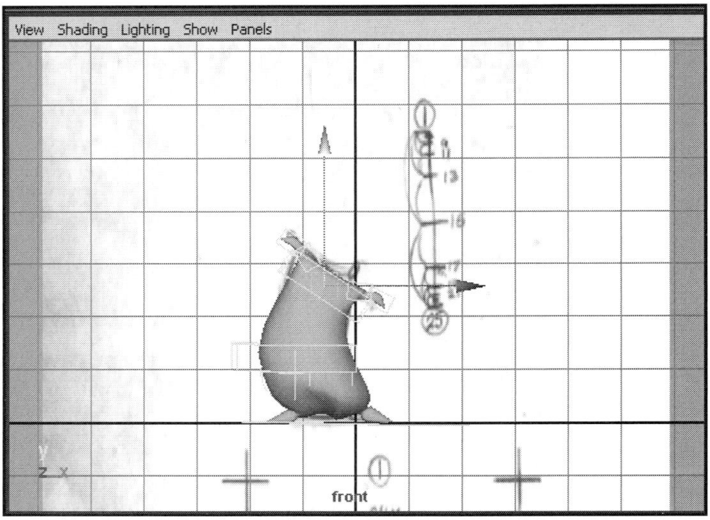

figure 5-33

The path to your Preferences.

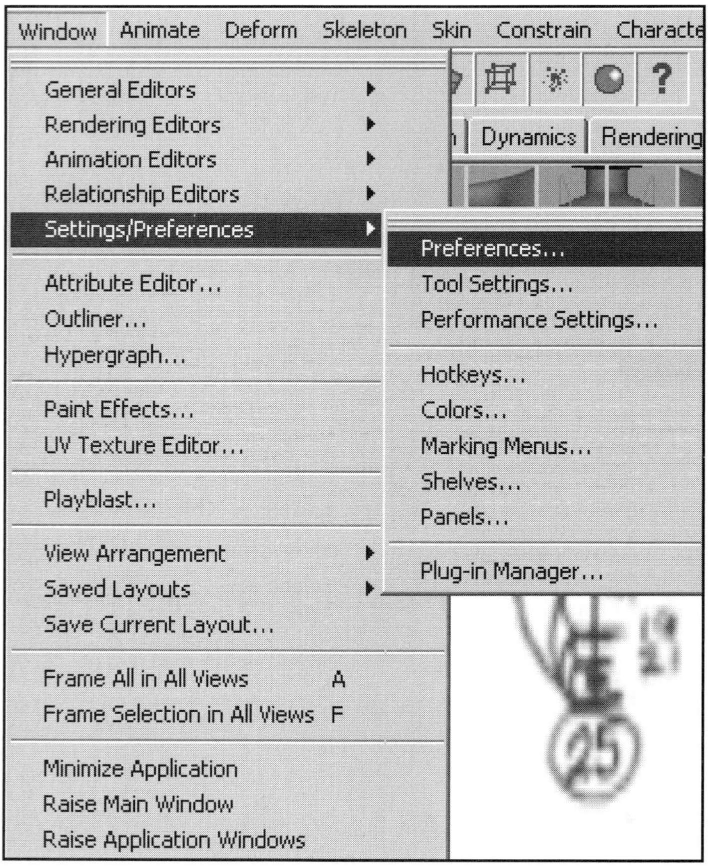

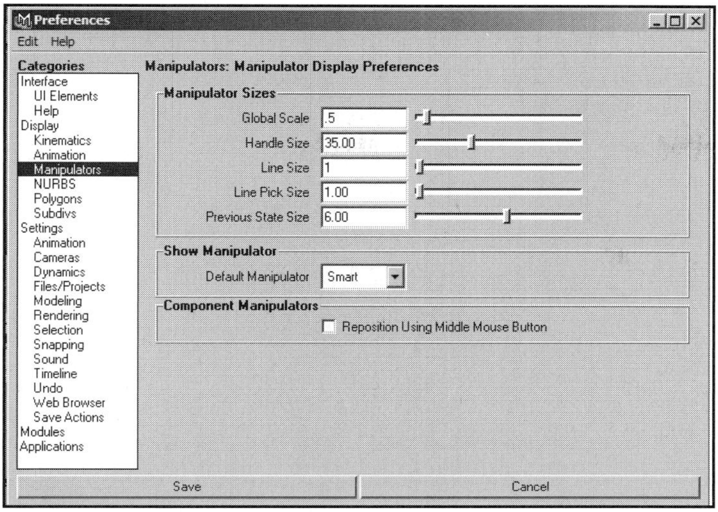

figure 5-34

Preference settings.

Now go to the shoulders and arms. Give Clyde a little bit of attitude. He is a confident guy, after all.

Now independently select each handle, and set a key frame for each. In the Channel Box, select every channel that you want to animate and then right-mouse click over the channels to set a key frame. You should remember this from the bouncing ball chapter.

Look at your Graph Editor. You should see curves started for every item for which you have set a key frame. These beginnings are demonstrated by a small black dot on the graph at frame 1.

Go through every key pose, and set up Clyde against the reference image. Be sure to move to the selected frame in your timeline before setting the pose. (You will be forced to get into this habit, as the reference image will not appear unless you move to the selected frame.) Make key frames for each pose on every handle, even those you do not move.

Staging

You will find reference images on these frames: 1, 25, 43, 57, 67, 75, 79, 87, 95, 99, 109, 113, 117, 121, 129, 143, 155, 167, 179, 189, 199, 211, 219, 223, 229, 235, 249, 255, 259, 261, 265, 267, 269, 271, 273, 275, 277, 279, 283, 287, 291. Set key poses on all of these frames.

While you are setting these poses, study them. They all give the viewer a piece of information. No pose should be wasted. Think of animation as a silent film or newspaper cartoon; most storytelling is done with the pose.

If you ever get into trouble, you can zero out the numbers in the Channel Box to get back to the starting position (see Figure 5-35).

figure 5-35

Returning to start.

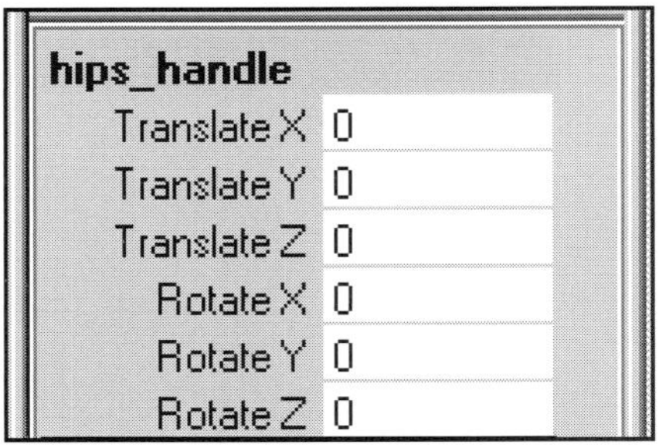

As a final housekeeping step, go to **Edit** > **Delete All by Type** > **Static Channels** (see Figure 5-36).

figure 5-36

The command to delete channels with no animation.

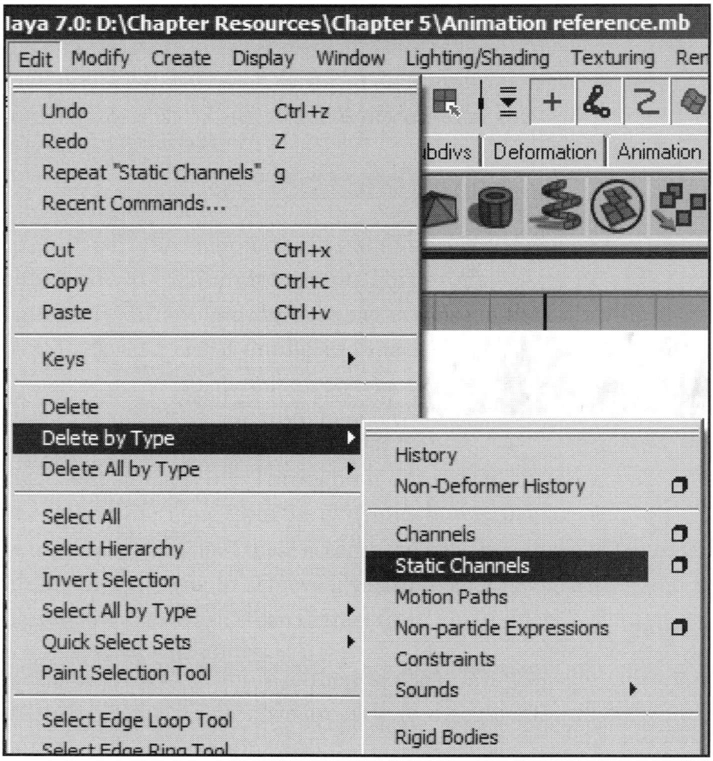

This cleans up your Graph Editor by deleting any unanimated curves. The procedure saves you time editing and in the final render.

Now make a playblast. Select the window view you want to see the animation in, and use the command **Windows > Playblast (options box).**

Set your controls as in Figure 5-37, but create a new path for the output of the file. You will find your movie in this file after it is created.

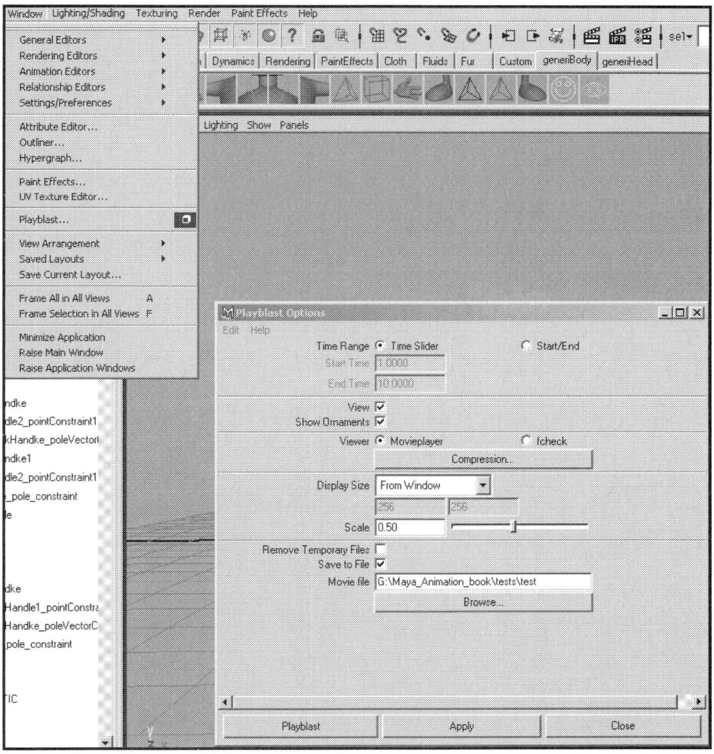

figure 5-37

Playblast interface.

You can play the file through any of your movie players on your computer.

Save your file. Save another copy, and name it **version 2.** Work with version 2 on the next assignment.

Timing Check

Now that you have entered all the key poses, you must do a timing check to see if it "reads." In production, this would be the point at which you wave down the director and get his input on the scene. If he gives you a thumbs up, it is on to the next step.

Suppose you do not get a thumbs up. Editing is easy at this stage because your curves are all stepped. Revisions will not be as painful here as they will be when you have set the arcs of your motion curves.

Next we will complete some editing. Make sure you have saved a version of your file with a different name before trying this next step.

Editing Curves 101

We will use this time to experiment with editing. Open the file practice_editcurves_start.mb on the enclosed CD, or use your file from the last exercise.

Editing the Slow Out, Fast In

Here you will practice creating in-betweens between two poses.

This is where those scribbled notations on every reference image gain critical importance. These are the timing references.

Look at the two timing charts in Figures 5-38 and 5-39.

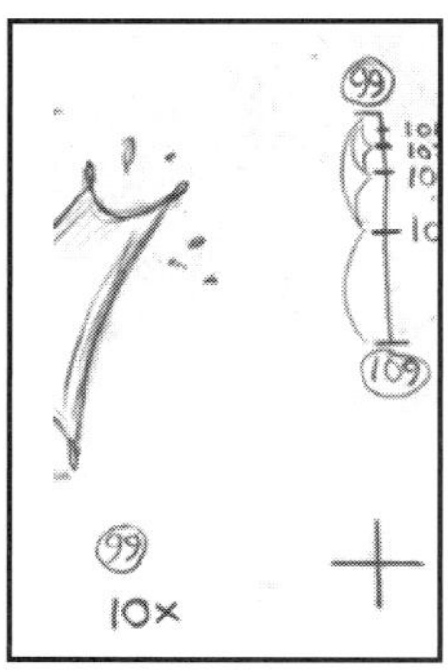

figure 5-38

Frame 99.

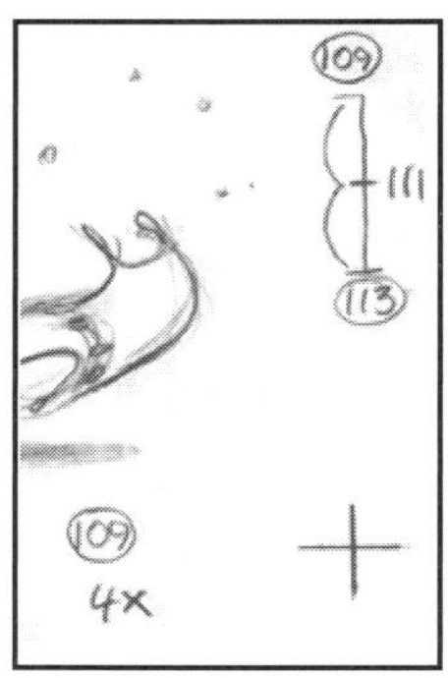

figure 5-39

Frame 109.

These timing charts are notations on the timing and spacing of the scene. They are frequently the only communications you will receive from the animation director.

As previously mentioned, objects that are closer together over a series of frames appear to be moving slower than a series of objects that get farther and farther apart over a series of frames.

At frame 99, you see notations for frames 99, 101, 103, 105, and 107. Frame 99 is the first key pose, and 107 is the last key pose. Any tick halfway between these two poses represents a character pose exactly halfway between the two keys. Which frame does this happen on?

The answer is 107 because frames 101, 103, and 105 are used to ease into the midpoint, which is 107.

The following frames are closer together on the chart: frames 99, 101, 105, and 107. What is the next farthest? The answer is frame 107 and then 109. This tells you that you are going to animate the key frames with a slow out and a fast in because the first five frames are slowly approaching the midpoint position.

What is the midpoint? The midpoint is the frame exactly between the two key frames. In this instance, the midpoint is frame 107. Mathematically, it would be 104, which is the wrong way to think. The lead artist created this midpoint to reflect his/her interest in the movement. This is very important to notice.

Frames 101, 103, and 105 are not evenly spaced either. Look at how they gradually ease away from each other. This is called a slow out. The image will change only slightly from frame to frame.

Because there are no keys between the midpoint and 109, this is called a fast in. The image changes greatly between these two frames.

Now look at the second graph. This graph represents only three frames—two key poses and one in-between. This in-between is directly between the two key poses.

Select the hips handle. Now go to the Graph Editor and select all the curves for the hips handle by drawing a marquee around the curves (see Figure 5-40).

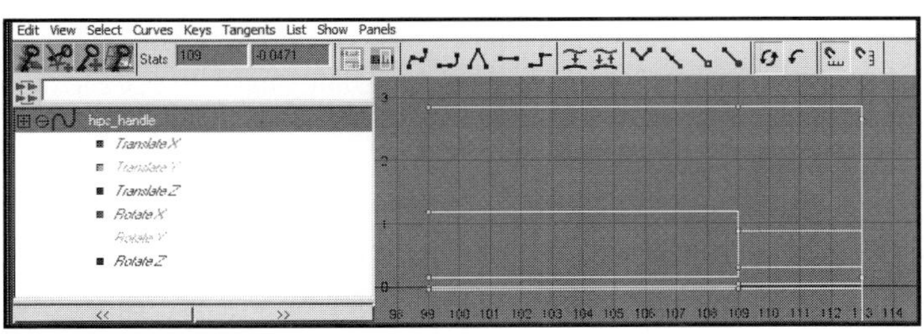

figure 5-40

Stepped curves.

In the drop-down menu bar of the Graph Editor, select **Tangents** > **Clamped** (see Figure 5-41).

Your curves will change.

Do this to every handle. When the entire puppet is changed to linear, play the animation. This will give you a rough idea of your timing.

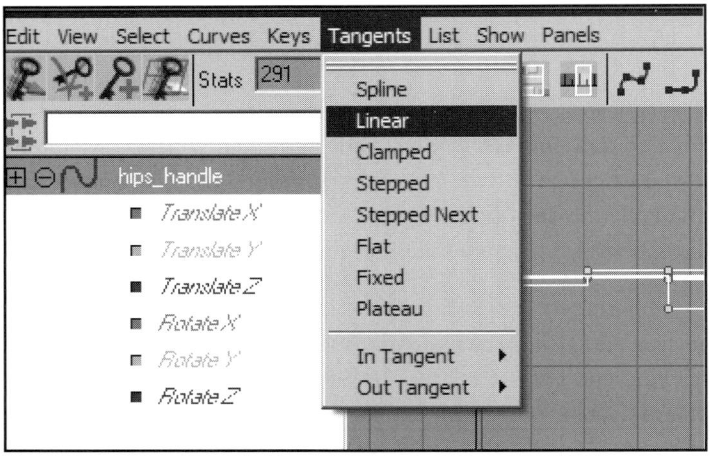

figure 5-41

Linear curves.

Play it frame by frame to make sure you have no crossing geometry. See the file practice_edit_curves.mb if you have any questions.

Now let us go back to the timing charts.

Look at the timing chart for 99. Here you see that Clyde has a slow out. Knowing that the left side of the Graph Editor represents value and the bottom numbers represent time, a slow out means the graph curve will stay close to the original value as it passes through time. Also happening during this slow out is a furiously quick stepping motion in the feet.

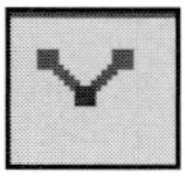

figure 5-42

The Break Tangent tool.

You will first work with the hips handle. It appears that the most noticeable movement is in the X Translate curve. This is the first thing you will modify.

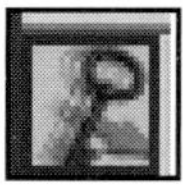

figure 5-43

The Move Nearest Key Picked tool.

Select the key frame at 99 for the X Translate curve. Break the tangent (see Figure 5-42).

Now select the outgoing tangent, which is the red bar leading away from the key frame. Select the Move Nearest Key Picked tool, and use the middle mouse button (MMB) to move the out tangent (see Figure 5-43).

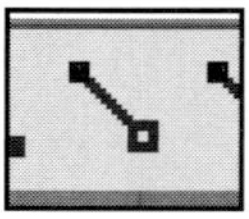

figure 5-44

The Free Tangent Weight tool.

The curve needs to be close to the initial value until it reaches 107, and then it should rise sharply. Right now, this process is not enough. You need to use one more tool. Make sure the X Tangent key at 99 is selected, and then press the Free Tangent Weight tool (see Figure 5-44).

Your tangent bar will appear different; it now has a square box on the tip. Select this box and pull. You can now make a much more efficient curve between the two key frames. An example is shown in Figure 5-45.

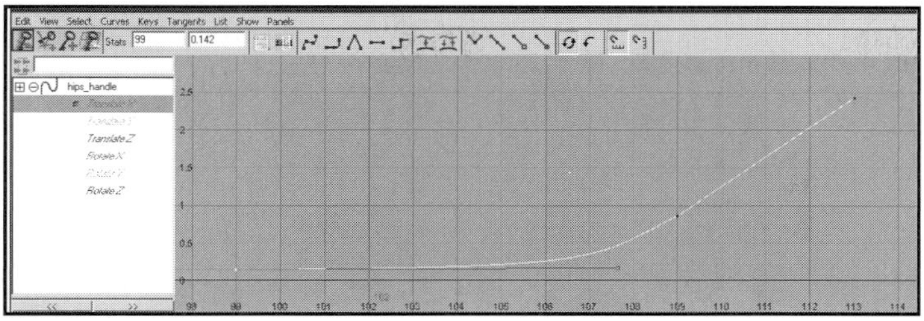

figure 5-45

Spline with weighted tangent edited.

In this example, we also broke the tangent at frame 109 and used the Free Tangent Weight tool to get this curve.

Next, you will work on the shoulder handle. The shoulders move down and to the right. Which curves would this motion require?

The correct answer is the Y Translate and the X Translate. You will edit the curves to look like Figure 5-46, and to represent the slow out.

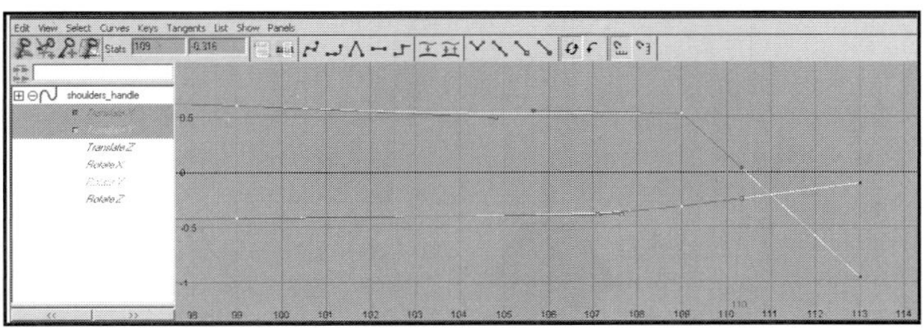

figure 5-46

Curves for X and Y Translate on the shoulders handle.

The next handle will be the right foot handle. Most of this handle's movement is also in X, Y Translate. The curves look like Figure 5-47.

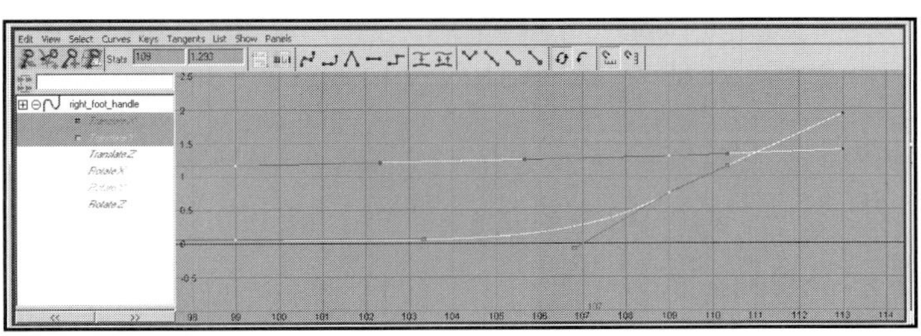

figure 5-47

Curves for X and Y Translate on the right foot handle.

The left foot handle is shown in Figure 5-48. Again, see the X and Y Translate.

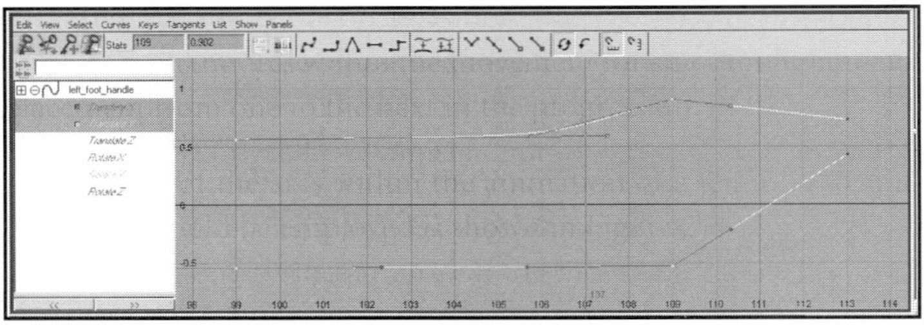

figure 5-48

Curves for X and Y Translate on the left foot handle.

Do the same process on the left/right arm and left/right shoulder handles.

Next we will key-frame your midpoint, which will require a little bit of thought. To complete this function, you must understand the mathematical midpoint versus the artist-chosen midpoint.

First, derive the mathematical midpoint by doing the following: Key frame 109–key frame 99 = 10 frames of action. Then, divide 10 frames by 2 = 5 frames from key frame 99, which = the exact midpoint. Thus, 104 is the mathematical midpoint.

Make a key frame at 104. The curves will not change much because the computer already determined this as the midpoint for you. However, the computer is not human and does not understand the art as well as you are about to. The frame this midpoint value should happen on is really 107.

Next go to the Graph Editor and move this mathematical midpoint to the artist chosen midpoint, 107. Notice this on the timing chart. Enter 107 in the first Stats window of the Graph Editor. This will move the key frame that you entered at frame 104 to frame 107 and will update your curve. The midpoint that the computer computed for you is now in the correct place.

The next timing chart represents an even interpolation between frames, which is desirable. Since all the curves are linear, your work here is done. Linear curves create, by default, an even staging between frames. See the preceding to check out my curves.

Animating the Flipper Feet

Look at the key pose on frame 109. Those feet are moving very fast. You can separately animate these from the preceding curves now that you have all the geometry in place. Check with your art director to make sure of his/her intent with the sketch and then proceed with your interpretation. You do not have to do it exactly like this example, but read it as a good example to consider.

Start the feet moving at frame 104 to give Clyde a chance to ease out of his shock pose. First, go to your animation Preferences and change your tangents in and out to Clamped (see Figure 5-49).

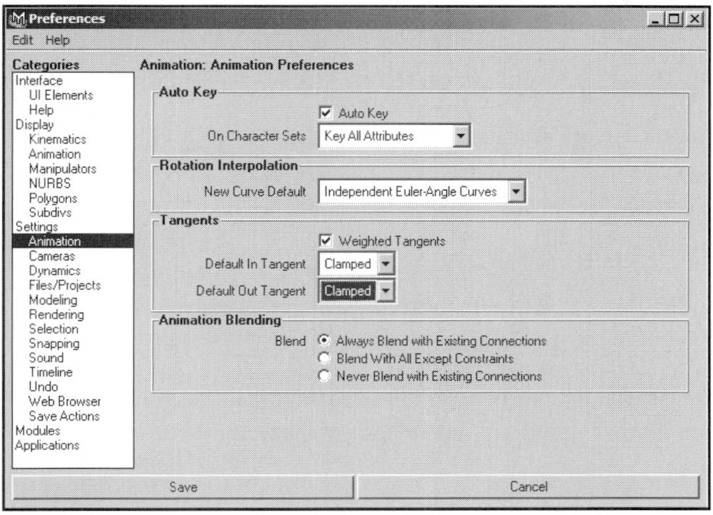

figure 5-49

Change tangent values to Clamped.

Begin with the right foot handle, and set a key frame for all values in the Channel Box at frame 103 because the next key frame you create does not influence the previous curve as much.

Set poses at frames 104, 105, 106, and 107 of the foot rotating in a circular arc (see Figure 5-50).

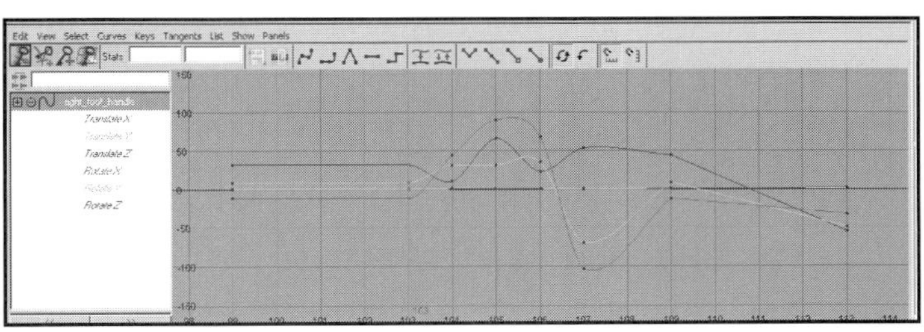

figure 5-50

Right foot handle curves.

Then move to the left foot handle, and set a key frame for all values in the Channel Box at frame 103. Set poses at frames 104, 105, 106, and 107 of the foot rotating in a circular arc (see Figure 5-51).

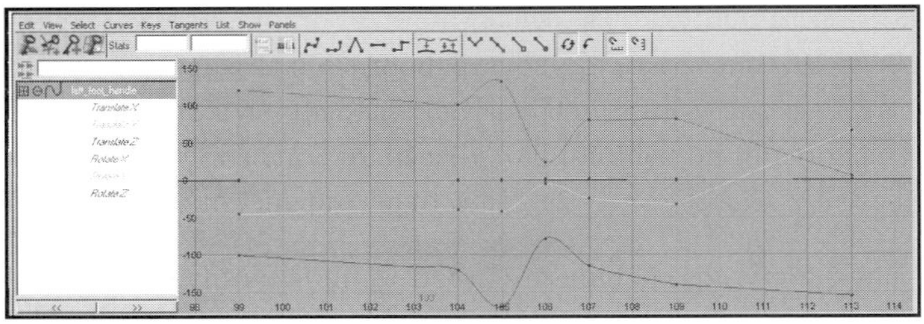

figure 5-51

Left foot handle curves.

Create a playblast, and check with your director for approvals.

From this point forward, do further tweaking based on notes you get from your director. More than likely, he/she will request an additional extreme pose at frame 111 to accentuate the speed and loss of balance. Check your work against practice_edit_cuves_final.mb on the enclosed CD.

More Ways to Edit in the Graph Editor

Suppose your director wants the entire scene to slow down. Does this mean you need to redo all of the key frames? No.

Select all your handles. The names show up on the left side of the Graph Editor (see Figure 5-52). Every animated curve on all of these handles will show up on the right side of the Graph Editor.

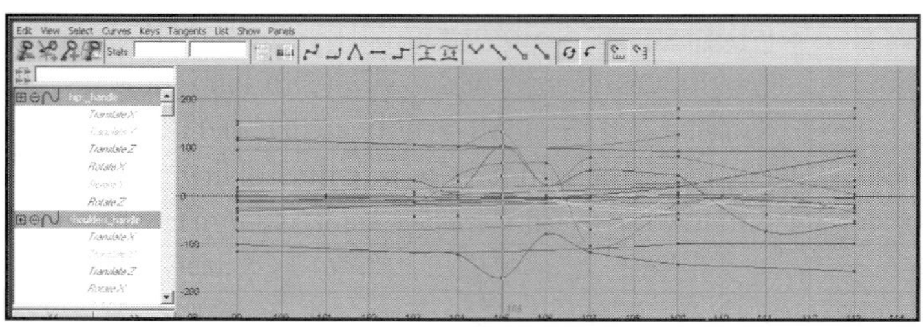

figure 5-52

Graph Editor with curves.

Now turn on the Scale tool by going to **Edit** > **Transformation Tools** > **Scale Keys Tool (options box)** (see Figure 5-53). Make sure "manipulator" is checked in the options box.

A box surrounds all of the curves (see Figure 5-54).

If you left-mouse drag on one of the circles in the scale box, you can scale the values of the curve up and down.

Now your director wants one part of the animation to be offset from the rest.

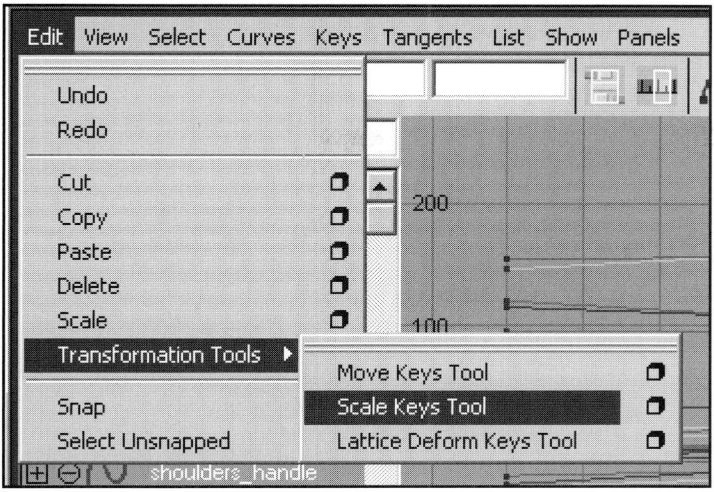

figure 5-53

The Scale tool.

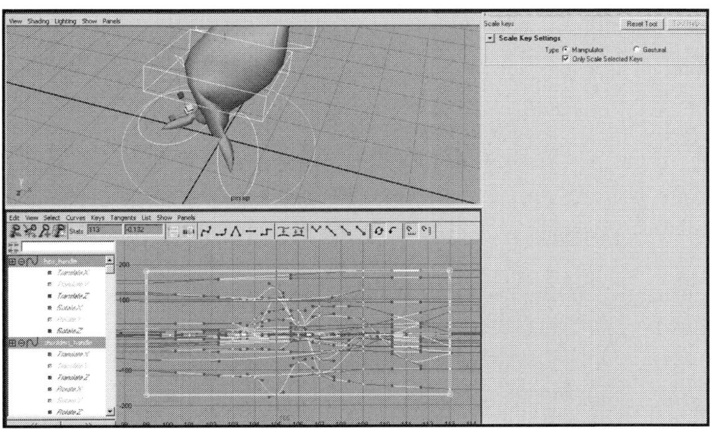

figure 5-54

The Scale tool in Graph Editor.

You can use the lattice tool to scale the animation curves to offset frames (see Figure 5-55). This is a quick and dirty way to do it, under the pressure of deadline. For high-quality work, pick and choose the offset animation manually. There *is* a method to the madness, and you can tell when an animator does not know the method. Go to **Edit > Transformation Tools > Lattice Deform Keys Tool (options box).**

This places a lattice around all of your key frames. Each circle on the lattice can be moved to adjust the curves beneath it. You can adjust how many sections are available in your lattice by adjusting the Columns and Rows in your Lattice tool options box. (See the right side of the image.)

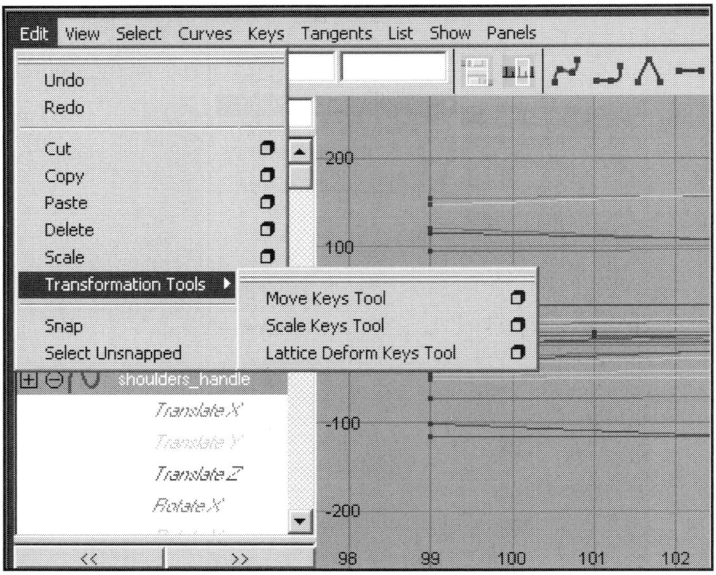

figure 5-55

The Lattice Deform Keys tool.

SUMMARY

Congratulations! You have animated your first multi-handle puppet down to the slow-out of the curves. Now you have a 300-frame scene. Practice your new skills by finishing the animation against the reference images.

Once you are done, let another pair of eyes review it. Look for floaty movement. If something looks like it is moving too evenly, check the curves.

The chief mistakes apparent in a beginner piece of CG animation are as follows:

- **Floaty movement.** This often is caused by simply changing your curve tangent to Spline after setting the key poses with Step, which is a common beginner's mistake.
- **No weight.** This is often caused by not animating the slow in or fast out as required by the action and a lack of follow-through. These curves are crucial to establishing weight.
- **Too many poses.** The character flies around the scene with no set purpose. The arms flail and the eyes wander because the animator wants to avoid making the puppet appear static. There are other ways to do this, which you will explore later.

- **Too many key frames.** You ought to be able to read the action in your scene just by looking at your curves. Too many key frames dirty the curve, making it jump and jitter when it is meant to be a smooth arc. If you can edit the curve with the handles to achieve the motion, be sure to do so since it will allow you to avoid excessive key framing.

TIP

When the reference images of Clyde go below the line, this means Clyde must move forward in Z space. Do no move Clyde below the line—he will appear to go through the floor.

in review

1. How do you set a key frame on just one channel?
2. Which handle is the main handle to animate with Clyde?
3. Which handle is saved for when the puppet is imported into another scene and needs to be repositioned?
4. What does a translate curve with a slow out and fast in look like in the Graph Editor?
5. When you first block out the animation with key poses, what should the default curves be set to? Should they be weighted or unweighted?
6. When you are ready to decide the speed of the curves, after setting the key poses, what should the curves be changed to?
7. What is inverse kinematics?
8. What is a sculpt deformer?
9. How do you delete curves that have no animation on them?

EXPLORING ON YOUR OWN

1. Finish setting key poses for the entire 300 frames of animation.
2. Edit the curves leading into each pose. Choose which curves represent the most movement, and animate those first. Make sure to pay attention to the timing charts.
3. Import images captured off of old cartoons, and animate against them to learn timing.

notes

Adventures in Design

ADVENTURES IN DESIGN

MAKING THE ANIMATIC

In this exercise, you will adapt your storyboard to After Effects, making a moving animatic as the skeleton of your short. An *animatic* is a moving storyboard with sound, a movie that helps you decide the length of your shots before you commit to animating sequences. It is imperative that you create this before beginning a short film—it can save you a ton of work!

I encourage you to learn After Effects or any other compositing program, as you must be able to edit your movies and add titles and credits once you have animated them. I am going to assume a basic understanding of the software in this exercise, as compositing in After Effects requires a whole book in itself. Learn to render in passes and composite your elements. This way, you will only have to re-render elements that need improvement, instead of entire shots.

Begin with a storyboard on paper.

Scan each panel as a separate image. We will bring these images in one by one to After Effects.

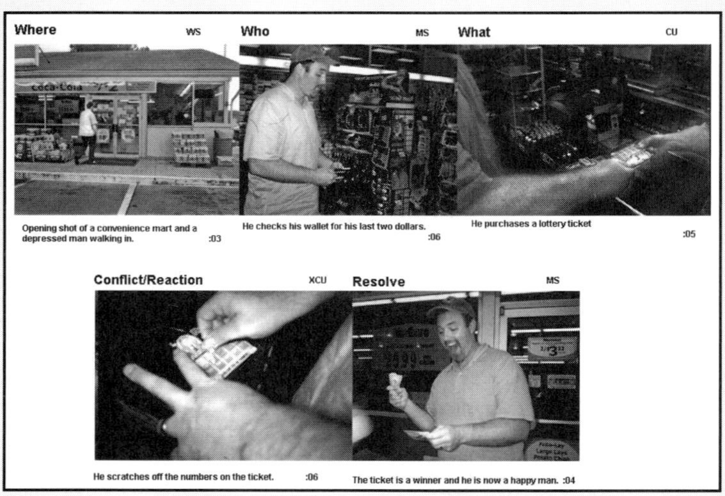

B-1 Man wins lottery.

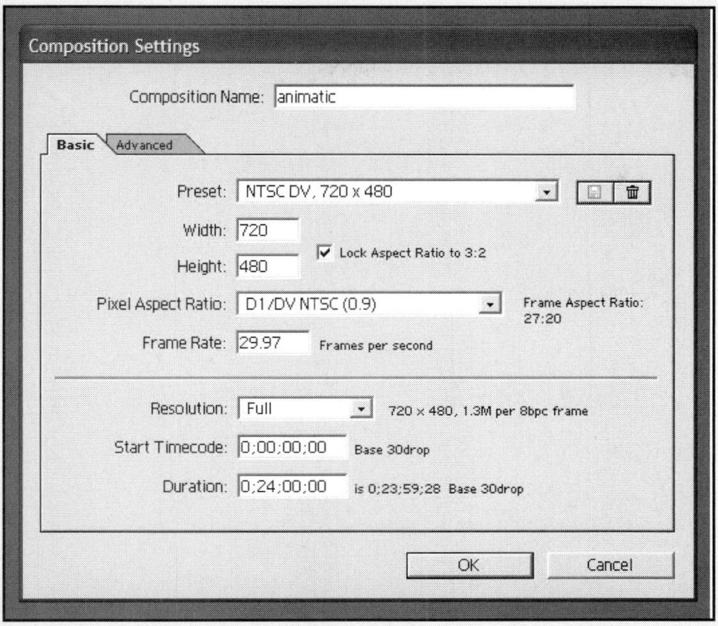

B-2 Creating the :24 composition in After Effects.

Open After Effects.

Set up your composition so that it is long enough to contain the timing of your intended animatic. Our example is :24.

Import the five scans that make up your five-panel storyboard. After importing, they will appear in your Project folder.

Place them on the timeline. Adjust the timeline for each shot, to match the timing you created in the initial storyboard.

Import the soundtrack and place it into your timeline. I have found that sound created as a .wav works best.

Render the movie.

You now have a basic animatic for production. As you create shots, render them out and replace the storyboard drawings/photos in your animatic with the new images. Your film will then create itself, and problems can be spotted before committing too much work to a shot.

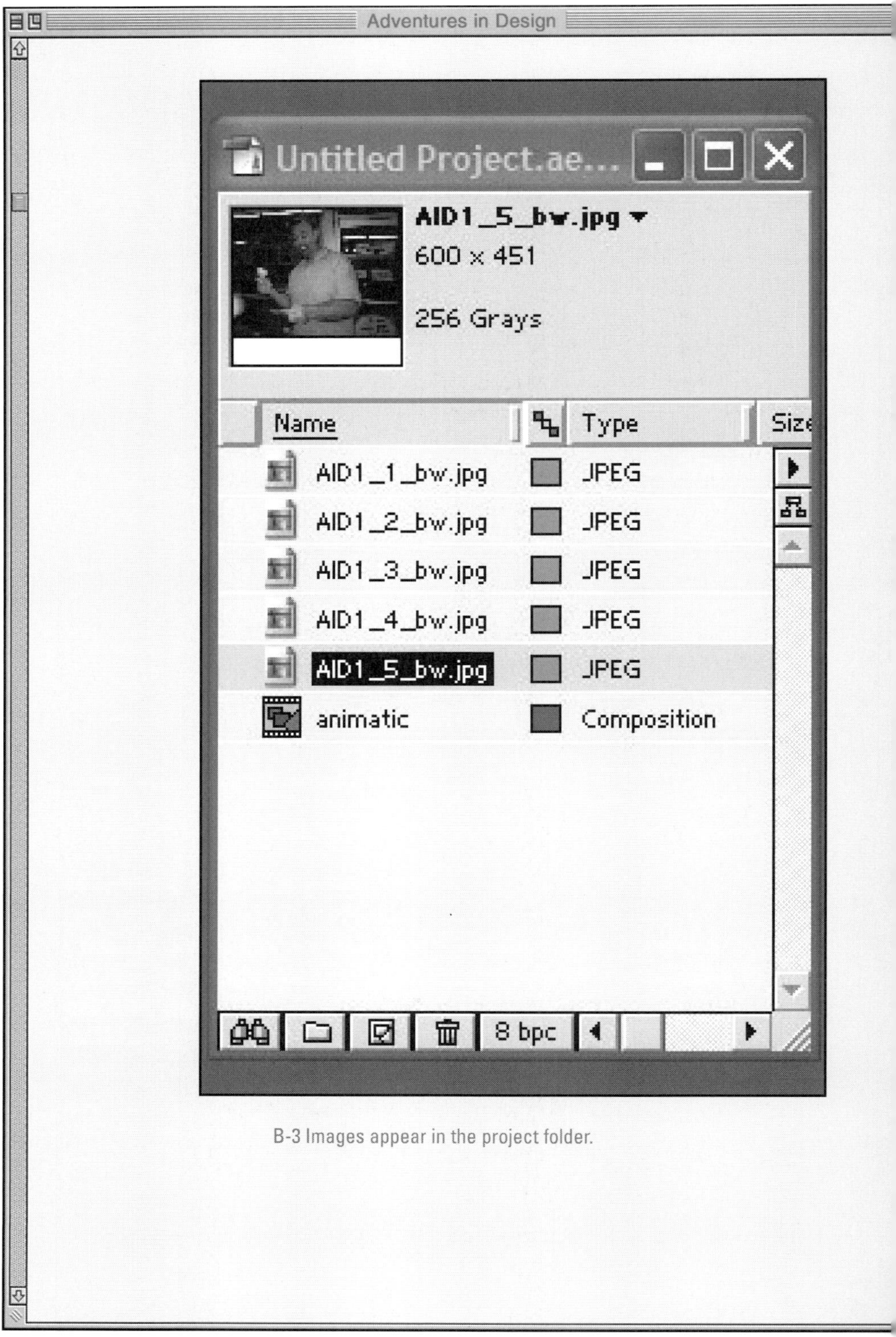

B-3 Images appear in the project folder.

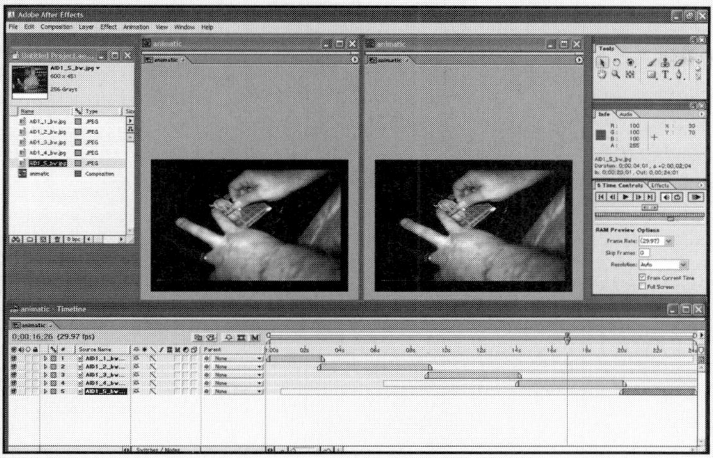

B-4 Images placed in the timeline corresponding with the time allotted for each shot.

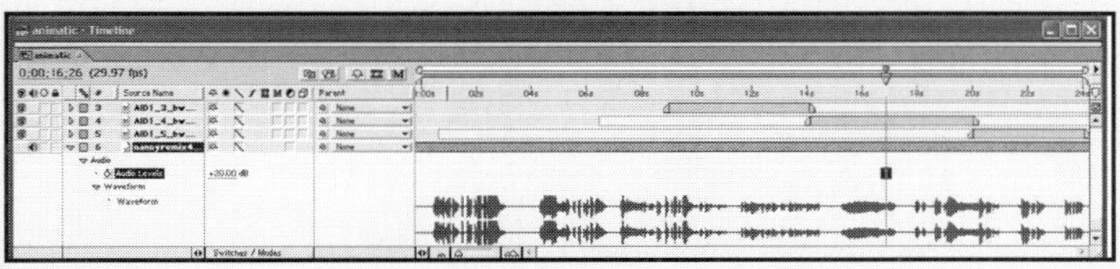

B-5 Audio imported into the timeline.

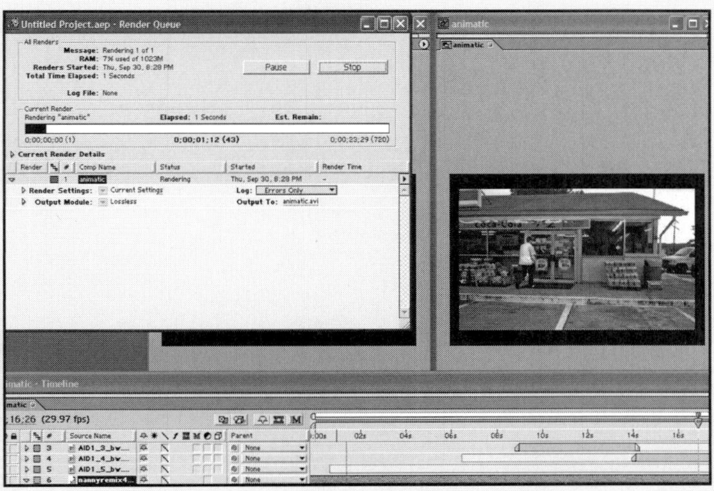

B-6 Rendering the movie.

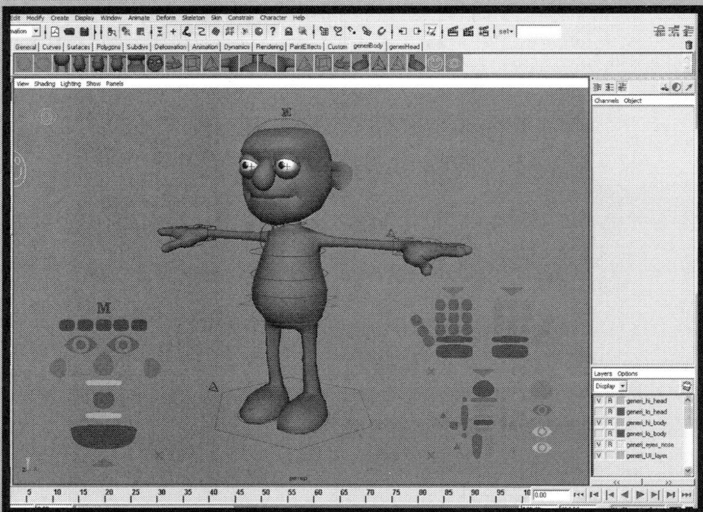

6 the generi rig

charting your course

Get to know your puppet before you do any complex animation exercises. Make sure you can identify the main body masses and what controls are available for each mass. A technical director is usually assigned to create such a puppet, but it is well worth your while as an animator to learn as much rigging as you can.

On the job, you will be in constant communication with a technical director. Get to know the basics of what you need in a puppet so that you can communicate effectively. That entails working with multiple rigs and training yourself in some basic rigging.

goals

In this chapter, you will:

- **Learn how to work with a pre-rigged character.**
- **Learn how to toggle between a high-resolution (hi-res) and low-resolution (lo-res) model.**

TOOLS USED

- **The Generi Rig.** You will explore your first complex character rig. Generi has the capability to switch between inverse kinematics(IK) and forward kinematics (FK), be lip-synched, and refer to locators.
- **Switching between IK and FK.** You will have the ability to use both forward and inverse kinematics on the arms. You will practice going between them.
- **Locators.** The knees and elbows can be manipulated so that they are pointing in the right direction when limbs are animated.
- **Hi-res vs. Lo-res models.** Lo-res models exist to make animating faster. Hi-res models are for the final render. You will learn how to use each.

THE GENERI RIG

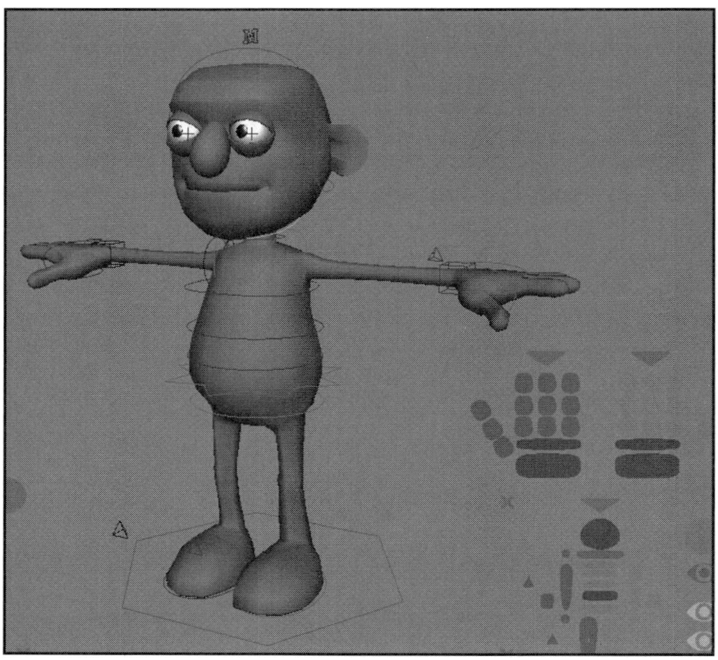

figure 6-1

The Generi Rig by Andrew Silke.

Generi is a complex rig; however, with practice, you can master it. You can already start animating when you learn the first basic controls. Once you understand these, you will then appreciate some of the more subtle attributes available. (Note: Andrew includes most of the following directions in his read me file, found in the generi_rigv1.1.zip file.)

Basic Setup

Unzip the file generi_rig_v1.1.zip using WinZip or some other decompression software.

Follow these directions to set up your Maya software interface to look like Figure 6-2.

NOTE

Andrew Silke generously created the Generi rig as a free rig for all practicing animators. Additional Mel scripting and rigging was contributed by Hamish McKenzie. You can see more of their work at www.cane-toad.com. They allow animators to use this rig as a learning and practice tool, but it may not be used for commercial production.

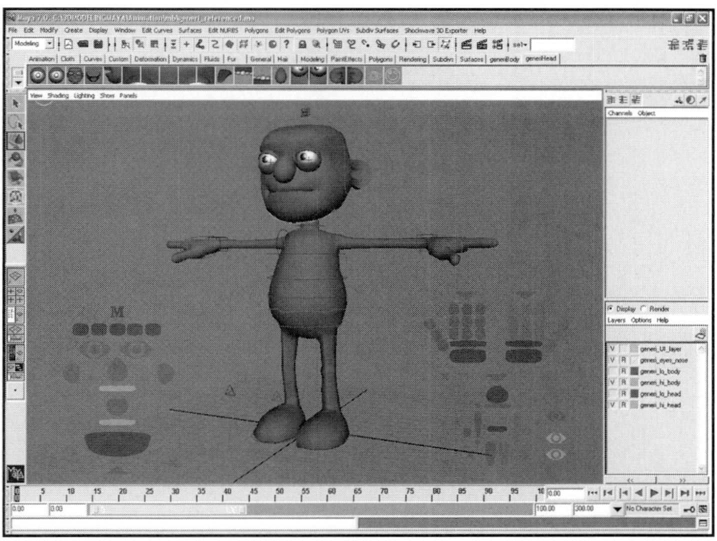

figure 6-2

Interface ready for animation of rig.

1. Unzip the file (keep the directory structure when unzipping). You can use the software WinZip. An evaluation copy of WinZip can be found at www.downloads.com.

2. Move both the .mb and .ma files to your project's Scenes directory (see Figure 6-3). If you do not know how to find this directory, refer to Chapter 1 of this book.

3. Move the contents of the prefs\icons folder to your Icons directory (see Figure 6-4). You will typically find your icons directory under C:\Program Files\Alias\Maya7.0\icons.

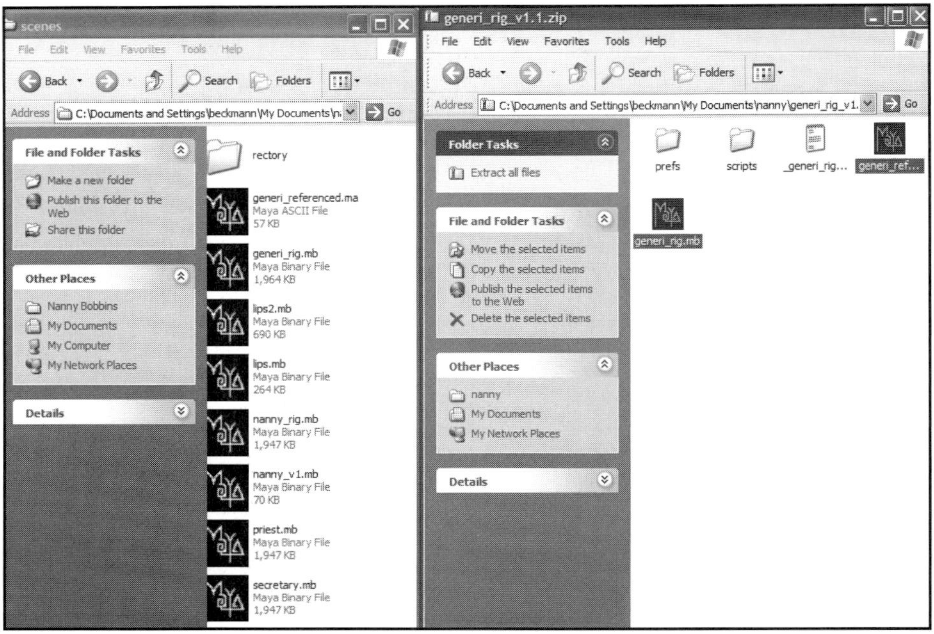

figure 6-3

Moving files.

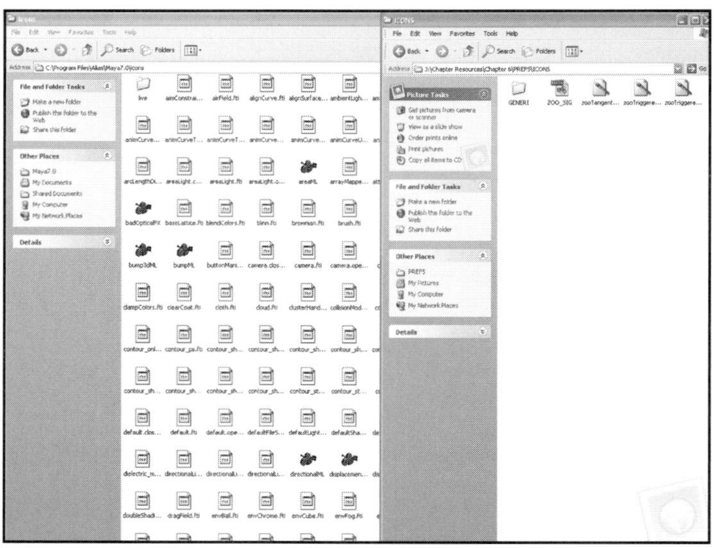

figure 6-4

The icons directory.

4. Move the contents of the prefs\shelves folder to your Shelves directory (see Figure 6-5). You will typically find your shelves directory under C:\Program Files\Alias\Maya7.0\shelves.

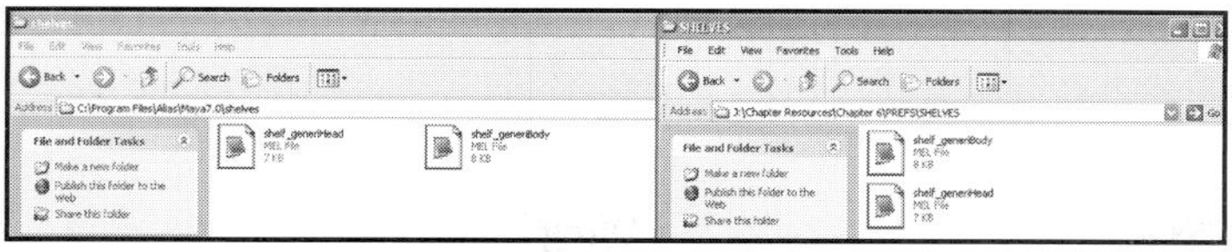

figure 6-5

The shelves directory.

5. Move the contents of the scripts folder to your Scripts directory (see Figure 6-6). You will typically find your scripts directory under C:\Program Files\Alias\Maya7.0\scripts.

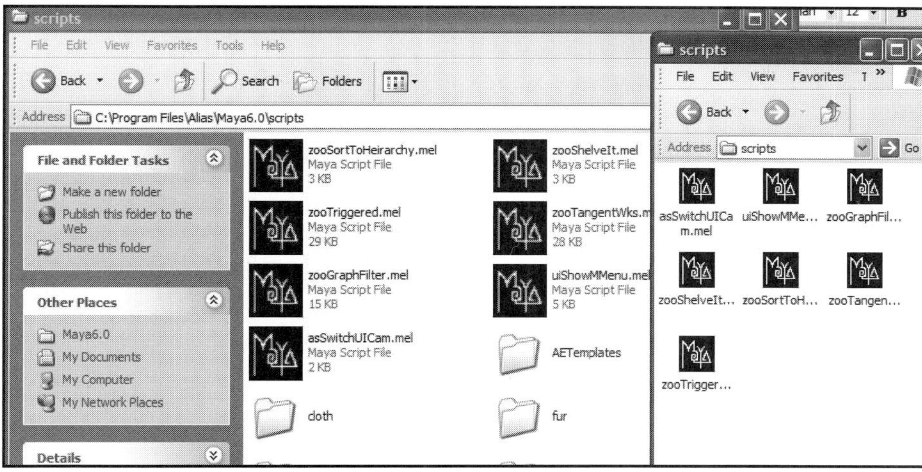

figure 6-6

The scripts directory.

The rig will work without any scripts; however, the trigger User Interface requires scripts to run.

You are done loading your files.

6. Start Maya, and load both shelves. To load the shelves, go to the left side of the shelf and click on the black triangle and then Load Shelf (see Figure 6-7).

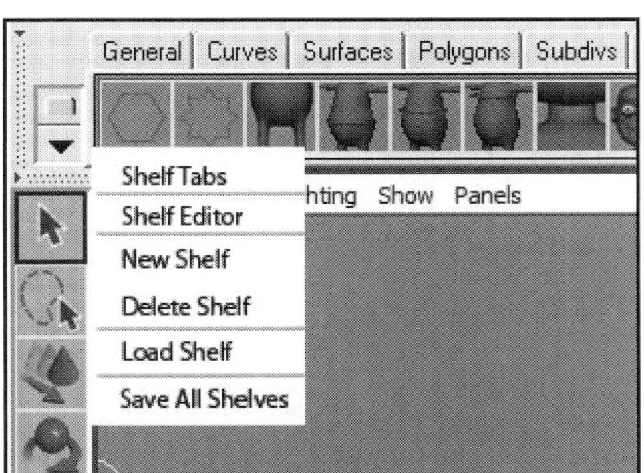

figure 6-7

The Load Shelf icon.

Then navigate to the shelves folder where you moved the shelves: C:\Program Files\Alias\Maya7.0\shelves (see Figure 6-8).

figure 6-8

The shelves folder.

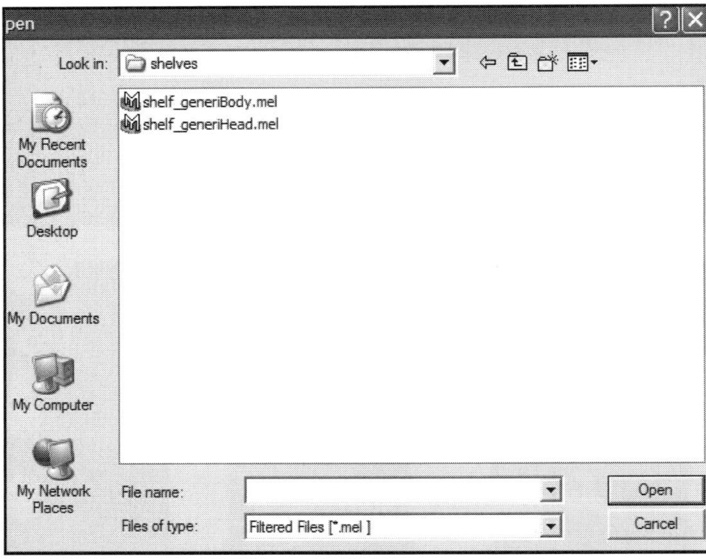

Click on the files you have just placed there: shelf_generiBody.mel and shelf_generiHead.mel. Select open. You are done loading your shelves.

7. In Maya, open generi_referenced.ma. This setup uses referenced files. When you reference a file, the actual model/rig is in another file and cannot be damaged regardless of what you do to the referenced rig in your scene. Also, you can update the original rig at any time in the animation (like changing textures, moving control vertices [CVs], etc.) by working on the puppet in the original file.

Generi 101

Once the file has loaded, it is best to show only polygons, NURBS, handles, and curves in your view window (see Figure 6-9).

It is also recommended that you change the select priority of nurbs Curves to a higher level so that you do not accidentally click on the mesh when you try to select a curve. To do this, go to the **Window > Settings/Preferences> Preferences window** and click on the Selection category. Then go to the Priority Presets drop-down menu, and switch to Custom. Scroll down to nurbsCurve, and change its priority value to **10** (see Figure 6-10). If you are using the trigger interface, you might also set NURBS to **11** so that you do not select through the user interface (UI) objects. Click on Save.

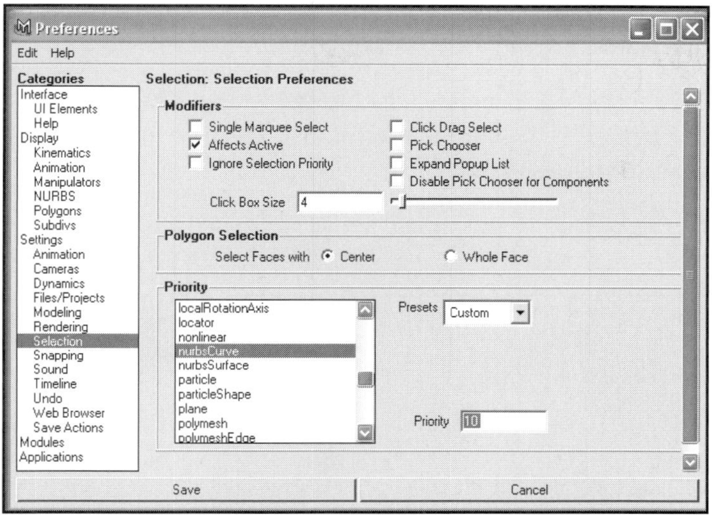

figure 6-10

Change the nurbsCurve preset to 10.

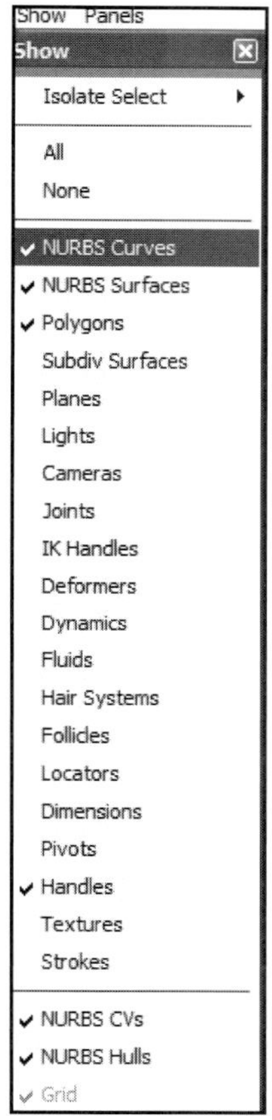

figure 6-9

Turn on NURBS, handles, and curves.

Selecting the Controls

You have three ways to select the puppet controls:

1. Select the curves/handles on the rig.
2. Select the trigger interface objects.
3. Use the shelf icons (see Figures 6-11 and 6-12).

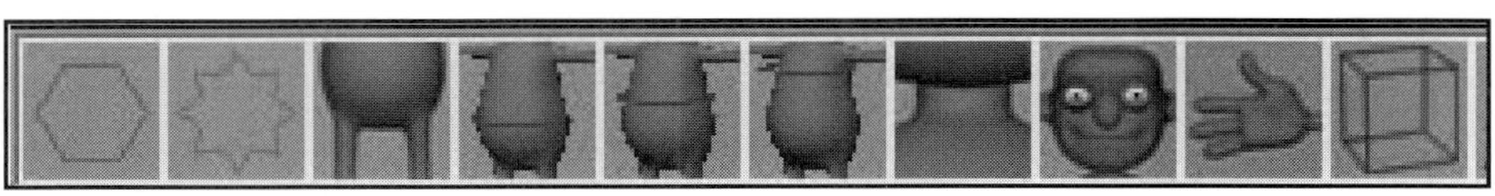

figure 6-11

Shelf buttons for body.

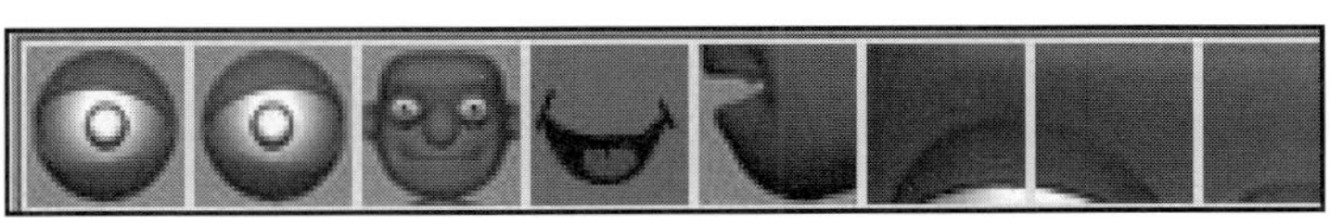

figure 6-12

Shelf buttons for face.

The shelf buttons toggle on/off so you can select more than one object at a time. Be careful; once you select something, it is selected until you deselect it. If your shelves are not filled with pictures, your icons are not loaded properly. Repeat that portion of your setup.

The animatable attributes for each control are in the Channel Box. In Figure 6-13 the head is selected, and the animatable controls show up in the Channel Box.

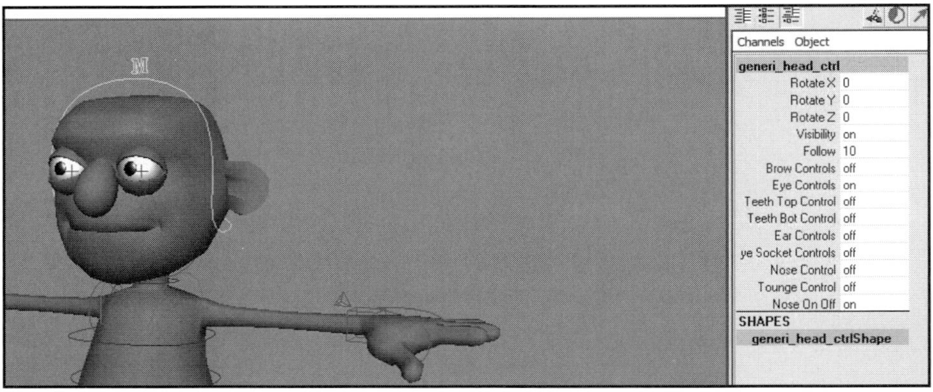

figure 6-13

The Channel Box shows what can be animated.

It is important to use the middle-mouse click+drag functionality of the Channel Box. To do this, click on the attribute you wish to change (found in the Channel Box), and then middle-mouse click and drag left/right in the 3D viewport. This provides slider-like interactivity. Important!

Toggle Hi-Res/Low-Res Model

A low-res body and head are included to speed up animation playback (see Figure 6-14). Figure 6-15 shows another version for comparison.

They look a lot alike until you move them. Then you will notice that the low-res model is chopped up. The hi-res model is smooth all over. When you animate, work with the low-res version, as it will be quicker. The low-res version is made with polygons, so it will render more quickly and use less memory to playblast. Switch to the hi-res version when you are ready to render.

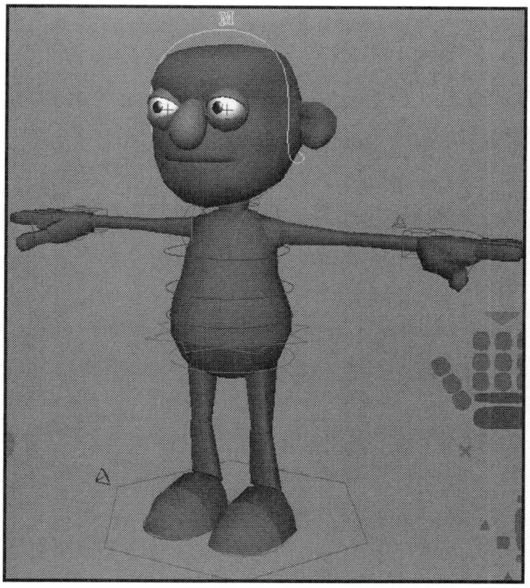

figure 6-14

Low-res body.

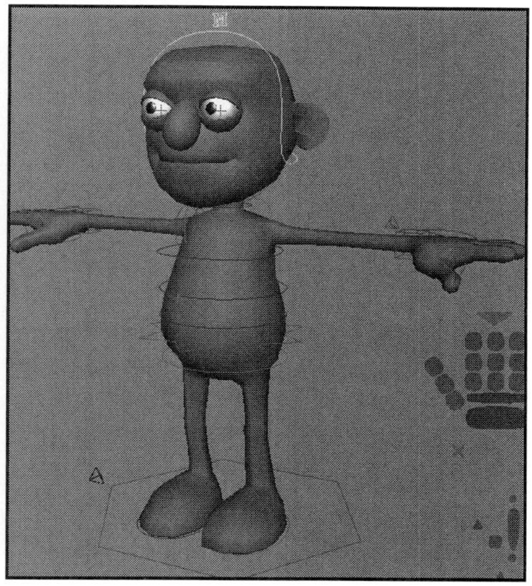

figure 6-15

Hi-res body.

To switch between hi- and lo-res, toggle the visibility of the layers in the layer bar (see Figures 6-16 and 6-17).

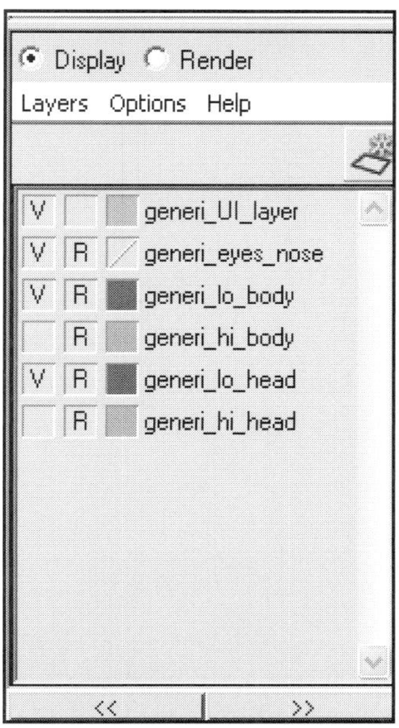

figure 6-16

Lo-res visibility toggled on.

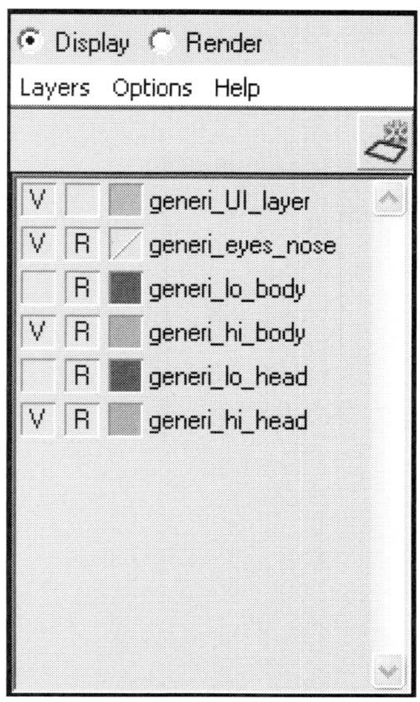

figure 6-17

Hi-res visibility toggled on.

To Smooth the Hi-res Mesh

Click on the cog_ctrl (red star) at the waist (see Figure 6-18).

figure 6-18

The cog_ctrl is found at the hips.

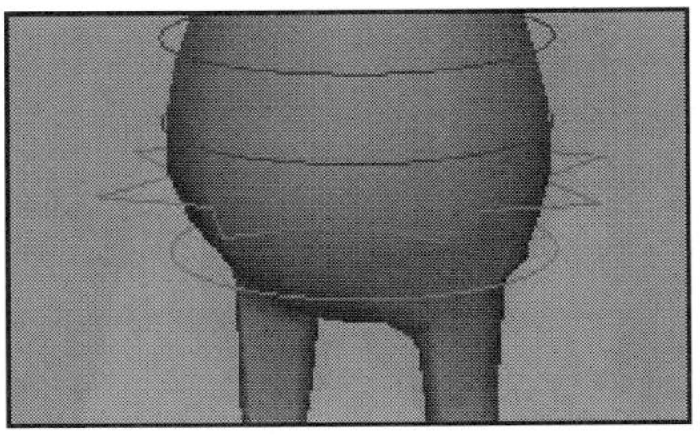

Change the Smooth Head, Smooth Body, and Smooth Lids attributes (see Figure 6-19). You can also change the opacity of the Trigger UI here.

figure 6-19

Attributes available for the cog_ctrl.

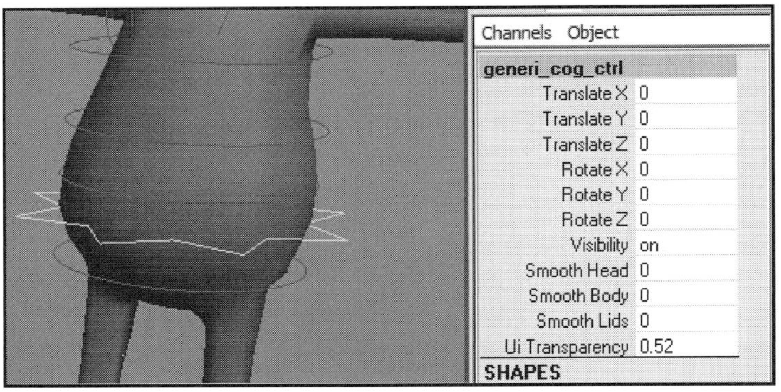

Moving the Rig Around

There are two ways to move Generi through space:

1. If Generi is animated and you want to position him in a scene you have just imported him into, use the moveAll_ctrl (see Figure 6-20). This is the hexagon-shaped control at the bottom of the puppet.

figure 6-20

The moveAll_ctrl.

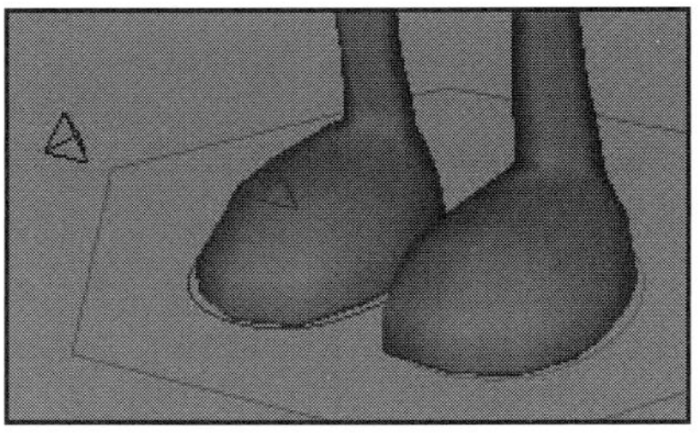

Do not animate this control when creating a walk or other repositioning movement. This control is your safety net. You only use this to reposition your character in the scene.

2. If you want to start blocking out a walk cycle for your character and you need to move him across the scene, use the cog_ctrl function (see Figure 6-21). This way you are still able to effectively use the IK on the legs.

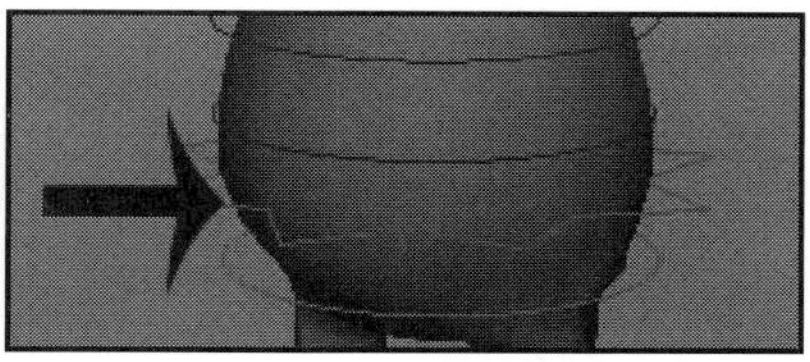

figure 6-21

The cog_ctrl.

Fingers

With Generi, you must individually rotate finger joints. You can use the selection sets in the Outliner to select finger joints, but it is much easier to use the Trigger UI controls (see Figure 6-22).

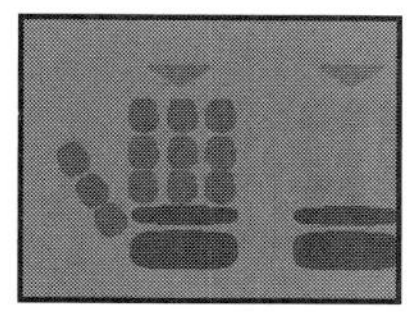

figure 6-22

Trigger UI for fingers.

If you want to use selection sets, they are found in the Outliner just below the geo files (see Figure 6-23). The sets are _anim_fingers_L and _anim_fingers_R. Make sure you have sets visible in the Outliner. Open each set in the Outliner for easy access. Rotate the finger bones accordingly.

You can easily build your own set-driven keys if there are some common hand positions you would like to animate. We will discuss set driven keys in an advanced animation book.

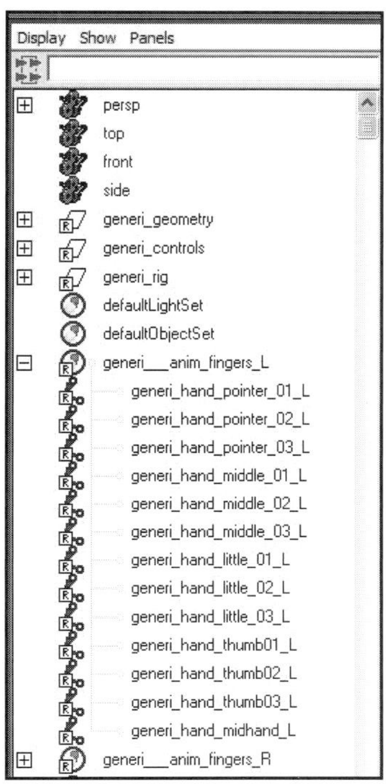

figure 6-23

Look in the Outliner for the finger controls.

Arms

Arms can be either forward kinematics or inverse kinematics. The IK/FK switch is found on each hand rotation control (see Figure 6-24).

The controls will show up in the Channel Box (see Figure 6-25).

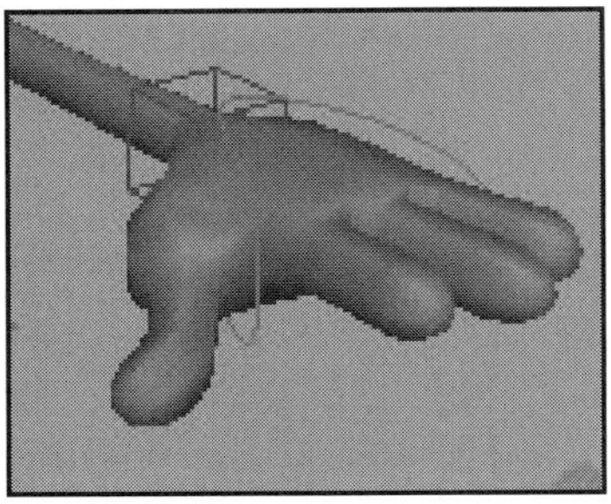

figure 6-24

Hand control is the curved object on the hand.

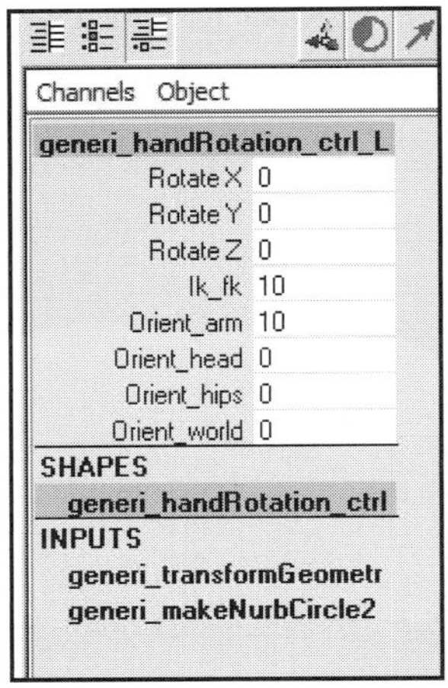

figure 6-25

See IK_FK.

A setting of 10 means IK is turned on, and you can select the box at the wrist to move the arm. A setting of 0 means FK is turned on, and a circle control will appear at the shoulder. This circle leads you to a Channel Box wherein you can access the rotate controls for the arm and elbow (see Figure 6-26). We will do FK in Chapter 7.

figure 6-26

Use the box for IK.

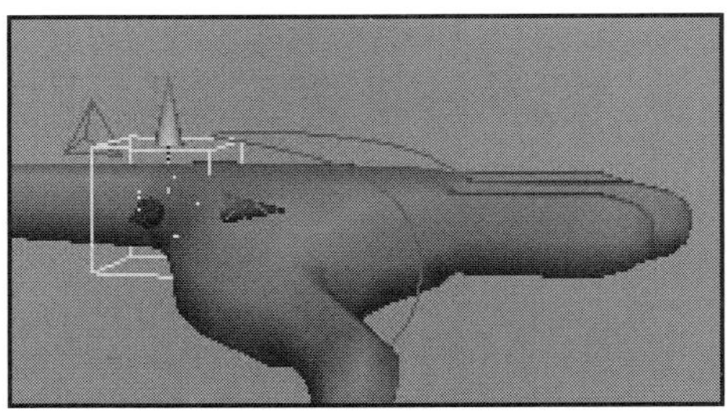

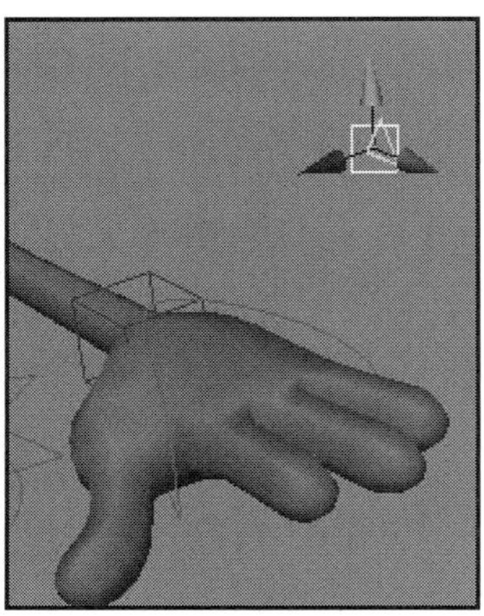

figure 6-27

Elbow pole vectors.

Inverse kinematics: The IK box will not appear at the wrist if you are set for FK.

Use the triangular pole vectors to point the elbows (see Figure 6-27). Often the arms will twist around on themselves due to something called a "pole vector," which you will learn about in your rigging studies. The pole vector allows you to limit this twisting and even animate the way the elbow points.

Look at the Orient controls on the hand. These allow you to set the hand orientation, which keeps the hand from twisting around when you move the puppet. We prefer to keep Orient_arm at a value of 10.

Forward kinematics: FK shoulder control will not appear if you are set for IK. You only get the shoulder control if you turn the FK value to 0 (see Figure 6-28).

The elbow bend is found on the shoulder control. Use the middle drag functionality of the Channel Box to change the values for the elbow bend, or simply type in a new value.

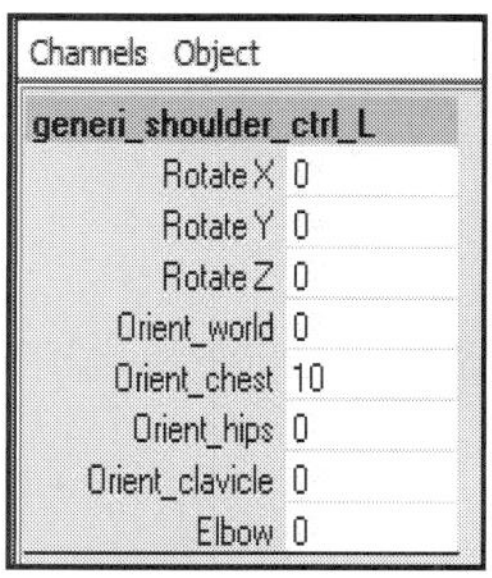

figure 6-28

The controls for FK.

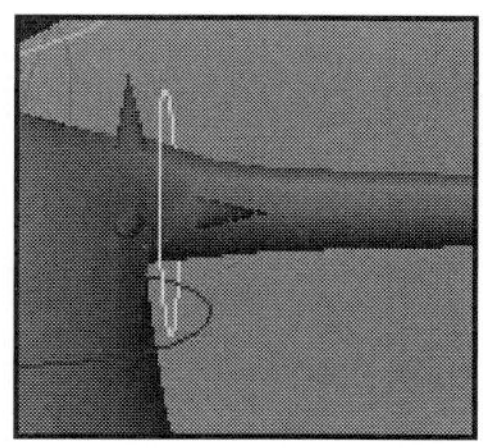

figure 6-29

Use the arm control for FK.

Most of the arm controls have parent constraints, so the hierarchy of animation can be altered (see Figure 6-29). These attributes can be animated midway through an animation. The attributes start with Pos_ or Orient_. Make sure the values of these attributes on each control add up to a total of 10 to keep anything odd from occurring.

You can also animate between FK and IK within the same scene by key-framing the IK/FK value.

Legs

You have the same FK/IK options available in the legs. Use the triangular-shaped knee constraints to point the knees (see Figure 6-30).

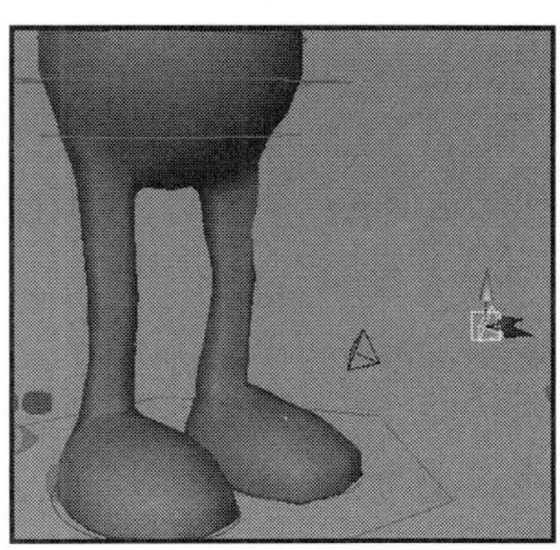

figure 6-30

To point the knees, move these.

You also have a few controls available to assist you with animating the role of the foot when walking. Notice the options available for heel, lift heel, toe, and bank (see Figure 6-31).

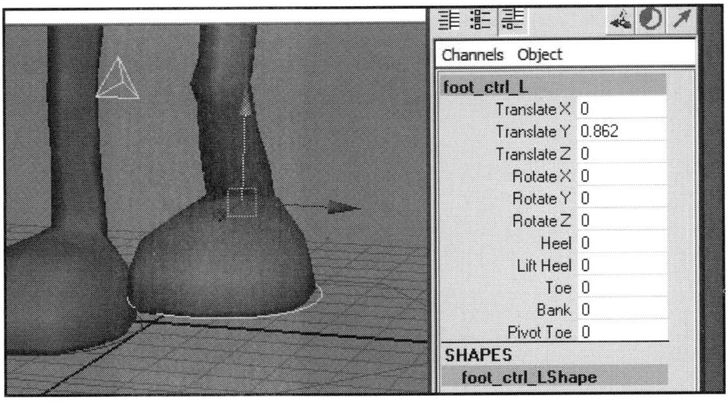

figure 6-31

Foot controls.

Change up the values here to see what happens to the foot. You will work with these in depth when you do the walk cycle.

Spine, Neck, and Hips

The spine, neck, and hips can only be rotated (see Figure 6-32). These are purely FK.

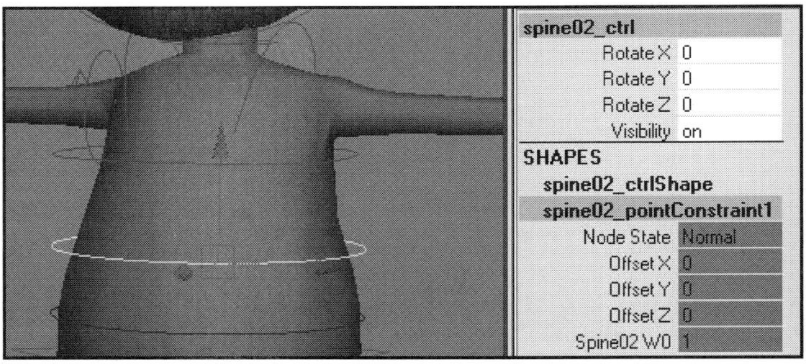

figure 6-32

Spine, neck, and hips.

The face controls will be described in Chapter 9 when you try a bit of facial animation.

SUMMARY

Generi is a wonderfully complex rig. You can just deal with the basic controls for simple animation, or you can dive into the advanced controls for more specific gestures. Make sure to experiment with the different controls a bit before you attempt any animation. Use this rig for the following chapter exercises.

in review

1. How do I switch from hi-res to low-res?
2. Why would I want to work in low-res?
3. When would I use hi-res?
4. Which appendages have pole vectors?
5. What UI control is visible on the puppet when you have set the limb to IK?
6. What UI control is visible on the puppet when you have set the limb to FK?
7. Can you animate between FK and IK?

EXPLORING ON YOUR OWN

1. Try a simple hand wave.
2. Pose the rig a few different ways to gain an understanding of the controls. Make Generi sit, lie down, or appear to leap in midair.
3. Make Generi achieve a few ballet positions.

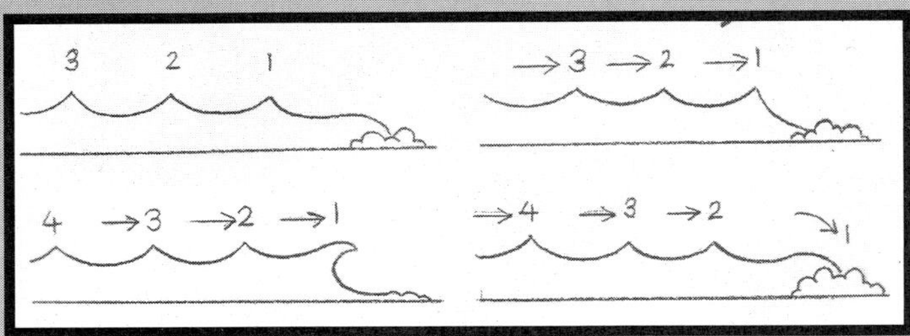

7 practicing principles

PRACTICING PRINCIPLES

charting your course

Believable character animation requires an innate understanding of follow-through and overlapping action. In this chapter, you will practice these skills with a few short exercises in preparation for our eventual walk cycle.

goals

In this chapter, you will:

- Understand forward kinematics and how it differs from inverse kinematics.
- Learn about ghosting.
- Practice follow-through and overlapping action.
- Successfully edit a more sophisticated set of curves.
- Learn how to set motion blur.

TOOLS USED

- **Forward kinematics.** Forward kinematics (FK) involves moving each individual skeleton joint to achieve movement. It works a lot like stop-motion animation. Imagine a doll that has movable joints, such as GI Joe. Move the arm at the shoulder for an upward arc, then move the elbow, and cock the hand in a wave. This is how FK works.
- **Ghosting.** Ghosting is a technique that allows you to see the entire animation in one image. A wireframe of each image in the animation is composited onto one frame and can be interactively edited.
- **Motion blur.** You can add the illusion of speed with a bit of motion blur. Motion blur smears the moving parts of the image to infer speed.

FORWARD KINEMATICS

Open the file ArmFK.mb on the enclosed CD (see Figure 7-1).

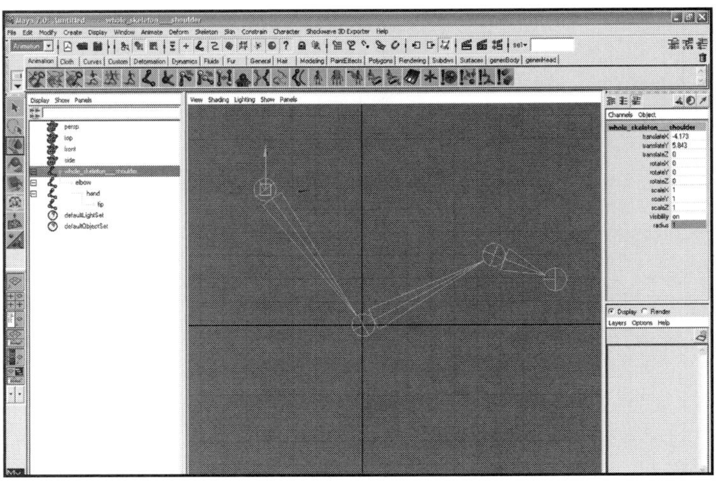

figure | 7-1 |

The interface of the whole_shoulder file.

This is a basic skeleton rig for an arm. You are expected to animate it using FK. Next you will do a simple demo. Set your tangents in Preferences to spline, weighted, and use the S key to set your key frames.

First, look in the Outliner window. You will see a skeleton object named whole_shoulder (see Figure 7-2).

This is the top node of the skeleton rig. If you select the top node of the skeleton and then Shift + left-mouse click over the plus sign, the entire hierarchy will be displayed.

Go to the first frame of the animation. Select the top node (whole_shoulder), and set a key frame at frame 1 by pressing the shortcut key S or by using the interactive tool **Animate** > **Set Key** (see Figure 7-3).

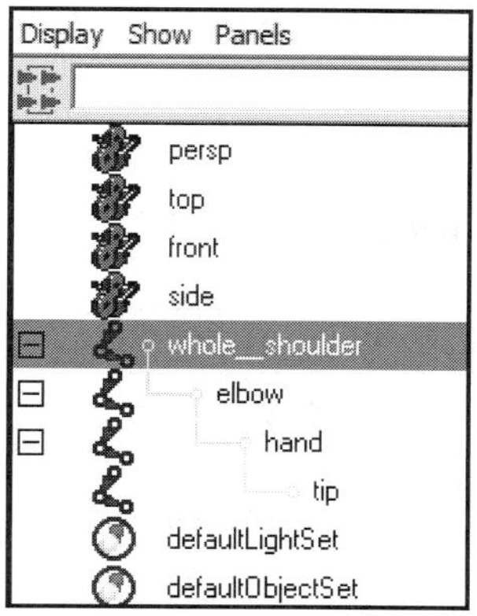

figure 7-2

The whole_shoulder object.

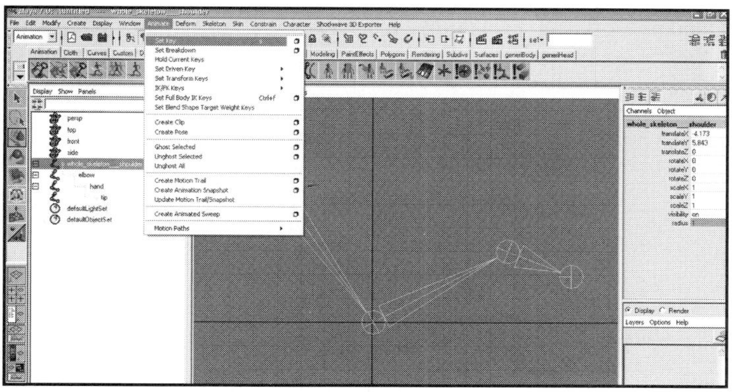

figure 7-3

Set a key frame for the shoulder.

Then open your Channel Box. Go to frame 30. In Rotate Z of the Channel Box, type **70** (see Figure 7-4). Create a key frame.

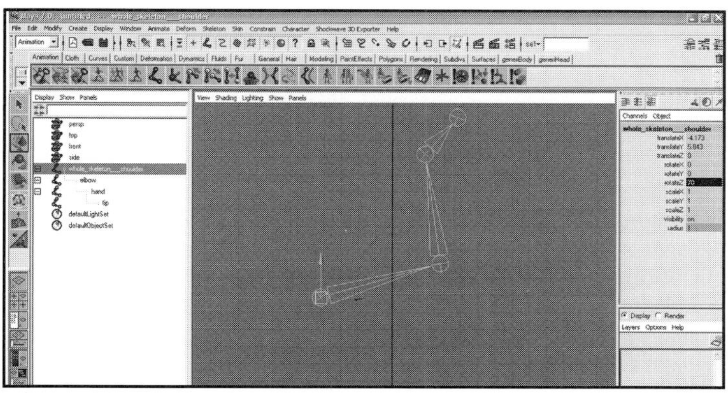

figure 7-4

Rotate Z at 70.

Now play your animation using the controls at the bottom of the interface (see Figure 7-5). They look like those on a VCR.

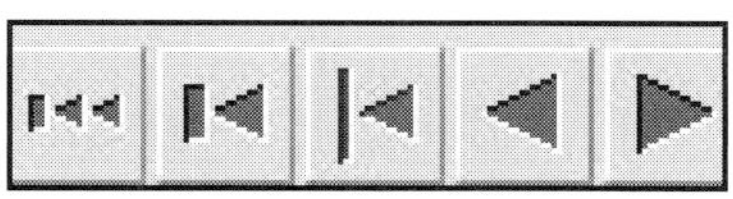

figure 7-5

Playback Controls.

The arm rotates. Now you will work with the elbow and the hand. Go to frame 2, and select the elbow joint. Set a key frame.

Go to frame 28, and select Rotate Z in the Channel Box. Set the value to **45** in Rotate Z. Set a key frame (see Figure 7-6).

Select the hand, and go to key frame 22. Set a key frame.

figure | 7-6 |

Rotate Z at 45 on frame 28.

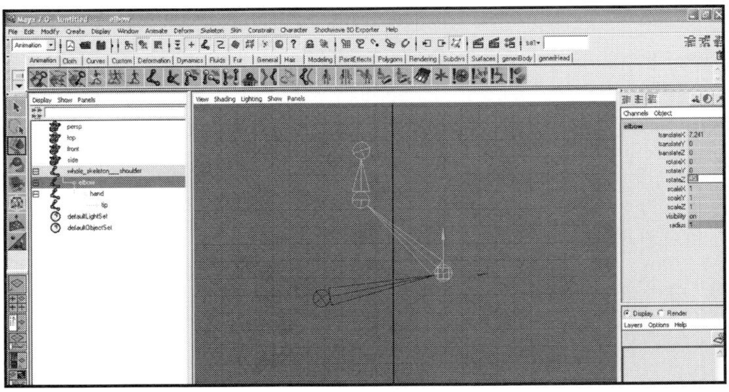

Go to key frame 26, and in the Rotate Z Channel Box, enter the value **70**. Set a key frame. At frame 30, set a key frame for Rotate Z for **−20**. Play the animation, and you will have a little wave (see Figure 7-7). Before ghosting it, we tweaked the Graph Editor curves, which is what a good animator does. This presentation is simple and does need work, but is satisfactory for a simple FK demonstration.

That is how you animate using FK.

For character animation, arms are usually animated using FK. They tend to look more natural. When inverse kinematics (IK) is used on arms, they tend to look like marionettes. The hand tends to direct the movement of the arm. With FK, the shoulder leads the arm, which is more natural to human movement.

Legs tend to use IK, which has a built-in constraint that locks the limb to a point in time. If the torso or body moves, the limbs still stay locked to the point in time to which they were key-framed. You can pull them away, but the limbs will always point to the constraints. FK does not have a constraint, so the limbs move with the torso.

Think of it like this—with IK, it is like using tacks to hold your limbs in place, and the body follows. With FK, it is like animating limb by limb in stop motion.

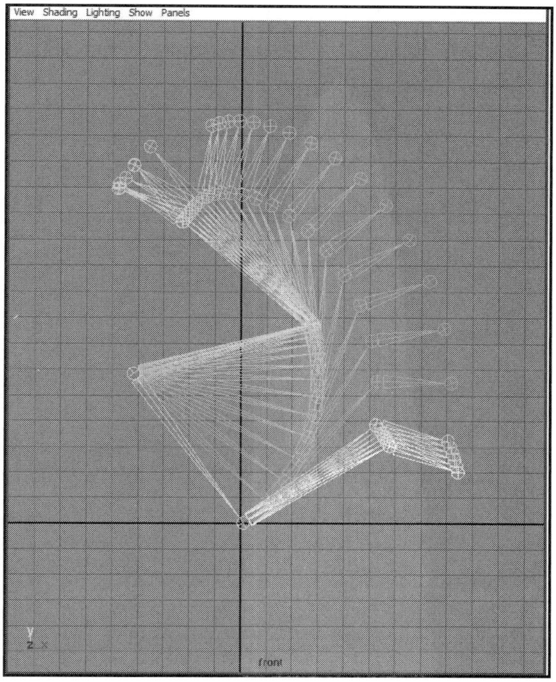

figure 7-7

A wave, using ghosting.

GHOSTING

Open the file ball_bounce.mb on the attached CD.

Here you have a 13-frame bounce. If you press Play, you see the bounce. Now you will ghost it.

Make sure you are in the Animation module. Select a Camera view as your active window. Select your ball as the ghosted object.

Select **Animate** > **Ghost Selected** > **options box** (see Figure 7-8).

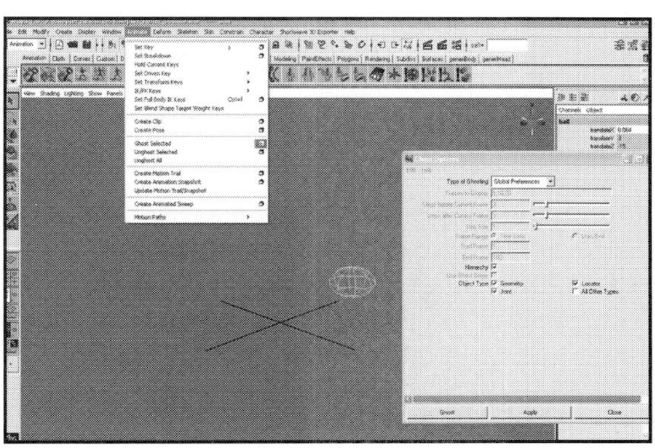

figure 7-8

How to get the ghost.

The new interface that opens has several options for ghosting. Choose the option Keyframes so that every key pose is viewable (see Figure 7-9).

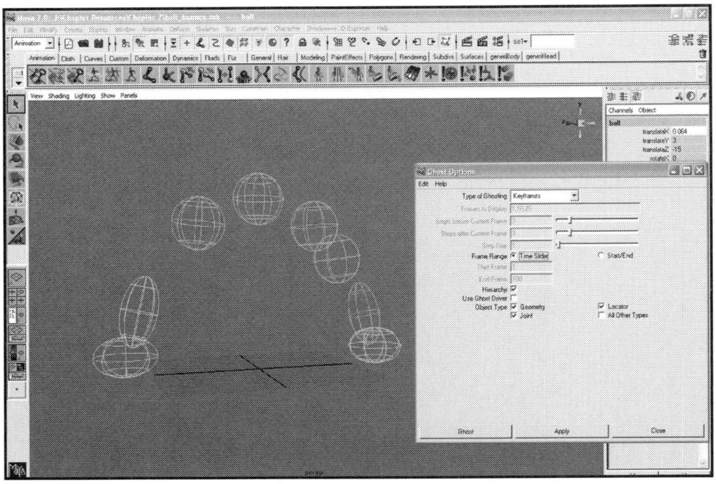

figure 7-9

Ghosted key frames.

You can change your key poses and watch the changes automatically update. Go to a key pose, and translate the ball up or down. Notice that the curves leading in and out will not change. This is because you are not viewing the interpolated images.

To view the interpolated (in-betweens that the computer creates) images, change your ghosting preferences. In the Ghost Options window, select Global Preferences (see Figure 7-10). You will now

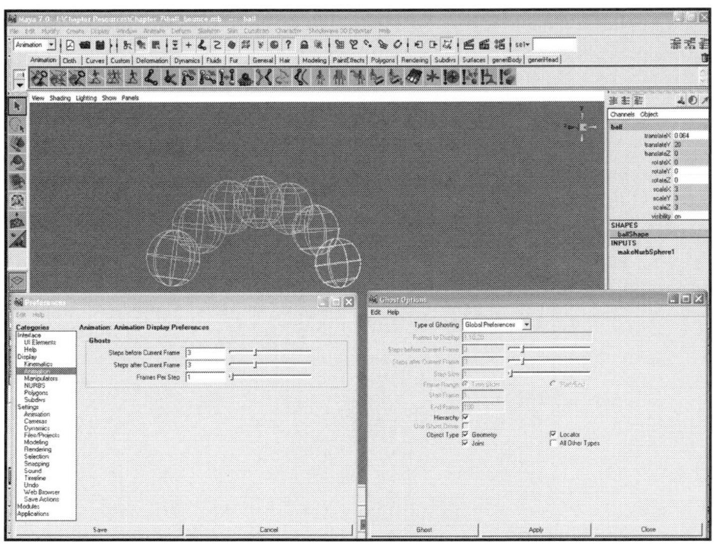

figure 7-10

Global preferences.

see a ghost based on the images interpolated three before and three after the image.

If you want to see more, go to your Preferences under Animation and increase the steps. Now move your key frame. The interpolated images leading in and out will change in accordance with the key pose.

PLAYBLAST

Open the file ball_bounce.mb on the attached CD. Select **Window** > **Playblast** > **options box** (see Figure 7-11).

You will get the PlayblastOptions box (see Figure 7-12).

We prefer to make a series of images and then play them in Fcheck. To set up options to allow this, select Fcheck, and

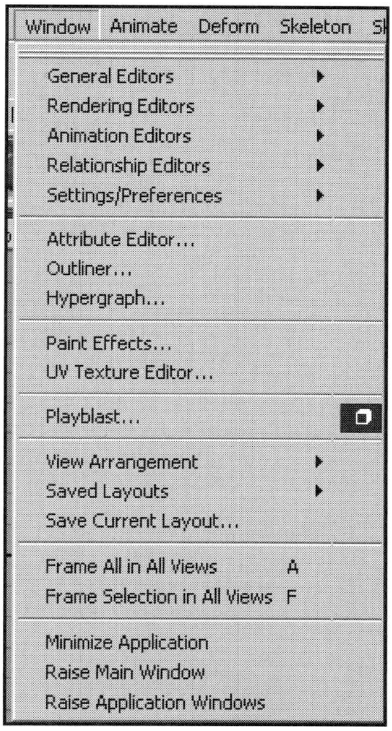

figure 7-11 How to get to Playblast.

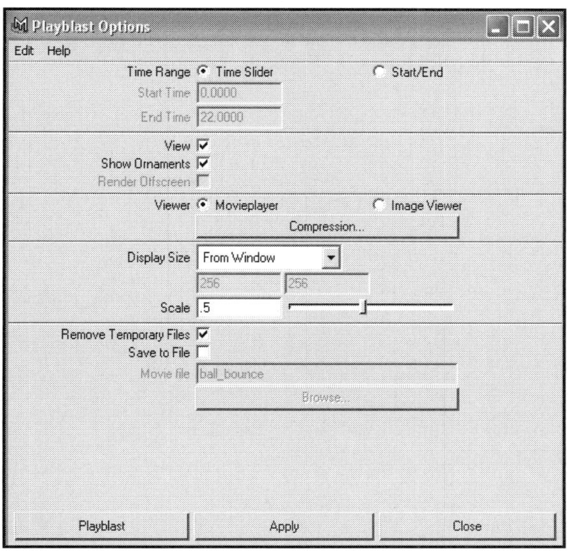

figure 7-12 The Playblast Options box with default settings.

Save to File. Then find the directory path to store these images (see Figure 7-13).

figure 7-13

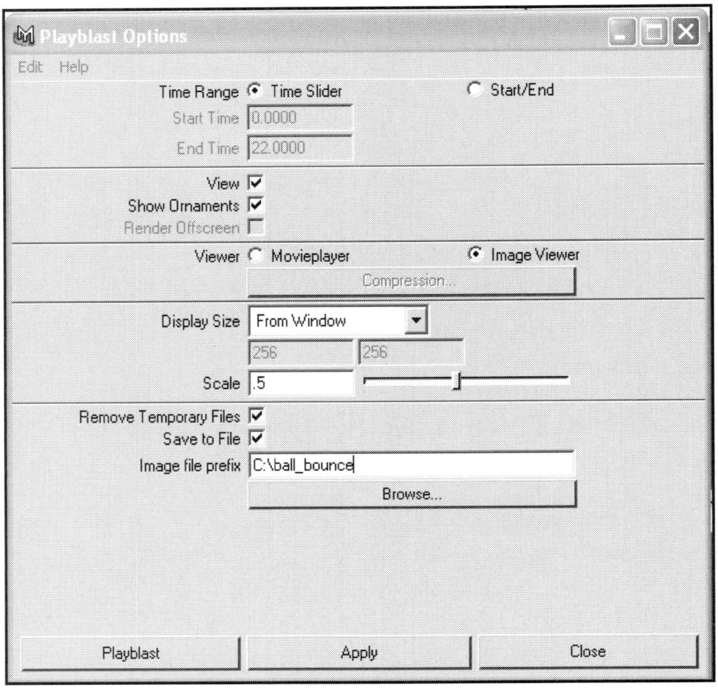

Change the options.

Then click on Playblast to create the files. A player should automatically open in your window on completion.

SKELETON, JOINTS, AND SKIN

This section shows you the basics on how the skeleton, joints, and skin work in Maya. You are encouraged to study rigging in addition to movement.

DON'T GO THERE!

Don't enter the field of animation with the sole expectation of getting a job as a character animator. The understanding of movement is only one part of the job. You should also have an understanding of rigging, modeling, texturing, and story. When the deadline for a project hits, it is all hands on deck. Your employer will need you to fill multiple positions in a pinch.

First we will get to know what a joint is. "Joints" is the technical term for the "bones" of the puppet. They make up the skeleton. The actual puppet is attached to these bones through a process called skinning.

Skinning involves attaching the model to these bones. These bones then aid in controlling the puppet. To do this, we will create clusters from the control vertices (CVs) that make up the model and attach them to the bones.

Close this file, and create a new file.

We next make a simple cluster from CVs and attach them to a joint. Make a NURBS sphere. Look at it in Component mode with CVs visible (see Figure 7-14).

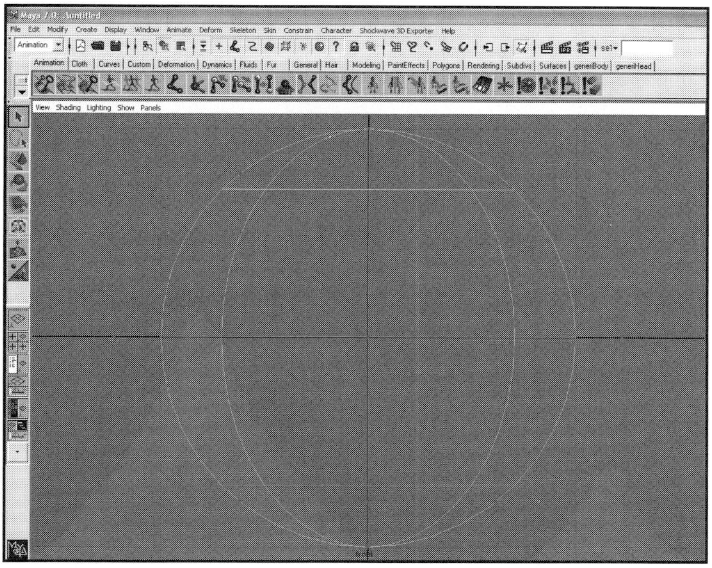

figure | 7-14 |

NURBS sphere in component mode.

Select the upper two rows of CVs (see Figure 7-15).

You will group these vertices into a cluster. A cluster operates like a ponytail holder. When hair is loose, it moves as the head dictates. When you gather it into a braid and enclose it with a ponytail holder, individual hairs move as one, even though they are still attached to the head.

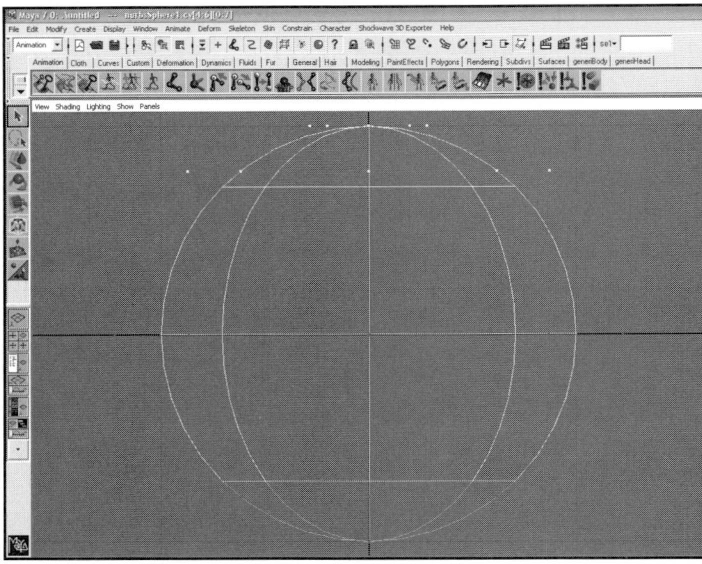

figure 7-15

Select CVs.

Use the command **Deform > Create Cluster** (see Figure 7-16).

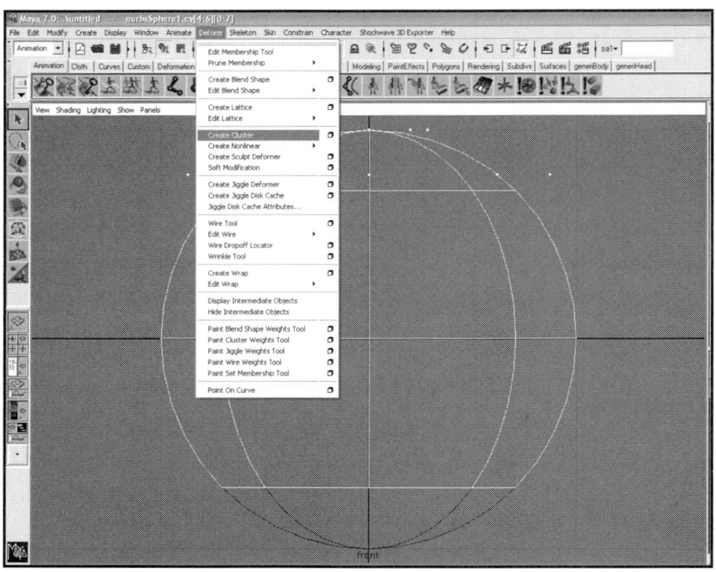

figure 7-16

Deform > Create Cluster.

Now look at your sphere. Look also in the Outliner (see Figure 7-17).

You will see a letter C in the middle of your Manipulator icon in the sphere. In the Outliner window, you will see a green cluster of grapes called cluster1Handle.

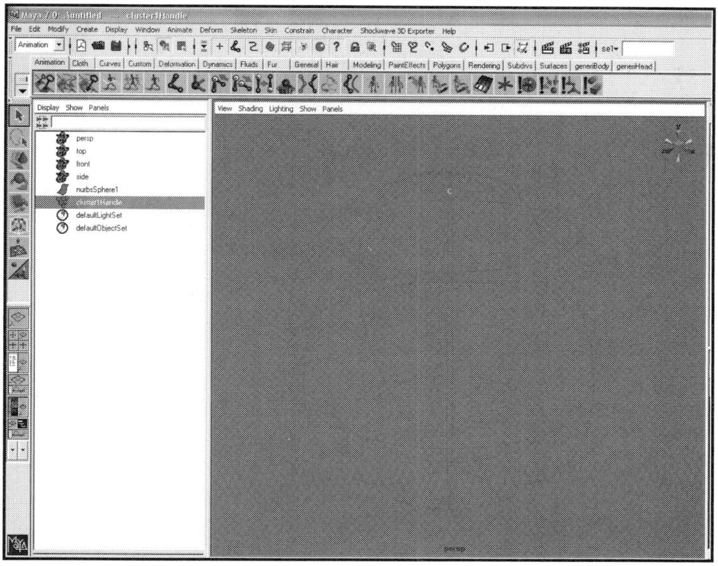

figure 7-17

The letter C appears, and a grape cluster shows in the Outliner.

Select the cluster1Handle in the Outliner, and move this cluster upward in the Y Translate (see Figure 7-18).

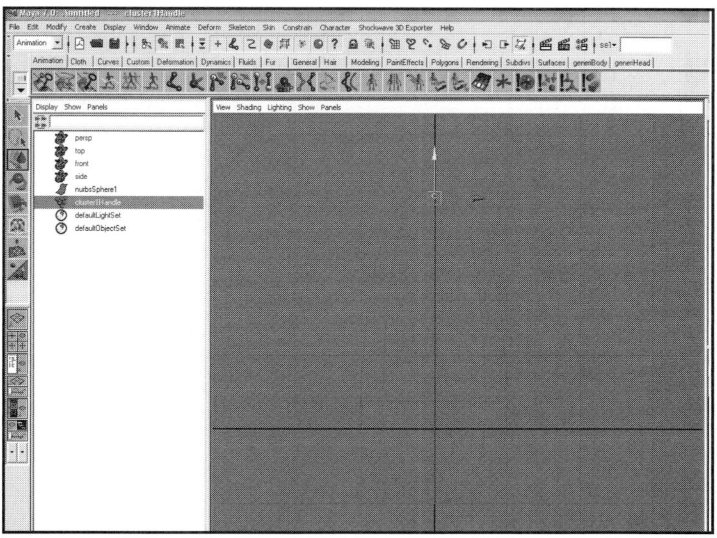

figure 7-18

Moving the cluster.

Notice how the rest of the sphere is stationary, though the cluster easily pulls the grouped CVs to a new destination. Now delete the cluster, and your sphere is back to normal (see Figure 7-19).

figure | 7-19 |

The deleted cluster does not affect the original model.

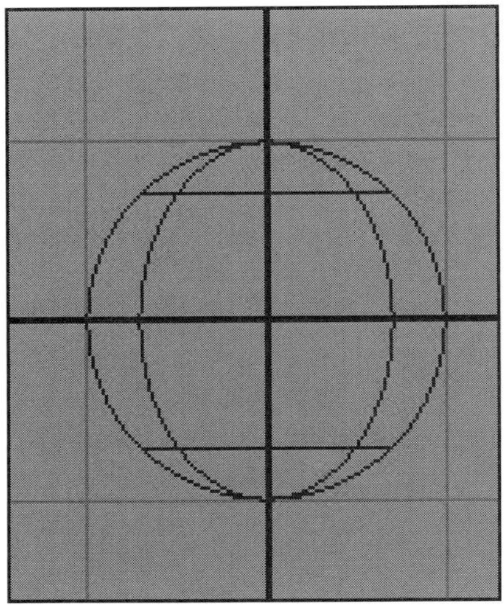

Joints work with clusters (see Figure 7-20).

figure | 7-20 |

Generi's joint skeleton.

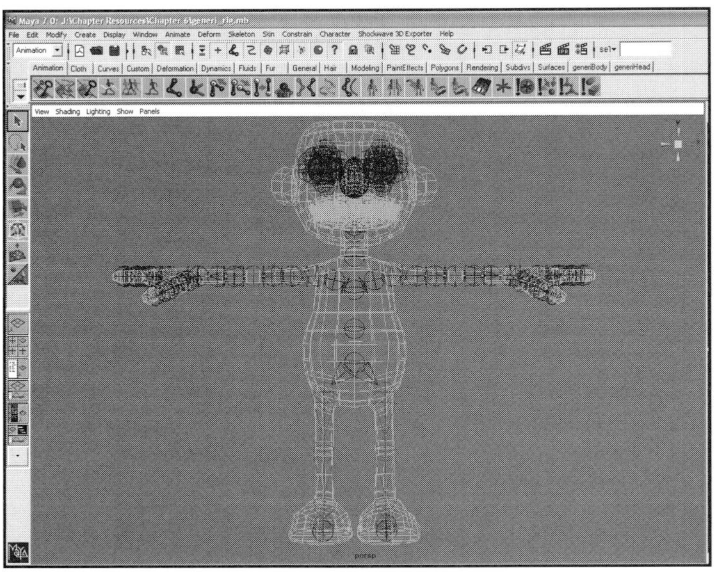

After the skeleton for a model is built, the model is attached to the skeleton. Maya groups the CVs of the model and connects them in clusters to the nearest joint. The joint then controls these clusters in weighted percentages. If you delete the skeleton and clusters, the original model still remains intact.

A lot of cleanup must happen after skinning. As with anything created by default in Maya, it must be tweaked to serve the end user's purpose. Clusters must be reassigned and weights altered. Often extra tools like lattices are used to make a cleaner bind. Again, learn rigging after you have tried out your animation skills.

In larger studios, animators work with technical directors responsible for creating rigs. They work closely together, translating the storyboard into an actual scene. In smaller studios, the animator must know how to build his or her own rig.

INITIATION OF MOVEMENT THROUGH CONNECTING PARTS

Next you will consider some principles of movement and how they work as the force of motion travels through an object or a series of objects in a process called a "wave pattern." This pattern runs consistently through all things connected with articulated or flexible parts and passes from primary actions into overlapping or secondary actions.

A fundamental example of a wave pattern can be seen in a cracking whip. In the whip, you find the movement initiated from the handle being put through a quick movement at one end. The movement then follows the length of the whip to the other end, causing a loud "pop" as the tip suddenly reverses as its inertia is broken (actually a miniature "sonic boom"!) (see Figure 7-21).

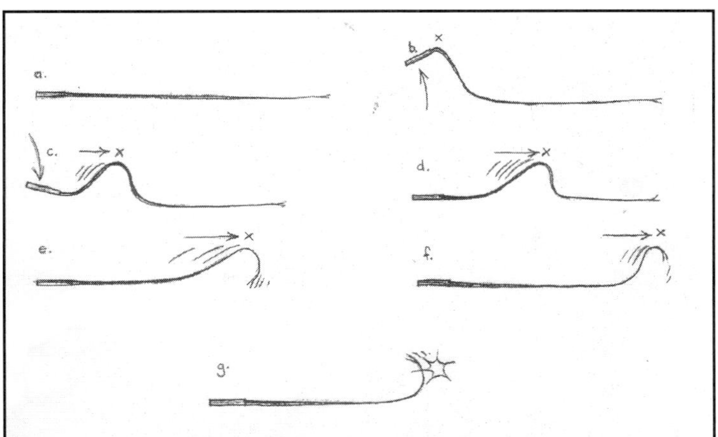

figure 7-21

A whip cracking.

Here is another good example of a wave pattern: the action of ocean waves traveling shoreward and resulting in surf breaking on a shoreline. As easily seen in Figure 7-22, the pattern of waves can be

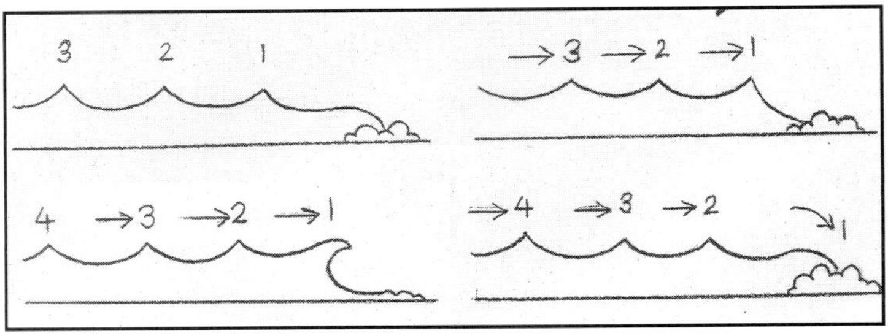

figure 7-22

A wave in motion.

tracked as they flow to the shore (we will use numbers at the top of each wave), and the end result once again is an exhibition of power, in this case the surf pounding the shoreline.

Now you will apply the wave pattern illustration to a living being, and you will find similarities to the other examples shown, as well as marked differences. The body is a series of connected, articulated parts. Although there are solid, non-flexing pieces within some bodily parts, there are also a multitude of flexible joints and soft tissues, allowing this structure to demonstrate the same sort of wave action in its movements.

Realize that the wave patterns in the whip and the ocean waves were produced outside of those subjects and were involuntary in those bodies. Wave patterns in a living organism are likewise initiated at one end of a connected chain, transmitted through successive parts, effectively producing a resulting reaction. The main difference is that in the motion demonstrated here, the action is voluntary and produced with a thought to accomplishing a result.

Try It in Maya

Open the file whip.mb on the enclosed CD. This simple rig will allow you to animate the wave pattern using FK. You will see a simple skeleton comprised of 10 joints.

Set your window to look like Figure 7-23, and set up the timeline from 1 to 30. For practice, also set your tangents to linear and stepped.

Select the entire skeleton. You will be setting key frames for each individual joint, so you will need to get used to moving up and down

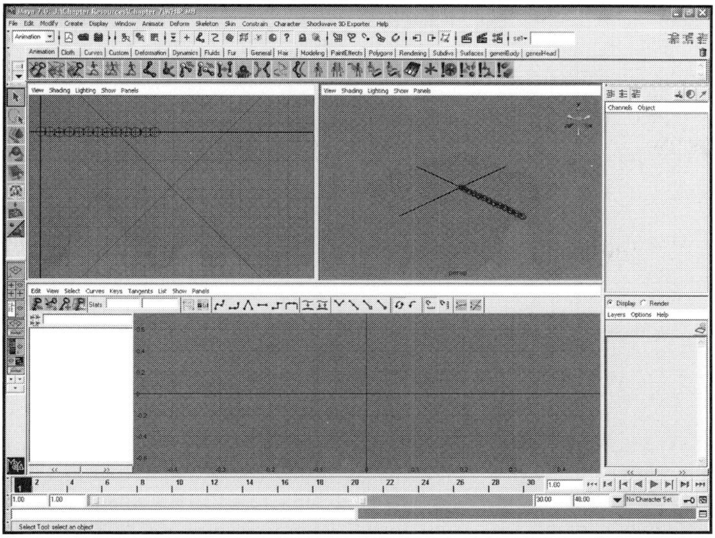

figure 7-23

The whip.

the hierarchy. With the entire skeleton selected, press the downward arrow key on the keyboard.

You will notice that one less joint is selected. Press the downward arrow key again. One less is selected.

When you set key frames for each wave pose, you will need to go down the hierarchy and set key frames for each joint. There is an easier way to do this, but it is important that you first learn the basics. Knowing this method and how it works will save you from some problems when working with a more complex rig. Use Figure 7-21 as reference for this exercise.

At frame 1, set a key frame for each of the 13 joints. You do not need to reposition the skeleton at this time.

Go to frame 8. Again, set the same key frames for the 13 joints for pose a.

On frame 22, set the pose for a because you will be looping this animation. In a loop, you need the start and end positions to match. Return to frame 10 and begin your animation.

You will work on twos. This means the next pose you set will be on frame 10, and you will set pose b (see Figure 7-24).

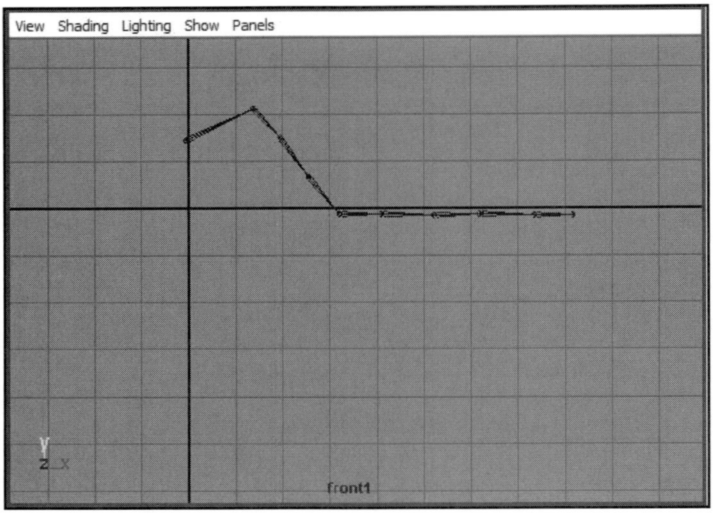

figure 7-24

Frame 10.

To set this pose, grab the root (joint1) and translate it up in the Y. Select the joint2 joint and rotate it in value to .77 in the Z to match pose b. If this value does not do that for you, adjust and use a value you think fitting. The third and fourth joints will not need to be rotated. The fifth joint will be rotated 50 in the Z. Using your up and down arrows, set key frames for the Y Translate and the Z Rotate of each joint.

On frame 12, using the same process, set the pose for c. Using your up and down arrows, set key frames for the Y Translate and the Z Rotate of each joint.

On frame 14, set the pose for d. Using your up and down arrows, set key frames for the Y Translate and the Z Rotate of each joint.

On frame 16, set the pose for e. Using your up and down arrows, set key frames for the Y Translate and the Z Rotate of each joint.

On frame 18, set the pose for f. Using your up and down arrows, set key frames for the Y Translate and the Z Rotate of each joint.

On frame 20, set the pose for g. Using your up and down arrows, set key frames for the Y Translate and the Z Rotate of each joint.

Play the animation using Playblast. You now have a loop of animation for a cracking whip.

Select the skeleton and turn on ghosting. Now you can analyze your motion curves by looking directly at a stop-action frame of movement.

Throwing a Ball

In this section, a simplified breakdown of the processes is used to accomplish the pitching of a ball, taken step by step through each part of the chain from start to finish.

Always use the best reference material you can get your hands on. You can always elaborate on the visuals, but without reference material, you can likely miss important details. For this example, we refer you to A-E shown in Figure 7-25.

Initially, the motion starts with the initiation of an anticipation move in the central part of the body, as the shoulder moves backward and the elbow comes up, the hand following. See A.

Now the elbow drops as the hand continues to rise to the top of its arc. See B.

The elbow now leads as the forearm comes forward. The hand reacts by tilting back in reaction to the move. See C.

The wrist begins to lead the move at this time. The momentum keeps the hand at a right angle to the forearm. See D.

The arm has extended into its full length, bringing about the final "snap" of the throwing action as the hand quickly straightens and releases the ball. See E.

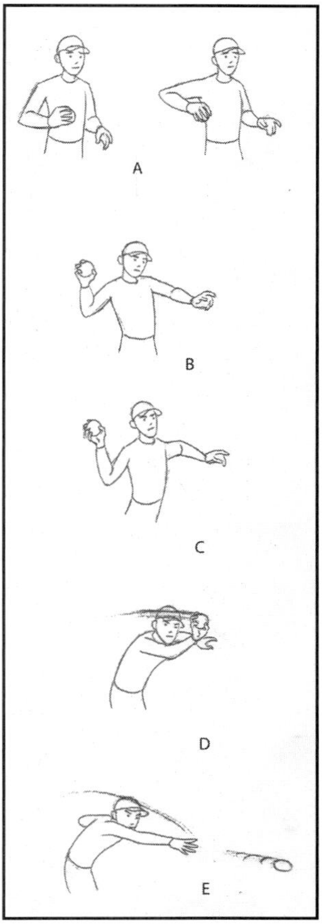

figure 7-25

The pitch in motion, steps A–E.

At this point, we can once again introduce the concepts of follow-through and overlapping action. This is one of the points where, as animators, we have the opportunity to enhance our work, unobtrusively making the action feel flowing and natural. Use the example of a batter hitting a ball, and notice what follows the actual hit.

As you have learned from the discussion of basic animation principles, an action presented successfully is not just a matter of getting from point A to point B and stopping. If you constructed the batting sequence in that manner, you would see the batter ready to swing, then the ball speeding in, then the swing, then the hit, and that would be the whole story. The batter could freeze right at that point with the bat in the middle of the arc of the swing (see Figure 7-26).

figure 7-26

The swing.

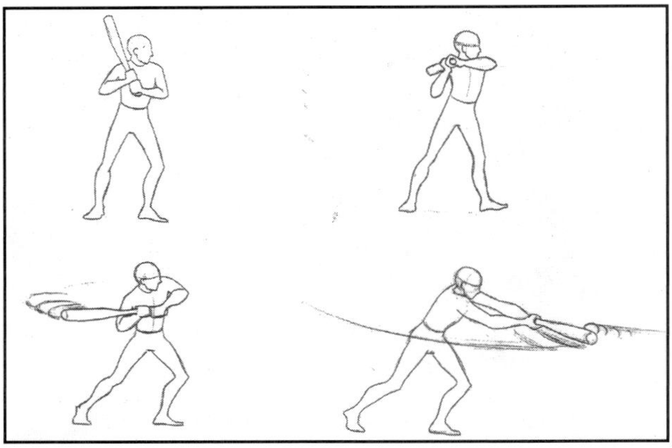

Now try it with points C, D, and so on added to finish the move.

One of the first things many animators discover in this type of action is that the actual "contact" drawing (the bat hitting the ball) is totally irrelevant in producing the desired effect. The dynamic of this kind of action is actually enhanced by an uninterrupted swing through the entire arc, letting the ball react to an implied hit, as shown in the following sequence. The whole action would play as explained here:

The batter is ready with the ball having been pitched. See A in Figure 7-27.

figure 7-27

The batter gets ready.

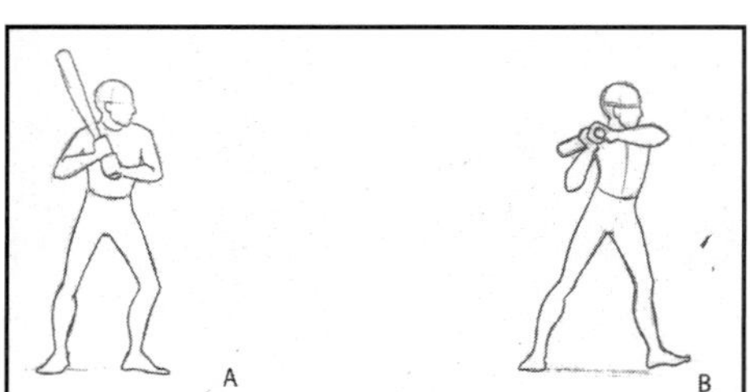

As the batter gets ready to swing, he steps in the direction of the ball, bringing the bat back in anticipation. See B in Figure 7-27.

Now comes the swing, quickly through the entire arc, with the reaction of the ball indicating the contact. See C in Figure 7-28.

At the extreme point of the swing, the batter's arms are wrapped around his body, his trailing hand having released the bat. See D in Figure 7-28.

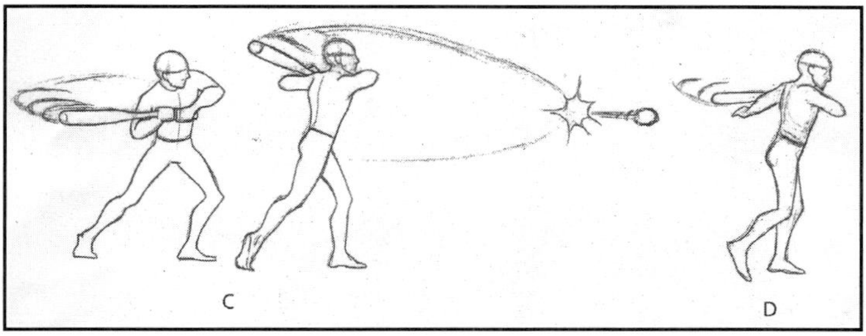

figure 7-28

The batter swings.

The hand holding the bat continues back in the opposite direction as the batter's body goes into anticipation for his run. See E in Figure 7-29.

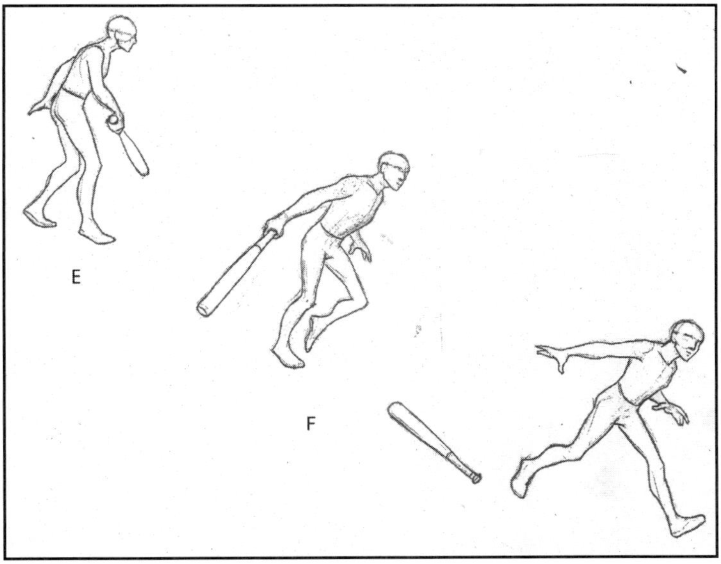

figure 7-29

Overlapping action.

Finally, in an example of interconnecting, overlapping action, the batter starts his run to first base, his hand continuing to swing to the rear in the same direction and releasing the bat. See F in Figure 7-29.

EDITING TIPS

Try the tools discussed in the following sections to enhance your editing skills.

Editing in the Timeline

The timeline can function as a handy editor. There are hidden tools available to you if you know where to look. Right-mouse click over the timeline to reveal a few (see Figure 7-30).

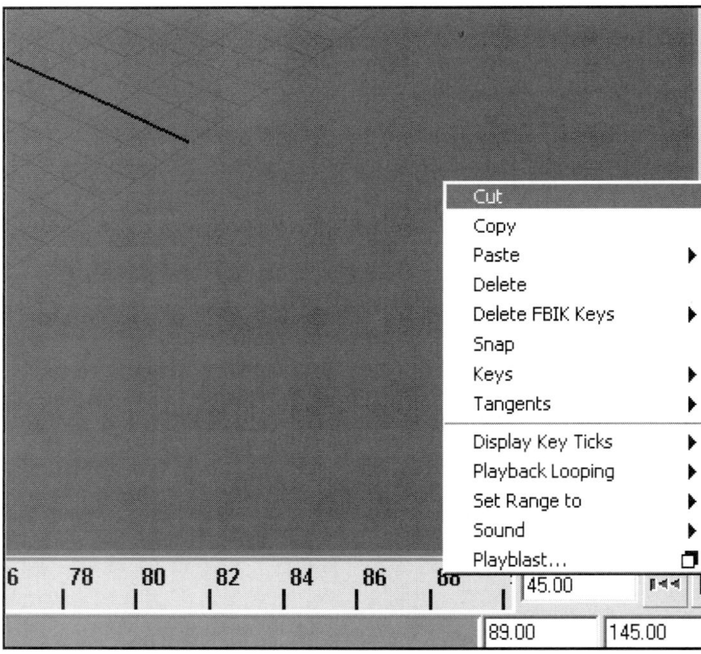

figure 7-30

The timeline and some of its secret controls.

Highlight a key, and select Cut from the secret menu. The key is no longer on the timeline. Select a new frame, and then select the Paste tool. You have taken the frame you cut from the last position and placed it in the new.

You have already used most of these tools before. Follow the arrows to the right of the tool to view your options. This menu is merely a shortcut, as Maya often stores tools in multiple places to speed your work process.

More editing tools exist in the timeline. Press the Shift button on your keyboard, then left-mouse select a frame on the timeline, and move your mouse to the right. You will see a red line take over your timeline (see Figure 7-31).

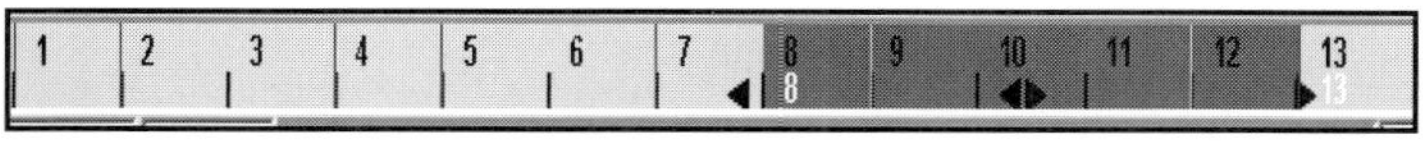

figure 7-31

Editing in the timeline.

This red area represents a workspace in which you can edit the placement of key frames. Everything inside the red area will be affected.

Left-mouse click the arrows in the middle of this red area to slide it back and forth. If you have key frames in this area, you will be moving them to a different place in time, but they will maintain their proximity to each other.

Left-mouse click the arrows on the outer limits of this red area to scale the frames up or down. The side you are not editing will not move; it will act as a pivot, and the frames will scale to it.

Click anywhere in the timeline to get rid of the red area.

Practice the use of this tool with your bouncing ball exercise. Try cutting and pasting key frames first. Then try to move the key frames.

Editing in the Graph Editor

Sometimes you will want to hold on a key pose. You only have one key frame for the pose, and you need to create a hold over six frames. The best way to create the hold is to create another key frame of the same value, six frames later in time.

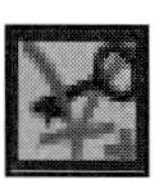

figure 7-32

The Insert Key tool.

You will use the ball_bounce.mb file for this example.

You want to hold the bounce in midair for three frames. You do not want the ball to move up and down in this time. Thus, you want to create holds in the Y Translate three frames after key frame 7.

Select the Y Translate curve, and use a tool in the upper left of the interface called Insert Key (see Figure 7-32).

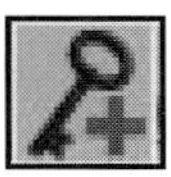

figure 7-33

The Add Key tool.

Then insert a key by middle-mouse clicking the curve and dragging the curve to where you want to insert the key. You can also use the Add Key tool (see Figure 7-33).

For Add Key, middle-mouse click the curve where you want to insert the key. All keys added to the curve will have the same tangent type as adjacent keys.

Suppose you want to move an entire section of keys to a different point in time. New tools have been introduced in Maya 6 to make this easier.

In the Graph Editor interface pull-down menus, select **Edit > Transformation tools.** You will see three new sets of tools available (see Figure 7-34).

figure 7-34

Transformation tools.

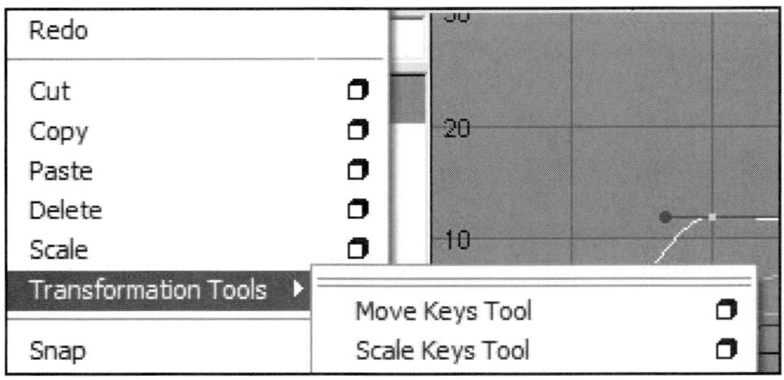

The Move Keys tool lets you select a group of keys and move them as a unit to a new place in time (see Figure 7-35).

figure 7-35

Move Keys tool.

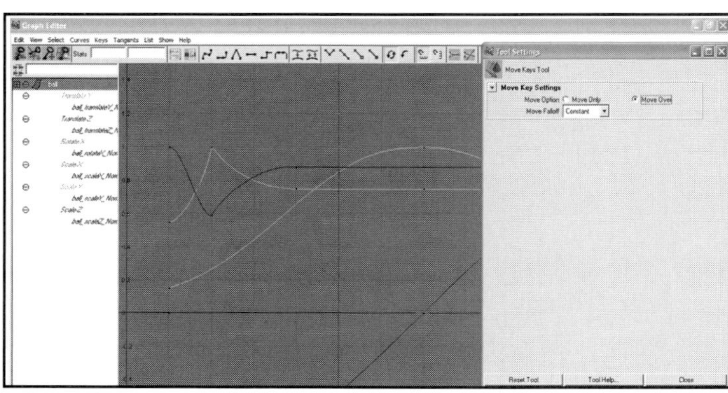

The Scale Keys tool lets you select a group of key frames and scale (see Figure 7-36).

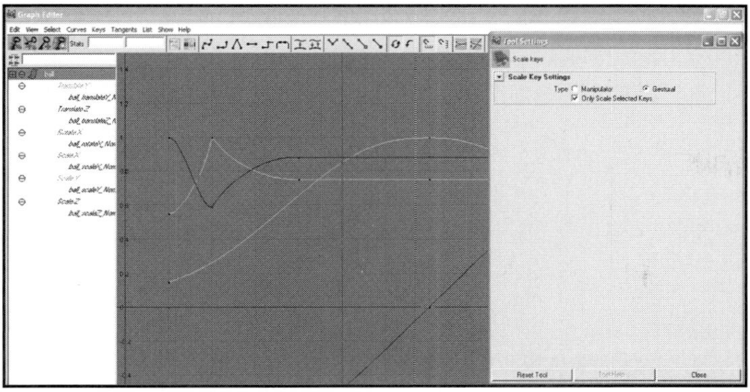

figure 7-36

Scale Keys tool.

Figure 7-37 shows the Lattice Deform Keys tool.

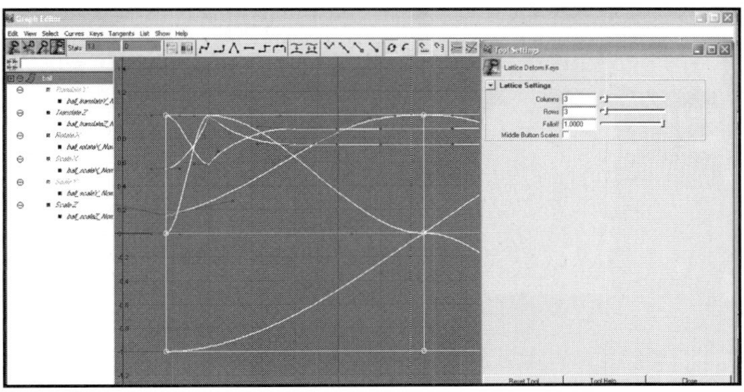

figure 7-37

Lattice Deform Keys tool.

THROWING WITH MAYA

Open the file Generi_rig.mb. Try to place the rig in the poses previously described. Follow the timing charts in Figure 7-38.

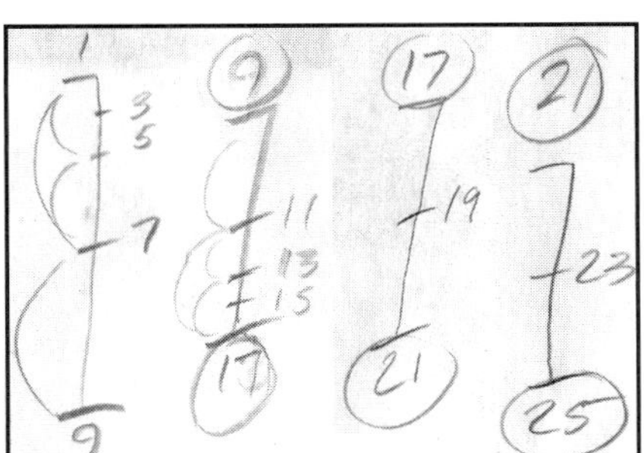

figure 7-38

Timing charts for the throw.

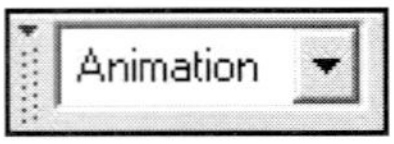

figure | 7-39 |

The Animation module.

Use FK on the arms and IK on the feet. You will notice that you have many more parts to keep track of, but just concentrate on the motion of the figure in this exercise.

Set up your interface to look like Figure 7-40. Under **Panels > Layouts,** choose Three Panels Split Top, and turn the lower window into the Graph Editor. Make sure to set up your tangency curves as linear and stepped.

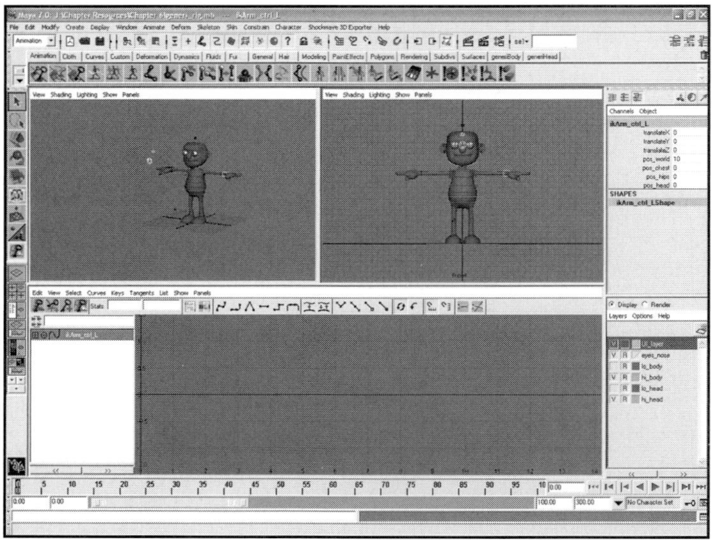

figure | 7-40 |

The interface to begin the throw exercise.

Now sketch a series of thumbnails for a throw and select your key poses. Refer to the drawings (see Figure 7-41).

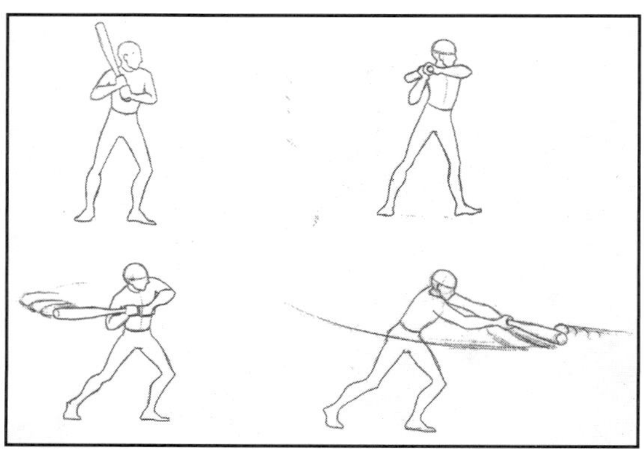

figure | 7-41 |

The drawn poses.

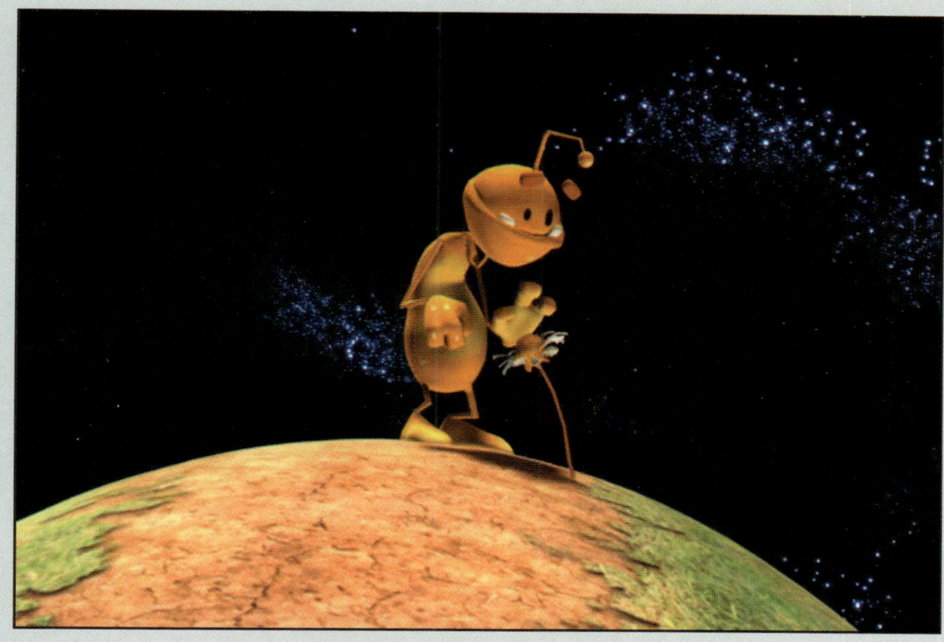

figure | 1 |

Benjamin Willis created "Quark" in Maya. Quark has been featured in many film festivals.

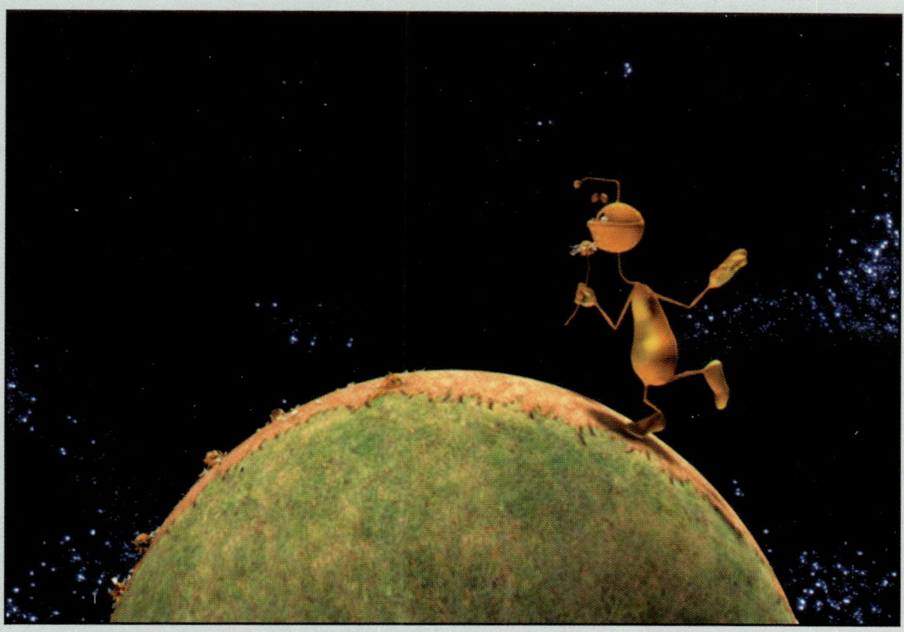

figure | 2 |

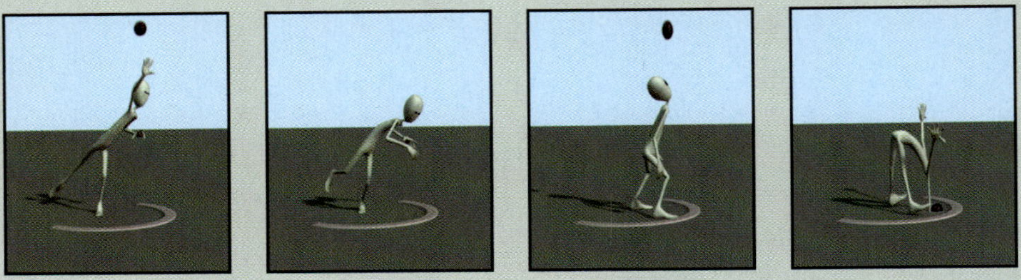

figures | 3–6 |

Mathew Munn created this thumbnail of action in Maya.

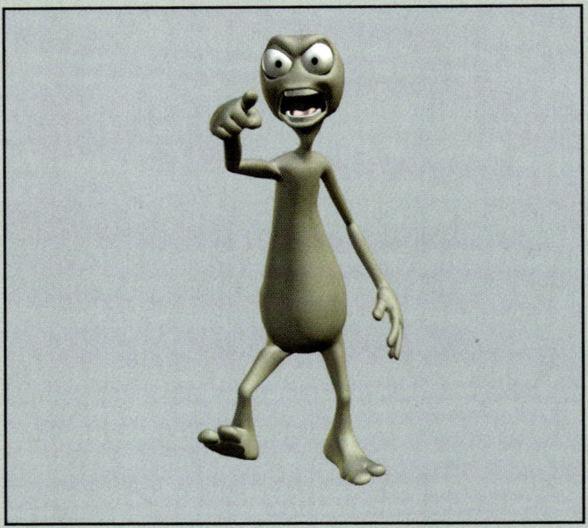

figure | 7 |

Mathew often reuses his characters in different acting scenarios.

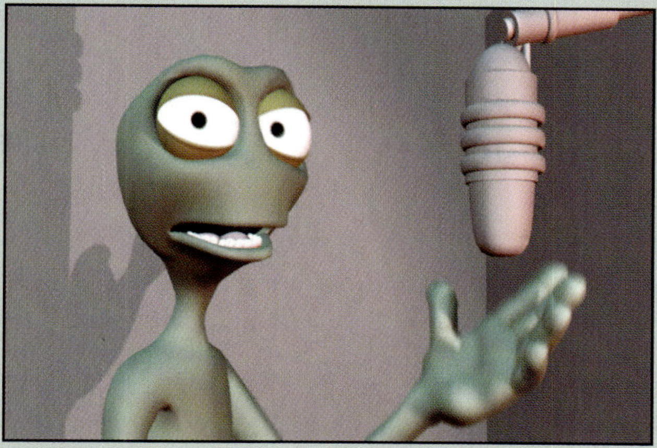

figure 8

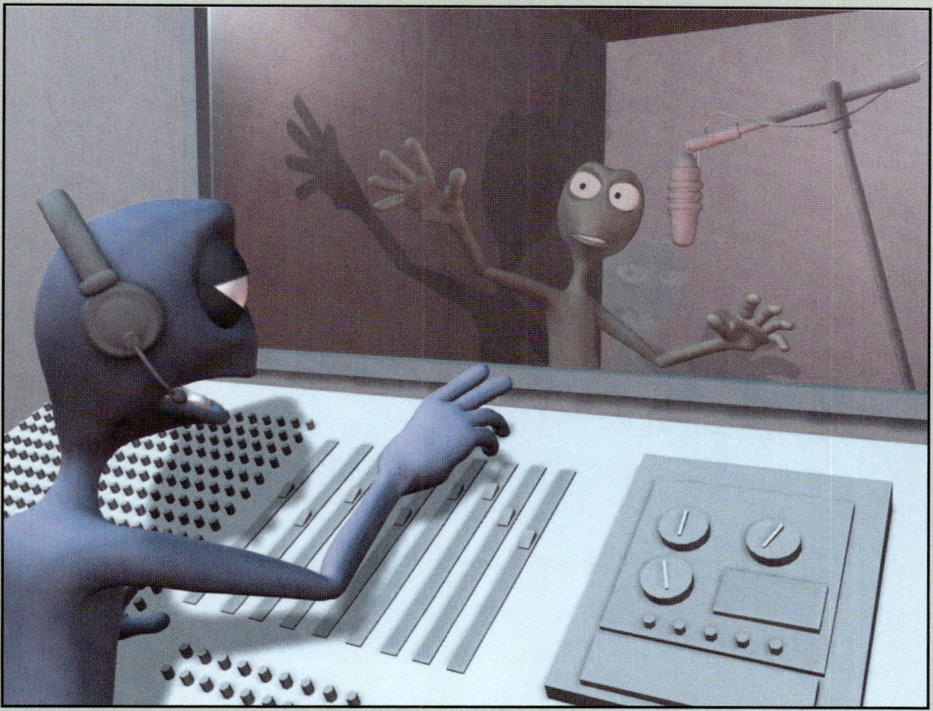

figure 9

Mathew Munn won the 10 Second Club contest on www.10secondclub.com for the month of December with this entry.

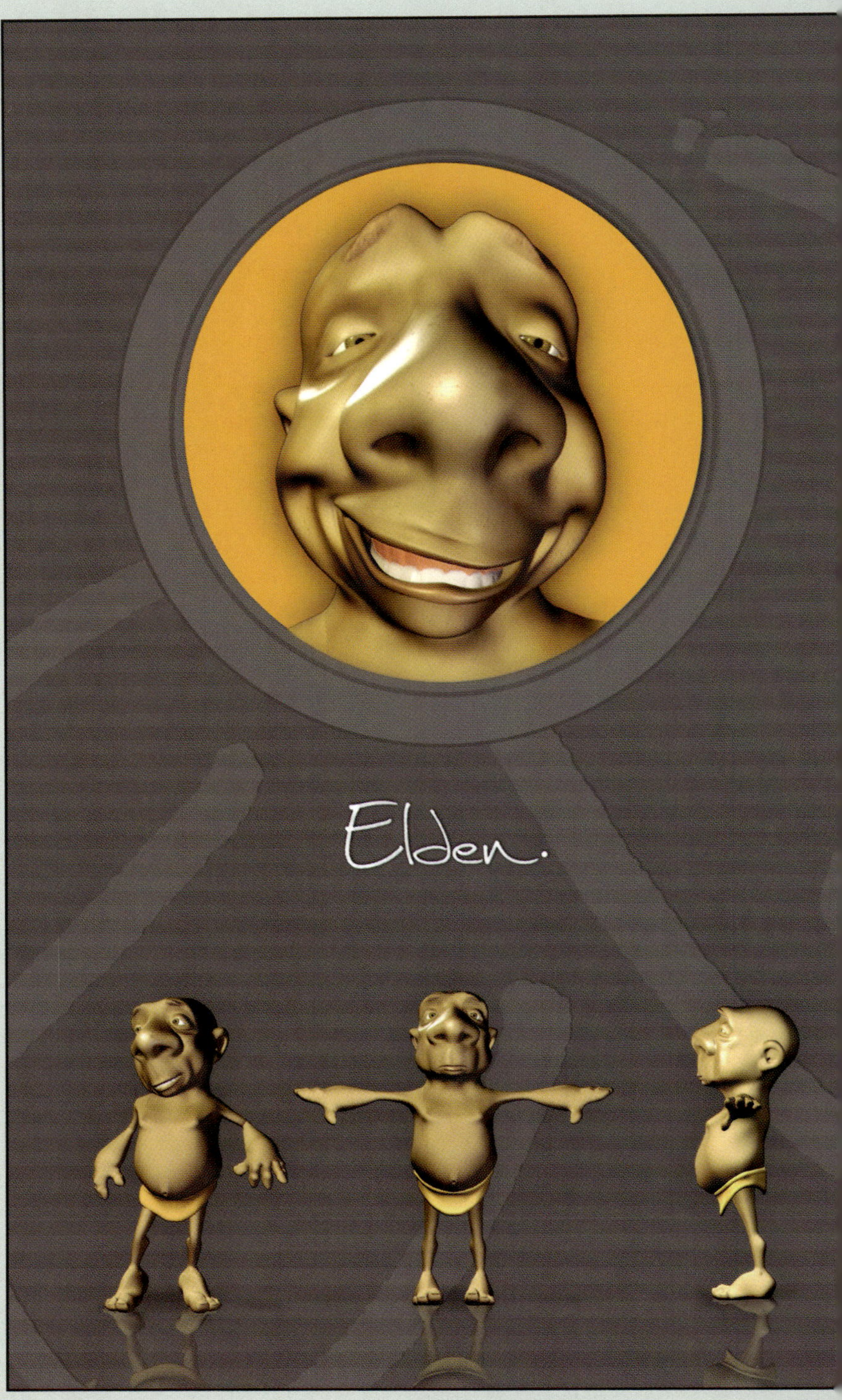

figure | 10

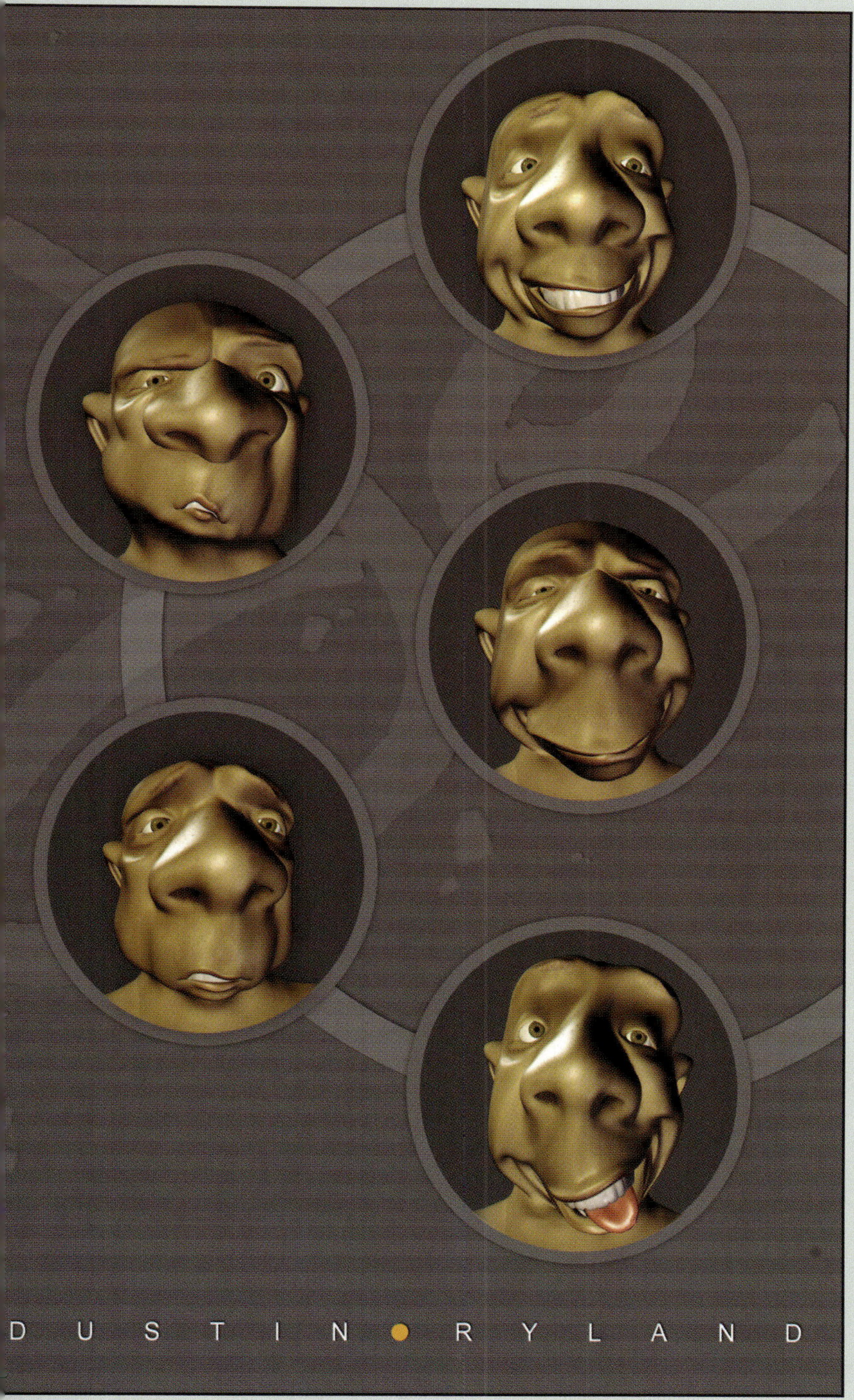
DUSTIN RYLAND

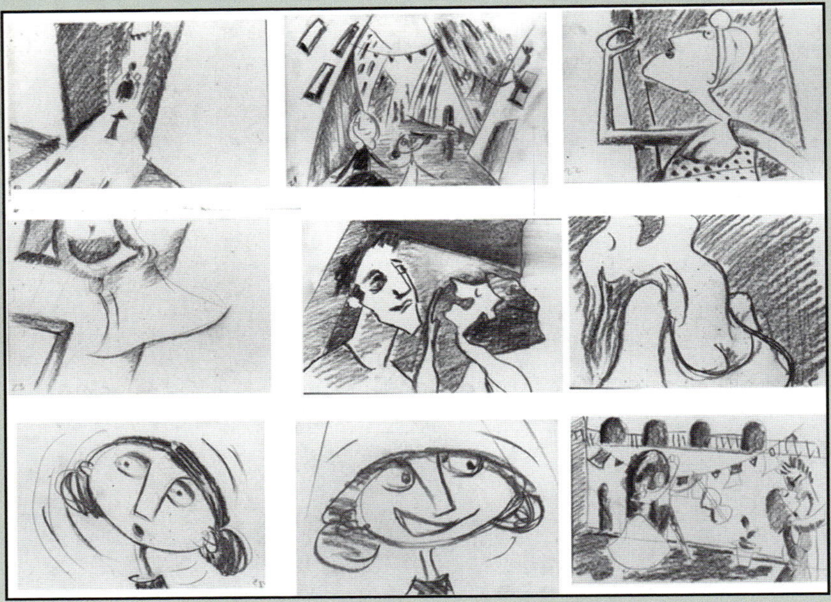

figure 11

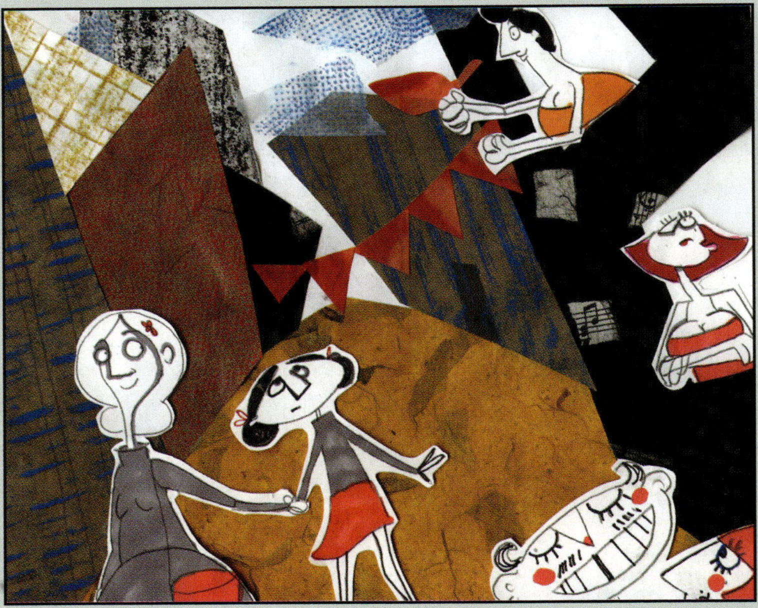

figure 12

Here we have storyboards (Figure 11) and final art based on the storyboards (Figure 12). Andrea Lira creates textures outside of the computer, then scans them. She imports them as textures onto flat planes in Maya to create an interesting collage effect. The end result looks a lot like cut-out animation.

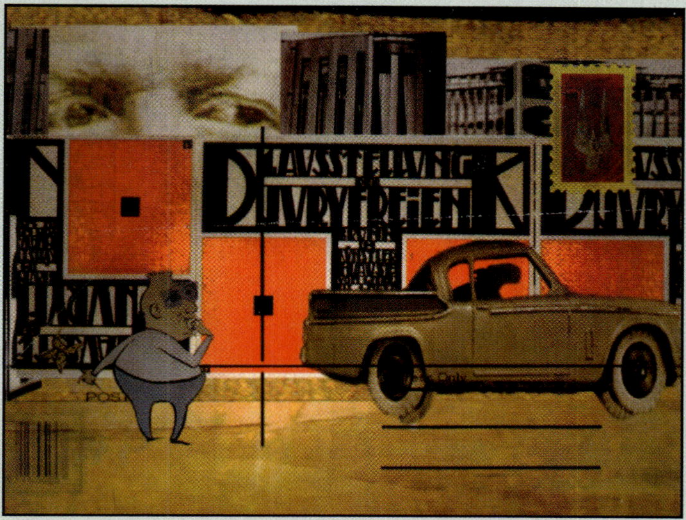

figure 13

Patricia Beckmann worked with Mark Mothersbaugh from the rock band DEVO to create an animation based on Mark's art. Mark is a wonderful visual artist (as well as a musician) and paints gorgeous mixed media/textural paintings. Much of his work was scanned and captured into the animation shown in Figure 13. You can see it online at http://www.mutato.com/mindlessbob.html.

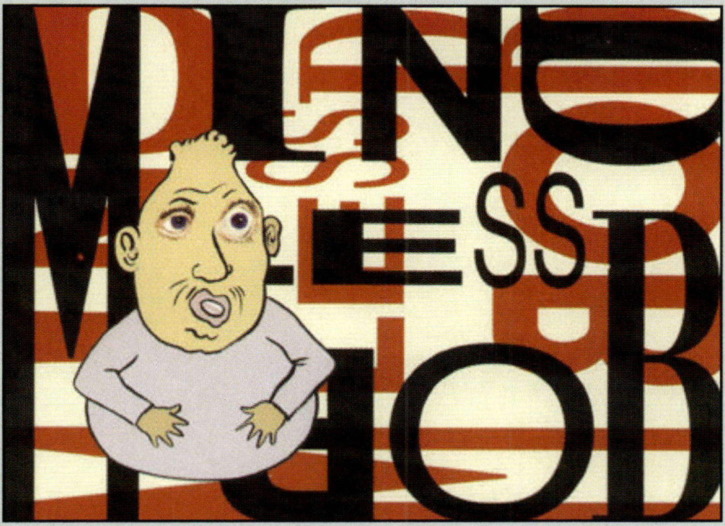

figure 14

Figure 14 is a sample of the original art (by Mark) that was used as reference for the animation.

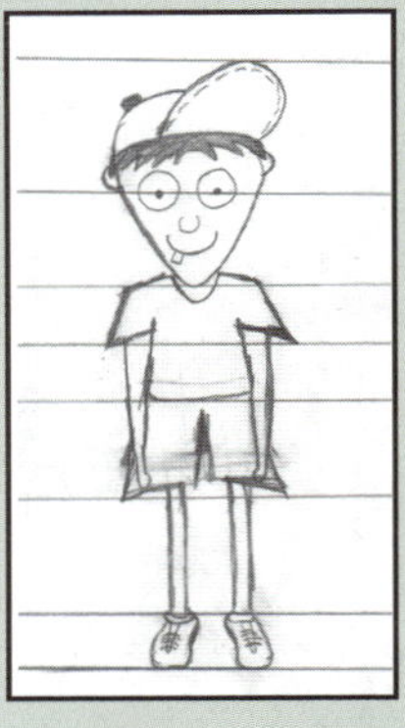

figure 15

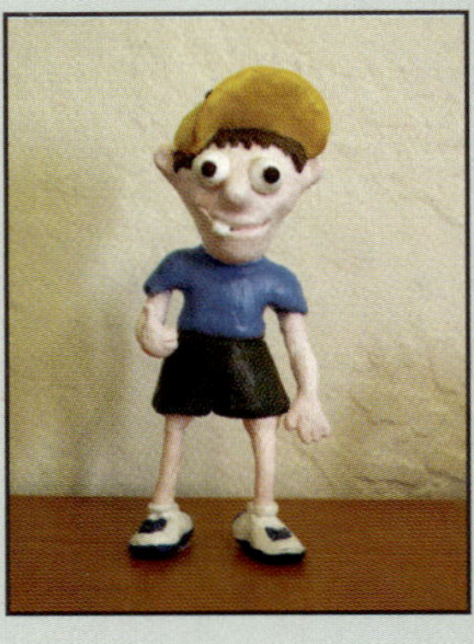

figure 16

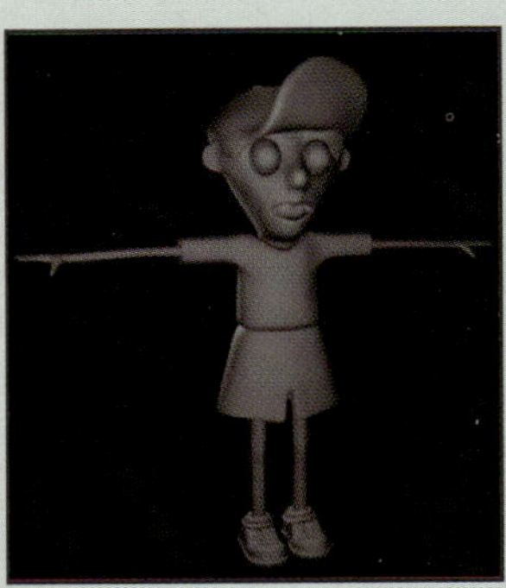

figure 17

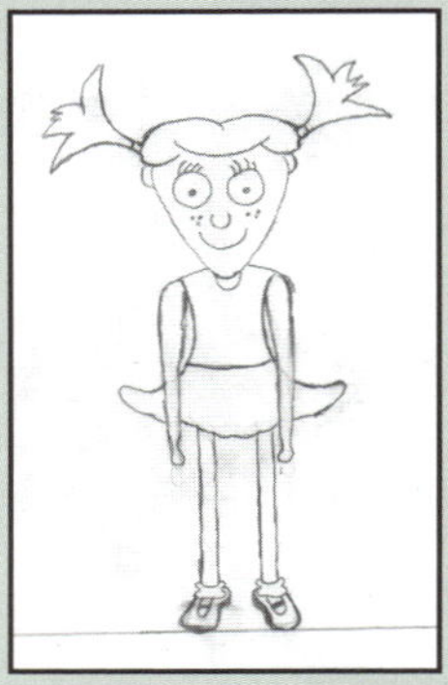

figure 18

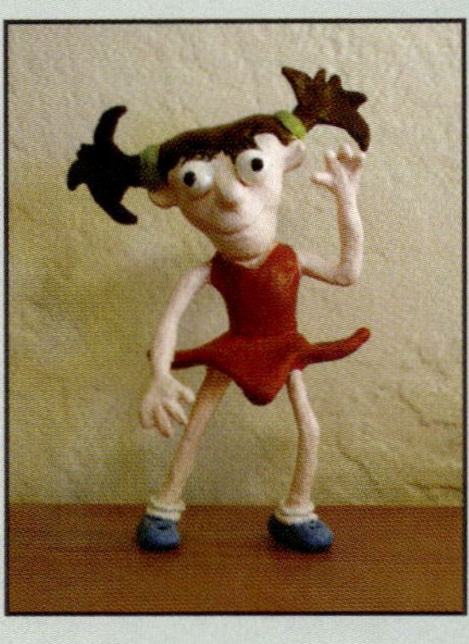

figure 19

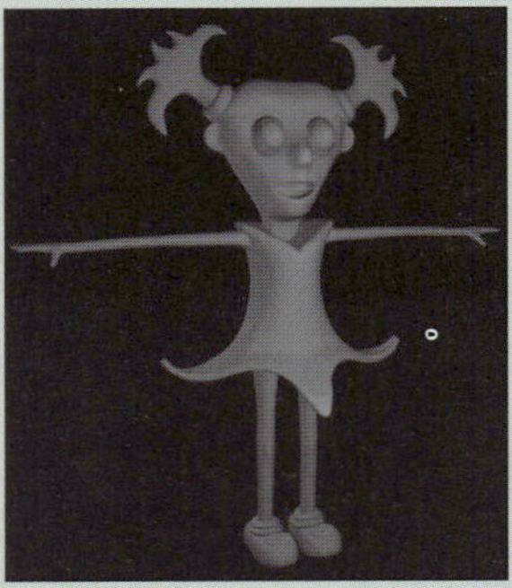

figure 20

Mark Gelfuso wanted a childlike look for his characters. He created character studies as drawings and maquettes prior to modeling them in Maya. He then created storyboards with low-resolution models, building up the look slowly as he worked with his characters.

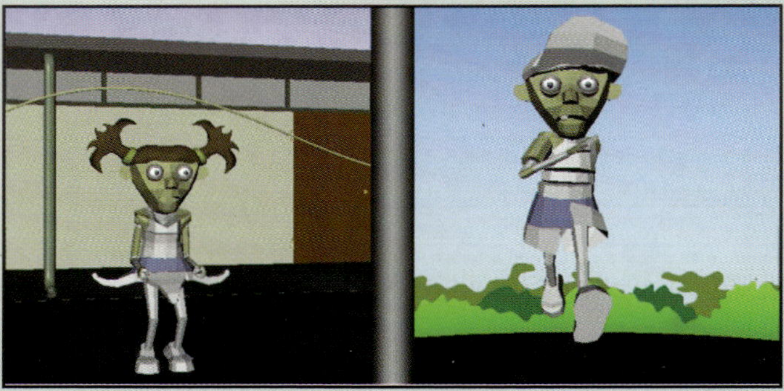

figure 21

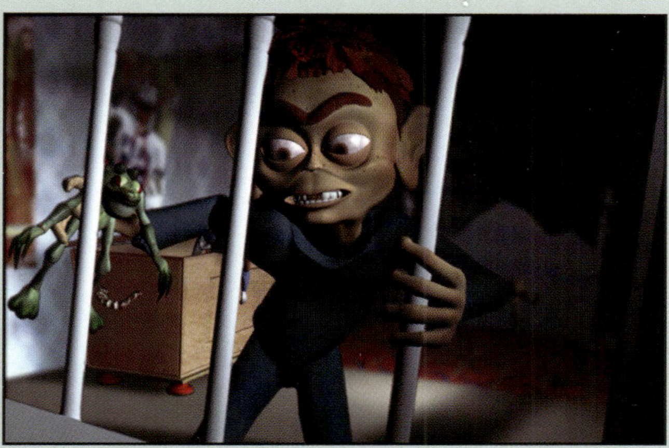

figure 22

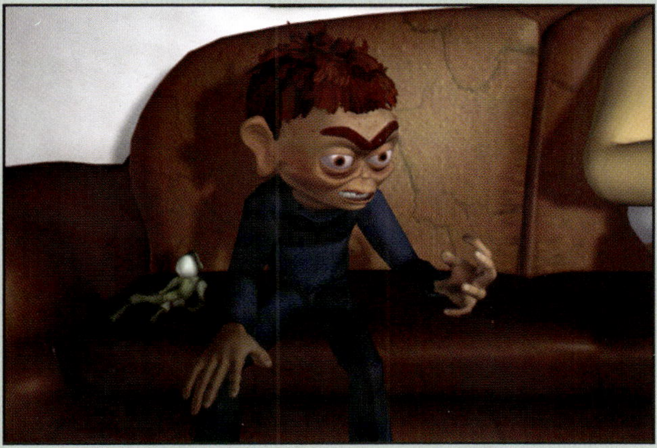

figure 23

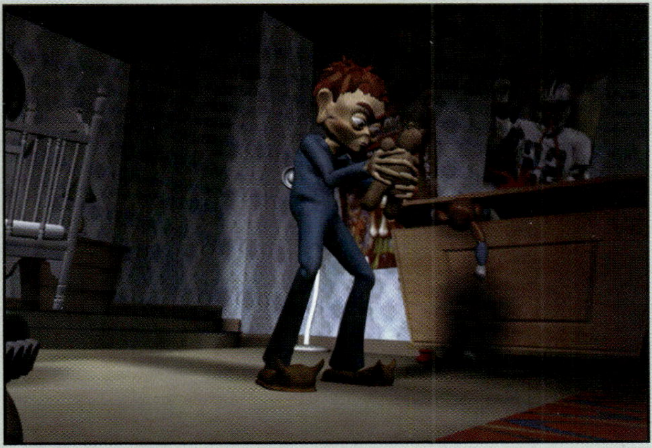

figure 24

Ryan Campbell created a dark animation about children learning to pattern themselves against others.

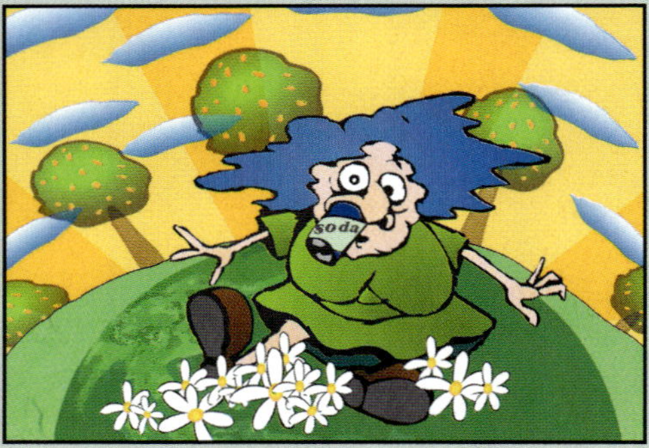

figure 25

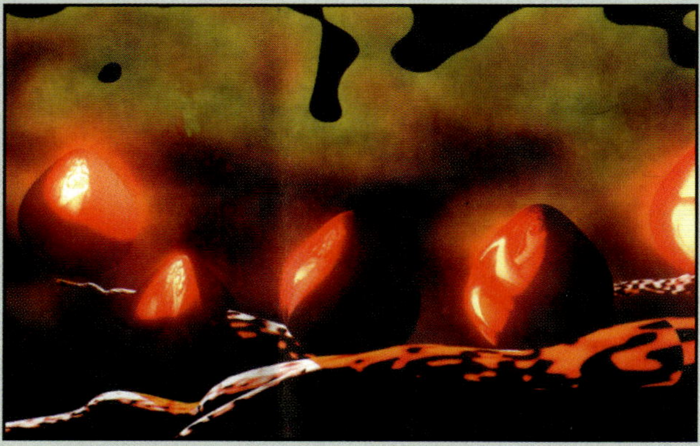

figure 26

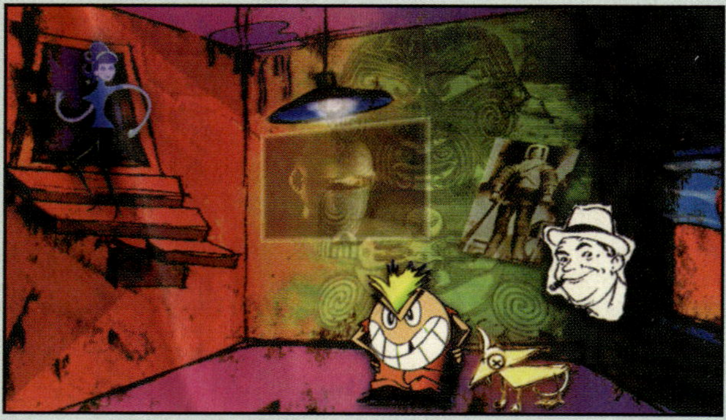

figure 27

Patricia Beckmann uses a variety of styles in her work. More of her projects can be seen at www.bunsella.com.

figure 28

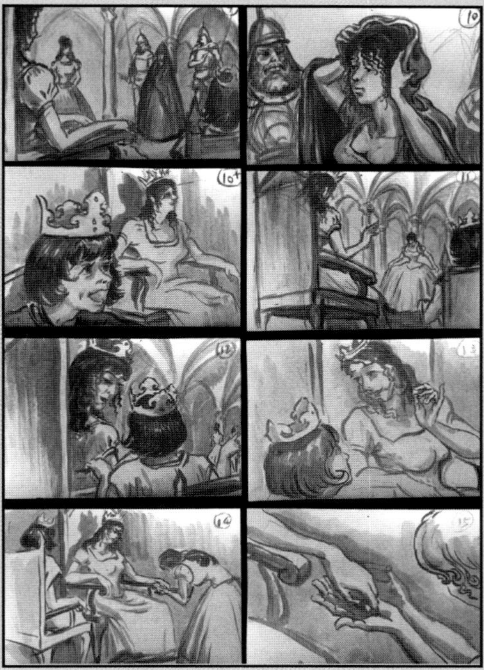

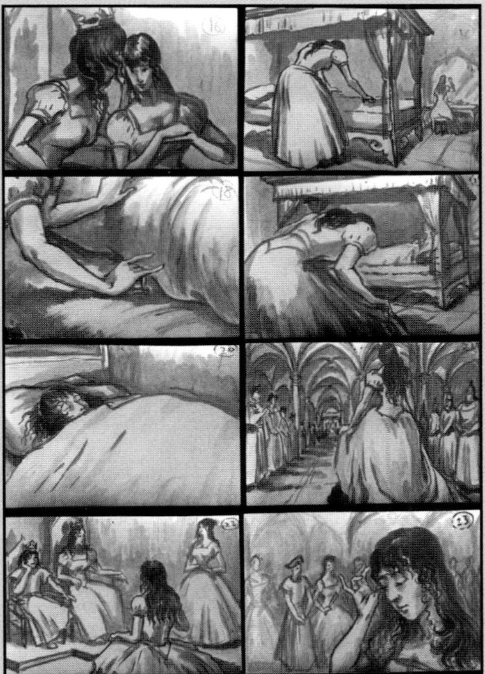

figure 29

Jian Cui created these storyboards for an adaptation of "The Princess and the Pea."

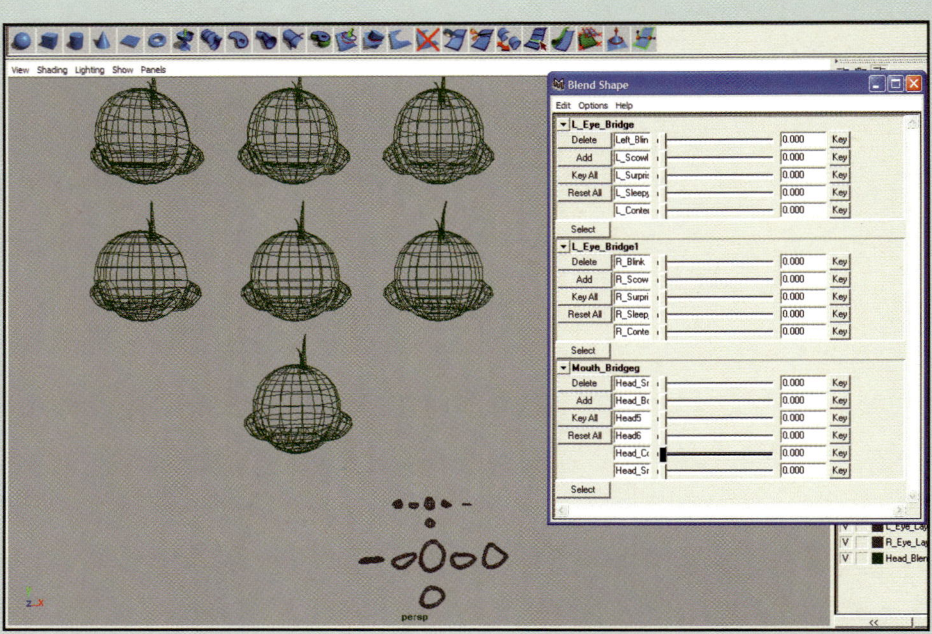

figure 30

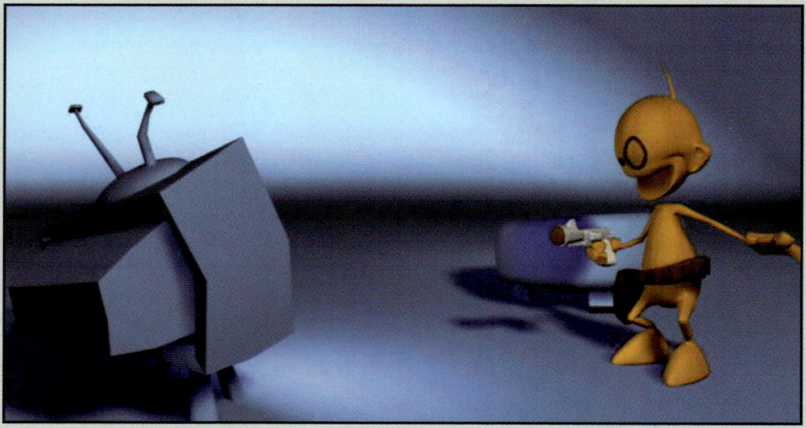

figure 31

Sean Danyi created a delightful simple character using deformations. The heads in the Maya interface picture are obviously the character, but below them you can see ring-like shapes. These are the eyes of the character. "Billy" is the name of the character featured in the short.

figure 32

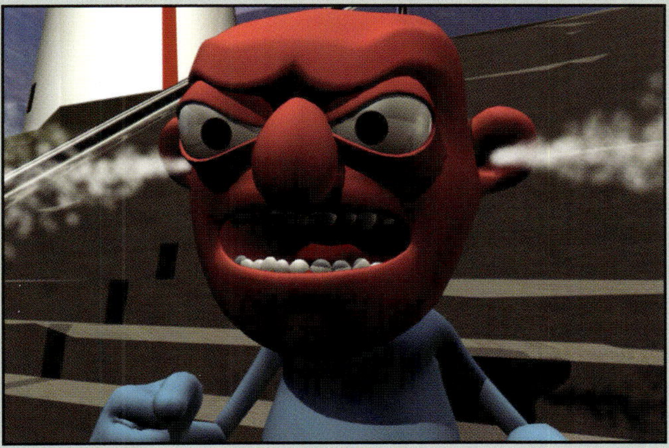

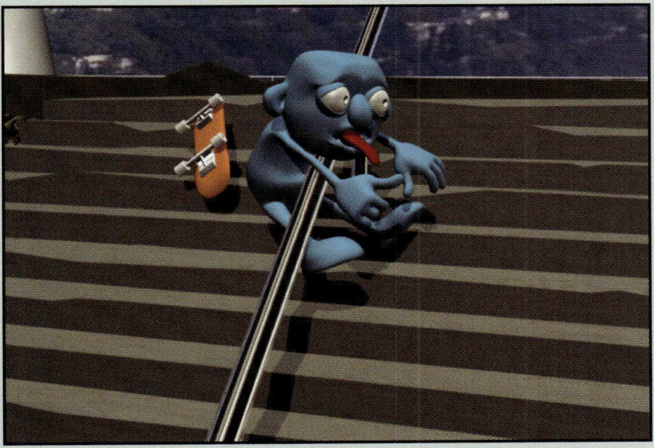

figure 33

figure 34

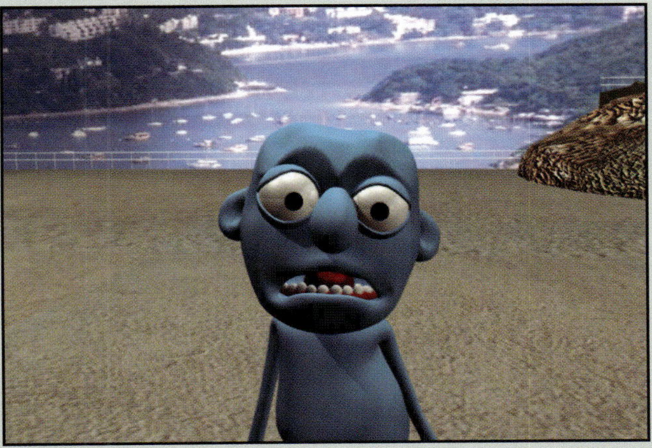

Samir Lyons used the Generi rig to create this hilarious animation about skateboard punks. He used original music from his band for the soundtrack.

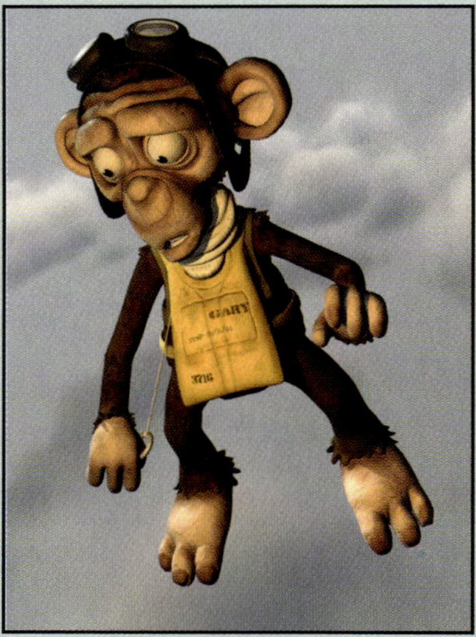

figure 35

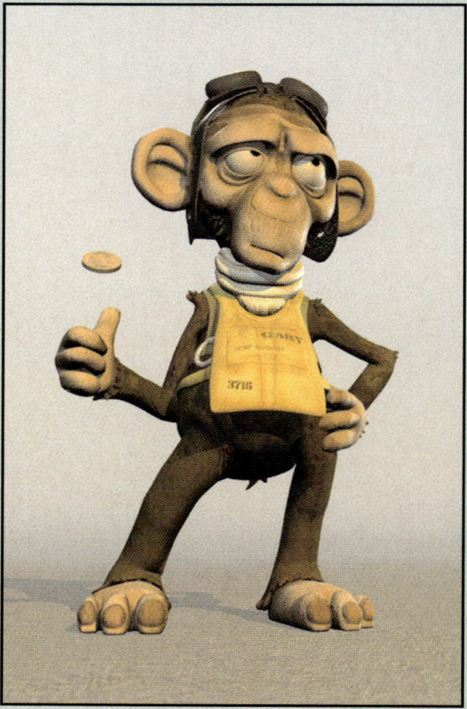

figure 36

Travis Gentry created this very fun monkey animation. Notice all of the expressions on his head deformations. More of his work can be seen at www.travisgentry.com.

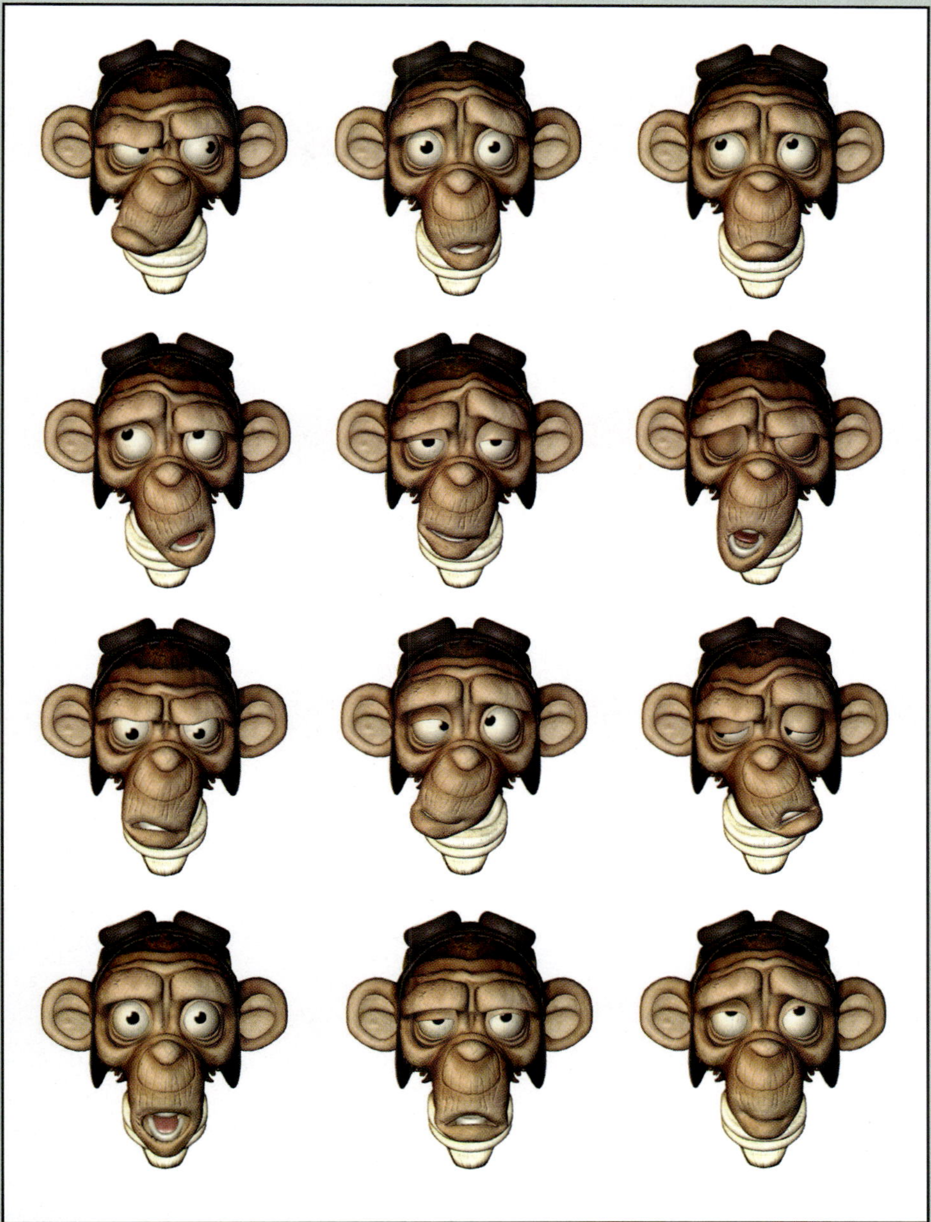

figure 37

figure 38

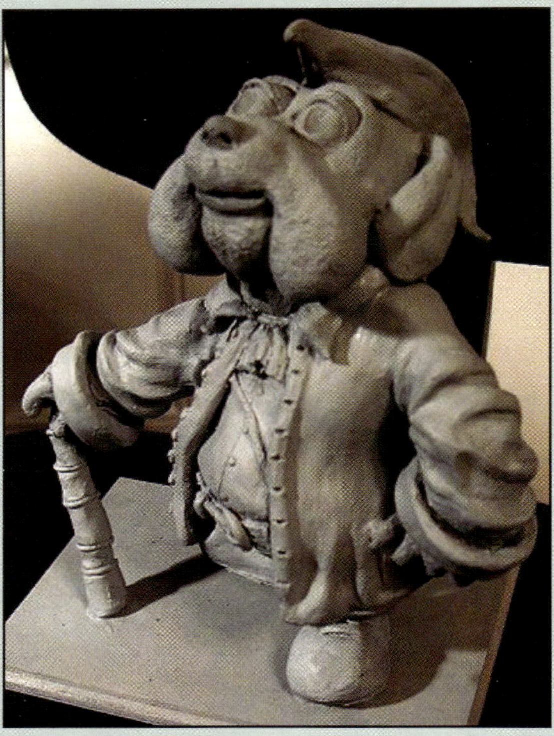

figure 39

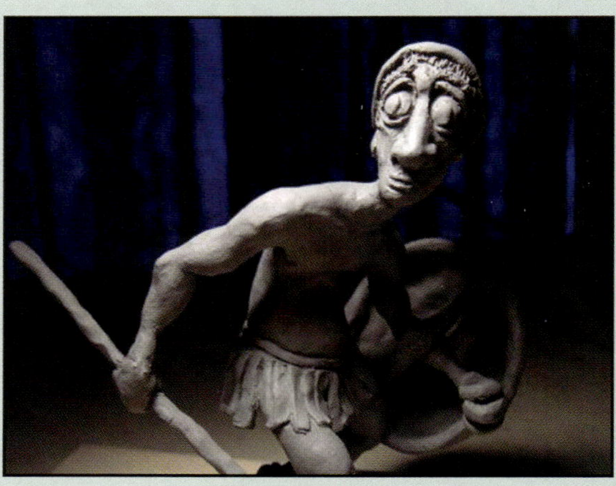

Sean Palmer created these two maquettes out of clay as character studies. Jean Petite is the dog-like character, and Trojan is the other.

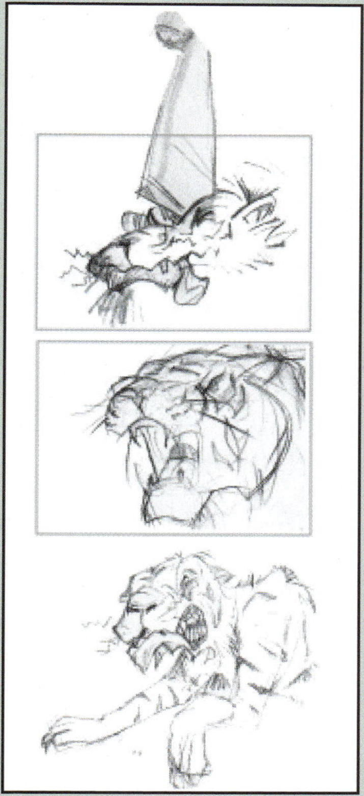

figure 40

Kishore Vijay created these thumbnail sketches of expressions for his tiger.

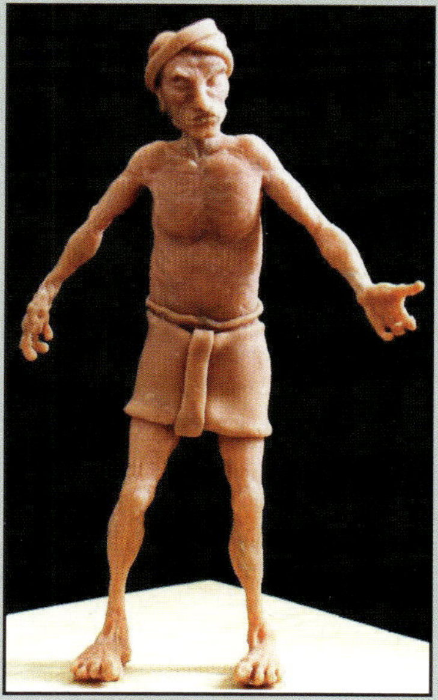

figure 41

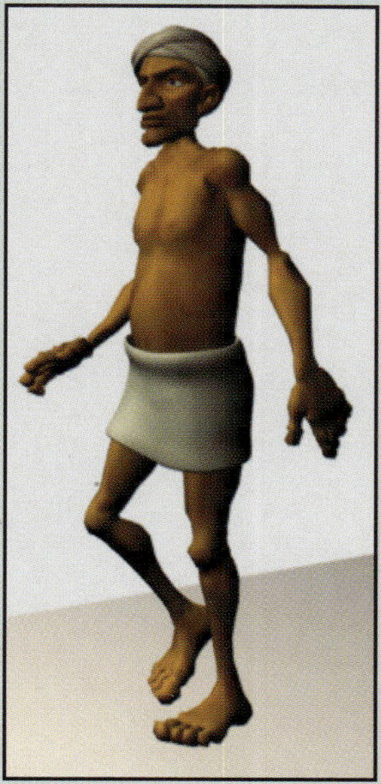

figure 42

Here are Kishore's studies of an old man. First he created him in sculpey, then in Maya.

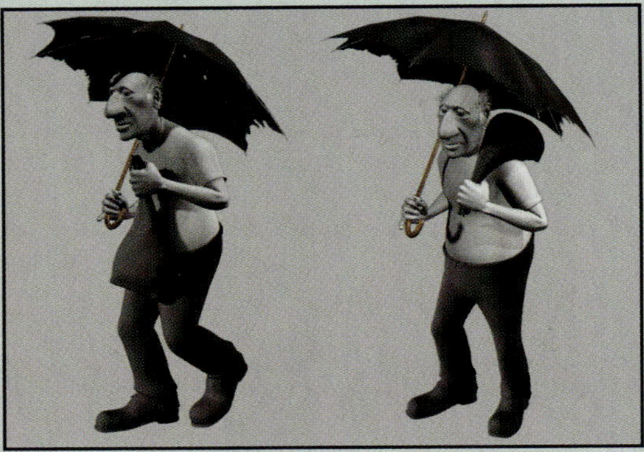

figure 43

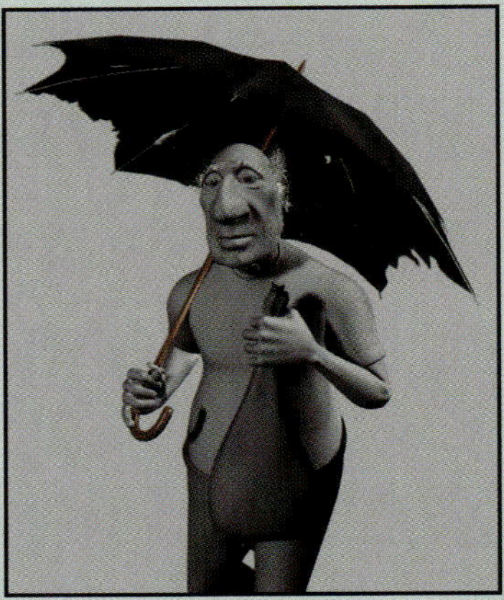

Kedar Dagade created these old man studies.

figure 44

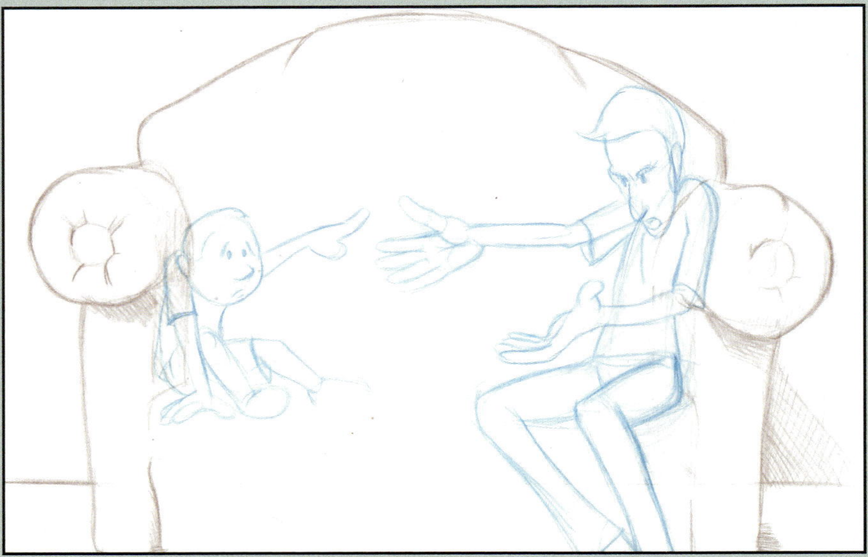

figure 45

Kevin Williams drew this sample layout page.

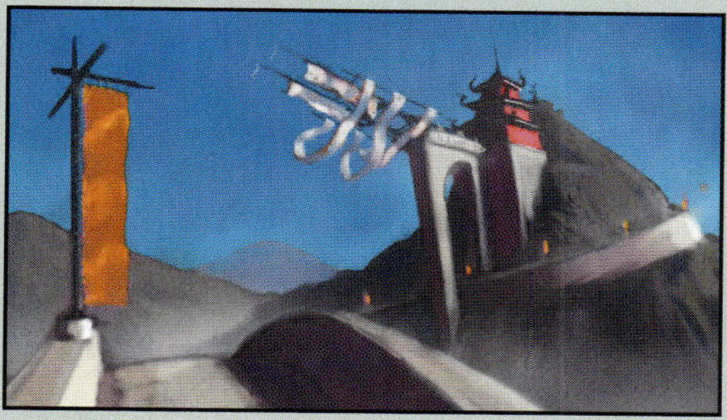

figure 46

figure 47

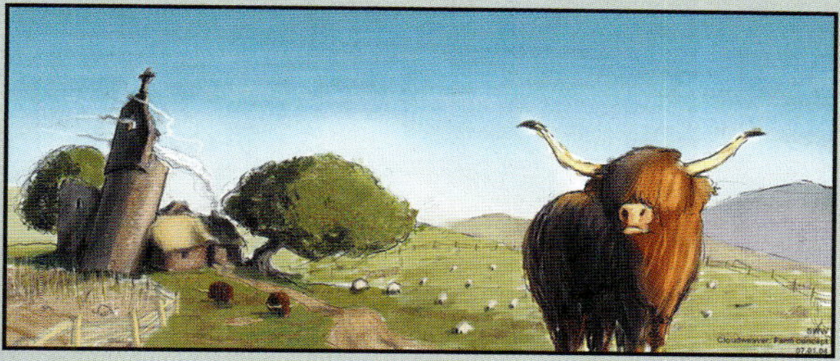

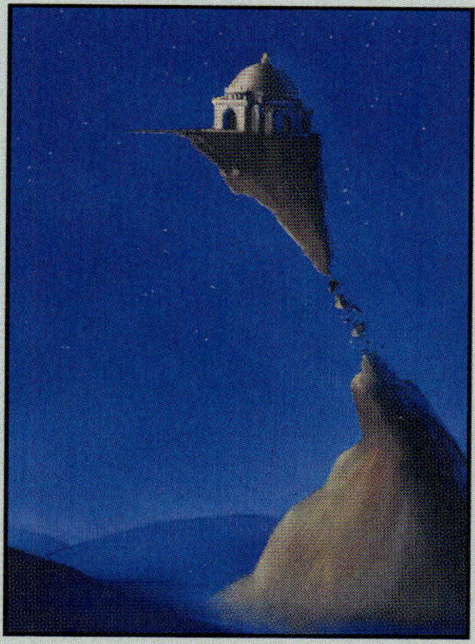

figure 48

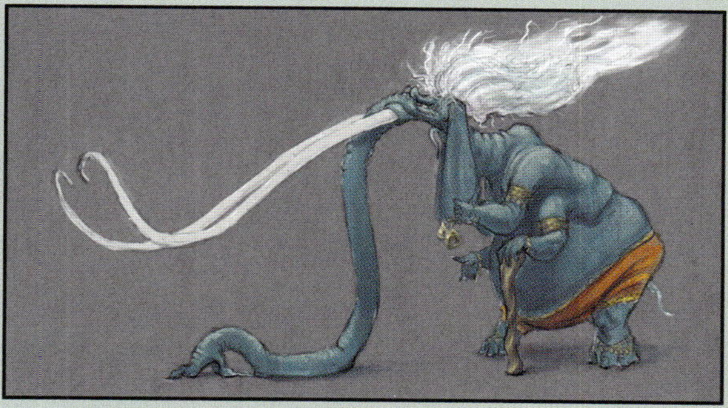

figure 49

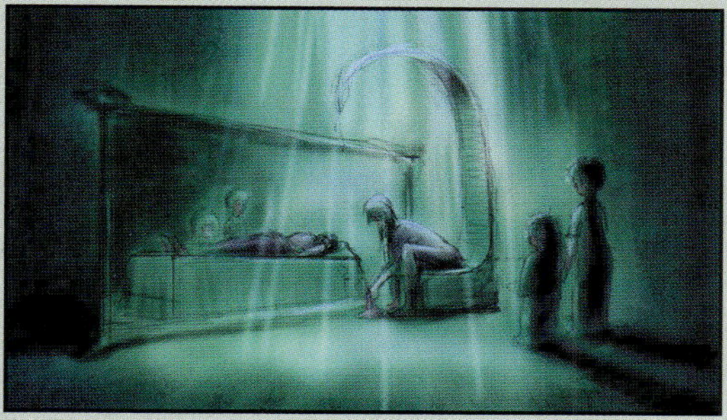

Scott Wells is working on this art for his thesis about children and grief. More of his work can be viewed at www.animax.com.

figure 50

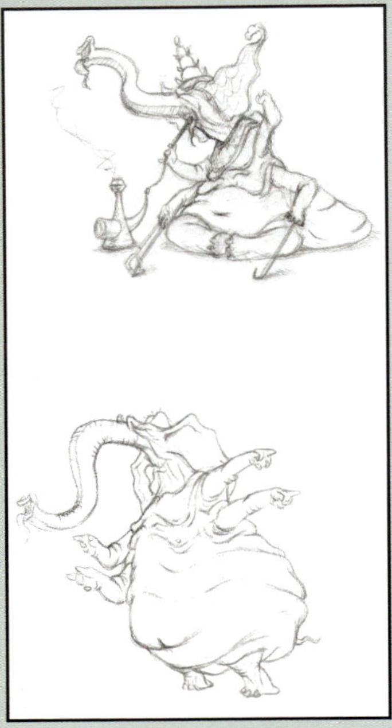

figure 51

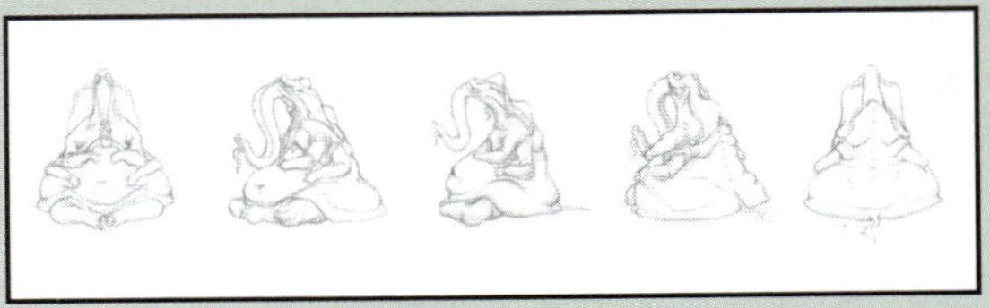

figure 52

figure 53

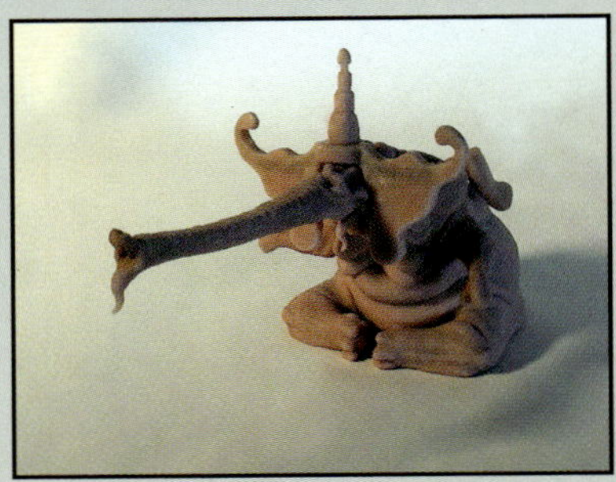

figure 54

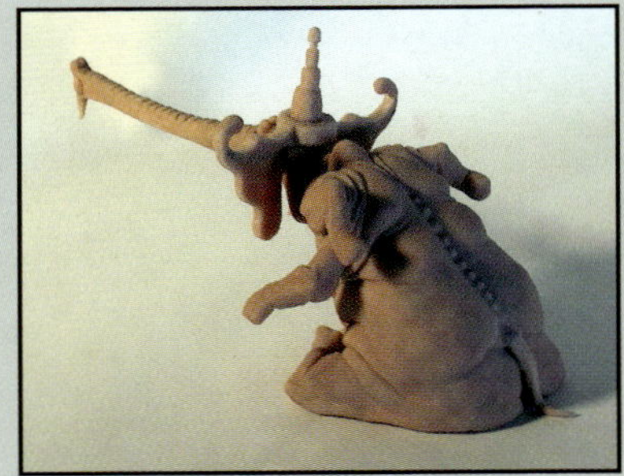

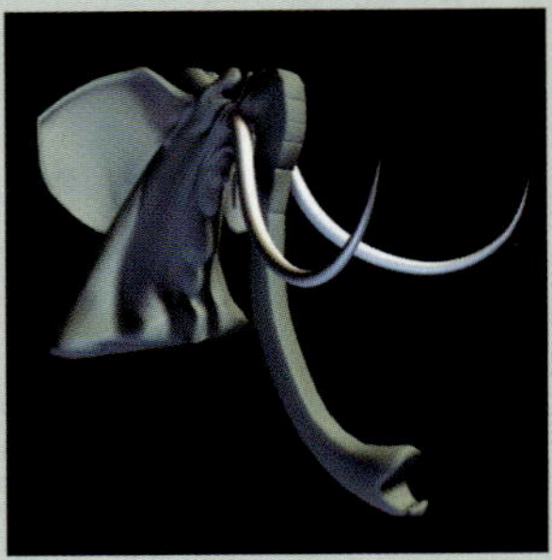

figure 55

figure 56

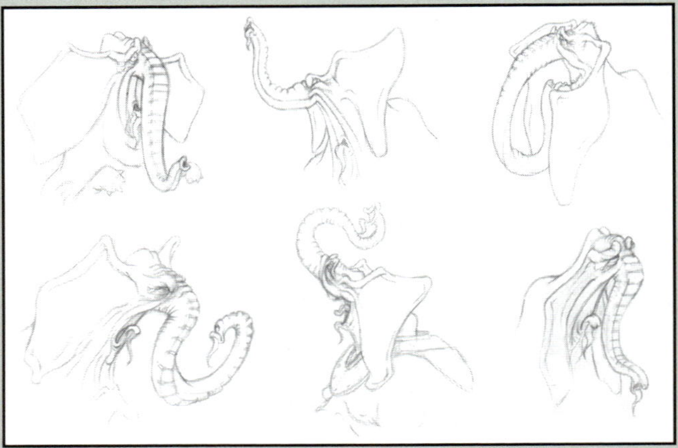

Scott Wells uses Asian, Indian, and Celtic influences in his character design. Here are studies of an elephant character.

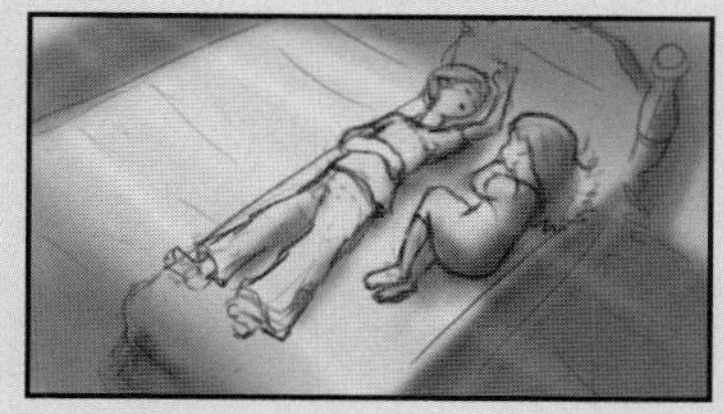

figure 57

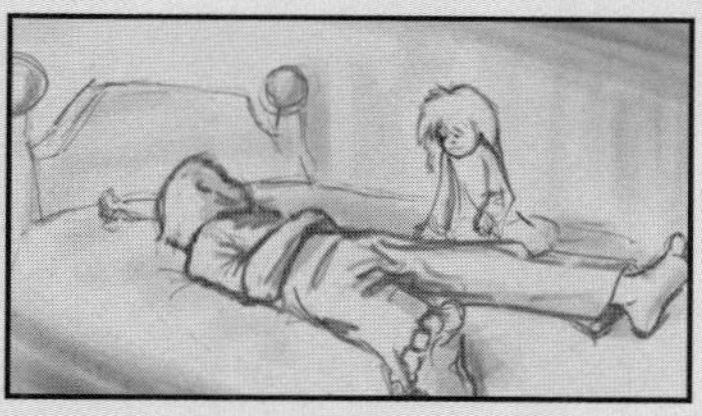

figure 58

Here are concept sketches for the thesis film that Scott Wells is creating.

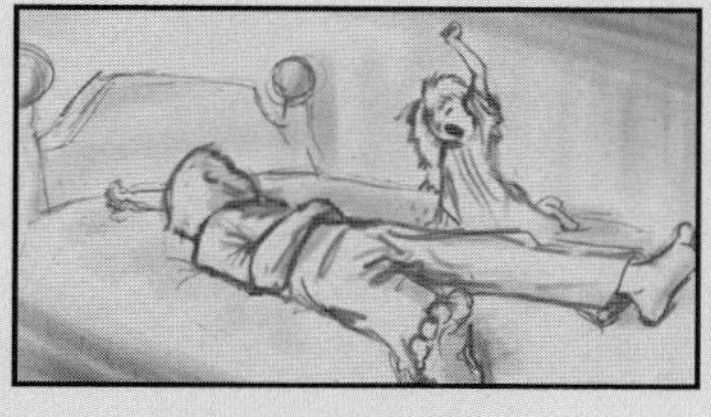

figure 59

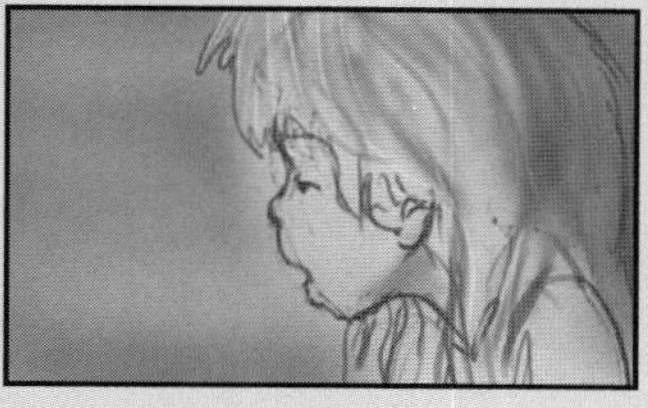

figure 60

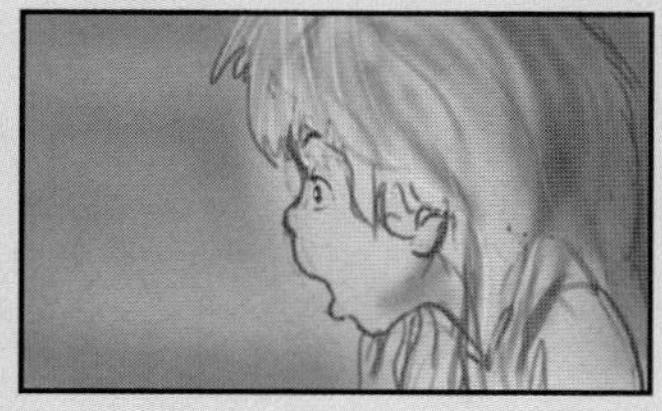

figure 61

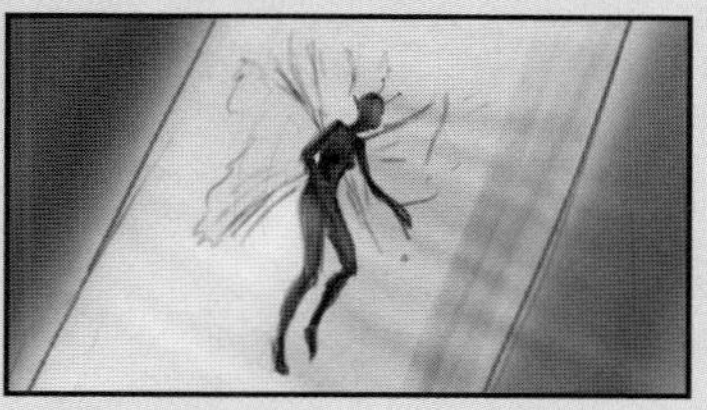

figure 62

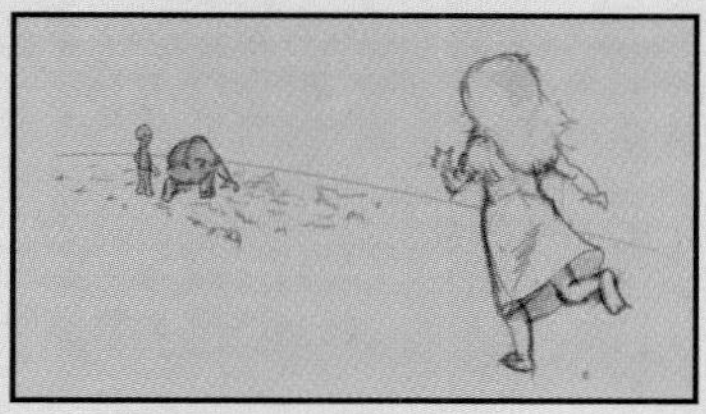

figure 63

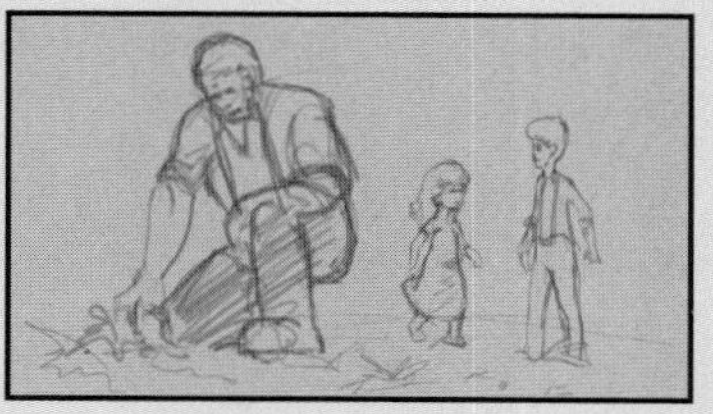

figure 64

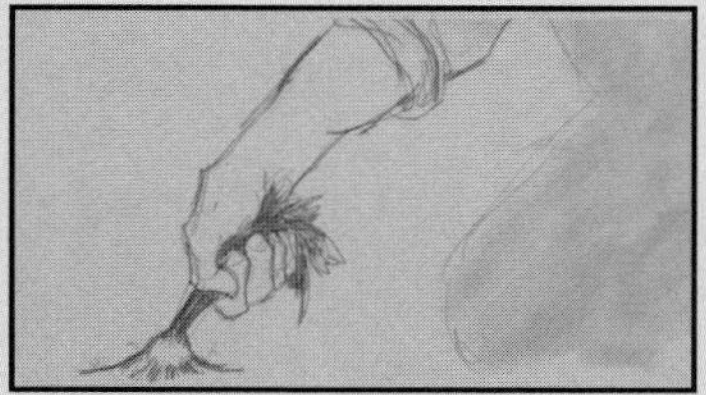

figure 65

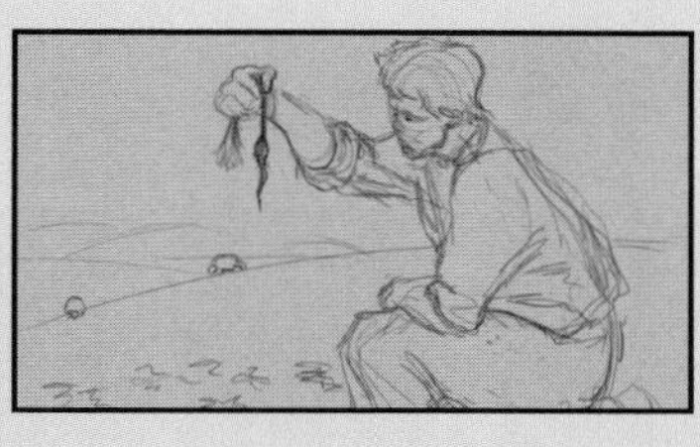

figure 66

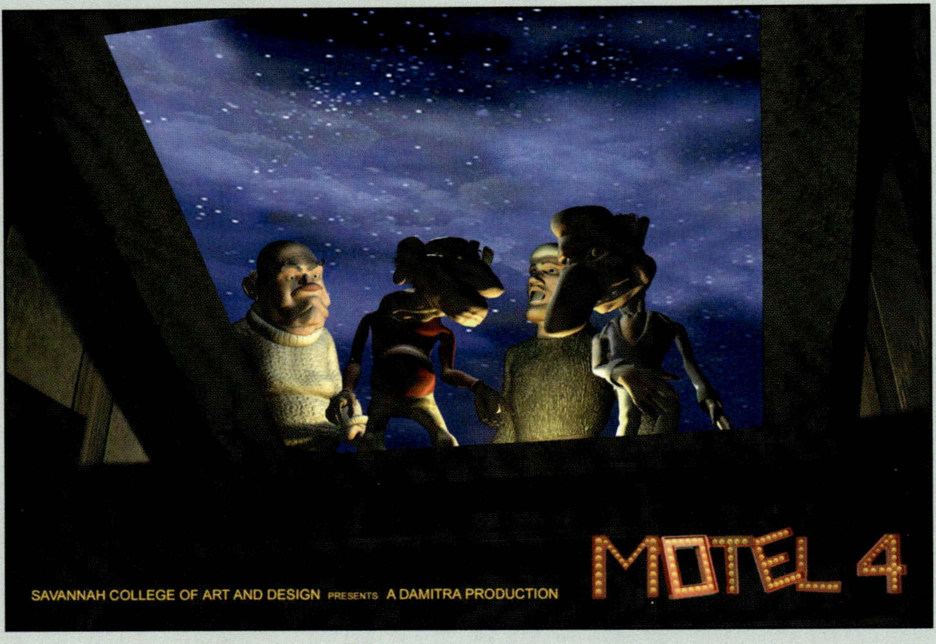

figures | 67–75 |

Three weary travelers stop at a motel for the night, only to find there are no vacant rooms to be had. With some persuasion, the old motel clerk puts the three up for the night in his room, the cellar. Lit only by candlelight, the three turn in for the night. Realizing the candle is keeping them from a good night's sleep, each has a go at blowing it out.

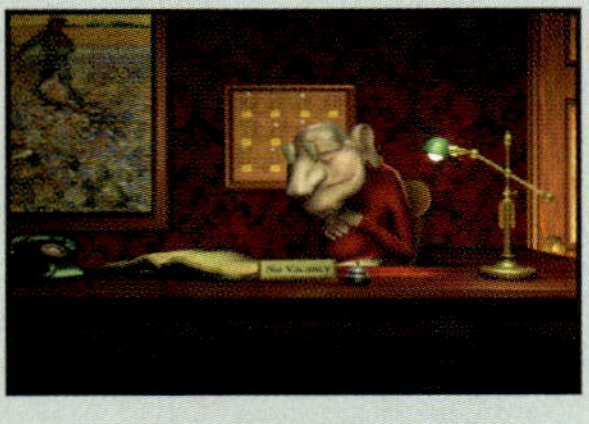

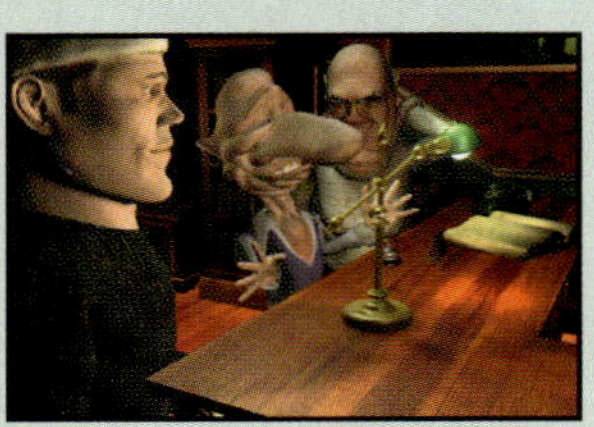

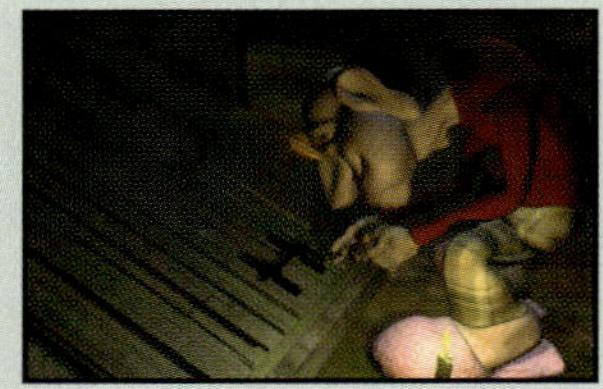

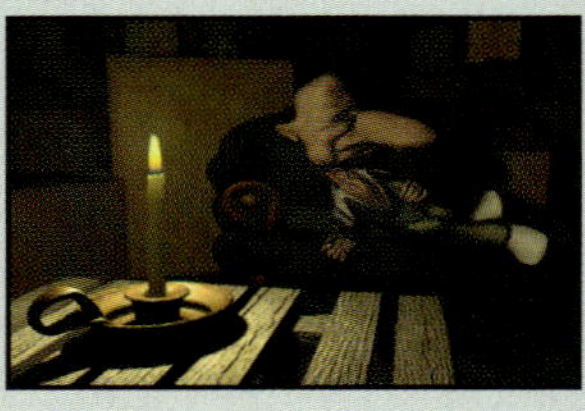

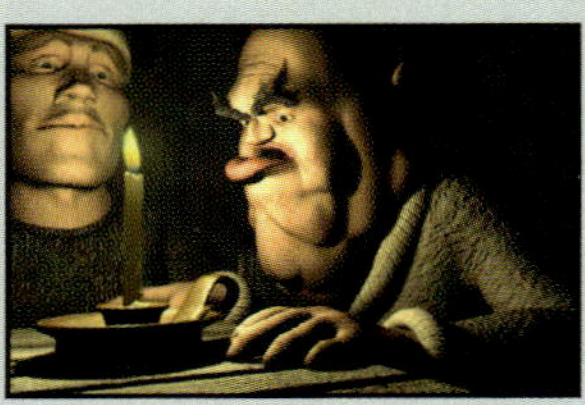

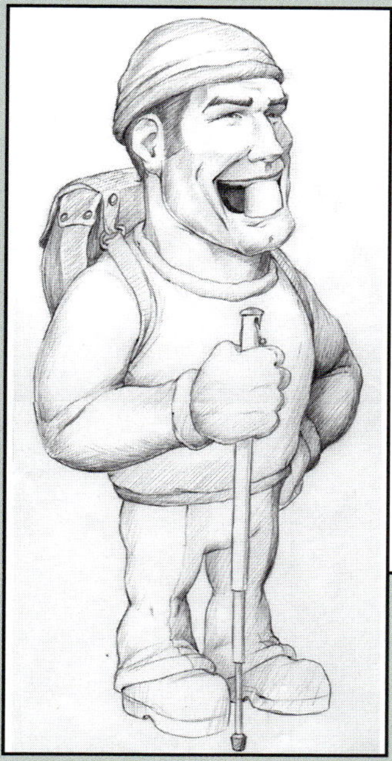

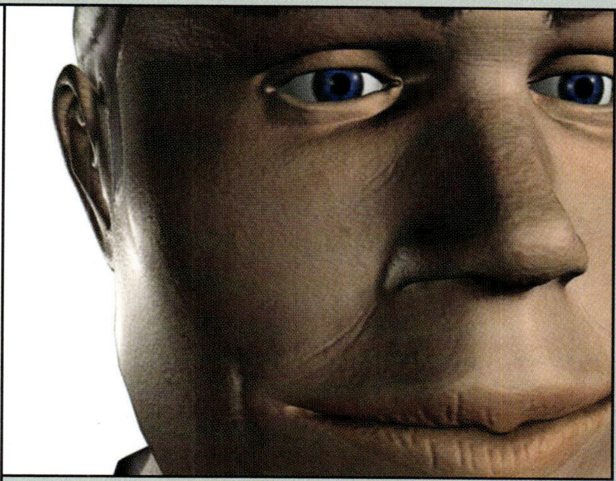

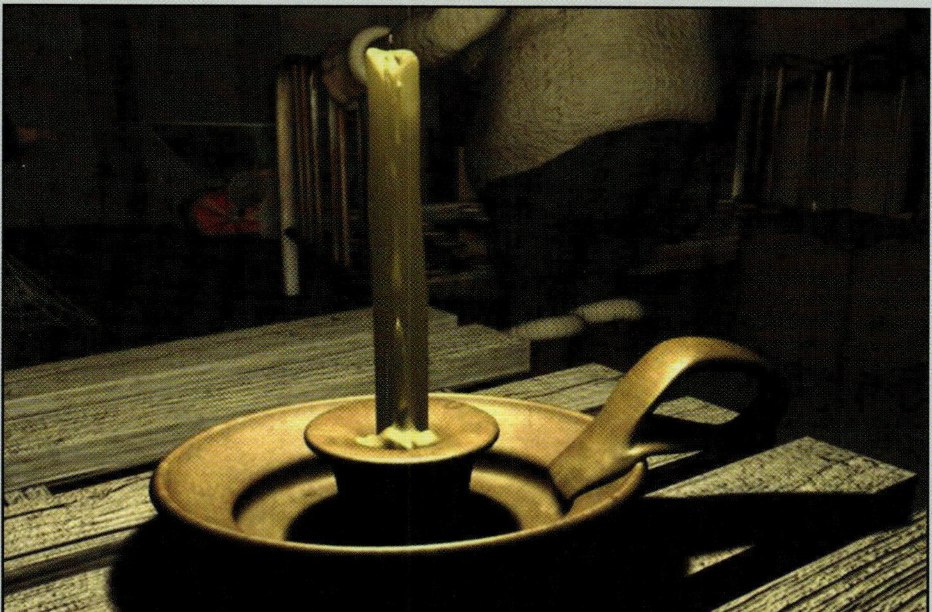

figures | 76–82 |

These are images showing the progression of the Old Man's character design.

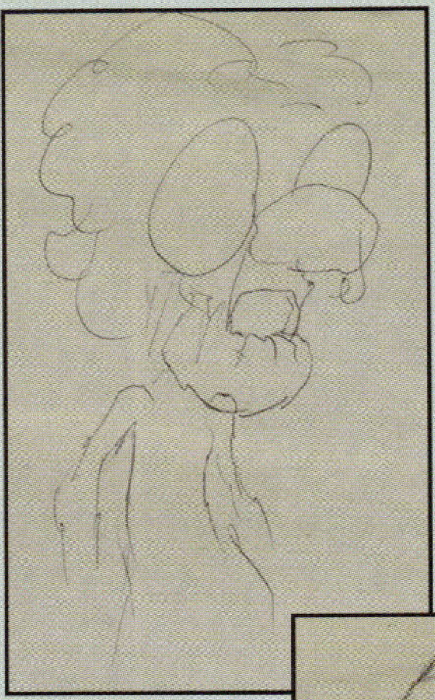

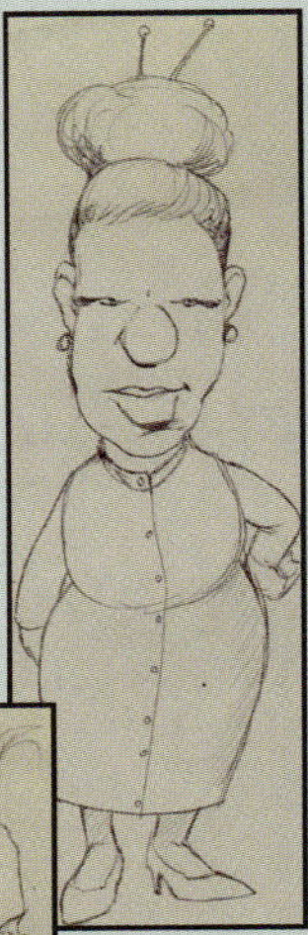

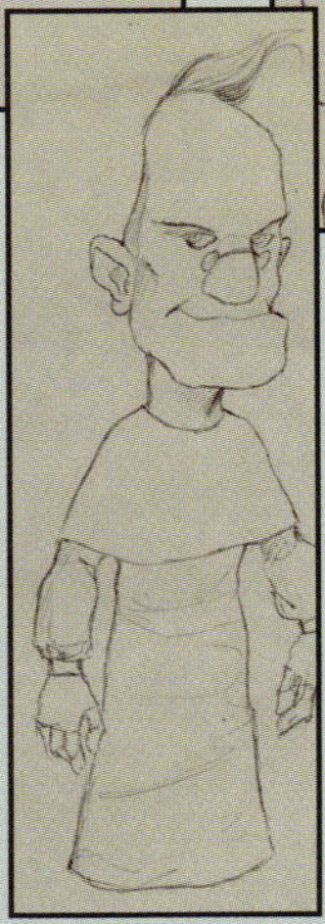

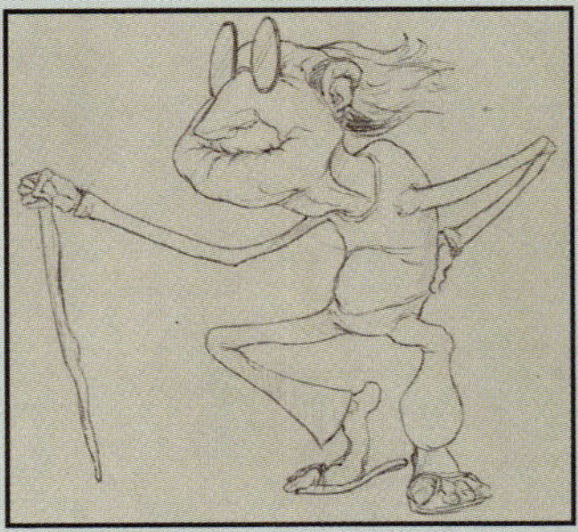

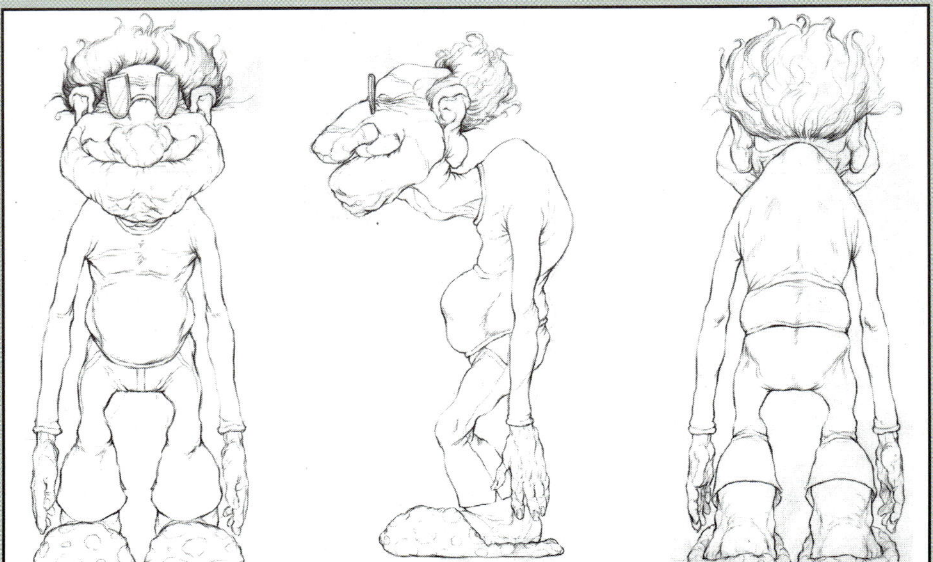

figures | 83–86 |

These are additional character studies of the Old Man.

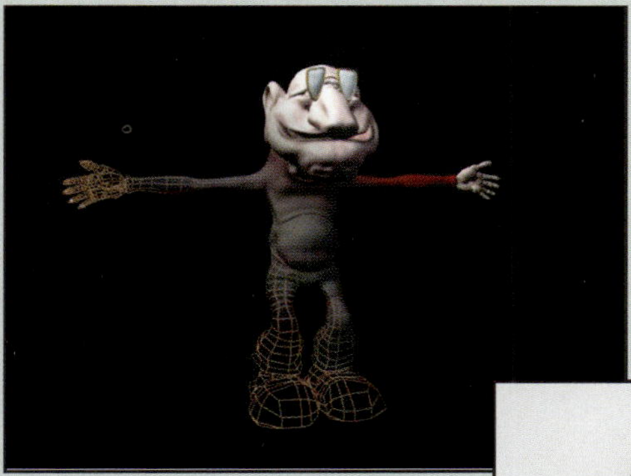

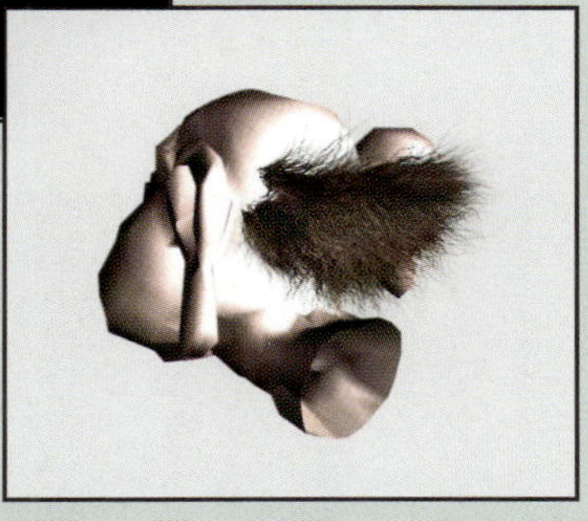

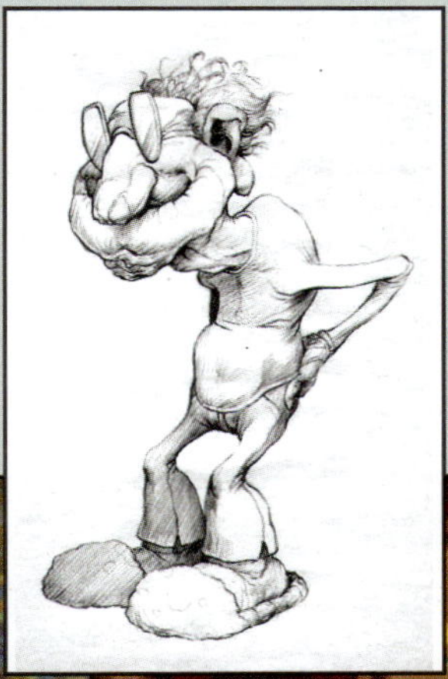

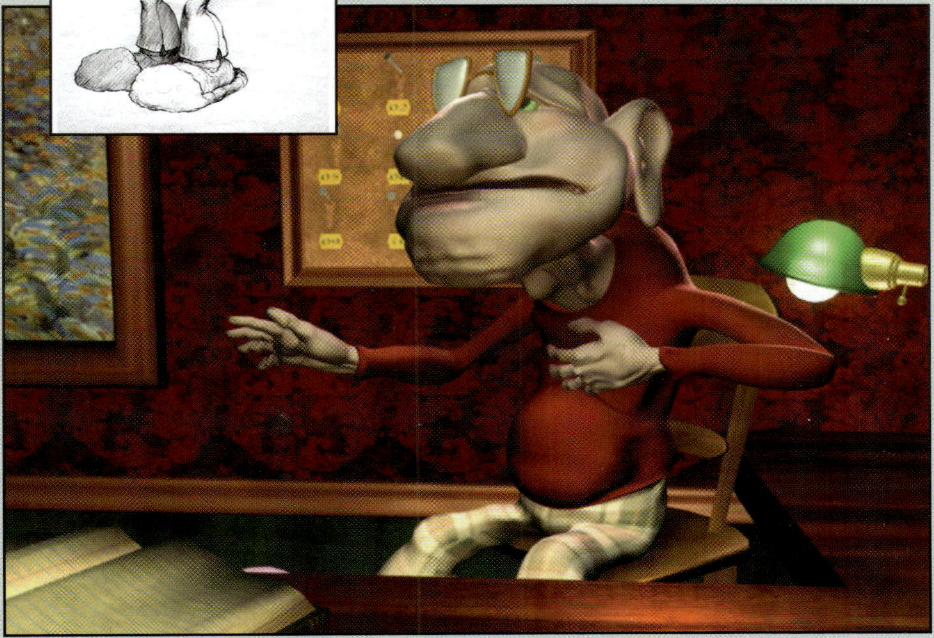

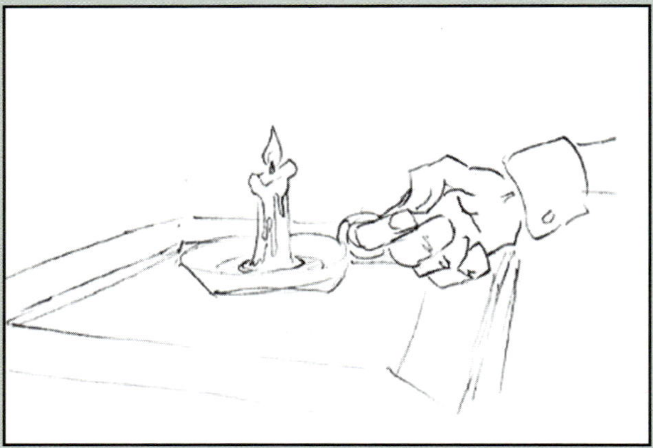

figure 87

figure 88

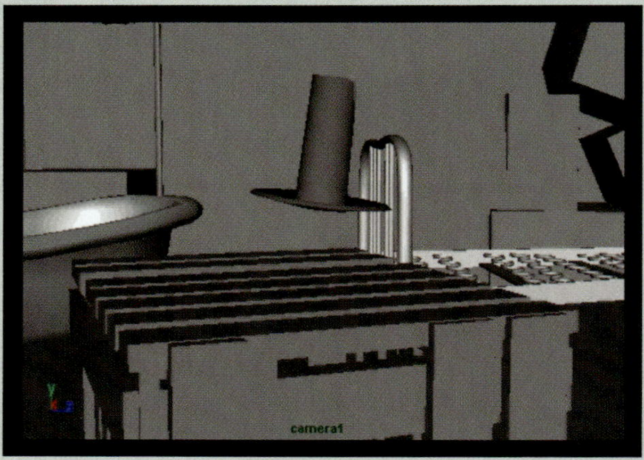

The 3D animatic is an important reference guide. It is always good to go back and compare original storyboard ideas against the animatic to see if certain shots are going to work. These pages show a couple of examples where the original idea held up throughout the entire production and one where there were some camera shot changes.

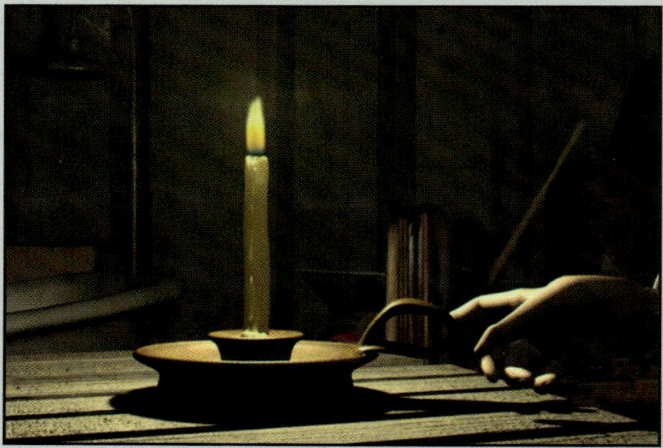

figure 89

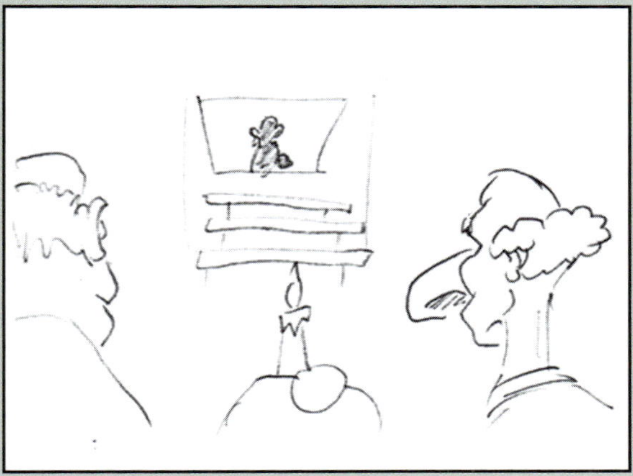

figure 90

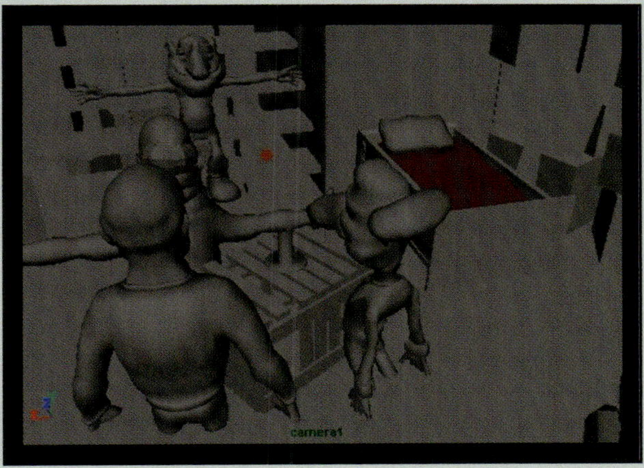

figure 91

figure 92

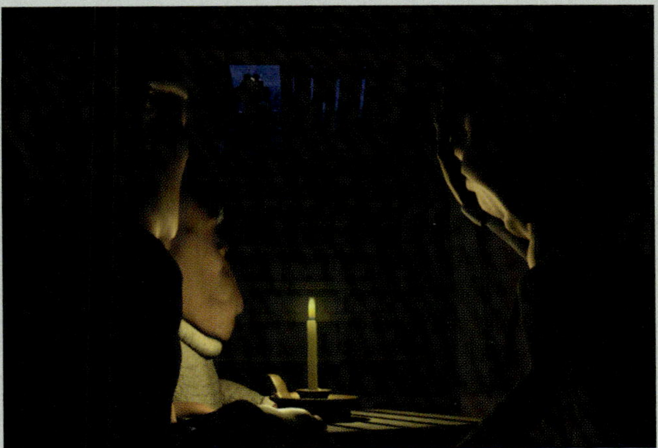

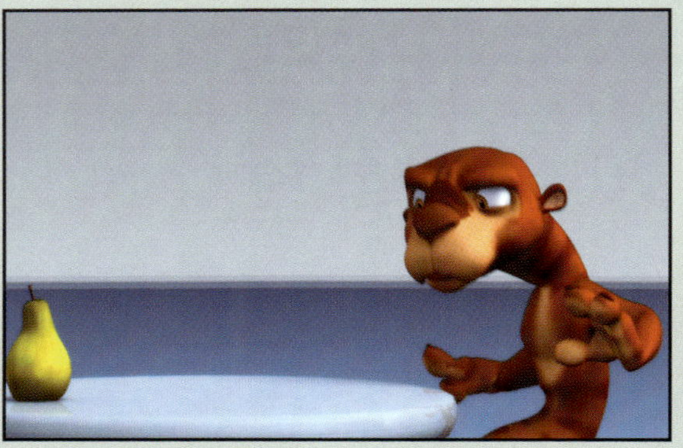

figure 93

Josh Burton created this short, called "Much Ado," in Maya. He used a number of traditional animation techniques to create the movement, completing several pages of storyboards and character design before beginning production.

figure 94

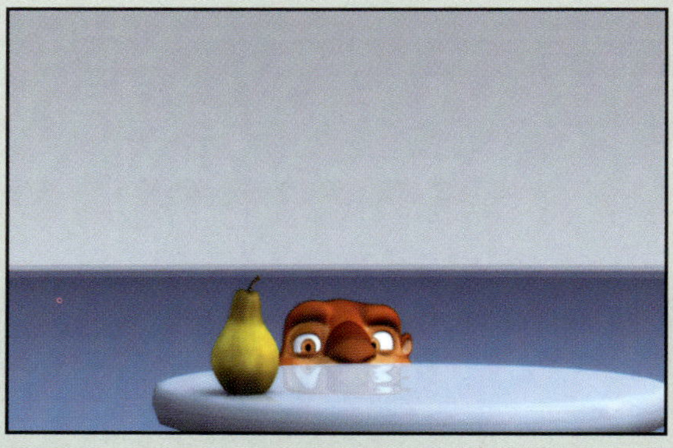

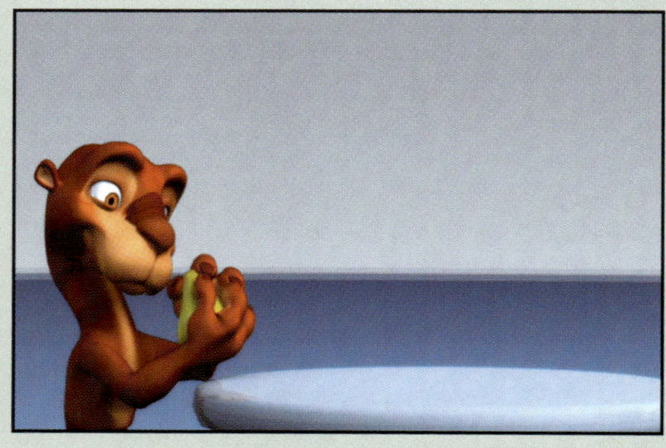

figure 95

figure 96

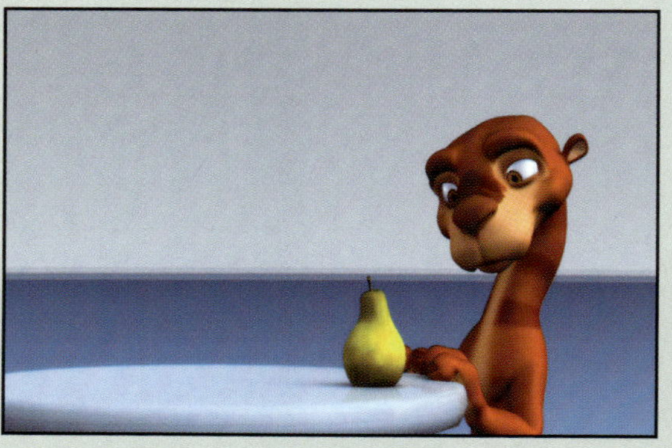

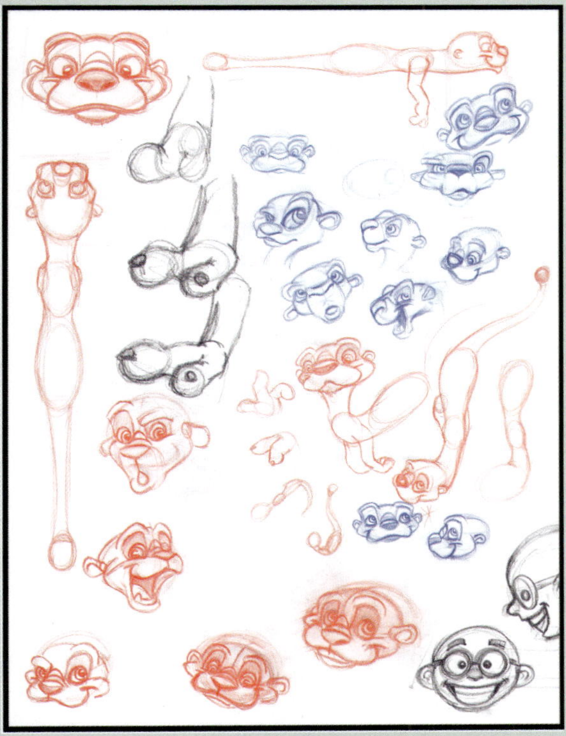

figure 97

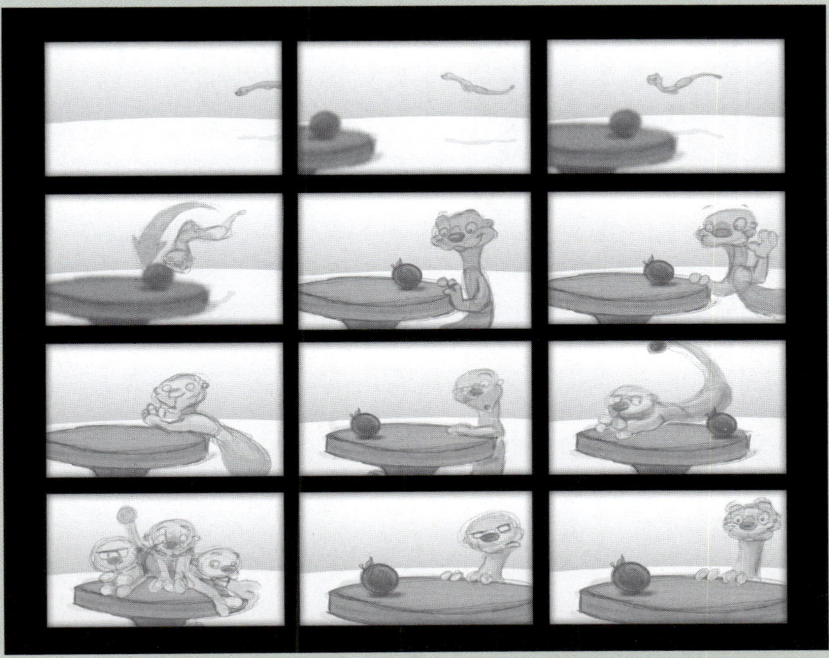

figure 98

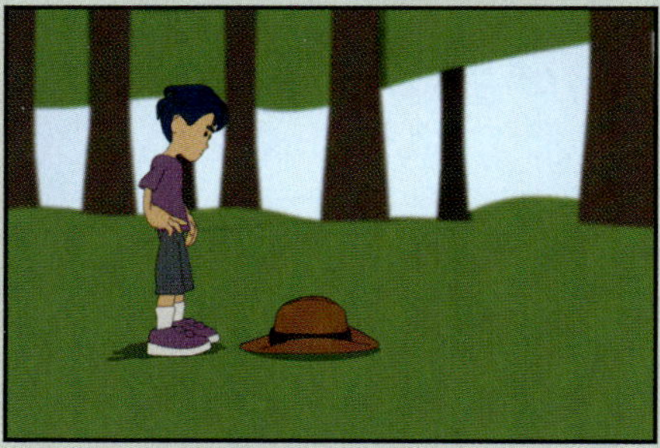

figure 99

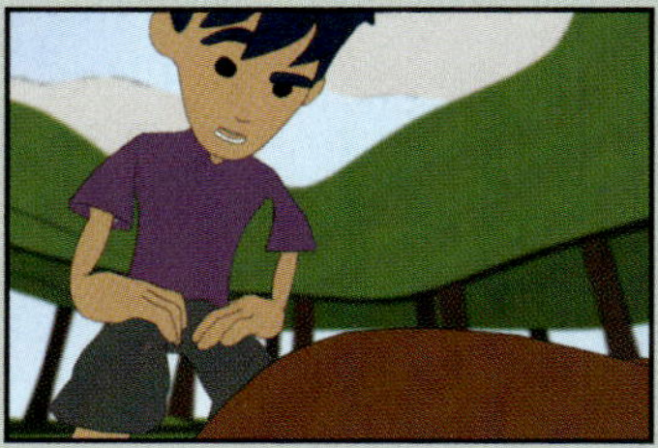

figure 100

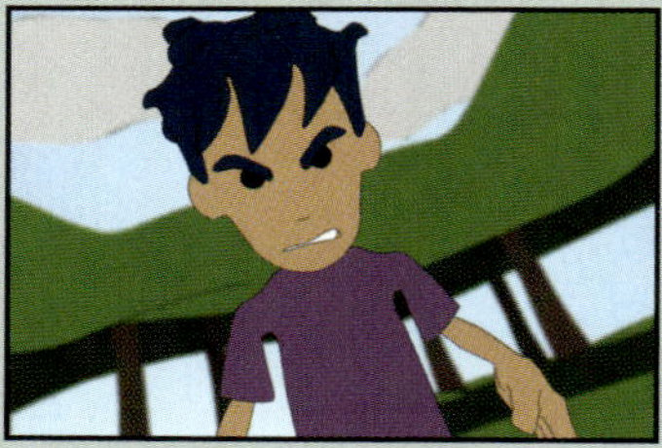

figure 101

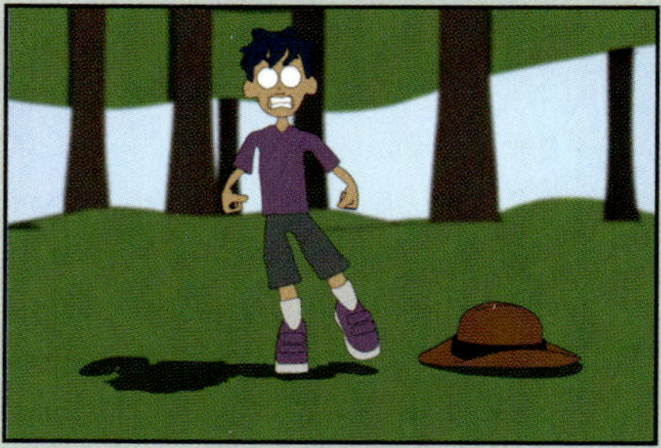

figure 102

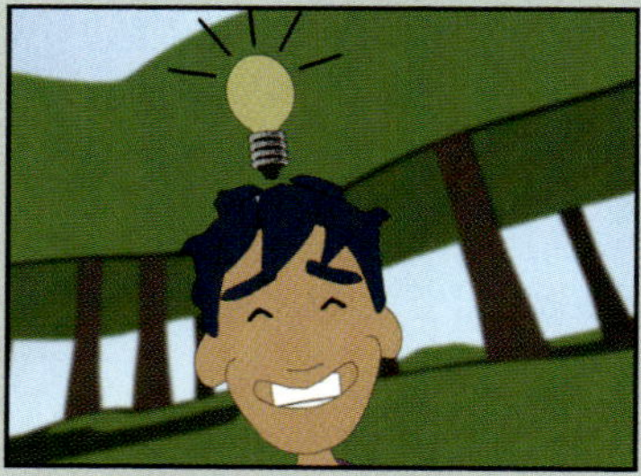

figure 103

Ricardo Tobon created "Luka's Hat" as the visual component of his M.F.A. thesis. He experimented with limited animation techniques commonly used in television animation. He used Maya vector rendering to obtain a cartoon-like look. The characters were rendered with outlines—and the background without—so one would stand out more than the other. The character only produced shadows on the ground to keep things visually simple.

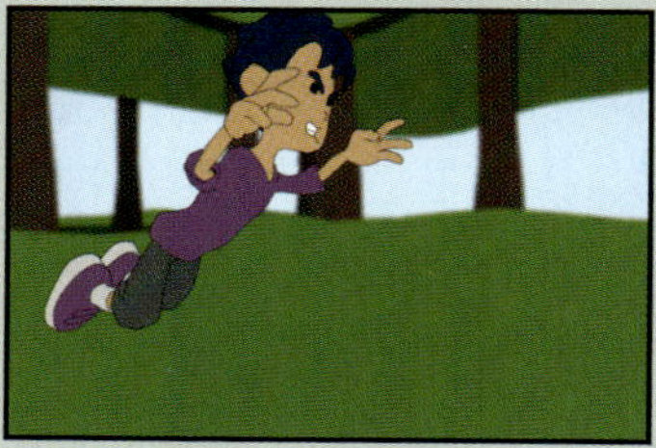

figure 104

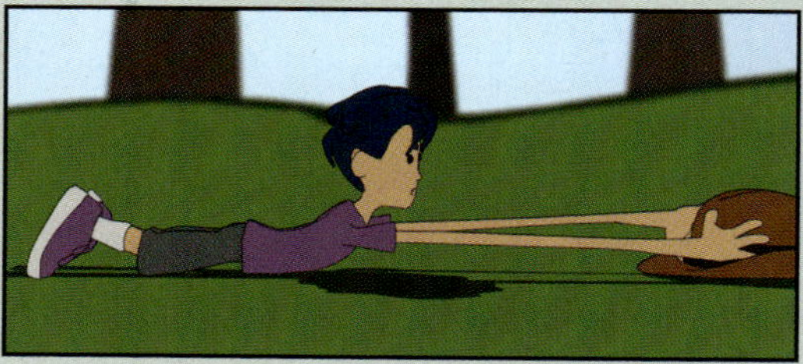

figure 105

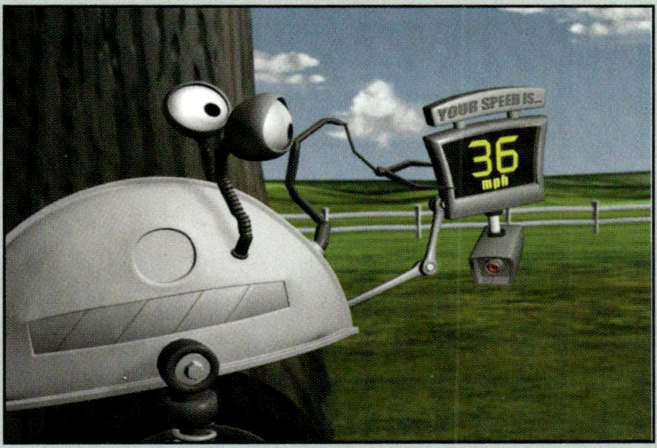

figure 106

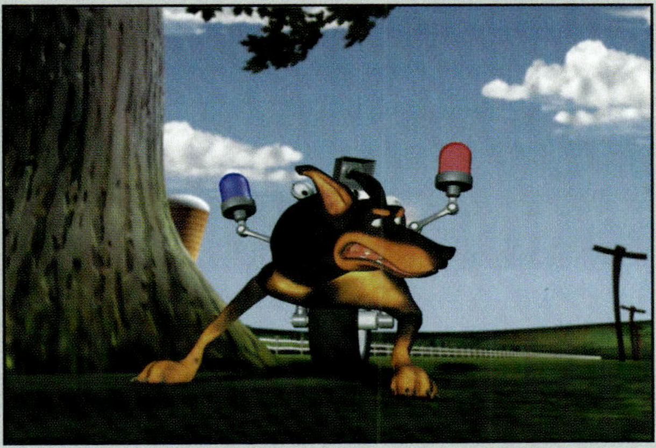

figure 107

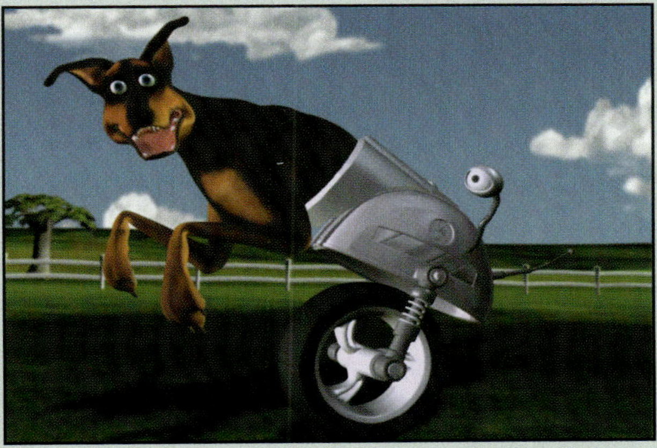

figure 108

Marty Clayton created Gumshoe with a team of graduate students as part of his thesis. Gumshoe is half dog and half machine. Here we see him on the job as a traffic cop. Marty created this piece for a children's programming pitch.

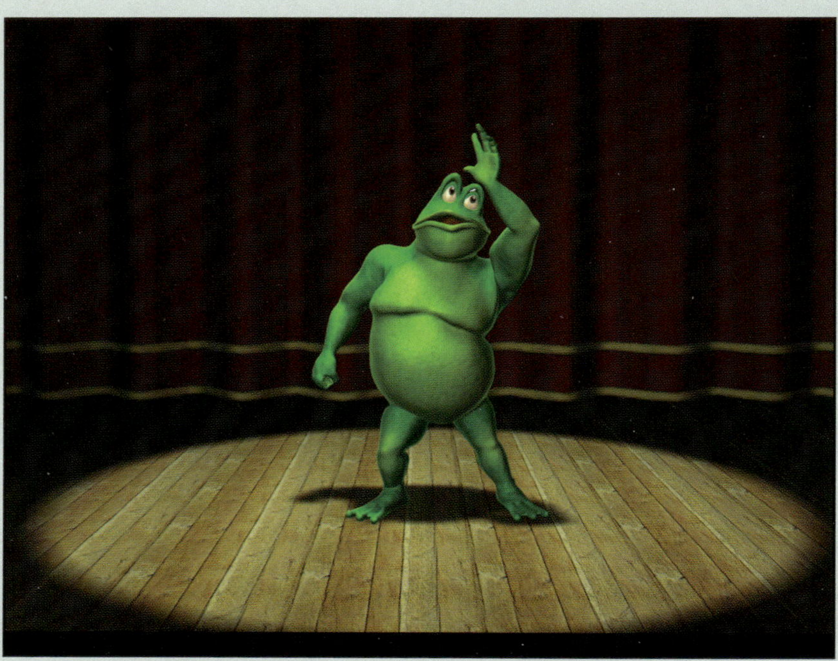

figure 109

Christoph Malessa created this dancing frog character. You can see the work in action at www.malessa.de.

Create a timing chart (see Figure 7-42).

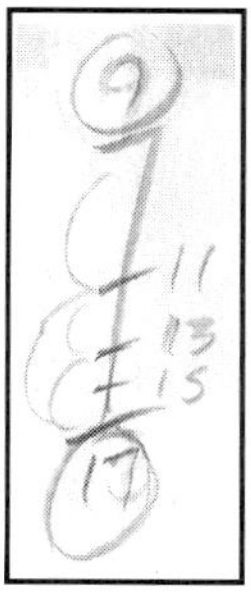

figure 7-42

A timing chart.

Now pose your character in relation to the thumbnails.

Use the following process for beginning your full-body animation. You will identify the big leading motion first and then go down the chain of responding motions to the final affected limbs.

1. Set the key poses with linear, stepped curves. Be sure to work in the low-resolution version of the puppet: Look for the lo_res selection layers in the Layer Editor and turn on their visibility. Turn off visibility for hi_res. The torso is the leading mass in this activity.

2. Play the animation for a timing check.

3. Edit key pose timing until approved.

4. Select Curves for Leading Motion, and change these to Clamped. You should be using the cog_ctrl for this action on Generi because it is the parent control of the spine. Pay attention to the rotate and translate curves. These are the most important elements in your puppet for implying weight and strength for this exercise.

   "The motion starts with the initiation of an anticipation move in the central part of the body."

5. Create the anticipation by setting a few extra key frames before the key pose. Tweak the in/out of each curve in reference to the timing chart. Think about where the speed and momentum are at each frame. Be careful that you do not have any parts of the rig "floating," in other words, slowly moving from one keyed point to another with no reason. Make definite movement choices.

6. Take the next large controlling mass—the three spines—and change these curves to Clamped. You are now working with spine01_ctrl, spine02_ctrl, spine03_ctrl. Notice that you can only rotate in the X, Y, and Z. Think of the wave principle when animating the spine. You may want to move your key frames up one frame on each spine control to create a wave of motion responding to the initial force.

7. Tweak the in/out of each curve in reference to your timing chart. Think about where the speed and momentum are at each frame. The cog_ctrl is leading these spines, and this motion precedes the motion in the arms. Make sure the movement is smooth for the entire swing.

8. The head is next. Select head_ctrl, the retainer-like object wrapped around the head. You can only rotate the head. Notice that it is at a different angle and rotation from the spine, and it may even rotate in reverse of the spine because the eye will always be on the target—in this case the batter.

9. Arms are next. Use FK. Remember to set IK_FK to **0** in the handRotation_ctrl_L and handRotation_ ctrl_R so that you can access the shoulder_ctrl_L and shoulder_ctrl_R. Note how the right shoulder and arm rise through the throw. Anticipation is necessary at the start. Remember to consider slow out, slow in, and fast in-between. Remember the hard accent at the end. Remember the weight of the ball as it is released.

10. Elbows are the next concern. They are reacting to the shoulders, which are reacting to the torso. Select the l_elbo and r_elbo. Notice that you can only rotate in the X. Set curves to Clamped and tweak the in and out speed.

    "*Now the elbow drops as the hand continues to rise to the top of its arc. The elbow now leads as the forearm comes forward.*"

11. Now address the follow-through and 'thinking' of the character with the hands. Take this time to address the basic wave principles and apply them to the hand and fingers. The hands begin to lead as the batter comes in contact with the ball, and then they fall back as the momentum of the body takes over.

"*The hand reacts by tilting back in reaction to the move. The wrist begins to lead the move at this time. The momentum keeps the hand at right angles to the forearm. The arm has extended to its full length, bringing about the final 'snap' of the throwing action as the hand quickly straightens ad releases the ball.*"

Play back the scene for a timing check. Is it too slow or fast? Edit your Graph Editor to make fixes. Now you should understand that poses are easier to fix in the stepped-curve phase, where less damage is done to curves already edited.

How Can I Imply Speed?

Sometimes the timing and movement are just right, but something is still missing. Film captures motion blur, and you are used to seeing it. In Maya, you must ask for it. You can add motion blur during the render in Maya.

Motion blur is found in your Render Settings (see Figure 7-43) on the Maya Software tab.

When you are ready to render out the scene, you can set these to On.

To save yourself rendering time, only set motion blur for the objects you want blurred. To change motion blurs per object, go to the Attributes window for the actual geometry and check or uncheck the settings as per your preference (see Figure 7-44).

NOTE

You may be beginning to pick up that animation is hard. It requires as much, if not more, time as rigging, modeling, and texturing. Too often I see people's use of all of their time constructing the scenario and the puppets, and then they rush through the animation.

A great deal of information can be gleaned from traditional animation and applied to 3D. Take the time to draw things out and study them before entering the 3D phase.

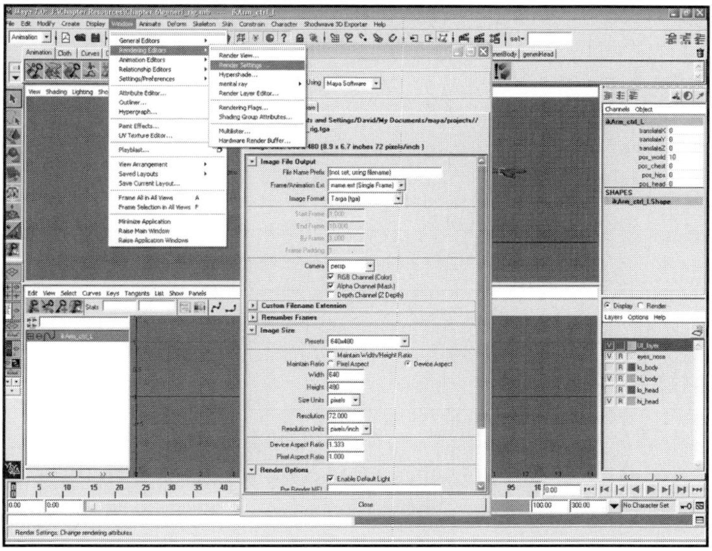

figure 7-43

Motion blur.

figure 7-44

Motion blur is under the Render Stats.

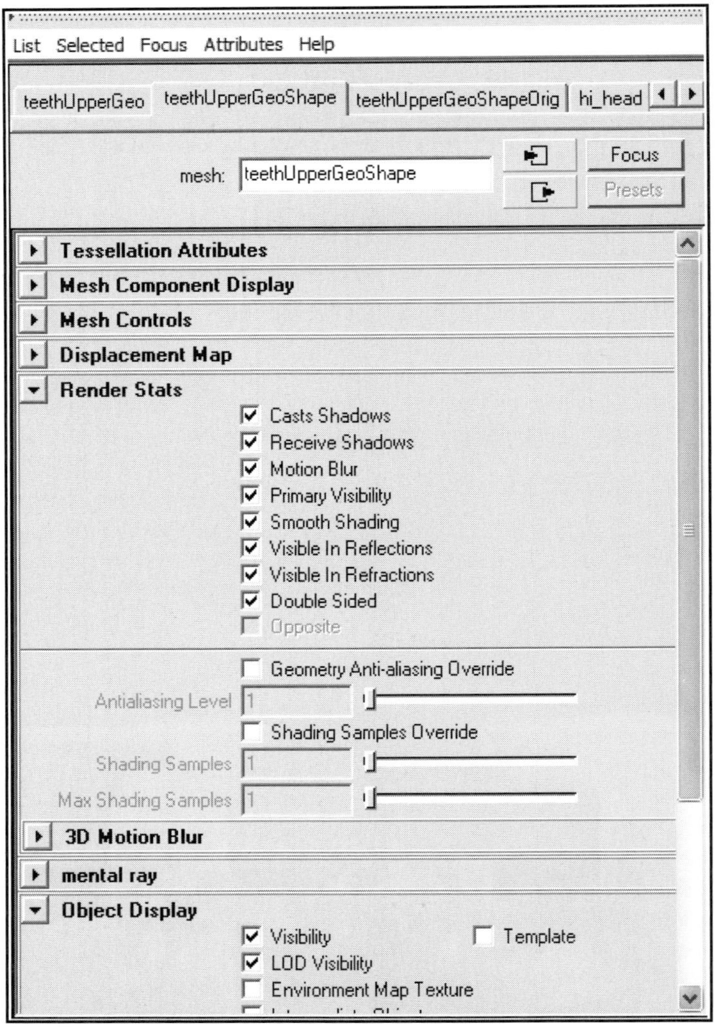

SUMMARY

The wave pattern applies to a great deal of animation. A base object determines motion, and all attached objects follow. Often there are multiple leading objects. Physics step in after initial propulsion and participate in the overlapping action and follow-through.

Work through your 3D puppet to determine the main thrust, and then work through the hierarchy to define the wave pattern to achieve believable motion.

REFERENCE IMAGES

If you're interested, the reference images for the preceding traditional throw are on the attached CD. Load them in as reference images and practice your timing against them. Then get used to thumbnailing out your own reference images.

An excellent resource for thumbnailed animation is *The Animators Survival Kit* by Richard Williams. He has some beautiful, hand-drawn sequences that can be scanned and posed against in Maya.

I use a cheap web camera to take stills of my thumbnail references. I photograph them using the timing charts I create, and then I play them back using the Maya Fcheck. This helps me save a great deal of time, as I can finesse my timing before even opening the Maya package. Your art director will appreciate your increased productivity.

in review

1. What is forward kinematics (FK)?
2. How does it differ from inverse kinematics (IK)?
3. What are interpolated images?
4. What is ghosting?
5. What is the Image Viewer?
6. What is the wave pattern?
7. How do you draw in an Image Viewer window, and why would you?
8. What kind of editing can you do in the timeline?
9. How do you set motion blur?

EXPLORING ON YOUR OWN

1. Go back to the flour sack animation in the last chapter and look for opportunities to practice follow-through and overlapping action. Create smaller timing charts to add in between the larger ones, and edit your curves to accommodate them.
2. Go back to the flour sack animation, and look at the timing on your weight opportunities. Do you see anything you would fix?
3. Add motion blur to the flour sack in chosen areas where speed may be emphasized.
4. Try a hard accent and a soft accent with the ArmFK.mb file.

notes

8

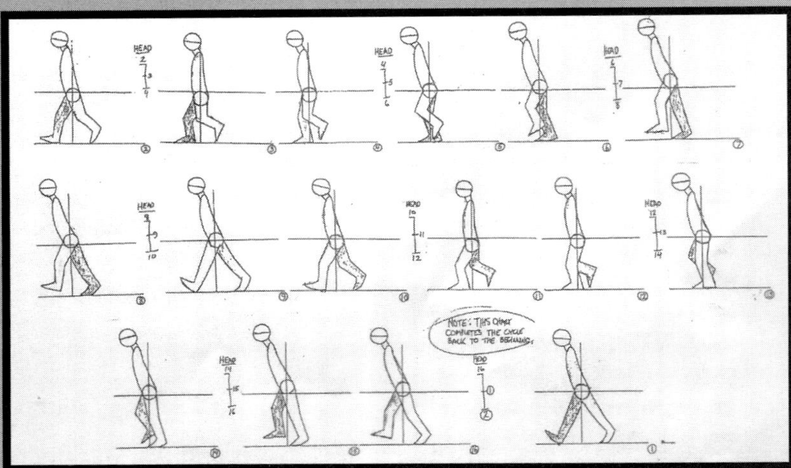

the walking cycle

charting your course

A walk cycle is one of the most difficult exercises that a beginning animator learns. Every joint is moving, and the character must be an identifiable personality—while all these limbs are translating, rotating, and showing weight—not to mention having a purpose to the walk. How does an animator give life while keeping track of all of the necessary movements?

Think of masses in motion.

goals

In this chapter, you will:

- **Learn how to work with a pre-rigged character.**
- **Examine the traditional construction of a walk cycle.**
- **Apply wave theory to the walk cycle.**

TOOLS USED

- **Switching between inverse kinematics (IK) and forward kinematics (FK).** You will have the ability to use both FK and IK on the arms. You will practice going between them.

- **Locators.** The knees and elbows can be manipulated so that they are pointing in the right direction when limbs are animated.

- **Hi-res vs. Lo-res models.** Low-resolution models exist to make animating faster. High-resolution models are for the final render. You will learn how to use each.

- **Foot controls.** You will practice using the Heel, lift Heel, Toe, Bank, and Pivot Toe controls found in the Channel Editor for the foot.

- **Extra arm controls.** You have access to a few more controls in the arms that have not been discussed yet. These will help you gain more control over the rig.

THE WALK CYCLE

Building Animation in Layers

You have arrived at what many animators consider to be one of the most complex issues in the animation process—the walk. For the purposes of this exercise, which will be a basic introduction to the mechanics of the process, you will be staging the figure in the center of your field of vision and in profile, held there throughout. In other words, the character will be striding along in place as the "background" slides along behind. In this way, you will get used to all the dynamics of the walking motion and also be able to put down a series of poses representative of one step with each foot, which you will then be able to repeat for as long as you require.

This process, although complex, will become clear through the "hands-on" process as you go through the exercise. So stay with it, and execute each step as delineated. You will get through it with no bruises!

To begin, you need to learn about "animating in layers." This will be an approach to utilize as you get into the more complex exercises you will confront throughout the rest of your time as an animator. It is best to get used to layering in the beginning, as you are going to need to rely on it as a way to check the various elements within your work as you get into more advanced acting and movements.

A Traditional Walk Cycle, Animated in Layers

The first thing you need is a sheet to establish guidelines to use as a template for your animated figure to move within. This guide sheet will be underneath your series of animation drawings and will remain on the bottom of the stack to refer to for alignments.

Ground Plane

This will represent the surface on which your animated figure will walk. Place this line at the bottom center of the sheet (see Figure 8-1). In Maya, you will use your grid as this ground plane.

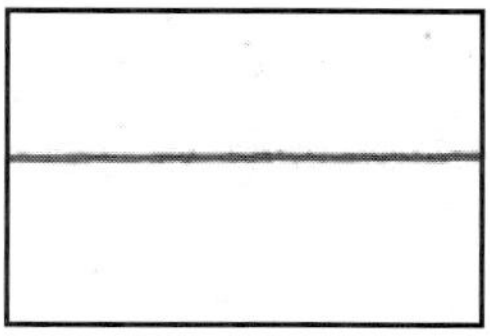

figure 8-1

The ground plane.

Vertical Centerline

The figure will need a line to represent a center of gravity for the up and down motion of the hips during the walk cycle. The hips will be represented in each drawing as a sphere. In Maya, you will use a curve for the vertical centerline (see Figure 8-2).

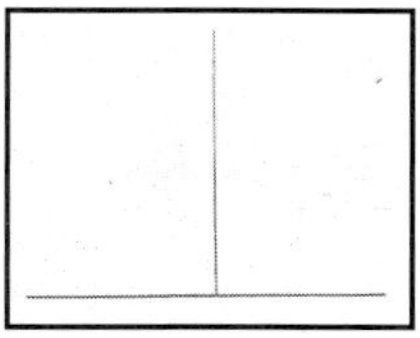

figure 8-2

Vertical centerline.

This up-and-down movement in the hips and body is the most important item to include in an animated walk, as it implies weight. Without this feeling of weight, a walk cycle will seem stiff and floaty. Lack of weight is the single most characteristic oversight in an amateurish-looking presentation, whether in traditional or CG animation.

Horizontal Centerline

This line will intersect the hips in the "neutral" position in order to establish the center of the up-and-down motion. In Maya, you will use a curve for the horizontal centerline (see Figure 8-3).

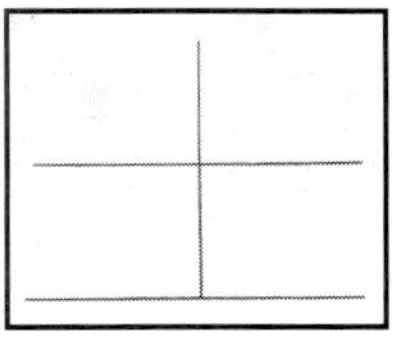

figure 8-3

The horizontal centerline.

You will be using 16 drawings to animate your two-step walk cycle. As you become more experienced in animating walks, you will find that there is no single "right way" to do it. This basic walk is merely a way to get something moving, and it is a fairly simple process for a beginning animator. We will first demonstrate how it is done in traditional animation.

A schematic drawing of the entire cycle to refer to as you go through the process of drawing it is shown in Figure 8-4. You can see why it is called a cycle, as number 16 perfectly hooks up back to number 1 with no interruption. If the concept is a bit foggy at this time, do not worry—it will become clear as you work through it.

figure | 8-4 |

The entire cycle.

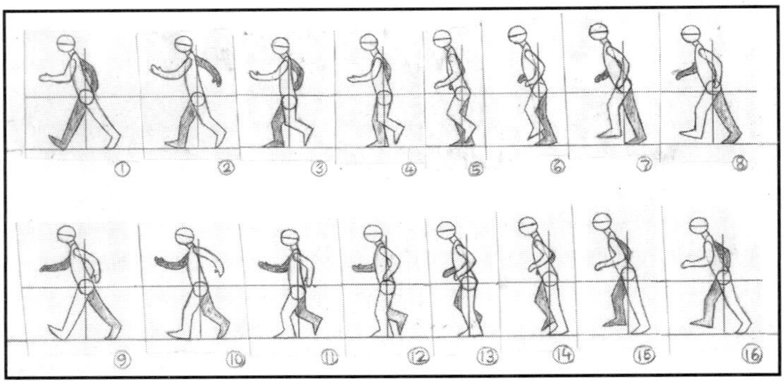

DON'T GO THERE!

Don't set four key poses for the walk cycle in 3D and assume you are done. There is so much more to consider when constructing the walk. In addition to everything else, there is overlapping action between all the limbs that requires offsetting keys. It can be one of the most complex movements to re-create in 3D.

Take the extra time to dissect the masses in motion. The art is in the subtle observations you are able to imitate.

Beginning the Drawings

You have arrived at the point where you can start the step-by-step process of making the drawings for your walk cycle.

1. Establish contact drawings (see Figure 8-5; numbers 1 and 9) for the right and left lead foot (hips sphere in "neutral" or center height). These are the most important drawings to establish at the beginning of your cycle. They determine the widest

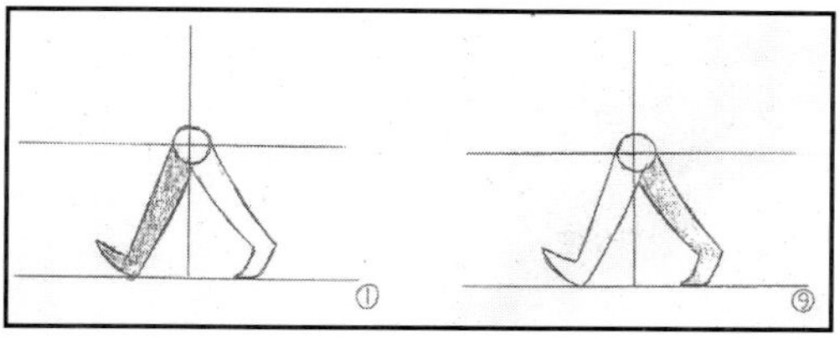

figure 8-5

Contact drawings.

part of the step and can be used later to determine how many steps it will take to get from one location to another on a layout. We will revisit this topic later.

It will help at this time to shade the upstage leg in all drawings to keep a clear idea of the location of each leg at all times. You will find this an issue as you work on walk cycles. Also, numbering each drawing as well as notes on the drawing indicating "high," "low," and any other description about a particular part of the cycle are well worth the effort and should become a habit. It is very easy to become lost animating when you don't make such notes.

2. Establish crossing drawings (see Figure 8-6; numbers 5 and 13) for each leading foot (hips center height).

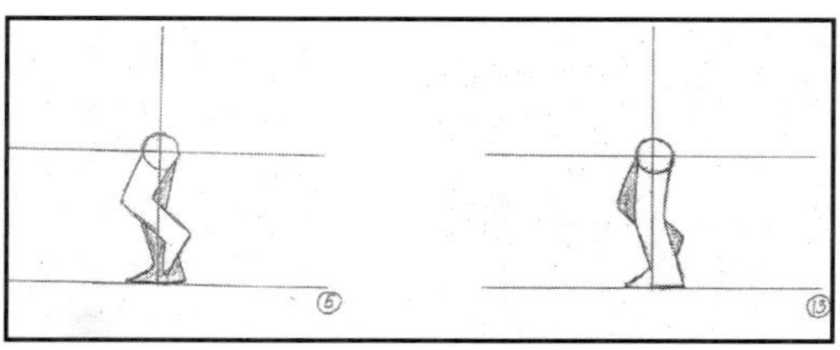

figure 8-6

Cross drawings for 5 and 13.

3. Establish low extremes for each foot. This is the point at which the leading foot catches the weight of the body in its forward movement and the body undergoes a drop downward (see Figure 8-7; numbers 3 and 11).

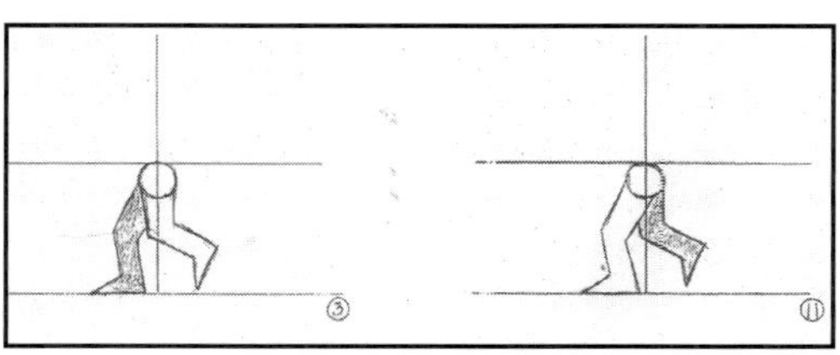

figure 8-7

Low extremes.

4. Establish high extremes for each foot (hips at highest position), as seen in Figure 8-8: numbers 7 and 15. This is the point at which the body is pushed to its highest position for the lead foot to be clear for its forward swing.

figure | 8-8 |

High extremes.

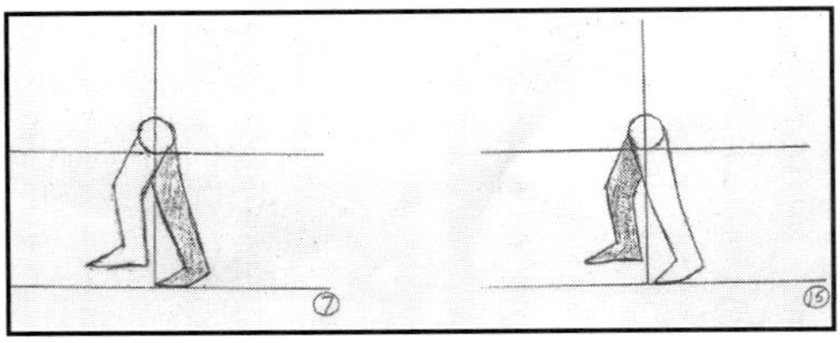

5. Complete the cycle by adding one drawing between each of the drawings. These extra drawings smooth out the action and make the timing about right to simulate a real walk. The numbers will be all the even numbers: 2, 4, 6, 8, 10, 12, 14, and 16. The charts will all be even timing; meaning each drawing will be exactly in the middle position between two extremes (see Figure 8-9).

figure | 8-9 |

The cycle with timing charts.

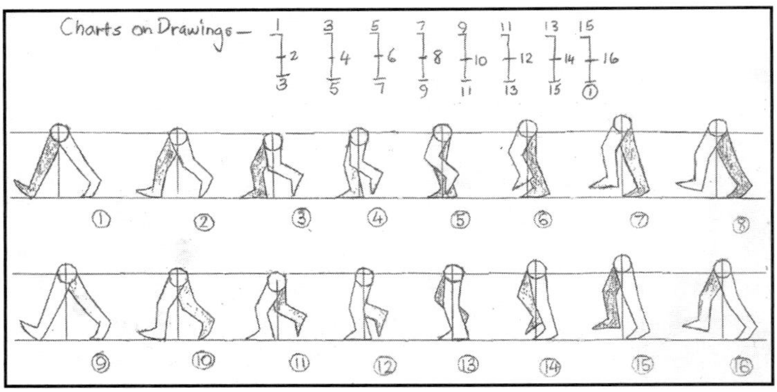

Now you have all the drawings you will need for your walk cycle. You can shoot the drawings and take a look at the action of the body from the hips down. Now move on to the next steps in completing your walking figure.

6. Add bodies (see Figure 8-10). Establish neutral position on the upper bodies. A walk is a forward movement; therefore, the neutral body should be leaning forward a bit. The drawings to receive the neutral body will be the contact poses (numbers 1 and 9), followed by the crossing poses (numbers 5 and 13).

figure | 8-10 |

Add bodies.

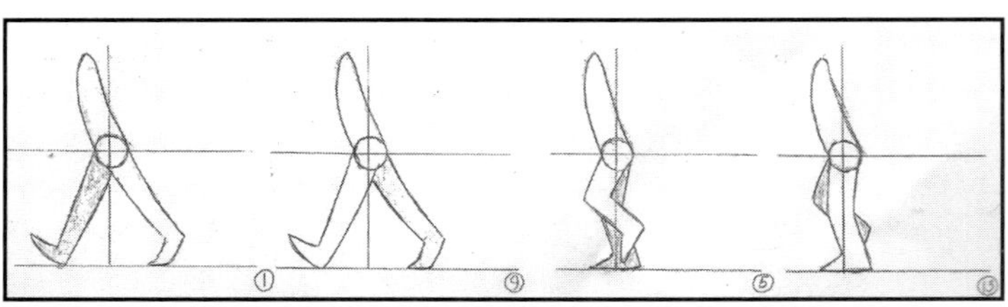

7. Now add bodies to the lowest and highest positions. First look at the lowest body position, which you will find by looking for the hip sphere below the horizontal centerline (see Figure 8-11). In this case, these will be numbers 3 and 11. In these drawings, the body will achieve its most vertical attitude. The reason for this will be seen when running the animation, which will come soon.

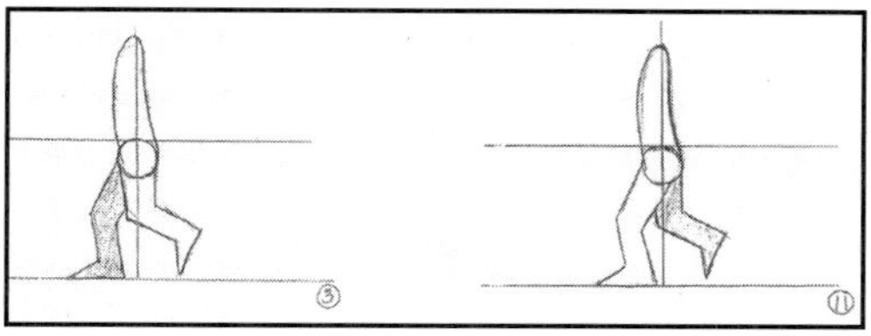

figure 8-11

The hip sphere below the centerline.

8. Adding the bodies to the highest drawings, the ones with the hip sphere above the horizontal centerline (numbers 7 and 15), you will reverse the procedure, making these the drawings with the farthest forward tilt (see Figure 8-12).

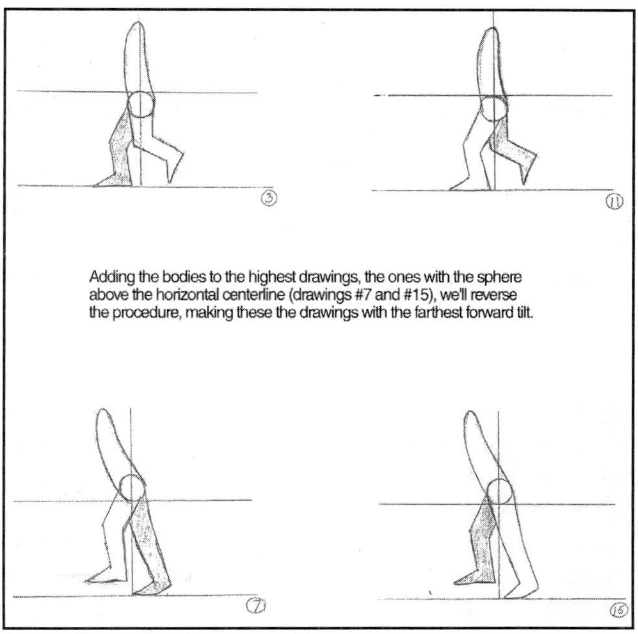

figure 8-12

The farthest forward tilt.

9. Once again, complete the cycle by adding bodies onto all the even-numbered in-between drawings, being careful to watch the arcs.

It is time to shoot the drawings and look at the cycle again. Adding the body in this manner has automatically given you overlapping action. It's starting to be fun now, isn't it?

10. It's now time to add heads, Attach heads to the bodies, starting with the contact drawings (see Figure 8-13: numbers 1 and 9). The neck makes a slight angle forward, as shown in figure A. Figure B shows the incorrect way of attaching the head.

figure 8-13

The correct way of attaching heads.

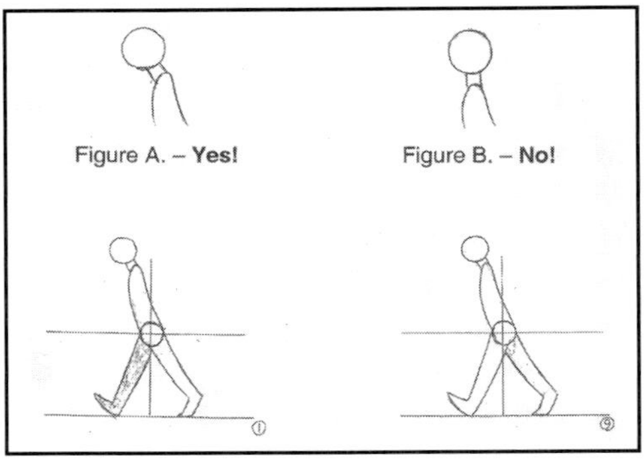

11. Now add the heads to the crossing drawings (see Figure 8-14: numbers 5 and 13), then the low extremes (numbers 3 and 11), and then the high extremes, (numbers 7 and 15). You now have heads on all the odd-numbered drawings (see Figure 8-14). The next step is to in-between the heads onto the even-numbered bodies. In this way, the action of the heads can be made smooth, and it eliminates the jumps and jerks that might happen otherwise.

figure 8-14

Adding heads.

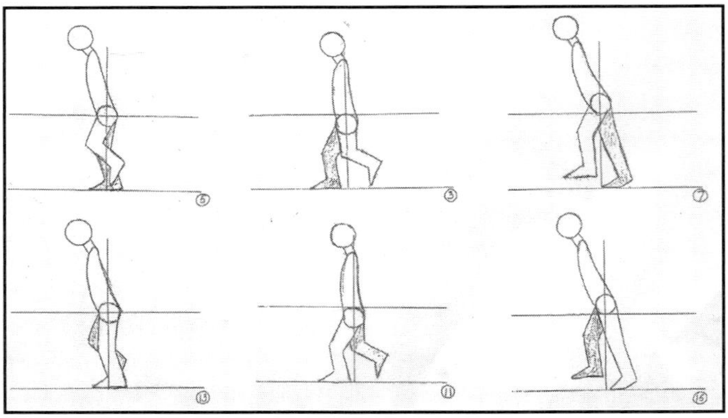

Here is where you get a bit more adventurous with overlapping action, delaying the head's reaction to the movement ever so slightly to indicate the wave action (Do you remember?) flowing from the central body outward, in this case to the head.

12. Now add a horizontal eye line through the center of the cranial sphere. The first ones to address will be completely level, and

they will be added to the first drawing past each high and low position in the cycle; in this case, those will be Figure 8-15, numbers 8 and 16 on the high end and numbers 4 and 12 in the low position. Explanation: By delaying the action of the head by one drawing, you have automatically instituted the wave action in the walking figure, slightly delaying the overlapping action as you get into the furthest articulating parts from the hips, which are the primary motivator.

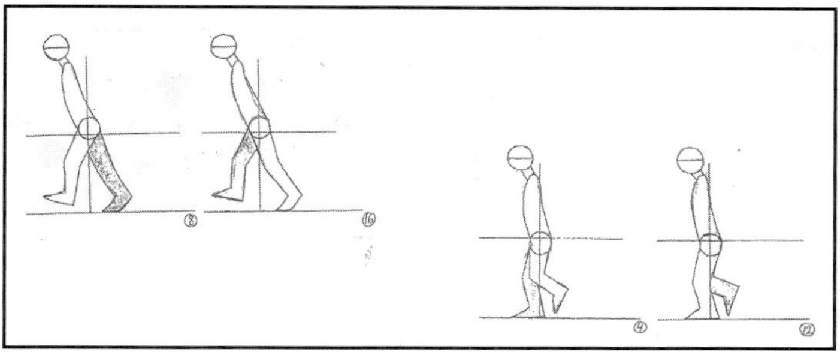

figure 8-15

A horizontal eyeline on 4, 8, 12, 16.

Once again, we beg your indulgence and ask you to bear with us if the concept still seems foggy. Once you have carefully followed the instructions and shot the resultant drawings, you will begin to see the method.

13. Next, you will need to locate the points at which the head will react to the up and down motion of the walk by tilting to its maximum positions for forward and back. Following the logic that the high and low points of the cycle are the most level position, then the middle (or neutral) positions would be the locations of the greatest tilt. (Stay with us!) This means that you need the two contact drawings and the two crossing drawings. But wait! Remember our one-drawing delay! So, going one drawing forward, you will pull aside drawing numbers 2, 6, 10, and 14.

14. In numbers 2 and 10 the body is dropping downward, so you will subtly tilt the head back in reaction to the drop (see Figure 8-16).

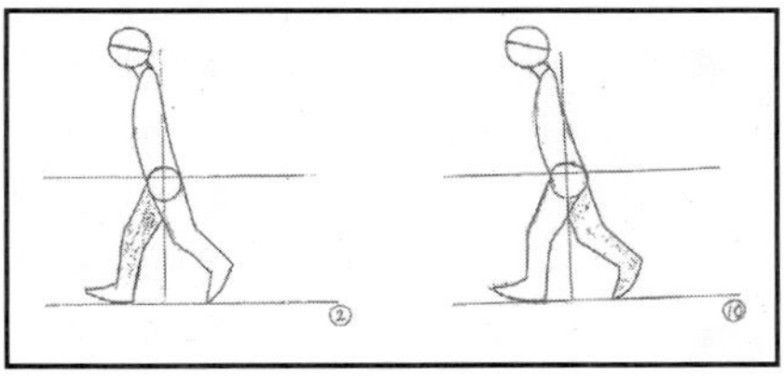

figure 8-16

Tilt the head back at 2 and 10.

15. As the body is rising in numbers 6 and 14 (see Figure 8-17), you will tilt the head forward in reaction to that motion (about the same amount of tilt as the back tilt).

figure 8-17

Tilt the head forward at 6 and 14.

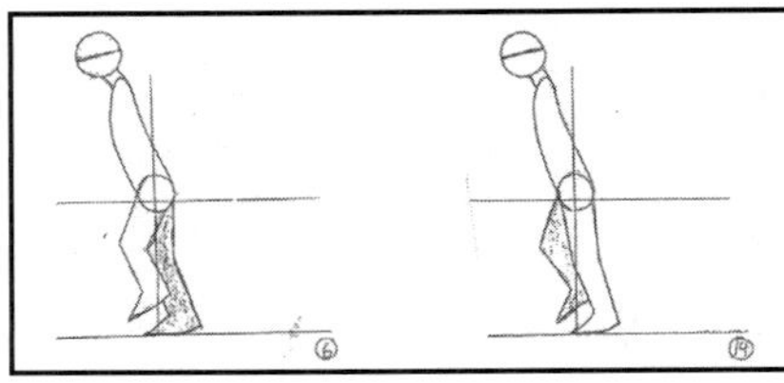

16. At this time, you will need to make charts for the heads (see Figure 8-18). The overlapping action you have used has made it necessary to consider all the even-numbered drawings as extremes so you can correctly in-between the head action. Make a note above each chart that says "head" so you will be able to keep track. Also remember that you are not in-betweening head position, just the angle of the eyeline. So, chart them and draw them.

figure 8-18

The whole chart.

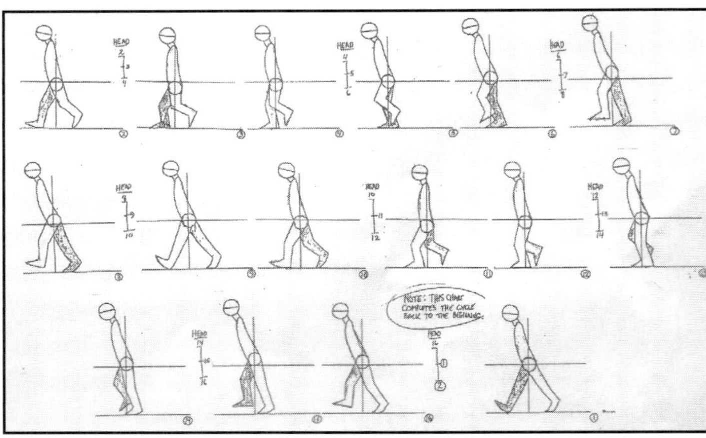

You now have a nifty overlap on the head action during the walk cycle. Remember to keep the tilt forward and backward subtle so that you do not end up with the character looking like he is trying to snap his head off while he is walking!

At this point, the only necessary part remaining is to add arms to the individual. In a straight profile shot like this, the motion of the arms needs to be thought of in the simplest form: right leg forward, left arm forward; left leg forward, right arm forward. Once again, use shading on all drawings to help differentiate the upstage arm from the downstage.

17. Locate the contact drawings. Now go one drawing past those and add the arms at their most extreme front and back positions, remembering that it is always the opposite arm forward from the leg (see Figure 8-19).

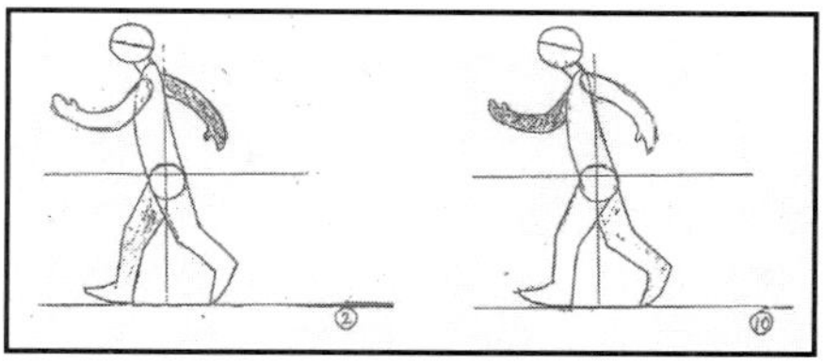

figure 8-19

Contact drawings, one frame past.

18. Now find the crossing drawings. Go one drawing past and add the arms at their closest middle position (see Figure 8-20).

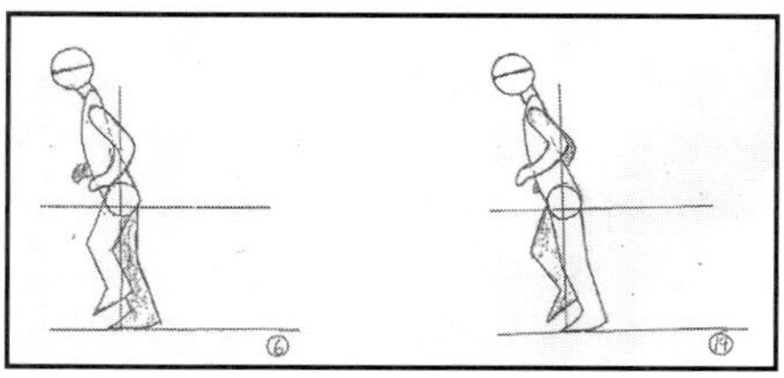

figure 8-20

Crossing drawings, one frame past.

19. Now for the final step! The four drawings on which you just added the arms (numbers 2, 6, 10, and 14) are now the extremes for the arm movements. Accordingly, you need to put charts on them as you did on the heads, this time specifying "arms" at the top of the charts. This time there will be three drawings between each extreme, and the charts will be done as shown in Figure 8-21. Chart and in-between all remaining drawings as indicated.

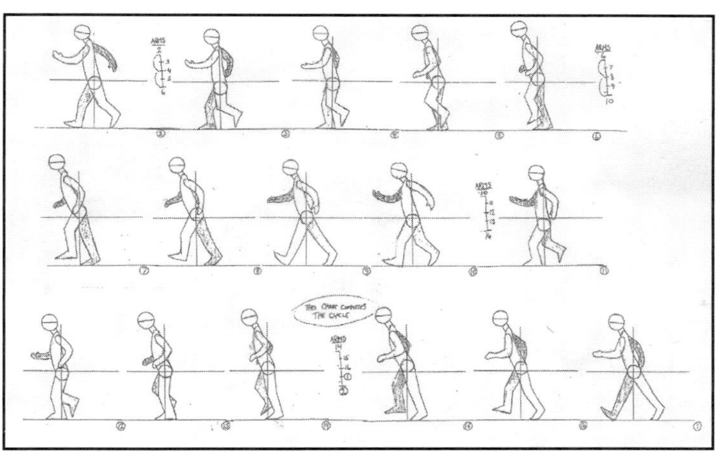

figure 8-21

Arms and charts.

That's it! Now shoot the drawings in the proper sequence, put them on a loop, and you can view the walk you have just animated as long as you want. Be critical, look for "glitches" (small jerks and pops in your walk pattern), and take the necessary steps to smooth them out. This can generally be accomplished by putting the offending section of drawings on the pegs, looking to see which ones seem "out of whack," and adjusting them to a smooth flow. This will become a routine part of the process, as there are usually small touches that can help any animated scene become better.

Armed with the things you have learned about the walk pattern, you are now ready to start experimenting with individual walks, turning a character into three-dimensional space and having it travel from one part of a layout to another. A number of good animation texts are available that lay out some interesting variations. Go forth and enjoy!

TECHNIQUES

The traditional method of animating is still important for CG animators. You will adopt many traditional techniques to the 3D platform as these theories are based on movement, not the type of tool you use.

IK and FK Blending

Sometimes you will want to use IK and FK on one control in the same scene. There is a very easy way to achieve this.

An animatable channel exists in the Channel Box when you select the handRotation_control (L or R; see Figure 8-22).

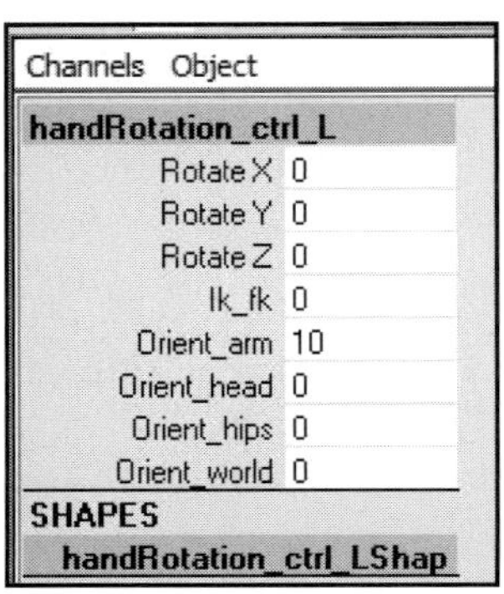

figure 8-22

The FK_IK channel.

A value of 10 means IK, and a value of 0 means FK. Open your rig, and select the handRotation_ctrl. Give yourself 10 frames to work with in the timeline. Go to frame 1. In the IK_FK channel, key frame a value for 0. Go to frame 10. Key-frame a value for 10. Change the position of the FK arm and elbow, and set a key frame.

You will see the arm respond to the FK_IK animated settings. The arm is changing from FK to IK control. See the file fk_ik_demo.mb on the enclosed CD. You can have this action happen over one or multiple frames.

You can also have an animation of a swinging hand in FK and the animation of a swinging hand in IK on the same limb. Animating between FK and IK will allow you to switch from one to the other in the same scene. This is handy when you want your walking man to grab ahold of a tree or some other locked-down element.

IK controls do not travel with FK-animated limbs, so when you view your IK handles in wireframe, they will be static when FK is in use. The limb will travel with the control when IK is in use. Check the color of the joints: The blue joint chain represents the skeleton with pure FK animation, the brown joint chain represents the skeleton with pure IK animation, and the magenta joint chain represents the animation blend.

Both FK and IK controls will be available for your use when a value greater than .01 exists in the Channel controls. Be careful with this setting to avoid confusion.

The Foot Controls

The foot controls contain some extra controls for the heel and toe movements (see Figure 8-23).

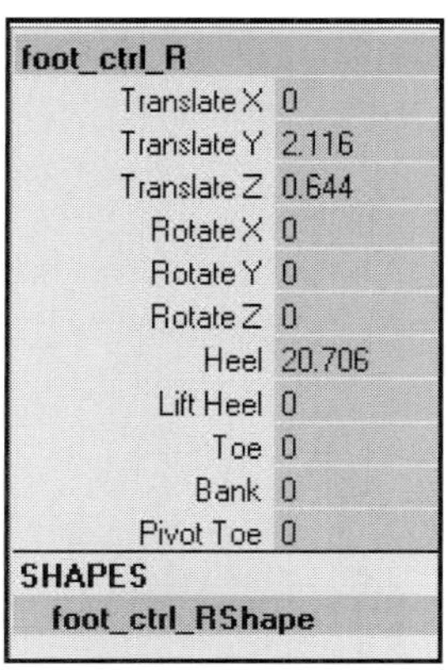

figure 8-23

Foot controls.

- Heel lifts the entire foot on one pivot.
- Lift Heel controls the back part of the foot, effectively lifting the ankle and not moving the toe.
- Toe moves the front half of the foot and does not affect the heel.

- Bank pivots the foot left and right on its axis.
- Pivot Toe does what it says—it pivots the foot on the toe axis.

These controls give you an increased flexibility in the foot for walking motion. You will rely heavily on these controls in the following walk exercise.

Locators

Locators exist to help you control which way the joints point, and they assist in reducing "joint flipping" (see Figure 8-24).

figure 8-24

Locators in front of the knees.

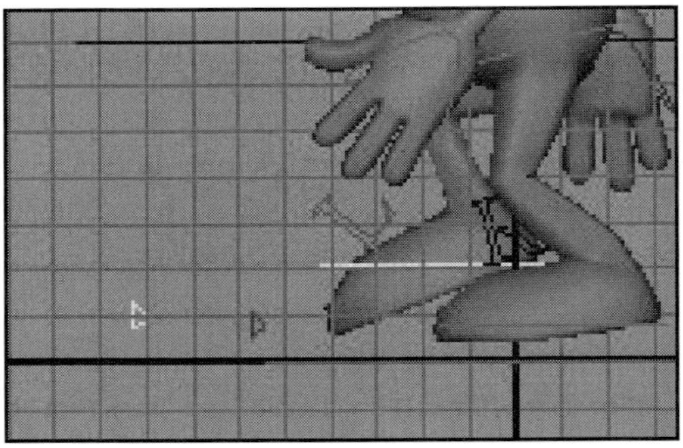

Your locators on this rig are named leg_Pole_V_ctrl_R, leg_Pole_V_ctrl_L, arm_Pole_V_ctrl_R, and arm_Pole_V_ctrl_L.

The leg poles affect the knees, while the arm poles affect the elbows. Select one and then move it around. Notice how the elbow or knee follows. These can be animated just like the limbs, and they are valuable in believably posing the character.

TUTORIAL

Open generi_walk_setup.mb on the enclosed CD, and set up your interface to look like Figure 8-25. This figure shows a Side view open, a Perspective view, and the Graph Editor. You should be using the low-resolution version of the model. Be sure that your Graph Editor curves are set to Linear and Stepped. Make sure you are in the Animation module.

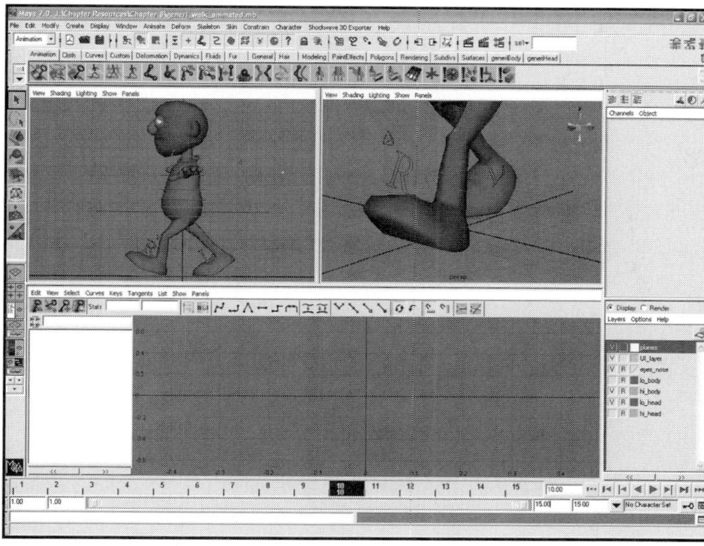

figure 8-25

The interface as it should now look.

Set the timeline from 1 to 15 (see Figure 8-26). This animation is shortened to 15 frames to compensate for the looping. If you kept it at 16, you would have an extra frame, which would add a stall to the animation.

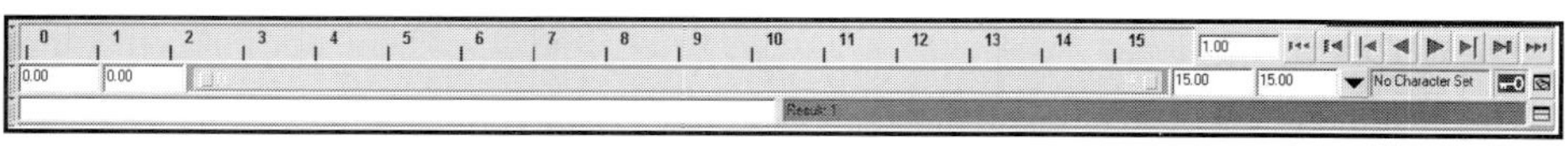

figure 8-26

The timeline set to 15.

Notice the vertical and horizontal centerline created using the EP (edit point) curve tool. Curves do not show up in the final render.

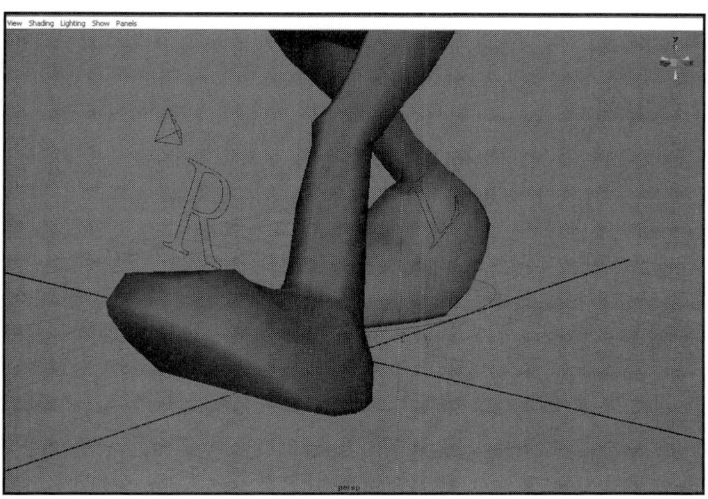

figure 8-27

Left and right feet.

Notice we differentiate between the left and right foot by attaching an "L" to the left foot and an "R" to the right foot. These letters are made of curves, so they will not render (see Figure 8-27).

The Extremes

You will need the same beginning and end pose. Go to frame 1, and create the pose referenced in Figure 8-20, the contact drawings. The file on the enclosed CD already has poses 1 and 9 in effect.

You will need to position the heel and toe. The numbers we used for this position are detailed in Figure 8-28. You can use your MMB and drag to change the numbers, or you can enter a numeric value. Notice the values in the Heel and Toe channels.

figure 8-28

Channel values for left and right foot at frame 1.

Channels Object		Channels Object	
foot_ctrl_L		**foot_ctrl_R**	
Translate X	0	Translate X	0
Translate Y	0.089	Translate Y	0
Translate Z	3.094	Translate Z	-4.764
Rotate X	0	Rotate X	0
Rotate Y	0	Rotate Y	0
Rotate Z	0	Rotate Z	0
Heel	-16	Heel	-0.8
Lift Heel	0	Lift Heel	10.8
Toe	25	Toe	0
Bank	0	Bank	0
Pivot Toe	0	Pivot Toe	0

Set contact key frames for 1 and 9 (see Figure 8-29). Select the cog_ctrl, and tilt the body forward in the direction of your walk using X Rotate.

figure 8-29

Drawings for frames 1 and 9.

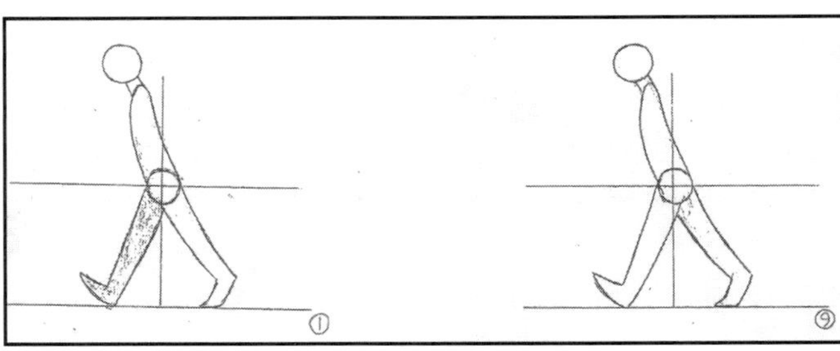

Rotate in the Y Rotate channel to allow the body to rotate in the direction of the step. Remember that your hips rotate and sway when you walk. The hip matching the leg moving forward should rotate forward. Set key frames for all Rotate and Translate channels at frames 1 and 9 (see Figure 8-30).

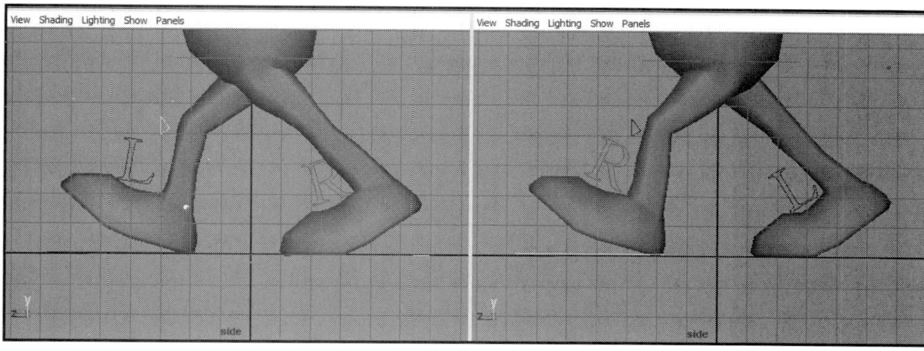

figure 8-30

Key-framed 1 and 9.

Now set the cross poses for each lead foot at 5 and 13 (see Figures 8-31 and 8-32). Notice that the body is constant at frames 1, 5, 9, and 13; so you are still only setting the controls for the feet.

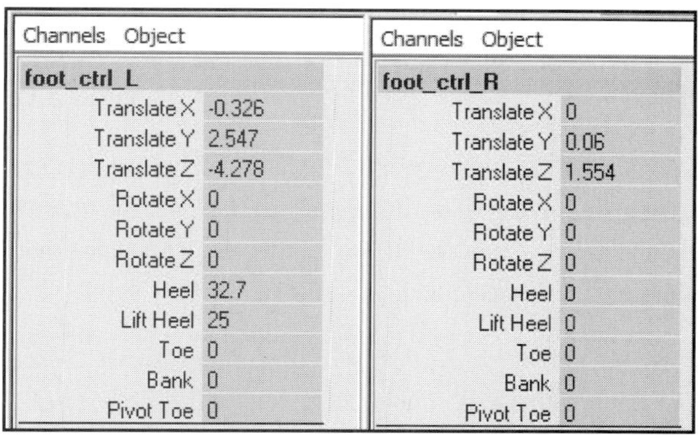

figure 8-31

Channel values for the left and right foot.

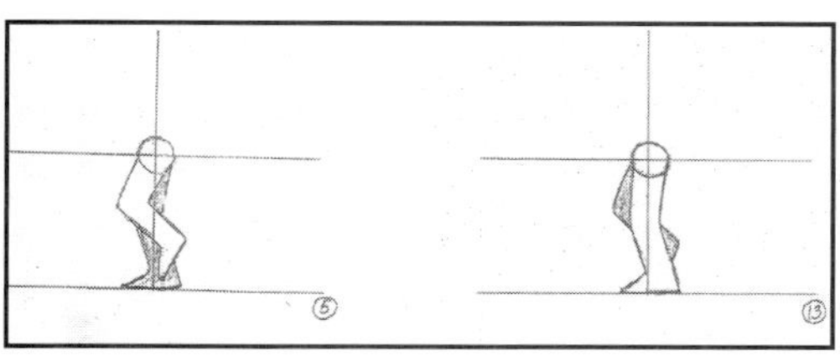

figure 8-32

Cross drawings for 5 and 13.

Select the cog_ctrl, and notice that the body should be in line with the legs. Set the Y Rotate to reflect the proper position of the body over the legs, which means the Y Rotate should be 0 or a value close to it. Set key frames for all Rotate and Translate channels at frames 5 and 13.

Now, go to the Graph Editor, and select the Rotate curves for the cog_ctrl. Change these curves from Stepped to Clamped (see Figure 8-33). Keep all other curves on other objects as Stepped.

figure 8-33

Channel values set to Clamped for the cog_ctrl.

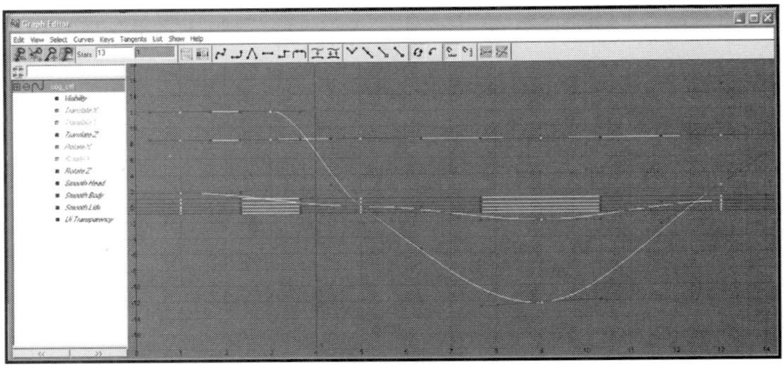

These curves need to represent the position of the body when creating subsequent foot placement. If the body is still holding a pose from a forward step and the legs are making a crossover step, you may overkey the placement of the foot.

Notice that there is a forward lean to the body in poses 1, 5, 9, and 13. The body is most vertical at 3 and 11. The body is tilted forward at 7 and 15.

The knee locators are placed away from the knees on purpose. You should be noticing some flopping in the legs. Go back through your animation and key the locators in their proper position so that the knees are pointed forward.

Play the animation. You should be seeing the walk in stepped poses. See the results in the file generi_walk_animatedv2.mb.

You will now set the low extremes at 3 and 11.

First, lower the body below the EP curve to match the drawings for frames 3 and 11 (see Figure 8-34). You can do this by setting the Y Translate value to −2.

figure 8-34

The hip sphere below the centerline.

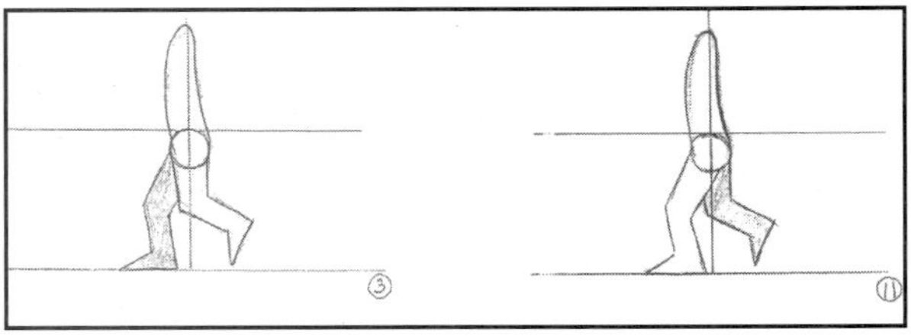

Look at the drawings. The body is no longer leaning forward. At frames 3 and 11, set the X Rotate value for the cog_ctrl to 0 (see Figure 8-35). It also should not have as much rotation in the Y Rotate value.

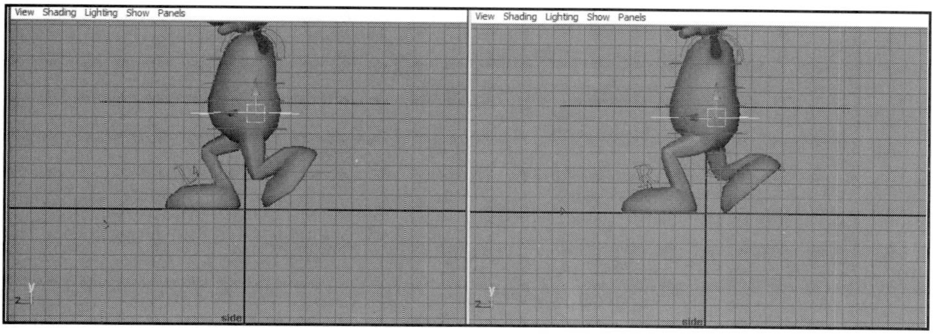

figure 8-35

Key-framed 3 and 11.

See Figure 8-36 for our settings for the feet at frame 3.

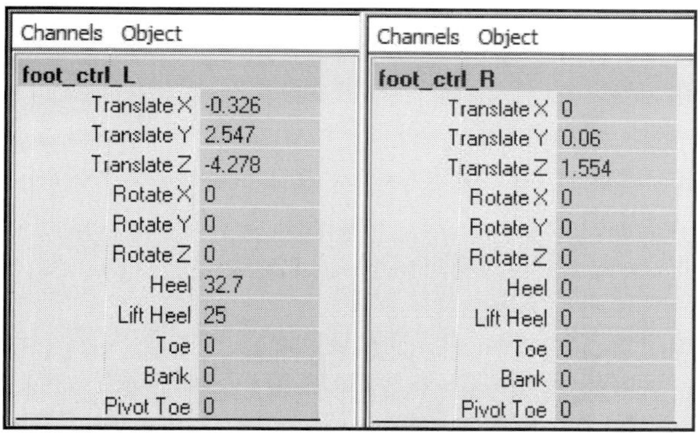

Channels Object

foot_ctrl_L	
Translate X	-0.326
Translate Y	2.547
Translate Z	-4.278
Rotate X	0
Rotate Y	0
Rotate Z	0
Heel	32.7
Lift Heel	25
Toe	0
Bank	0
Pivot Toe	0

Channels Object

foot_ctrl_R	
Translate X	0
Translate Y	0.06
Translate Z	1.554
Rotate X	0
Rotate Y	0
Rotate Z	0
Heel	0
Lift Heel	0
Toe	0
Bank	0
Pivot Toe	0

figure 8-36

Settings for cog_ctrl at frame 3.

You can see the results by opening generi_walk_animatedv3.mb. Now set the high extremes at 7 and 15 (see Figure 8-37).

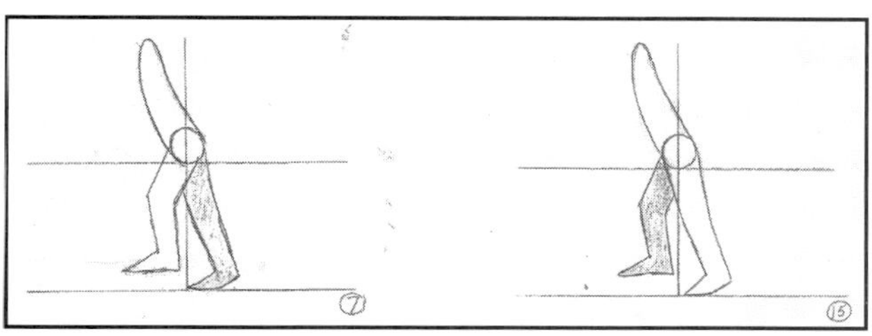

figure 8-37

High extremes drawn for frames 7 and 15.

Here you will raise the hip sphere above the horizontal centerline and will also put in the farthest forward tilt of the body (see Figure 8-38). On these frames, the puppet falls forward into its next step.

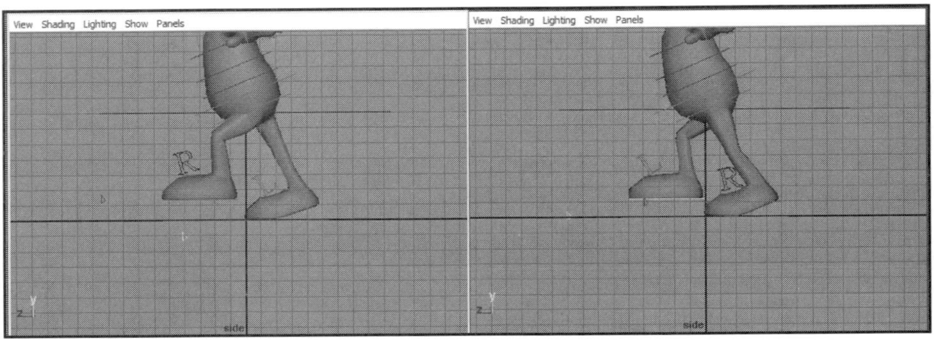

figure 8-38

Key frames for 7 and 15.

This file has been saved as generi_walk_animatedv4.mb.

The Head

You must tilt the head forward. To do so, you need to select the neck_ctrl and set the Rotate X value to **19** (see Figure 8-39).

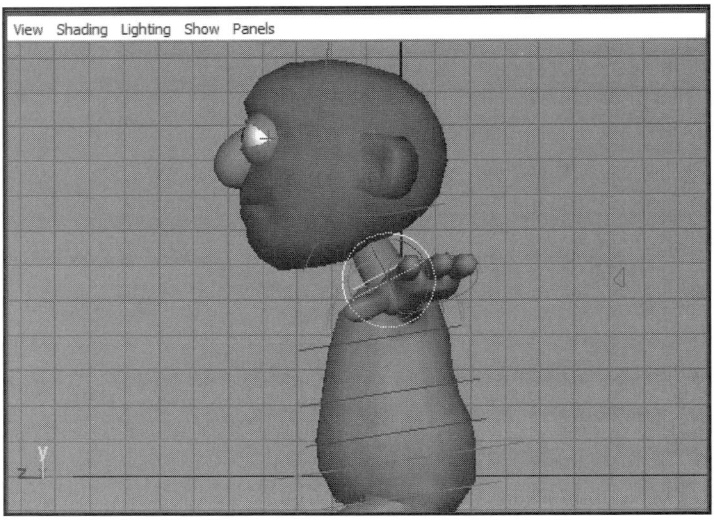

figure 8-39

Neck tilted forward using the neck control.

You do not use the neck control anymore.

Select the head_ctrl, and set key frames on 4, 8, 12, and 16. On these keys, he is staring straight ahead. Note that you are not working on the odd keys anymore. You are delaying the action one frame to accentuate the wave theory.

Now you will address the angle of the eye line and tilt the head further. On frames 2 and 10, tilt the neck_ctrl back (see Figure 8-40). Change the value in the Rotate X to **−6.**

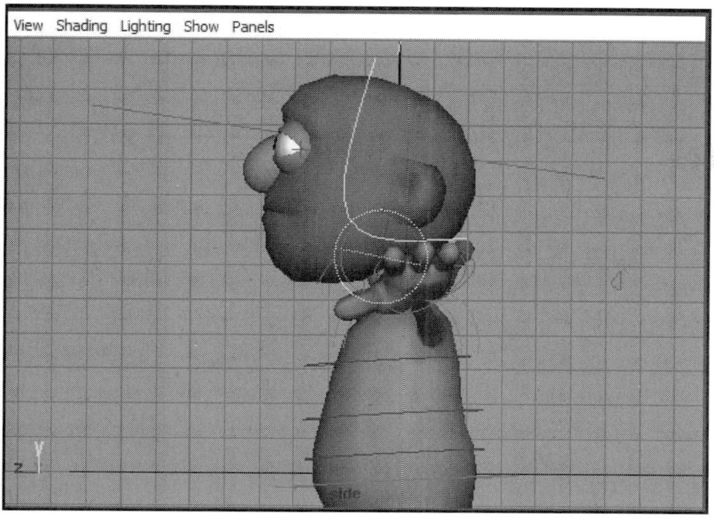

figure 8-40

Tilt the head back to –6.

To finalize the wave theory, you will tilt the head forward on keys 6 and 14 (see Figure 8-41). Change the value in the X Rotate to **6.**

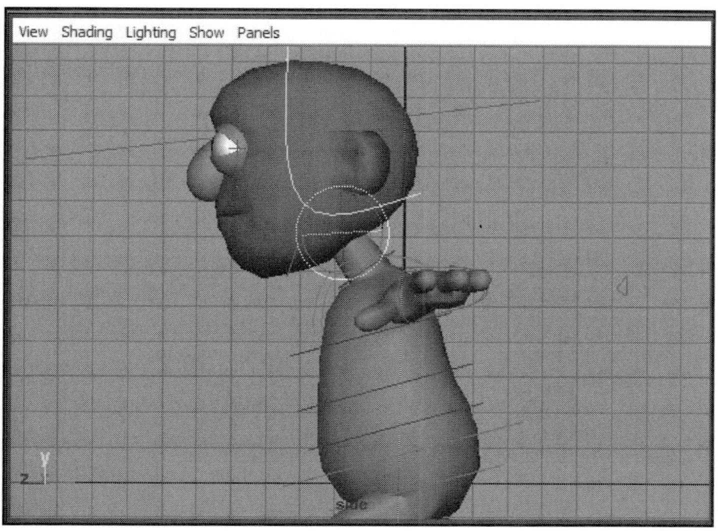

figure 8-41

Tilt the head back to 6.

Extra Arm Controls

Most of the arm controls have parent constraints so that the hierarchy of animation can be altered. These attributes can be animated midway through an animation. The attributes start with Pos_ or Orient_. Make sure the values of these attributes on each control add to a total of 10. Total values above or below the value of 10 will have a negative effect on the animation.

Basically, these attributes affect what the arms are parented to (position) or oriented to For an example, see the IK control set as follows:

Pos_ World **10**

Pos_Hips **0**

Pos_Head **0**

Pos_Chest **0**

It will act like it is not parented to anything (that is, world coords). However, if it is set as follows:

Pos_ World **0**

Pos_Hips **0**

Pos_Head **10**

Pos_Chest **0**

It will act like it is parented to the head (that is, when you rotate the head, the hand will move with it). You can also have combinations like these:

Pos_ World **7.5**

Pos_Hips **0**

Pos_Head **2.5**

Pos_Chest **0**

In this scenario, the IK control will be parented 75% to the world and 25% to the head. Be careful when there are values on more than one of these attributes, as the results are not always predictable. Also, when all of the values are added together, they should equal 10. The following example might not function properly because the values add up to 20:

Pos_ World **10**

Pos_Hips **10**

Pos_Head **0**

Pos_Chest **0**

These hierarchies were set up by the technical director who made the rig. They are created using "set driven key" or expressions.

The Arms

The arm extremes are explained next. Remember that the arm reacts opposite to the leg on the same side and in synch with the leg on the opposite side.

You will use FK to animate the arms. To set FK, select the hand-Rotation_ctrl and set IK_FK to 0 (see Figure 8-42).

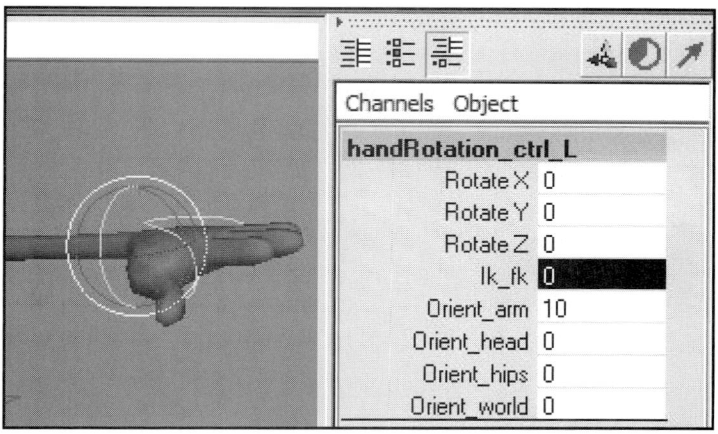

figure 8-42

Set IK_FK to 0.

You must now operate the puppet using the control found in the shoulder area (see Figure 8-43).

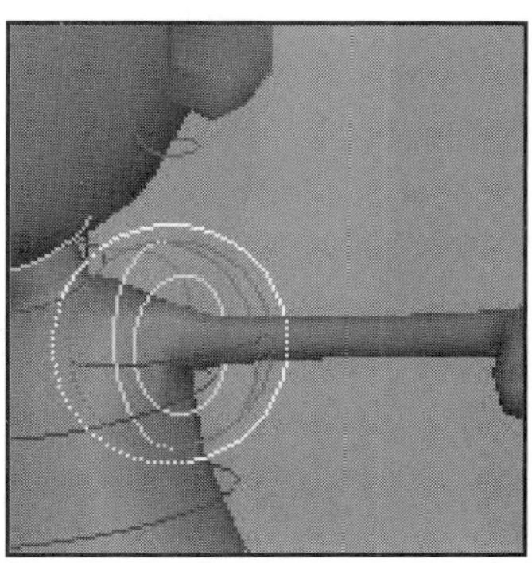

figure 8-43

The shoulder control.

Position the arms for the extreme positions one frame past the extremes for the legs (see Figure 8-44). Set key frames at 2 and 10.

figure 8-44

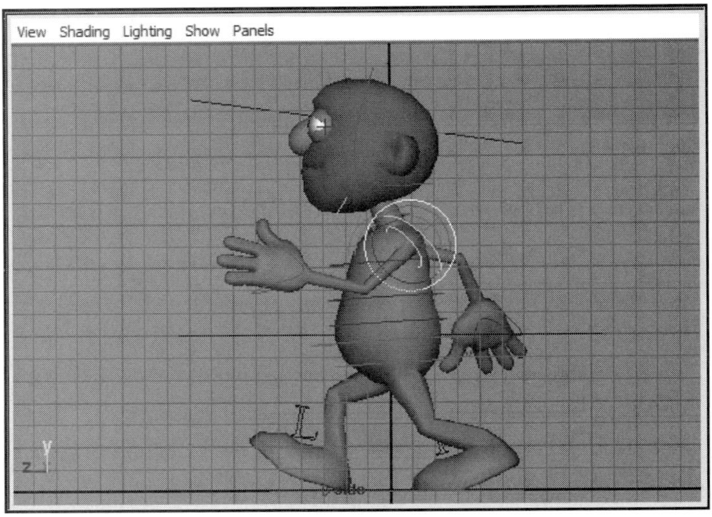

Extreme arms at frame 2.

Here are the Channel Boxes for the arms at frame 2 (see Figure 8-45).

figure 8-45

Channels Object

shoulder_ctrl_L	
Rotate X	-75
Rotate Y	0
Rotate Z	-50
Orient_world	0
Orient_chest	10
Orient_hips	0
Orient_clavicle	0
Elbow	-50

Channels Object

shoulder_ctrl_R	
Rotate X	-50
Rotate Y	0
Rotate Z	75
Orient_world	0
Orient_chest	10
Orient_hips	0
Orient_clavicle	0
Elbow	-50

Channel boxes for arms at frame 2.

Set the arm cross position, the closest middle position at frames 6 and 14 (see Figures 8-46 and 8-47).

figure 8-46

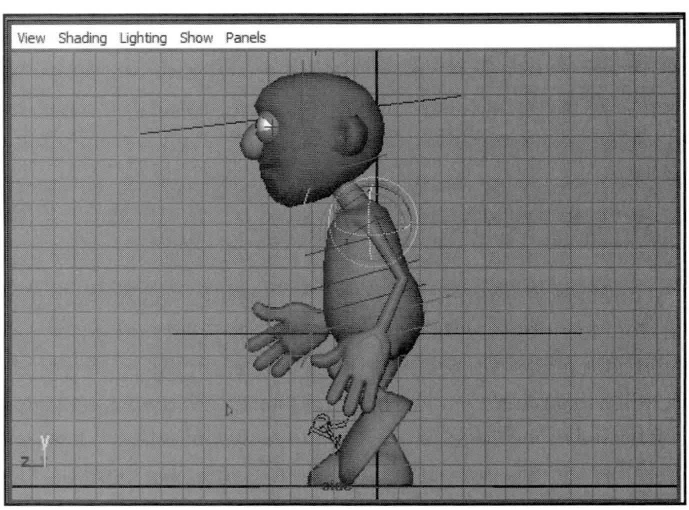

The arm cross position.

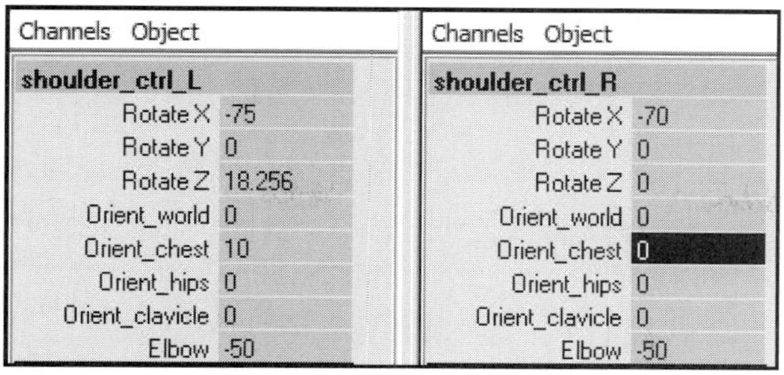

figure 8-47

Channel Box settings for the cross position at frame 6.

There is one last step. When you animate in 3D, curves are crucial. Right now, your curves start cold and end dead. You need to copy some keys into frames −2 and 18. Then, you will have motion going into the scene and leaving it.

DON'T GO THERE!

Don't start your animations on frame 1. Sure, the scene can start on frame 1, but try to start the motion a few frames before the first frame in your scene. The final result will look more natural.

This is because the shape of the curves entering and exiting the key frame depends on the placement of keys preceding it. If you don't key preceding the scene, you will have much more editing to do.

Save this file as generi_walk_animatedv5.mb.

GRAPH EDITOR

The key frames are all in place, and the walk already looks pretty good. Since most of your curves are still stepped, it is much easier to make changes to your timing at this stage. Let us presume you are happy with your timing and take the final steps to clean up your curves.

Now select each appendage that was animated, and change the curves associated with it to Clamped. At the same time you clamp them, break the tangents and free the tangent weights. You should now have relatively smooth motion when you play the animation. At this point you determine where the fast "ins" and "outs" are applied in order to achieve believable weight. Apply what you learned about weight when you edited the ball.

On your own, try to apply the wave theory you learned to the hands.

SUMMARY

The wave theory applies to the walk cycle. Applying it helps you create believable weight and overlapping action.

Creating animation in stages helps you to focus on parts of the body in fluid reactionary motion instead of thinking of the puppet as one stiff GI Joe doll. This is another reason why it is important to thumbnail out the action in a scene: It helps you stage what the primary motions will be.

in review

1. When animating in stages, what body mass do you begin with?
2. What is the wave theory?
3. What is overlapping action?
4. How do you animate FK and IK?
5. Why do you use a horizontal and vertical horizon line?
6. What did you use locators for?

EXPLORING ON YOUR OWN

1. Videotape yourself walking, and try to re-create it with Generi.
2. Look up Monty Python, and learn about the Ministry of Silly Walks. Then see what you can do with this important historical reference.
3. Try animating a larger person and then someone very thin.
4. Think about what animal a particular person reminds you of. A chicken? A duck? Videotape chickens and ducks and apply their movements to the walk of your character.
5. A few walk cycles are available in the color section of the book for your reference. Pick some attributes, and try your hand at re-creating them.

notes

notes

Adventures in Design

ADVENTURES IN DESIGN

THE COLLABORATIVE PROJECT

Working as a group is a difficult task. Opposite personality types coupled with disparate interpretations of story, characters, and design can lead to chaos, hurt feelings, and a project that never ends. Graduate students approached the concept of collaborative project with the goal of completing a good experience and a great short film.

Involved in the project were students Diony Cook, Timothy Farrell, Travis Gentry, Hsiang-Yu Hsu, Chih-Te Kan, and Dustin Ryland under the guidance of Professor Patricia Beckmann.

THE GROUP

We met previous to the quarter to discuss the goals of the class and get to know each other. We talked about the expectations and limitations of the class. All were told that if the project was not completed on time, then the whole group would receive a failing grade. (Gasp!)

On the first day of class, we each completed the Jung Personality test and shared our results with the group. This gave everyone an idea about who we were and how we

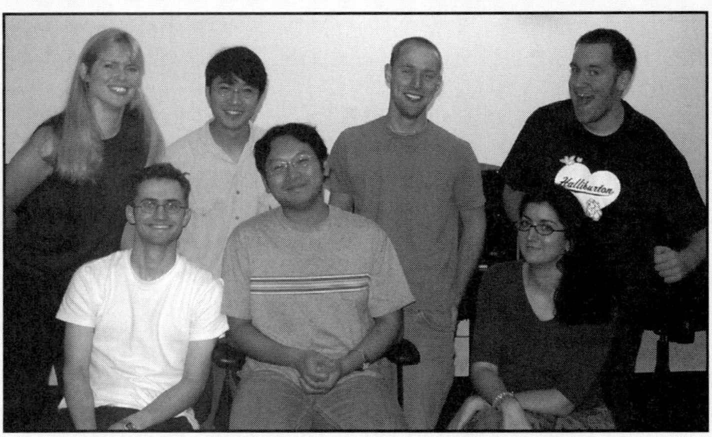

C-1 Group photo, clockwise from upper left: Professor Patricia Beckmann, Chih-Te Kan, Dustin Ryland, Timothy Farrell, Diony Cook, Hsiang-Yu Hsu, and Travis Gentry.

worked. Interestingly, everyone in our group was classified as an introvert, which could lead to communications problems. Two members identified that they would be likely to be at odds with each other because they were both leaders. One member was identified as a peacemaker. It was good to understand everyone's nature before the stress began. We then created a chart of our weaknesses and strengths in CG Animation and identified what each person would like to contribute and what they would like to learn more about. We identified production jobs and matched likely candidates based on this information, and looked for holes in the production staff that people could prepare themselves to fill.

Collaborative is a 10-week class. The students were made aware that the project had to be completed within ten weeks or they would all fail. Thus, they were aware of expectations at the onset, and warned to tailor the project to fit the 10-week production schedule.

Each student pitched a project to the rest of the class. Each unique project was supported by a storyboard or animatic, and art direction. Once all of the students pitched, they talked about each project, and shared ideas on how each could be improved. They then met outside of class in a casual setting without the professor to make a final selection.

THE PROJECT

Week 1

On the second day of class, they presented a group storyboard and the idea they had all agreed would be the focus of that quarter. All students had chosen a role for the project, and the Producer (Dustin Ryland) turned in a production schedule to Professor Beckmann.

The students decided to create a short one-character piece based on a narrative captured from an interview with a well-liked professor. They would take the narrative and add information to the film through visuals to create an entirely new interpretation of the edited voiceover.

Week 2

The graduate students interviewed four instructors. Assisting the group with recording were sound design graduate students Val Thielker, Joshua Green, and Ricardo Ochoa. They recorded in a professional audio studio. All professors gave a personal and

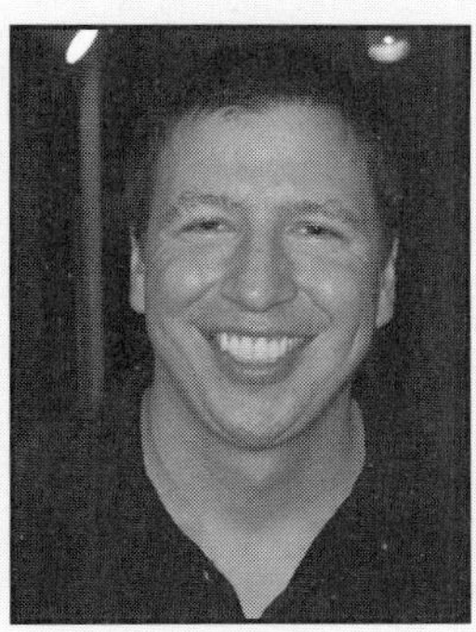

C-2 Dave Kaul, the voice of the janitor.

character-laden interview, but Dave Kaul was chosen for the character of his narrative.

Tim then took the sound and created an animatic, which is included on the attached CD. Dustin organized the production schedule and took on the role of director/producer. Diony took on art direction. Trevor created the character design and model, while Dustin and Hsiang-Yu finalized the rigging. Hsiang-Yu and Chih-Te modeled the classroom environment. The group built a production pipeline wherein they referenced the developing set and character. All agreed on naming conventions and file management. They met outside of class time to give each other input and ideas.

Week 3

Crisis! Communication was getting stilted due to the mixture of nationalities and English skills on the team.

Solution: The group talked it out and discussed solutions. English speaking members learned Chinese words to further understand the difficulty of understanding English. Communications took on a whole new friendly and effective result.

Week 4

Crisis! The group was getting behind.

Solution: The group put in extra hours and redefined the essential shots. The group met and found some shortcuts and then applied them to the animatic.

THE ANIMATION

Week 5

Keyframes have been added to all the scenes, and students are critiquing each other's work. The film is starting to take shape.

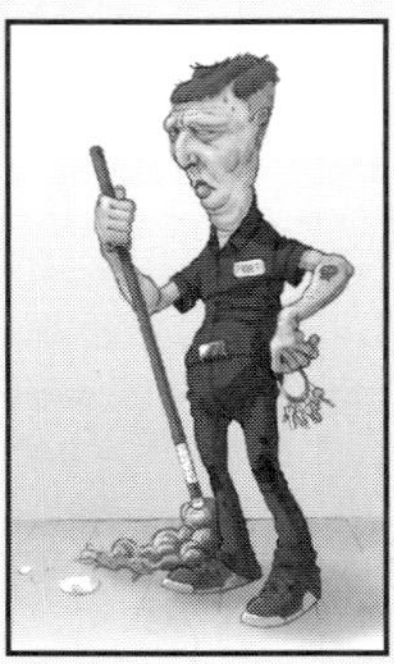

C-3 Character design of Janitor.

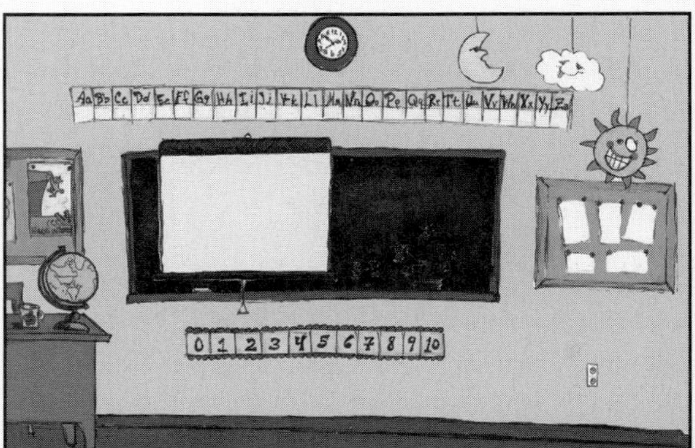

C-4 Drawn study of classroom environment.

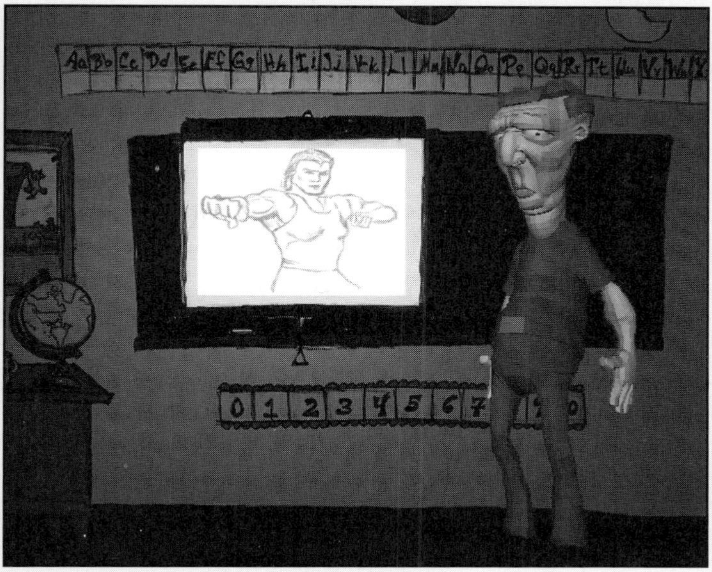

C-5 Model and classroom test.

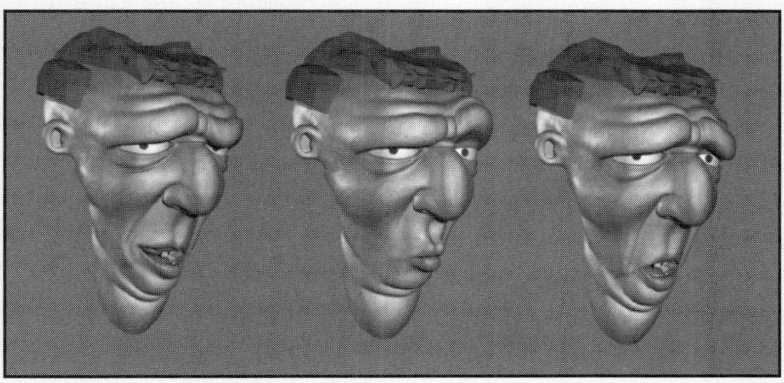

C-6 Facial tests.

The group decided on who would animate each shot. The short was broken down into 15 segments, and an animator was put in charge of each one. Students were instructed to supply a playblast of their key poses and camera edit to place in the animatic, so that all could watch and comment on the evolution of the character.

Sadly, we are just halfway through this project as I complete this book. However, if you go to www.bunsella.com, you will find a link to the final animation and a summary of the group progress.

Adventures in Design

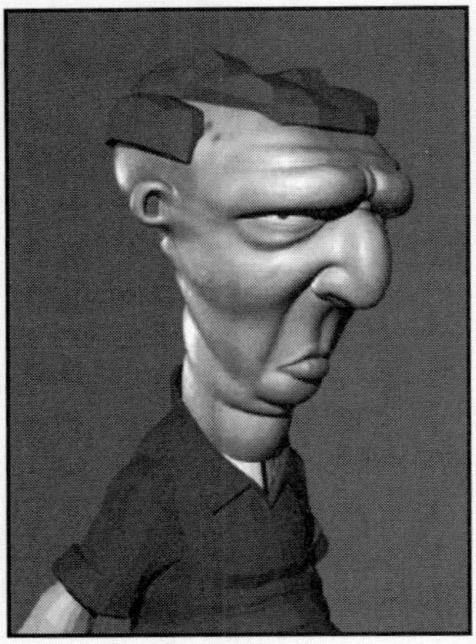

C-7 Test render.

Project Guidelines

Week 1

1. Setup and communications are essential to success. Know who are the members of your group. Take the Jung Personality test and share it with your group.

2. Have the group identify their strengths and weaknesses, then share their portfolios.

3. Decide on a storyline as a group. Allow the story to change based on member input and become an idea the whole group has grown.

4. Create an animatic with sound. Depending on the project, record the sound before or after this step.

5. Watch the animatic as a group. Show the animatic to friends and people you barely know, and ask them if they understand the story.

6. Edit the story. Look for shortcuts. Delete scenes that don't add information to the story.

7. Show the animatic again for input.

Week 2

8. Design characters and environment. Look beyond the obvious. Seek out favorite artists, children's books, and architecture. Make drawings, maquettes, and clay models—whatever helps you flesh out the character. Do not use the 3D program in this step. Get ideas together on color theory and composition.

9. When happy with the results of (8), start blocking out characters and environment in 3D.

10. Reference the set and character so that you can make changes throughout production and have them automatically update.

Week 3

11. Finish low-resolution model and give it to the rigger. Start texture studies for character.

12. Rig low-resolution model.

13. Finish environment tests.

14. Animators must begin improvisational studies of character. Thumbnail animation for scenes.

Week 4

15. Finish high-resolution model of the character and give it to the rigger.

16. Rig high-resolution model along with low-resolution model and finish rigs.

17. Add animator thumbnails to animatic. Animators should be practicing movement studies and study each other's work.

Week 5

18. Begin animating scenes. Do only the key poses for your first draft of animation. Make playblast .avi files and drop them into the animatic. Keep a copy of the original animatic, but keep a progressive animatic of the latest animation as a diary. You will begin to see more problems and solutions as this advanced animatic builds itself.

19. Edit the story. Look for shortcuts. Delete scenes that don't add information to the story.

20. You will begin to feel a lot of stress in the group. Meet and discuss communication strategies and roles.

Week 6

21. After another review, consider the camera, lighting, and pace of editing. Does the camera, lighting and edit add to the story? Is the pace fast or slow, does the camera lead the viewer's eye to what you want them to look at? What kind of mood is present, and how can you heighten it?

22. Continue with the animation and make secondary keyframes. Slide .avi files of these scenes into the animatic.

23. Edit the story. Look for shortcuts. Delete scenes that don't add information to the story.

Week 7

24. Start some rendering tests. Test lighting of the characters as they hit their marks.

25. Animators change curves from stepped to clamped and begin editing the ease-in and ease-outs of character arcs.

26. Slip new playblasts into animatic.

27. Group critique of project so far.

28. Consider Foley sound and extra sound effects.

Week 8

29. Finalize render tests, and begin to render background and characters in layers. Composite them in a compositing package.

30. Refine animations.

Adventures in Design

31. Finalize sound.

32. Finalize lighting.

Week 9

33. Finish animation and create final renders. Make changes as necessary.

34. Edit the story. Look for shortcuts. Delete scenes that don't add information to the story.

Week 10

35. Make final changes and match Foley sound with narrative sound.

36. Final render and composite.

THINGS TO CONSIDER

A collaborative project is as much a management exercise as it is an animation exercise.

1. Everyone has something valuable to contribute. If a member of the group has an important role and is not living up to your expectations, try changing the expectations. During production is not the time to attempt changing someone into a world-class rigger/modeler/animator. What you enter the group with is pretty much all you are going to have to work with. Find a creative solution.

2. Short cuts are good. If a painted background makes a good environment, then paint the background instead of modeling it. Whatever production time you save can be spent making a better story.

3. Show the animatic to people often. When you get too close to a production, you often lose sight of the story.

4. A sense of humor and forgiveness will help you to find creative shortcuts and solutions. The best art is grown out of limitations. Allow your group's limitations to become an asset instead of a fighting ground.

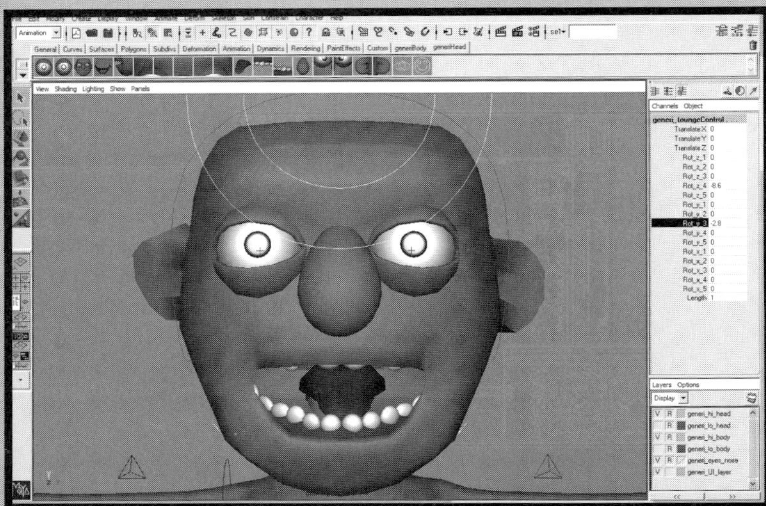
Animation
General Curves Surfaces Polygons Subdivs Deformation Animation Dynamics Rendering PaintEffects Custom generiBody generiHead
View Shading Lighting Show Panels
Channels Object
TranslateX 0
TranslateY 0
TranslateZ 0
Length 1
Layers Options
Display
generi_hi_head
generi_lo_head
generi_hi_body
generi_lo_body
generi_eyes_nose
generi_UI_layer

9

the face

charting your course

The face is capable of a million subtle expressions. Believability is contained in the fraction of a second that an expression is held. You can capture a great many of these expressions with a few well-keyed deformations.

In this chapter, you will attempt to re-create Generi as a speaking character, in combination with the walk you have just finished.

goals

In this chapter, you will:

- **Learn phonemes (mouth shapes for consonants and vowels) and how to accurately create them.**
- **Learn how to animate deformers.**
- **Understand how to work with a sound file.**
- **Understand how to work with an exposure sheet.**
- **Master the smooth, natural look of phrasing.**

TOOLS USED

- **The Generi rig facial controls.** Generi has a full-featured facial setup. You can move the eyes, nose, and ears in addition to the deformation-based facial expressions.
- **Deformations.** Deformations are a technique of morphing one shape into another. This is the most common way to animate faces.

THE GENERI FACE

You will continue to use the Generi puppet from the last chapter (see Figure 9-1). Let us explore the facial controls. Make sure you are working with generi_reference.mb; otherwise, the shelf may not work for selecting controls.

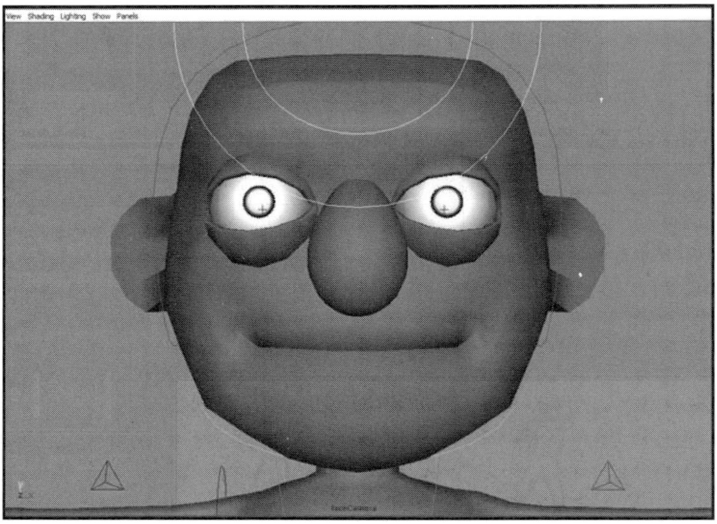

figure 9-1

The Generi face.

We find the facial controls by selecting the head control. Many of the face controls can be switched on and off inside the head control (see Figure 9-2). The user interface (UI) for the head control is the purple curve around the head that looks like a headphone.

Here you can turn on or off the tongue, eyes, brows, nose, teeth, or ears. To do so, you just type **on** or **off** in the Channel Box.

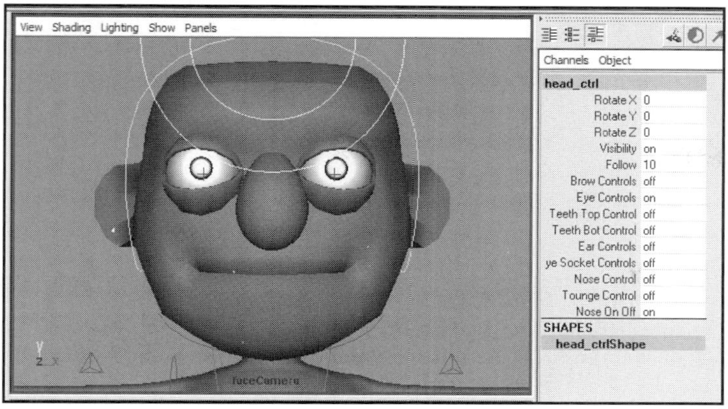

figure 9-2

The controls you can turn on and off inside the head control.

You can also select face controls from the generiHead shelf (see Figure 9-3) or the trigger user interface.

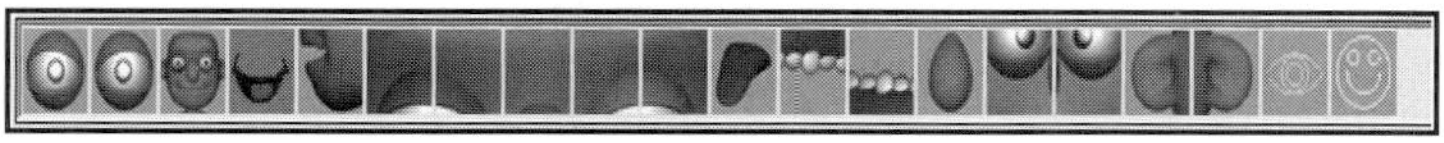

figure 9-3

The generiHead shelf.

Eyes

The eyes can be rotated individually by using the generi_eye_Rot_R or generi_eye_Rot_L found in the Outliner under the generi__anim_FaceControls or in the shelf (see Figure 9-4).

You can instead rotate both at the same time with the aim control (the eye icon; see Figure 9-5).

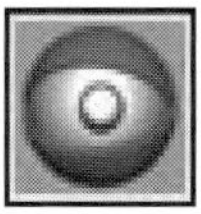

figure 9-4

Single eye selection in the shelf.

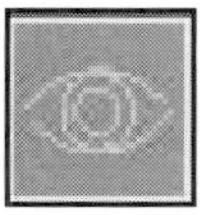

figure 9-5

The eye icon.

By selecting the generi_eye_Rot_R on its own, you have access to the eyelids. You will want to change the eyelid placement to match the acting your puppet needs to achieve.

Lid Follow is a value that lets the eyelids automatically follow the eyes (see Figure 9-6). An input value of .4 is suggested, even though the default is "1."

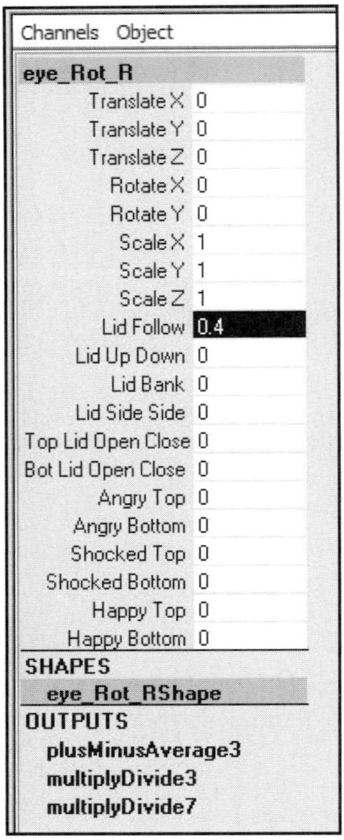

figure 9-6

The generi_eye_Rot_R Channel Box controls.

Brows

The eyebrows can be selected in the shelf as well (see Figure 9-7). You have five brow clusters to choose from that can be rotated and moved for a variety of expressions. They exist on the shelf in the same order that they exist on the face.

Each of these controls allows you to translate or rotate that particular brow region.

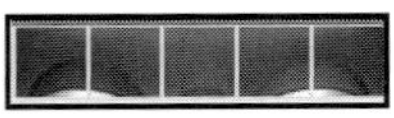

figure 9-7

Eyebrow controls in the shelf.

Mouth

Selecting the M on top of the Generi head accesses mouth shapes (see Figure 9-8).

You can also select the 2D image of the mouth from the shelf (see Figure 9-9).

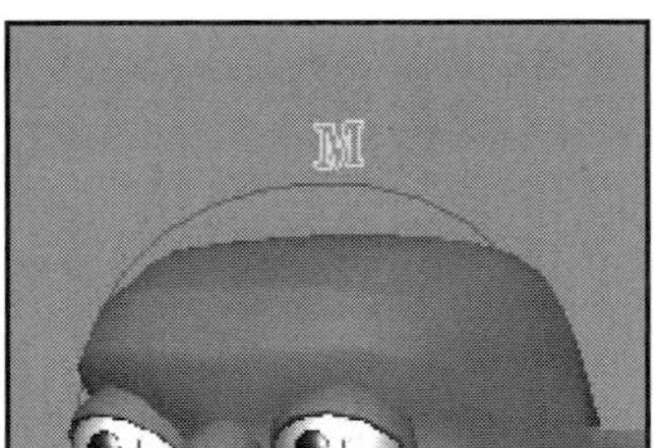

figure 9-8

The M at the top of the Generi head.

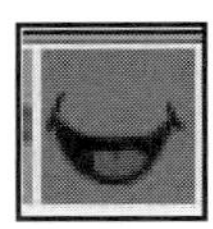

figure 9-9

The shelf icon for mouths.

Your Channel Box will reveal the controls shown in Figure 9-10.

Sliders are slow and take up too much screen space. Instead, the Channel Box middle-click + drag functionality was constructed to change shapes. You simply select a channel and then middle-mouse drag to change the value. You can also use numbers and type in a value. Some mouth shapes should be combined with an open jaw.

The maximum value for each shape is 10, but the values can go higher. Values higher than 10 will probably look odd and may distort the head. Some values also go into the negative. Highlight two values at once and then middle-click + drag in the viewport for changing multiple shapes at once. Some mixing of shapes will work; some mixing of shapes will not.

The technical director arbitrarily chose the values 1 and 10. These could be any two values, but the theory remains the same.

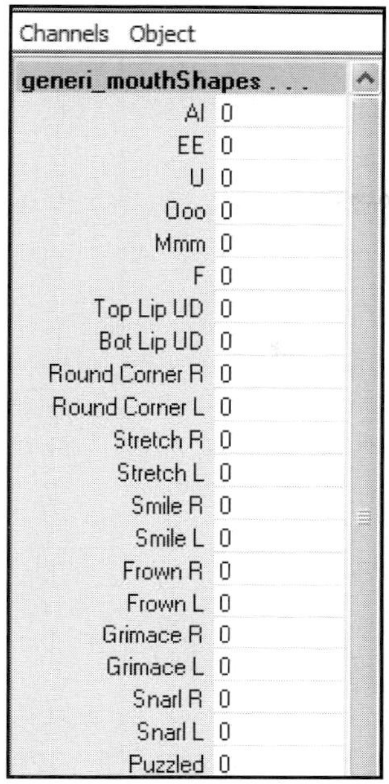

figure 9-10

Facial controls in the Channel Box.

The Jaw

The jaw features a three-bone setup. All the bones are controlled through the jaw control (jaw_ctrl; see Figure 9-11).

Use the Top Lip and Chin attributes to mix up the mouth positions (see Figure 9-12).

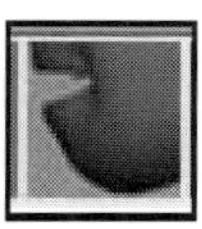

figure 9-11

The jaw icon on the shelf.

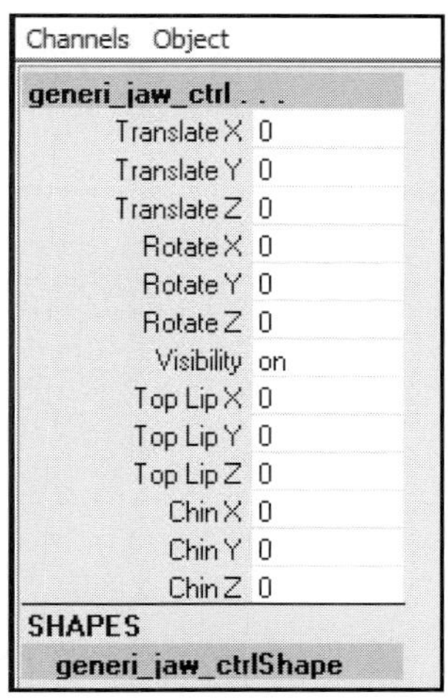

figure 9-12

Channel Box controls for the jaw.

Other Controls

Other controls include ears, eye sockets, nose, teeth, and tongue. These can be accessed through the shelf (see Figures 9-13 through 9-20). Be careful, the teeth do not move with the lips and must be animated separately.

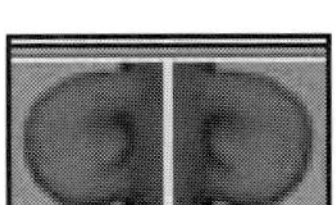

figure 9-13

Ears.

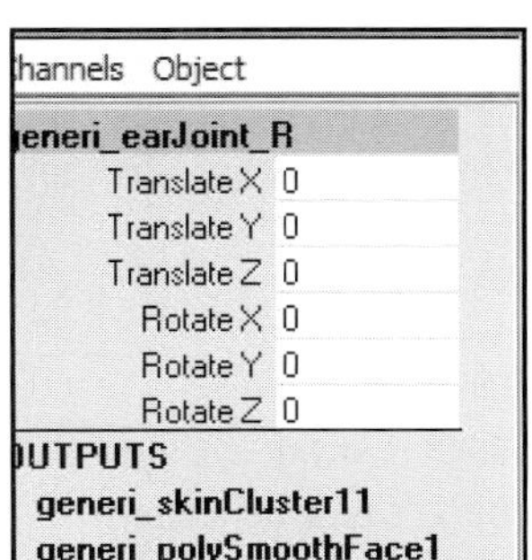

figure 9-14

Ears in the Channel Box.

figure 9-15

The nose.

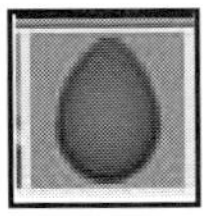

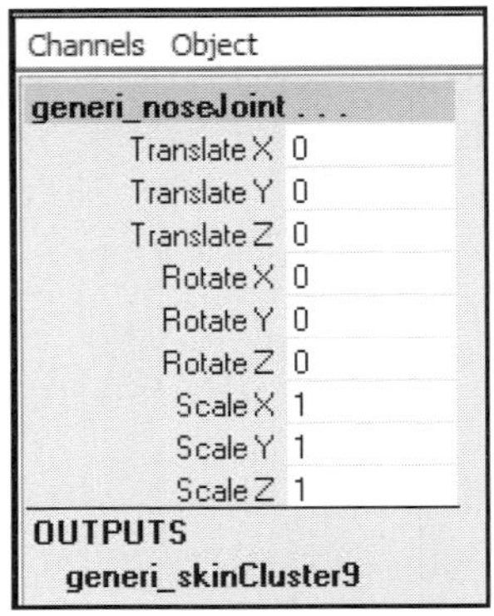

figure 9-16

The nose in the Channel Box.

figure 9-17

Teeth.

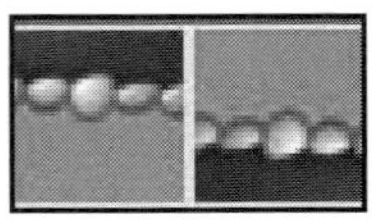

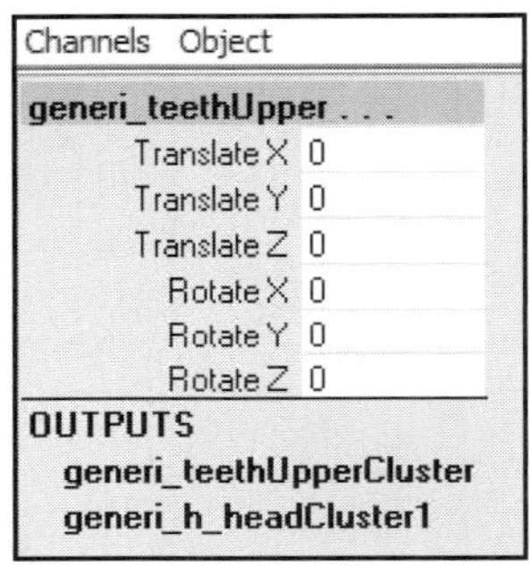

figure 9-18

Teeth in the Channel Box.

figure 9-19

The tongue.

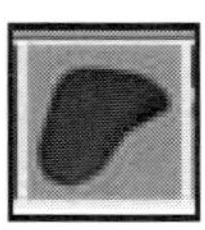

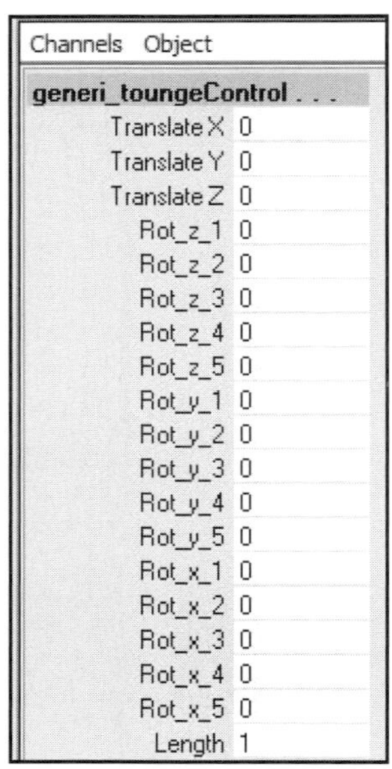

figure 9-20

The tongue in the Channel Box.

Note all of the extra controls available here for the tongue. The X, Y, and Z rotations allow you to make great use of phonetic positions for the letters s, l, t, and d, among others, as well as a variety of facial gestures such as sticking out and wiggling one's tongue while thumbs are inserted into one's eardrums.

The Length allows you to stick the tongue quite a distance outside of the mouth.

WORKING WITH SOUND

To get some use out of the face, you need a sound file to work with. Here is how you import a sound file.

Locate the sound file phil_book on the attached CD.

To import the file into Maya, select **File > Import** (see Figure 9-21).

Find your sound file in the directories, and select it.

Now, in Maya, go down to your timeline, and right-mouse click in the timeline. Your hidden menu will pop up. Select Sound from this menu, and make sure to select the arrow next to the word Sound (see Figure 9-22).

You will see the sound file phil_book .wav on this list. Select it. You should now see the .wav file in your timeline (see Figure 9-23).

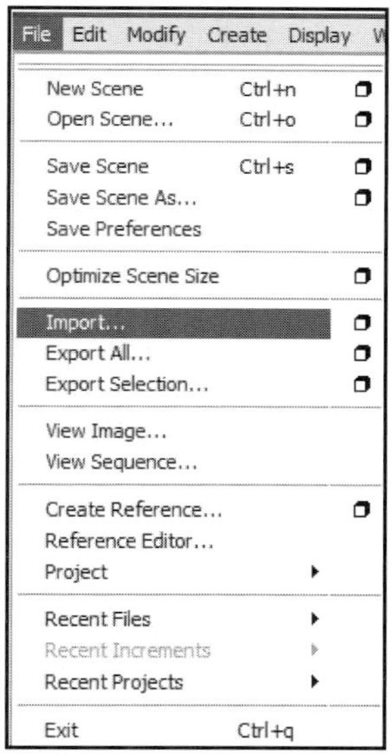

figure 9-21

File > Import.

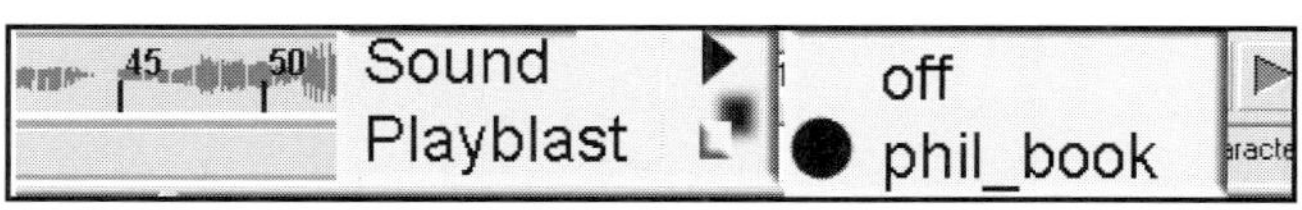

figure 9-22

Select your .wav file from the timeline menu.

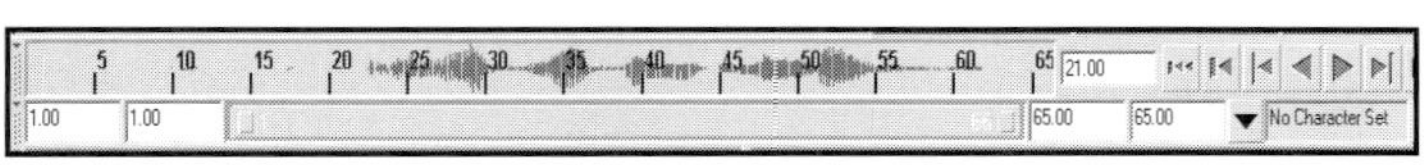

figure 9-23

The waveform shows in the timeline.

To make sure we are using the same settings, go to your Preferences and select Sound. Match your preferences to Figure 9-24. Make sure the sound is turned up on your computer.

figure 9-24

Match these preferences.

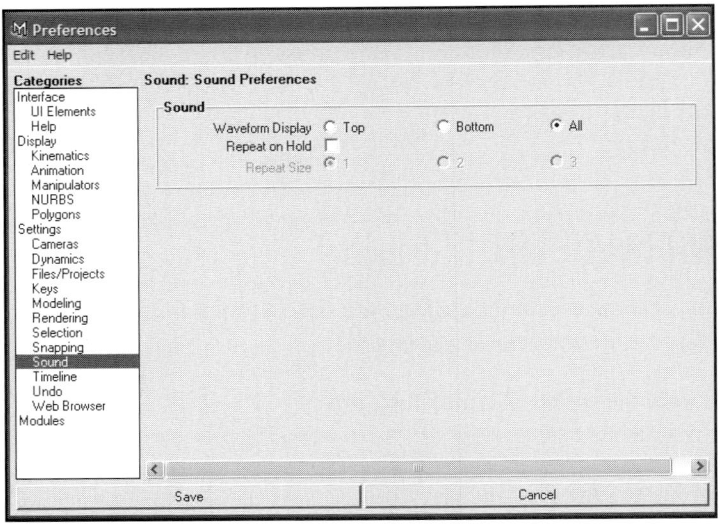

Go to Timeline, and match the on-screen preferences again (see Figure 9-25). You are increasing the height of the timeline so that the waveform is easier to see. This will be important when you try to see derivations in sound. Make sure your playback is correct by changing Playback to 24fps in the Preferences. If this is incorrect, you will not hear your sound when you press Play.

figure 9-25

Match these preferences.

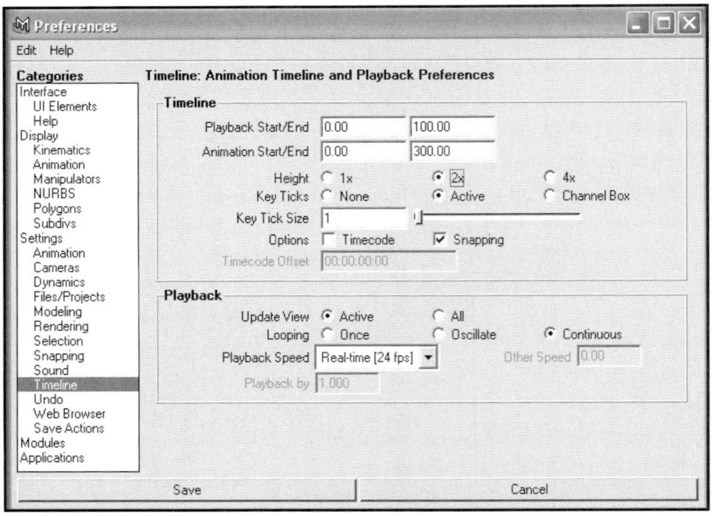

Press Play in the control panel.

Look at the waveform as it plays to get used to where the consonants hit.

Hold down your middle-mouse button (MMB), and rub over the timeline. You are now "scrubbing" the sound. You can target individual sounds and accurately match your facial poses using this method.

WHAT IS A DEFORMATION?

A deformation is a blend shape. If a sphere is made with 100 control vertices and a cone is created with 100 vertices, the two objects can be set up to morph into each other. They just need the same number of vertices.

LET'S TALK

There are a few points to make now on the art of verbally expressing ideas using animation. This chapter will deal with the technical aspects you need to be aware of when you have a character speaking on-screen. You will approach it with the goal of making the verbalization appear natural and appropriate to the manner in which the lines are read on the sound track.

The subject of acting will not be specifically dealt with at this time, as that needs a book in itself. Another aspect is facial expression, a subject that can fill volumes and that we will not get into at this time. Suffice it to say that acting is manifested in total-body attitude when posing out a character's movements, and facial expressions and dialogue can be regarded as the "icing on the cake" when it comes to expressing ideas. For now, we will deal with getting the words to come out in a natural looking manner.

The Natural Quality

Although there are an endless variation of ways to approach a line of dialogue, think for a moment of some of the ways the subject has been handled in the past.

In the early days of sound movies, animation went into a highly experimental period in which many methods were tried in having cartoon characters speak, with a great variety of results. It was standard practice at some studios to animate the dialogue first and then have the voice actors attempt to synchronize their reading of the lines to the film they were shown—while it was playing! Some of the most spectacularly unsatisfactory efforts were the result of the kind of technical problems that tended to cause the characters to over enunciate the words they were saying. The animation medium was, of course, fairly primitive at the time, and that factor, combined with the search for the right way to get the stuff onto film, made for some results that were humorous in their ineptitude.

The scary part of the story is that it is all too easy for a beginning animator to get into the same groove of over enunciation without intending to. The process of making a story one frame at a time, as you do in this book's process, can sometimes cause a kind of tunnel vision in which you put too much emphasis on each drawing, and suddenly you have created something capable of getting laughs for the wrong reasons! Here is an example of an over-enunciated line.

The line of dialogue is "I have nothing to say," and Figure 9-26 shows a series of over-enunciated drawings:

figure 9-26

"I have nothing to say,"

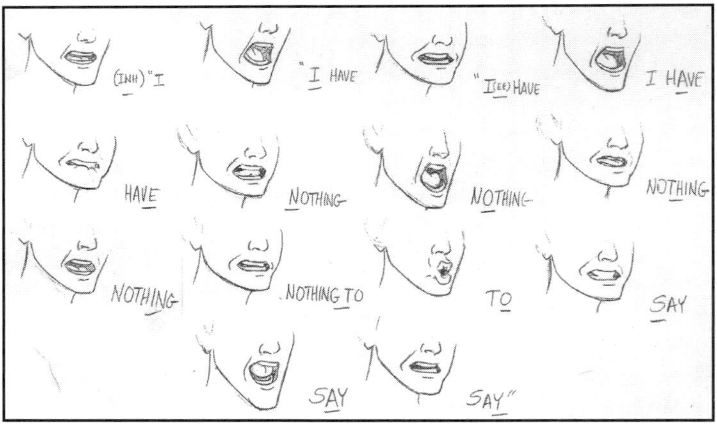

There is a possibility that a character may have a situation that calls for a rather weirdly enunciated version of that line, but chances are it will not be as over-the-top as this example. This approach is going to take the mouth through an unnatural series of gyrations when the drawings are shot as a series. Next you will look at some of the things that will help you to make the right choices.

Know Your Character

Work with the folks who have developed the character to find out as much as you can about the way that individual would analyze and approach a given situation. Listen to the recording of the dialogue several times before you begin any notes or thumbnails. Consider the situation in which the character is delivering the line. Try to form a mental image of the character delivering the line.

Consult the X-Sheet

Check the position of the dialogue in relation to the frame numbers. This is a necessary part of getting the dialogue worked out in order to synchronize the vowels and consonants to the appropriate drawings. The exposure sheet shows the vocal recording in real time as it will be translated onto film. The sheet is divided to show segments of time as well as overall film footage. Figure 9-27 shows the way the dialogue might look transcribed onto the exposure sheet.

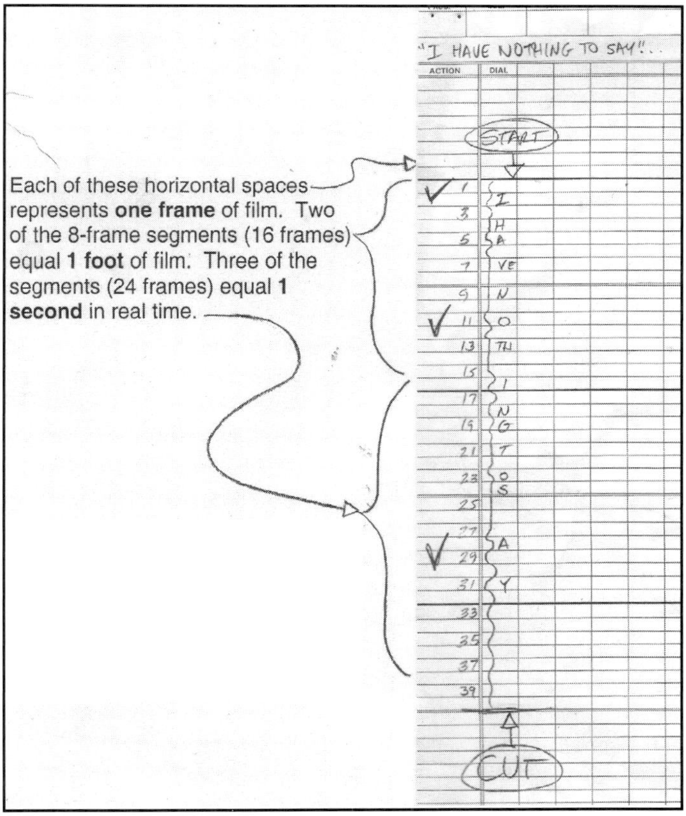

figure 9-27

The X-sheet.

The rule for placing dialogue is to place each vowel or consonant on the frame number in which it shows on the X-sheet. If there is a need to vary that plan, always anticipate, meaning start one or two frames ahead of the frame it hits on—never behind!

Phrasing

This term is used to denote the method for making the dialogue appear smooth and natural in the animation. Basically, phrasing consists of breaking the dialogue, or phrases, into groups as they are spoken. First, play the dialogue several times, lip-synching the voice actor while listening, and begin to experience the feelings of its delivery. Now look for accents or the places where the dialogue is expressed most strongly. (It takes a few times practicing this for it to become second nature.)

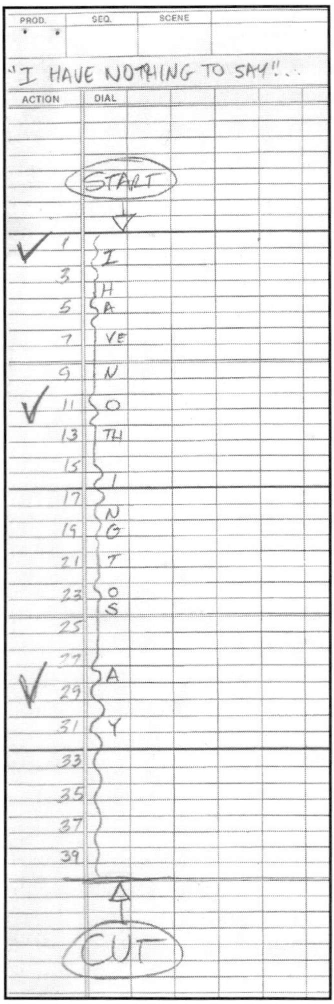

figure 9-28

Accent points are shown by the checkmark.

Next, mark the accents on the X-sheet in their proper position. Accent points are marked in Figure 9-28.

The accents are where the mouth is going to open to its maximum size in the scene, and the frames leading up to the accents are where, as a rule, the mouth becomes nearly or totally closed (on B, M, and P, for instance).

Now, using a mirror to watch the opening and closing of your mouth, play the recording and lip-synch a few times. You will now see how you are able to blend words so that you can execute this line of dialogue by smoothly opening and closing the mouth, about three times.

Take a look now at the same line of dialogue utilizing efficient phrasing (see Figure 9-29).

Simplify!

Consult the books available on drawing techniques for animation and learn the most simple, efficient mouth shapes for vowel and consonant sounds. Let the viewer clearly see the accented parts.

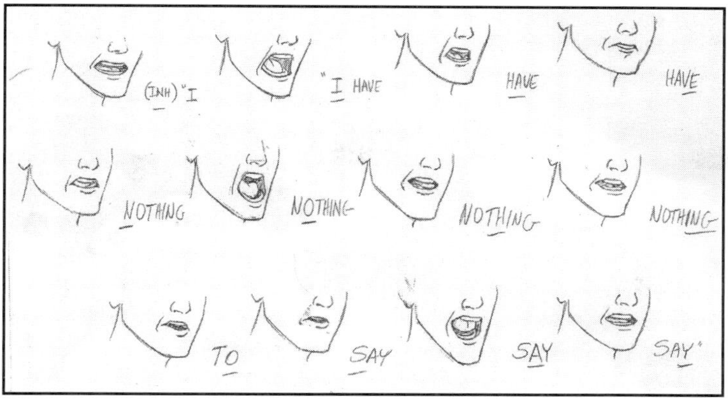

figure 9-29

Efficient phrasing of "I have ntohing to say."

Remember to exaggerate; it quite often takes a much broader approach to emphasize dialogue than one would expect.

This is animation. We have hopefully plugged you into some of the techniques to enable you to get started doing some great work.

USING THE GENERI FACE

Open the Generi rig exercise that you animated in the preceding chapter. You will animate Generi speaking using the same file you used to create the walk cycle. Make sure your interface looks like Figure 9-30 and that you are in the Animation module.

Select the shelf that has your facial tools illustrated.

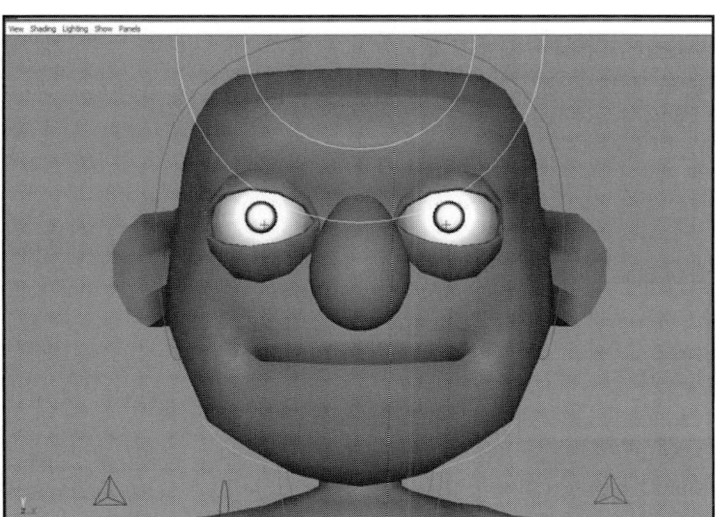

figure 9-30

Generi Face.

Each tool has an icon directly referencing the part it controls (see Figure 9-31).

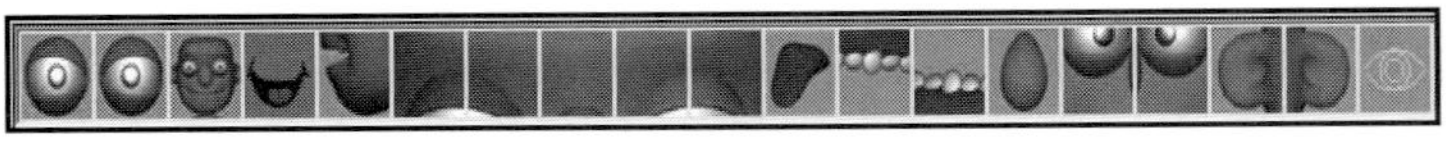

figure 9-31

Shelf with facial tool icons.

To see the facial deformations available, select the smiley face on the shelf and look in your Channel Box (see Figures 9-32 and 9-33).

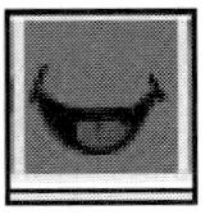

figure 9-32

The smiley face.

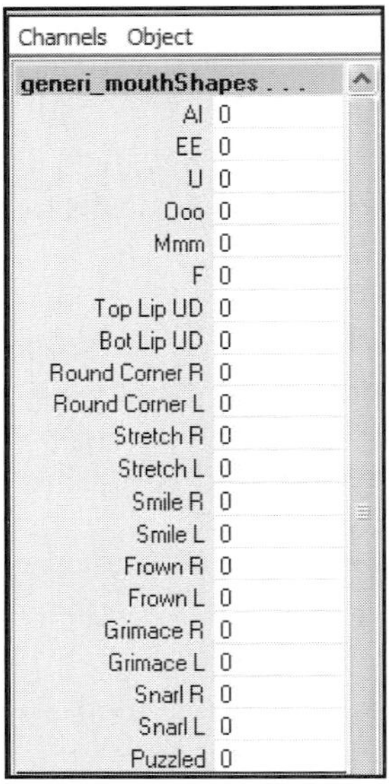

figure 9-33

The Channel Box.

Try a couple of these by changing the values in the channels and looking at the face of Generi. When you open Generi, his mouth may already be open. A UI shortcut to getting these controls in the Channel Box is to select the M over the generi rig head (see Figure 9-34).

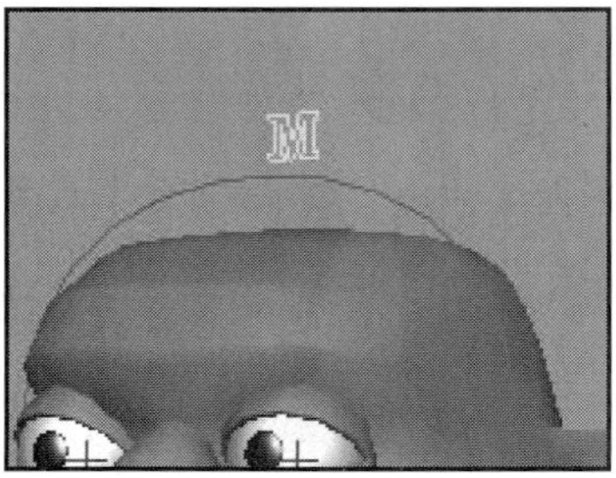

figure 9-34

The M over the Generi rig head.

Make sure your sound file is loaded and that you can see the waveform in your timeline.

Your file contains a face camera. Look for it under **Panels** > **Perspective** > **Face Camera** (see Figure 9-35).

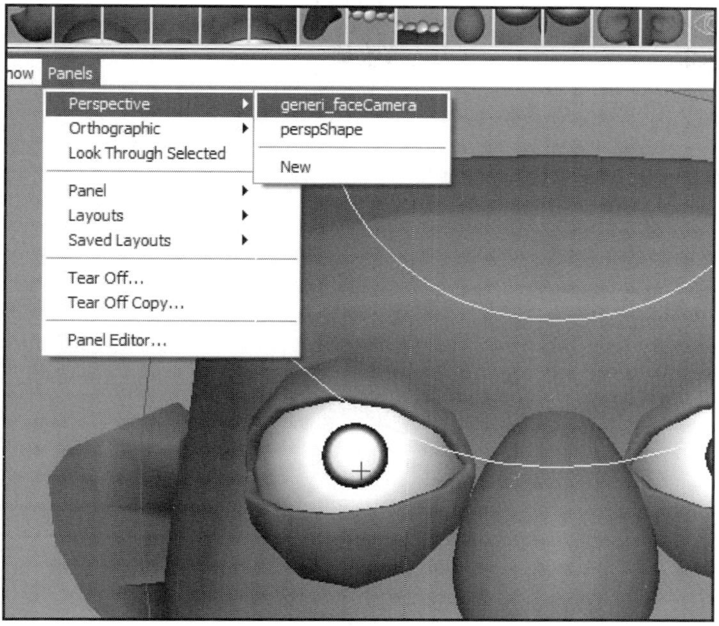

figure 9-35

How to find the face camera.

Select it. You have a traveling full-frontal view of your face (see Figure 9-36).

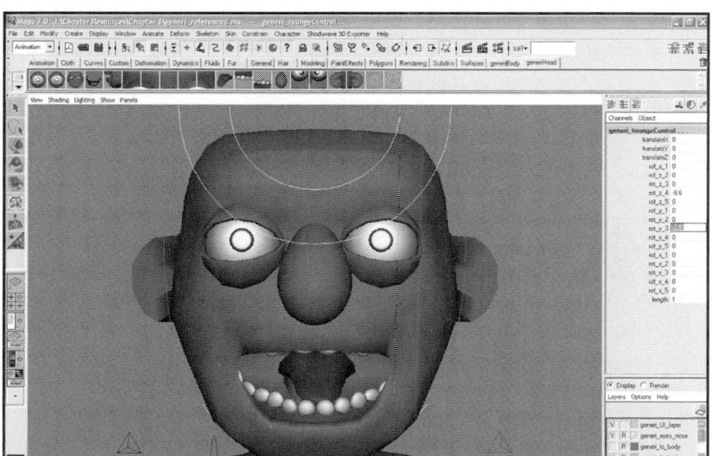

figure 9-36

Camera view of the face.

Most animators animate the physical motions of the puppet before animating the phonemes. It is important to physically communicate the scene before adding the facial shapes. Sometimes animators get lazy with the physical expressions once the lip-synch is done, and they fail to achieve the poses needed to keep the scene energized.

NOTE

It is a good idea to thumbnail out the mouth shapes, but I know that this takes a great deal of time. If anything, thumbnail out a typical phrase for your character and make note of any special mouth shapes that differentiate this character from others you are animating. Make note of the channel values used to achieve each default shape. Keep this chart nearby.

TUTORIAL

Use the Genri rig you animated walking in the last chapter. Select the face camera so that you are only seeing the face. Here, you will see the effects of your key-framing on the face.

When you are done with the facial animations, you will have a character walking and talking at the same time.

Import the sound clip. Offset the sound −22 frames by going into the Attributes editor for the sound file. This is detailed at the end of the chapter if you have problems. Go to frame 1. Now, let us consult the facial charts (see Figure 9-37).

If you set the channels values to 10 for each Generi channel, you end up with the facial

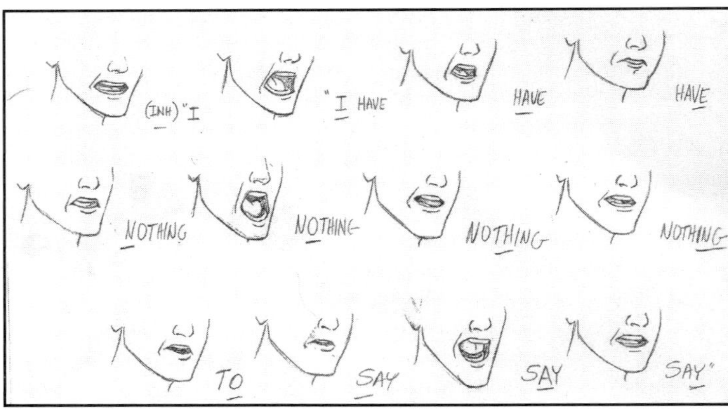

figure 9-37

The correct "I have nothing to say."

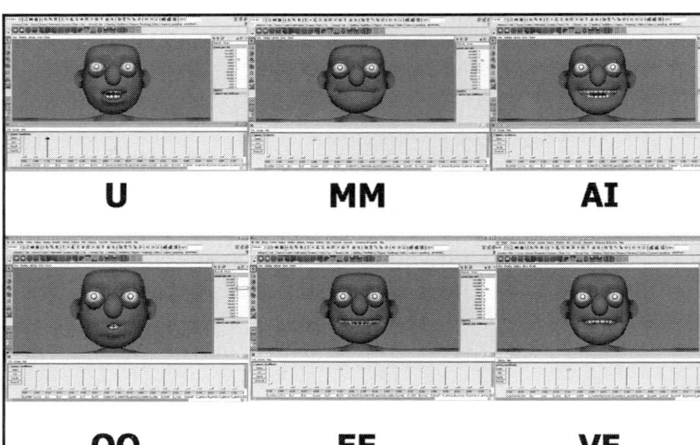

figure 9-38

Extreme poses of Generi.

shapes in Figure 9-38. Analyze these against the drawings. How would you mix and match them to achieve the phrasing shapes? We used the jaw control to open the mouth for some of the poses.

Reading the exposure sheet, you have 39 frames in which to complete this exercise. How many seconds is that at 24fps? The answer is almost 2. Set your timeline for an animation taking 39 frames. Remember to add a few frames to the beginning. Your timeline should go from −5 to 39.

You will create 12 basic mouth shapes to accommodate your phrasing.

The first mouth shape takes place between frames 1 and 5 on the exposure sheet. It will begin from a closed mouth, set at −5. Key-frame a closed mouth at −5 by selecting all the channels in the Channel Box and setting a key frame (see Figure 9-39). All the channels should turn orange.

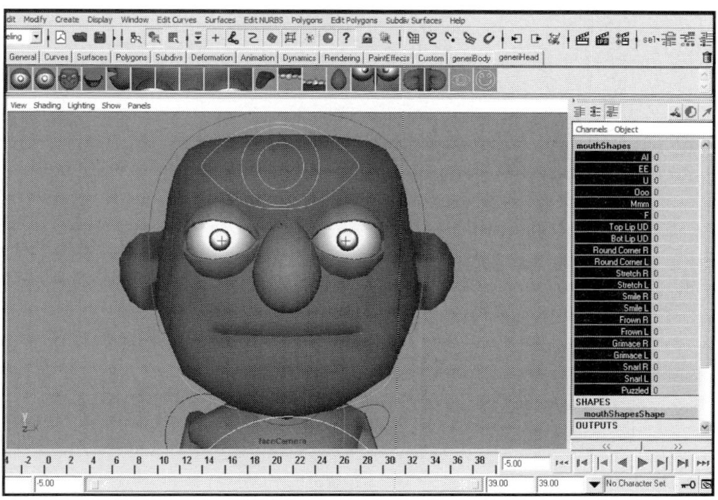

figure 9-39

Key-frame all mouth shapes to 0 at –5.

Then go to frame 1, and analyze the first mouth shape (see Figure 9-40).

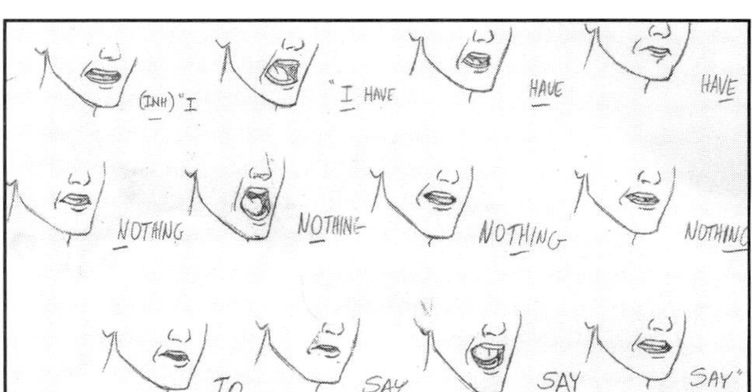

figure 9-40

The exposure sheet and first mouth pose.

When needed, you can use the jaw control to open and close the mouth.We often do that before setting the mouth shapes.

Figure 9-41 shows the mouth shapes we came up with in Maya. You can approximate mine by mixing the facial deformations.

figure 9-41

12 mouth shapes.

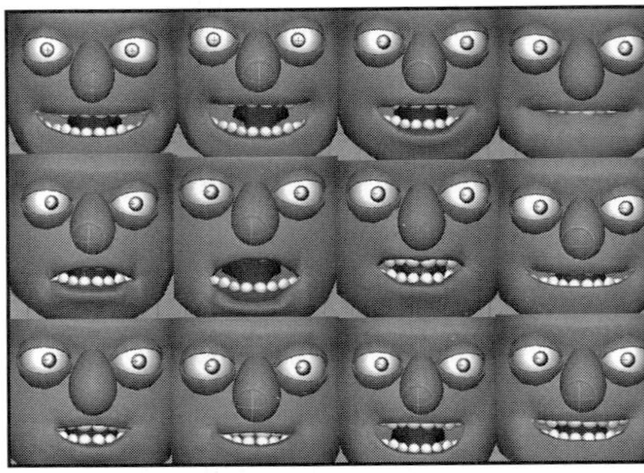

Following the exposure sheet, I keyed shape 1 at frame −1 (see Figure 9-42).

figure 9-42

The channel value for shape 1.

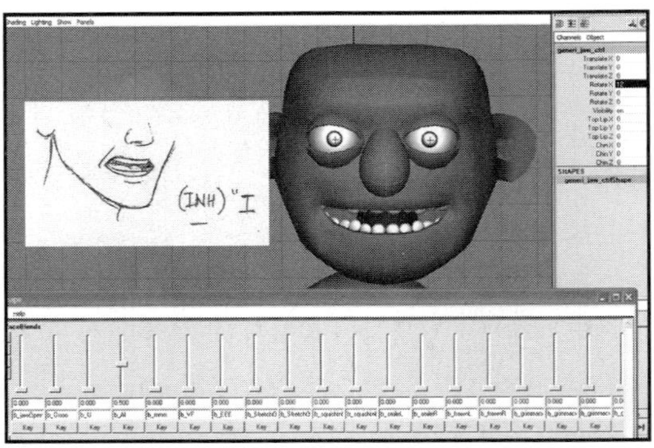

Shape 2 is keyed at frame 2 (see Figure 9-43).

figure 9-43

The channel value for shape 2.

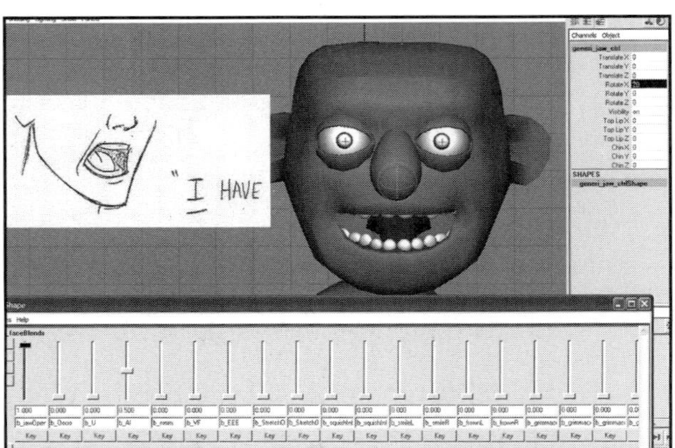

Shape 3 is keyed at frame 4 (see Figure 9-44).

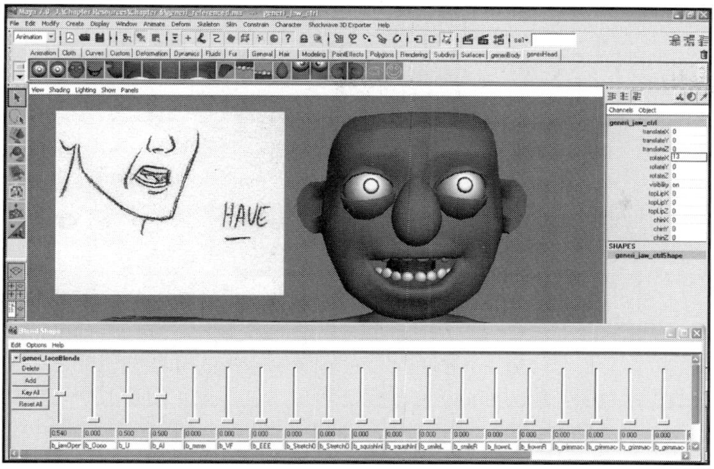

figure 9-44

The channel value for shape 3.

Shape 4 is keyed at frame 7 (see Figure 9-45).

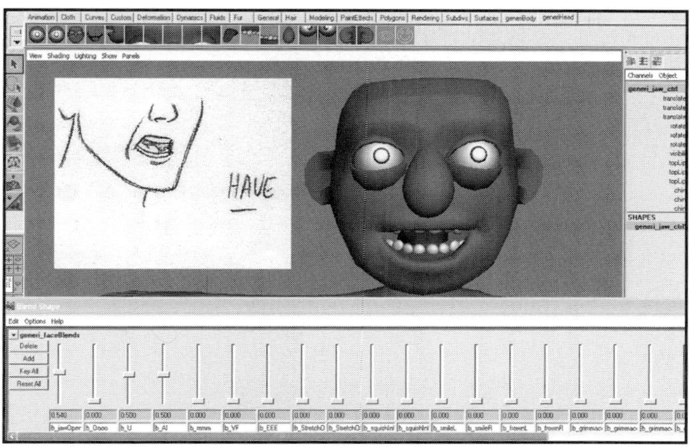

figure 9-45

The channel value for shape 4.

Shape 5 is keyed at frame 9 (see Figure 9-46).

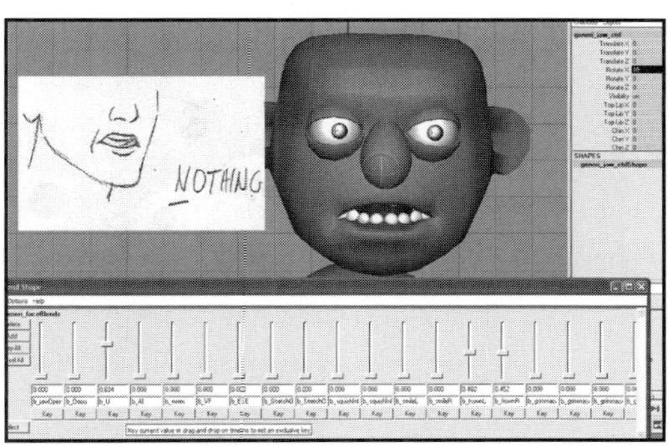

figure 9-46

The channel value for shape 5.

Shape 6 is keyed at frame 11 (see Figure 9-47).

figure 9-47

The channel value for shape 6.

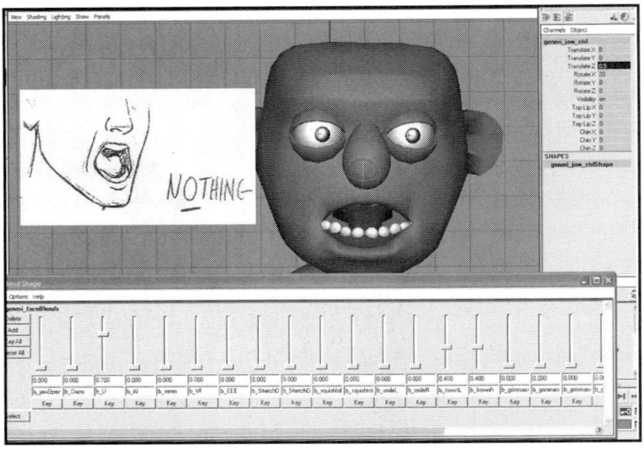

Shape 7 is keyed at frame 13 (see Figure 9-48).

figure 9-48

The channel value for shape 7.

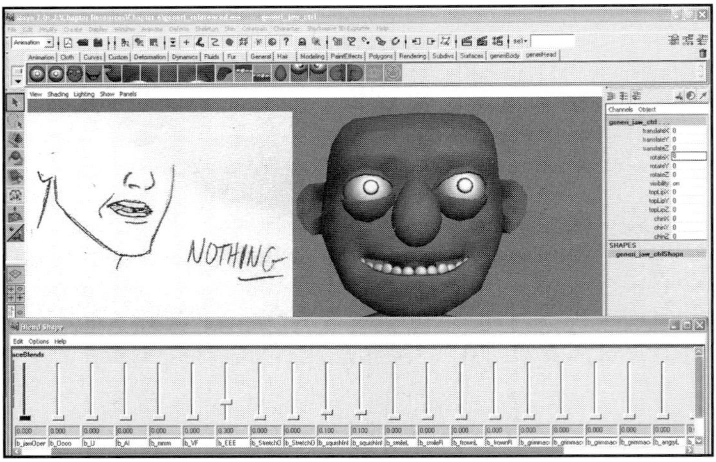

Shape 8 is keyed at frame 18 (see Figure 9-49).

figure 9-49

The channel value for shape 8.

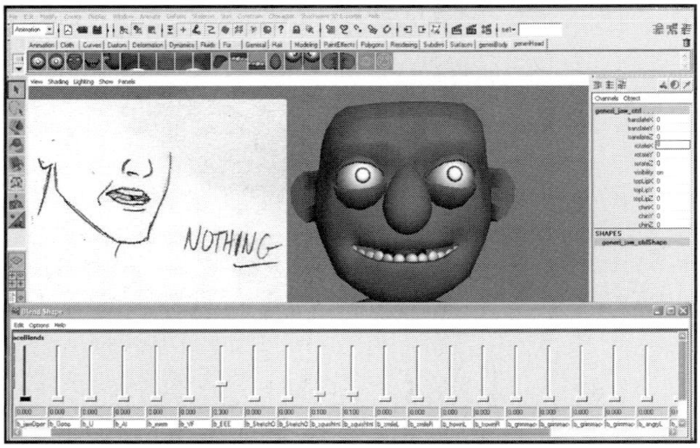

Shape 9 is keyed at frame 23 (see Figure 9-50).

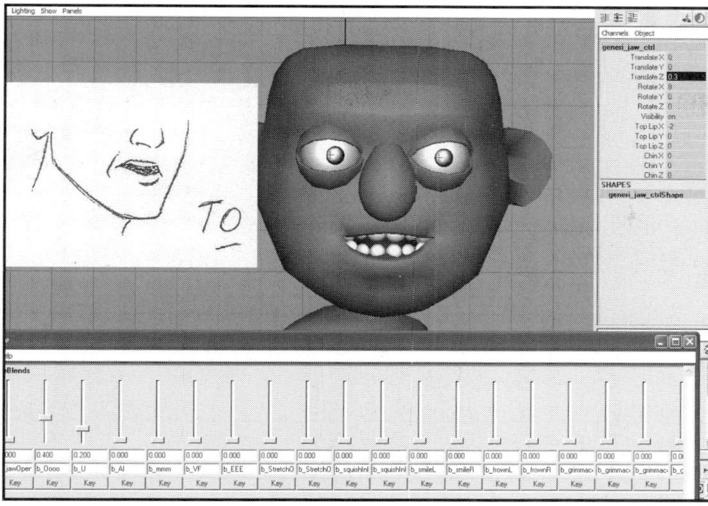

figure 9-50

The channel value for shape 9.

Shape 10 is keyed at frame 25 (see Figure 9-51).

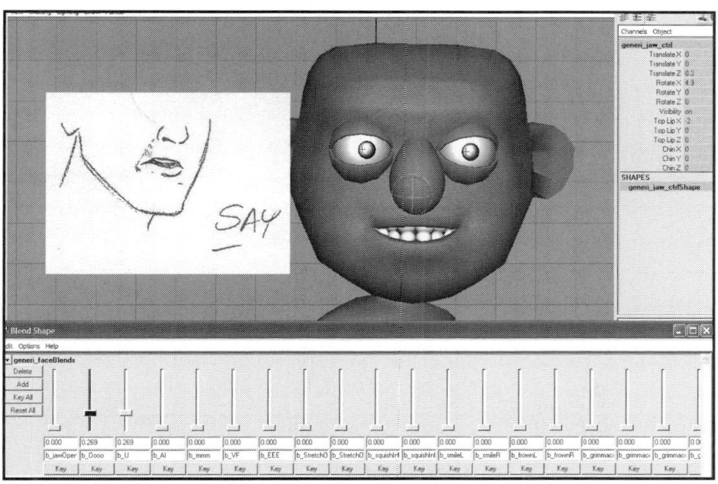

figure 9-51

The channel value for shape 10.

Shape 11 is keyed at frame 28 (see Figure 9-52).

Shape 12 is keyed at frame 31 (see Figure 9-53).

Our Graph Editor looks like Figure 9-54. We used stepped curves at first, then changed to clamped and edited the ins and outs. Now we can adjust the curves depending on the look we are trying to achieve.

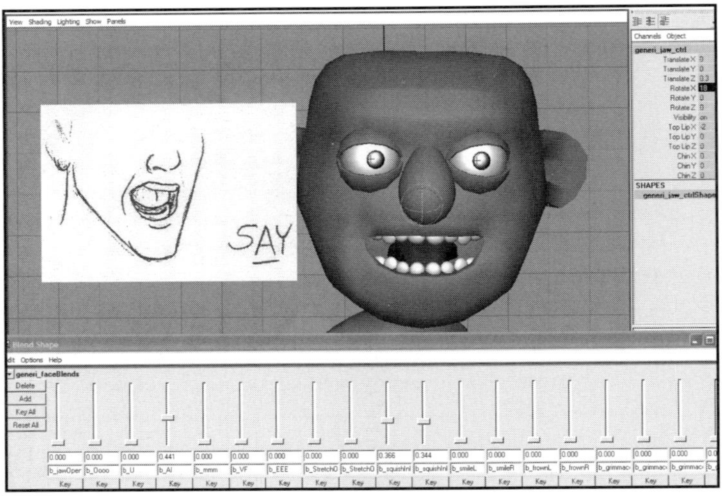

figure 9-52

The channel value for shape 11.

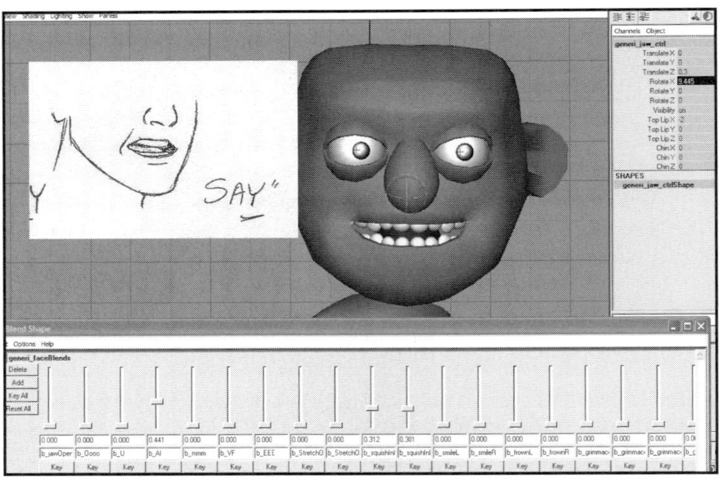

figure 9-53

The channel value for shape 12.

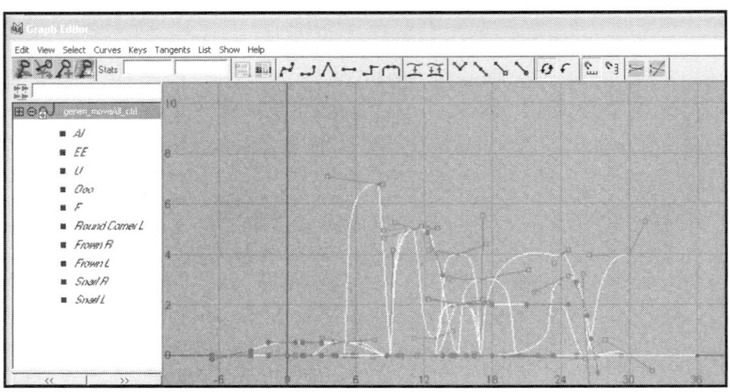

figure 9-54

The Graph Editor for "I have nothing to say."

It is okay to use either stepped or spline curves when keying mouth shapes. Always start with stepped, though. Spline curves tend to cause problems and require advanced editing.

Be aware of the rules of in/out so that it does not look floaty or robotic. Edit the curves like you did in the bouncing ball exercise to achieve a believable look based on the sound.

Notice that we edited the curves so that they did not go below the 0 limit or above the 10 limit. Had those limits been exceeded, the face would have stretched and possibly broken. When you switch from stepped to clamped, you will experience overshoot where the curve goes beyond the key pose. Correct this.

We also used the command **Delete all by type > Static actions** to remove the curves for any blend shapes that we did not use. We also deleted any static key frames on each curve. This makes the graph easier to read and edit.

We analyzed all of the facial poses in between the key frames and edited the curves to negate any unappealing crossover effects between facial poses. Mixing two, three, or four mouth shapes can create some undesirable in-betweens. You will notice that we may have moved a few key frames for specific shapes to earlier frames to avoid problems. We also edited the jaw to be open when checked on the exposure sheet.

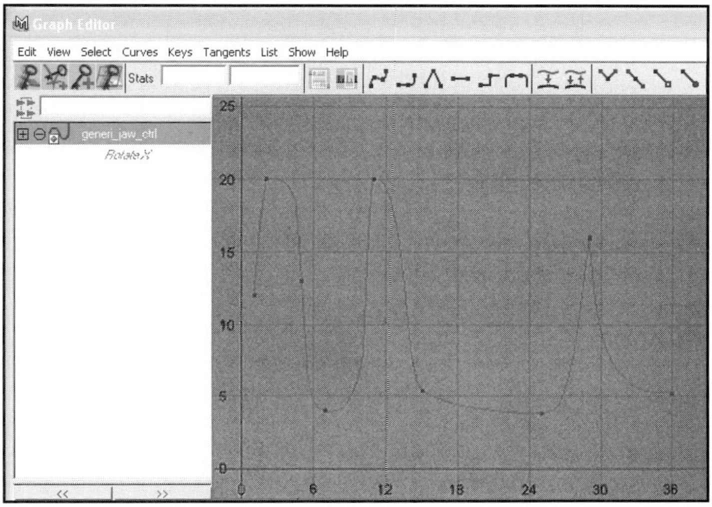

figure 9-55

The jaw is open at frames 1, 11, and 29—as per the checkmarks on the exposure sheet.

We edited the ease in and ease out depending on how a word was spoken. Sometimes the mouth moved quickly to a pose or held a shape longer. Had we left the default curves, we would have been left with very even, robotic lip movements.

When we noticed a curve that moved forever (perhaps we missed a key pose), we went in and assigned it a zero value in the statistics box above the Graph Editor and made a key frame where we felt it should stop moving.

Once you have the body poses and the lip synch, you can concentrate on facial expressions. Try your hand at animating the nose, eyes, eyebrows, and ears to add personality to this animation.

How to Offset Sound

Right-click in the timeline, and go to **Sound > Phil_book,** which is the audio you used for the exercise. Go to the square options box next to the audio clip to access the Attribute Editor (see Figure 9-56). In the Attribute Editor, under Audio Attributes, change the value in Offset to −22. The audio will match this exercise.

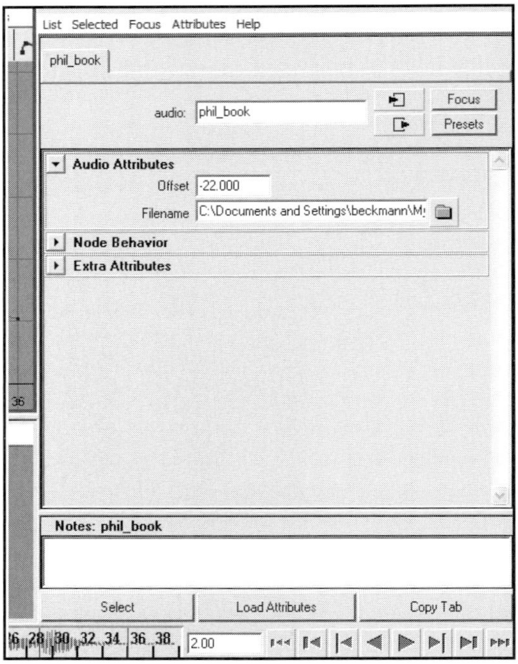

figure 9-56

Offset sound set to −22 in the Attribute Editor.

SUMMARY

Facial animation is best when simplified. Avoid over-enunciating by animating in phrases.

When you use 3D, watch your curves so that they do not overextend or cross over each other. You can use spline or step curves when animating dialogue, depending on the accent you are trying to achieve.

in review

1. How do you get to the mouth shapes? What icon do you select to get mouth shapes in the Channel Box?
2. How do you avoid over-enunciating?
3. What is a deformation?
4. How many frames are in a foot of film?

EXPLORING ON YOUR OWN

1. Try your hand at animating a sound clip from the www.10secondclub.com web site. Upload it. You will get feedback from your peers here.
2. Try animating one of the extra sound clips available on this book's CD.
3. Record yourself in different emotional states saying the same sentence. Try animating those emotions with lip-synch.

notes

notes

index